T0321974

Resource Allocation in Next–Generation Broadband Wireless Access Networks

Chetna Singhal
Indian Institute of Technology Kharagpur, India

Swades De
Indian Institute of Technology Delhi, India

A volume in the Advances in Wireless
Technologies and Telecommunication (AWTT)
Book Series

www.igi-global.com

Published in the United States of America by
IGI Global
Information Science Reference (an imprint of IGI Global)
701 E. Chocolate Avenue
Hershey PA, USA 17033
Tel: 717-533-8845
Fax: 717-533-8661
E-mail: cust@igi-global.com
Web site: http://www.igi-global.com

Library of Congress Cataloging-in-Publication Data

Names: Singhal, Chetna, 1987- editor. | De, Swades, 1969- editor.
Title: Resource allocation in next-generation broadband wireless access
  networks / Chetna Singhal and Swades De, editors.
Description: Hershey, PA : Information Science Reference, [2017] | Includes
  bibliographical references (pages) and index.
Identifiers: LCCN 2016052522| ISBN 9781522520238 (hardcover) | ISBN
  9781522520245 (ebook)
Subjects: LCSH: Radio resource management (Wireless communications) | Radio
  frequency allocation. | Wireless communication systems.
Classification: LCC TK5103.4873 .R47 2017 | DDC 621.3845/6--dc23 LC record available at https://lccn.loc.
gov/2016052522

This book is published in the IGI Global book series Advances in Wireless Technologies and Telecommunication (AWTT) (ISSN: 2327-3305; eISSN: 2327-3313)

British Cataloguing in Publication Data
A Cataloguing in Publication record for this book is available from the British Library.

For electronic access to this publication, please contact: eresources@igi-global.com.

Advances in Wireless Technologies and Telecommunication (AWTT) Book Series

Xiaoge Xu
The University of Nottingham Ningbo China, China

ISSN:2327-3305
EISSN:2327-3313

MISSION

The wireless computing industry is constantly evolving, redesigning the ways in which individuals share information. Wireless technology and telecommunication remain one of the most important technologies in business organizations. The utilization of these technologies has enhanced business efficiency by enabling dynamic resources in all aspects of society.

The **Advances in Wireless Technologies and Telecommunication Book Series** aims to provide researchers and academic communities with quality research on the concepts and developments in the wireless technology fields. Developers, engineers, students, research strategists, and IT managers will find this series useful to gain insight into next generation wireless technologies and telecommunication.

COVERAGE

- Digital Communication
- Broadcasting
- Cellular Networks
- Grid Communications
- Network Management
- Telecommunications
- Mobile Web Services
- Radio Communication
- Wireless Broadband
- Virtual Network Operations

IGI Global is currently accepting manuscripts for publication within this series. To submit a proposal for a volume in this series, please contact our Acquisition Editors at Acquisitions@igi-global.com or visit: http://www.igi-global.com/publish/.

Titles in this Series

For a list of additional titles in this series, please visit: www.igi-global.com

Big Data Applications in the Telecommunications Industry
Ye Ouyang (Verizon Wirless, USA) and Mantian Hu (Chinese University of Hong Kong, China)
Information Science Reference • copyright 2017 • 216pp • H/C (ISBN: 9781522517504) • US $145.00 (our price)

Handbook of Research on Recent Developments in Intelligent Communication Application
Siddhartha Bhattacharyya (RCC Institute of Information Technology, India) Nibaran Das (Jadavpur University, India) Debotosh Bhattacharjee (Jadavpur University, India) and Anirban Mukherjee (RCC Institute of Information Technology, India)
Information Science Reference • copyright 2017 • 671pp • H/C (ISBN: 9781522517856) • US $360.00 (our price)

Interference Mitigation and Energy Management in 5G Heterogeneous Cellular Networks
Chungang Yang (Xidian University, China) and Jiandong Li (Xidian University, China)
Information Science Reference • copyright 2017 • 362pp • H/C (ISBN: 9781522517122) • US $195.00 (our price)

Handbook of Research on Advanced Trends in Microwave and Communication Engineering
Ahmed El Oualkadi (Abdelmalek Essaadi University, Morocco) and Jamal Zbitou (Hassan 1st University, Morocco)
Information Science Reference • copyright 2017 • 716pp • H/C (ISBN: 9781522507734) • US $315.00 (our price)

Handbook of Research on Wireless Sensor Network Trends, Technologies, and Applications
Narendra Kumar Kamila (C. V. Raman College of Engineering, India)
Information Science Reference • copyright 2017 • 589pp • H/C (ISBN: 9781522505013) • US $310.00 (our price)

Handbook of Research on Advanced Wireless Sensor Network Applications, Protocols, and Architectures
Niranjan K. Ray (Silicon Institute of Technology, India) and Ashok Kumar Turuk (National Institute of Technology Rourkela, India)
Information Science Reference • copyright 2017 • 502pp • H/C (ISBN: 9781522504863) • US $285.00 (our price)

Self-Organized Mobile Communication Technologies and Techniques for Network Optimization
Ali Diab (Al-Baath University, Syria)
Information Science Reference • copyright 2016 • 416pp • H/C (ISBN: 9781522502395) • US $200.00 (our price)

Advanced Methods for Complex Network Analysis
Natarajan Meghanathan (Jackson State University, USA)
Information Science Reference • copyright 2016 • 461pp • H/C (ISBN: 9781466699649) • US $215.00 (our price)

www.igi-global.com

701 E. Chocolate Ave., Hershey, PA 17033
Order online at www.igi-global.com or call 717-533-8845 x100
To place a standing order for titles released in this series, contact: cust@igi-global.com
Mon-Fri 8:00 am - 5:00 pm (est) or fax 24 hours a day 717-533-8661

Editorial Advisory Board

Table of Contents

Detailed Table of Contents

There is a massive upsurge in data traffic over the Internet due to multimedia services. The upcoming heterogeneous broadband wireless access networks (BWANs) provide higher data rates, increased capacity, and enhanced network coverage. Since the smart phone usage and multimedia service demand is increasing at a much faster pace as compared to the capacity and resources of the underlying network technology, adaptive multimedia services are essential to provide satisfactory quality of experience (QoE). The focus of this chapter is to discuss the adaptive techniques to provide better multimedia services to heterogeneous users in next-generation networks. These techniques consist of video streaming optimization using MPEG-DASH, video caching schemes, quality aware video transcoding, web optimization of multimedia services, and user-centric cross-layer optimization.

Chapter 2

Recent measurements on radio spectrum usage have revealed the abundance of under-utilized bands of spectrum that belong to licensed users. This necessitated the paradigm shift from static to dynamic spectrum access (DSA). Researchers argue that prior knowledge about occupancy of such bands, such as, Radio Environment Maps (REM) can potentially help secondary networks to devise effective strategies to improve utilization. In the chapter, we discuss how different interpolation and statistical techniques are applied to create REMs of a region, i.e., an estimate of primary spectrum usage at any arbitrary location in a secondary DSA network. We demonstrate how such REMs can help in predicting channel performance metrics like channel capacity, spectral efficiency, and secondary network throughput. We show how REMs can help to attain near perfect channel allocation in a centralized secondary network. Finally, we show how the REM can be used to perform multi-channel multi-hop routing in a distributed DSA network.

Chapter 3

Ravikant Saini, Indian Institute of Technology Delhi, India
Swades De, Indian Institute of Technology Delhi, India

Mobile connectivity these days is no more a privilege but a basic necessity. This has led to exponentially-increasing data rate demands over the network, causing tremendous pressure to the access network service planners. Orthogonal frequency division multiple access (OFDMA) is being considered for resource allocation in higher generation communication networks, where spectrum efficiency improvement while fulfilling the users' data rate demands is a key aspect of interest. Normally resource allocation is considered from the viewpoint of users, with the users selecting their best available subcarriers. In this chapter, the resource allocation problem is approached from the subcarrier's perspective. Besides the conventional user-based scheme, a recent subcarrier-based shared resource allocation scheme is presented that selects the best user(s) for each subcarrier and assigns the subcarrier either to a single user or more than one user on time-shared basis according to their current SNRs. Unlike the user-based schemes, in the proposed scheme each user can contend for any subcarrier.

Chapter 4

Naveen Gupta, Indraprastha Institute of Information Technology Delhi, India
Vivek Ashok Bohara, Indraprastha Institute of Information Technology Delhi, India
Vibhutesh Kumar Singh, Indraprastha Institute of Information Technology Delhi, India

In this chapter, the authors present the simulation and measurement results for direct and single hop device-to-device (D2D) communication protocols. The measurement results will further argument the development of D2D communication and will also help in understanding some of the intricate design issues which were overlooked during theoretical or computer simulations. The measurements were taken on a proof-of-concept experimental testbed by emulating a cellular scenario in which a Base station (BS) and many D2D enabled devices coordinate and communicate with each other to select an optimum communication range, transmit parameters, etc. A testbed (Multi-carrier) was developed using Software Defined radio which incorporates the concept of Spectrum Sharing through static sub-carrier allocation to D2D user by cellular system which will eventually enhance the performance of cellular as well as D2D communication system. Our purposed and deployed protocol have shown significant improvement in received Signal to Noise Ratio (SNR) as compared to conventional direct transmission schemes.

Chapter 5

Nalin Dushantha Kumara Jayakody, National Research Tomsk Polytechnic University,
*   Russia*
Dang Khoa Nguyen, Aalborg University, Japan

Wireless Power Transfer is a promising solution to increase the lifetime of wireless nodes and hence alleviate the energy bottleneck of energy constrained wireless networks. In this Chapter, we discuss two power transfer policies; dual-source and single fixed-source, two bidirectional relaying protocols; multiple access and time division broadcast, and two relay receiver structures; time switching and power splitting, are considered to derive closed-form expressions for the outage and throughput of the network in the context of delay-limited transmission. This framework assists the reader not only to quantify the degradation of outage probability and throughput of the networks due to the impairments of realistic transceiver but also to provide realistic insight into the effect of power transfer policies, relaying protocols and receiver structures on outage and throughput of the networks.

Chapter 6

Prashant Kallappa Wali, International Institute of Information Technology, India
Amudheesan Aadhithan N, International Institute of Information Technology, India
Debabrata Das, International Institute of Information Technology, India

Mobile operators are showing a growing concern for energy efficiency in cellular networks in the recent past not only to maintain profitability, but also to tackle the overall environment effects. Such a trend is motivating the standardization bodies, network operators and researchers to aggressively explore techniques to reduce the energy consumption in the network. This trend has stimulated the interest of researchers in an innovative new research area called green cellular networks which is a vast research discipline that needs to cover all the layers of the protocol stack and various system architectures. Since Long Term Evolution-Advanced (LTE-A), which promises better support to richer applications, is fast emerging as the next generation cellular network standard and expected to aggravate the energy consumption problem, various techniques have been proposed and researched to improve its energy efficiency. This chapter discusses three link level techniques that attempt to reduce the energy consumption of a LTE-A cell with intelligent MAC layer algorithms.

Chapter 7

Zhi Liu, Waseda University, Japan
Mianxiong Dong, Muroran Institute of Technology, Japan
Hao Zhou, University of Science and Technology of China, China
Xiaoyan Wang, Ibaraki University, Japan
Yusheng Ji, National Institute of Informatics, Japan
Yoshiaki Tanaka, Waseda University, Japan

HetNet is a hot research topic in the next generation broadband wireless access network and mitigating the intercell interference could improve the system throughput. Users care whether their requested data rates can be satisfied or not the most. Hence a user-centric intercell interference coordination scheme (i.e. resource allocation scheme considering user request) is necessary. In this paper, at each specific subframe, when users have data requests, the corresponding base station first selects which user to serve based on each user's 'instant data rate', data rate request and capacity gained. Then given the users selected, a method is proposed to help choose which intercell interference coordination scheme to use in order to maximize the users' data rate satisfaction ratios. Intensive simulations are conducted and the results demonstrate that the proposed scheme achieves considerable gains over competing schemes in terms of the data rate satisfaction ratio and system capacity in Config.4b scenarios defined by 3GPP.

Chapter 8

Alexandra Bousia, University of Thessaly, Greece

The focus of this chapter is centered on the network underutilization during low traffic periods (e.g., night zone), which enables the Mobile Network Operators (MNOs) to save energy by having their traffic served by third-party Small Cells (SCs), thus being able to switch off their Base Stations(BSs). In this chapter, a novel market approach is proposed to foster the opportunistic utilization of unexploited SCs capacity, where the MNOs lease the resources of third-party SCs and deactivate their BSs. Motivated by the conflicting interests of the MNOs and the restricted capacity of the SCs, we introduce a combinatorial auction framework. A multiobjective framework is formulated and a greedy auction algorithm is given to provide an energy efficient solution for the resource allocation problem within polynomial time. In addition, an extensive mathematical analysis is given for the calculation of the SCs cost, which is useful in the market framework. Finally, extended experimental results to estimate the potential energy and cost savings are provided.

Chapter 9

Bighnaraj Panigrahi, Tata Consultancy Services, India
Hemant Kumar Rath, Tata Consultancy Services, India
Bhushan Jagyasi, Pristine Retail Solutions, India
Anantha Simha, Tata Consultancy Services, India

With the advancement of smart phone technologies cellular communication has come to a stage where user bandwidth has surpassed the available bandwidth. In addition, the well-organized but stubborn architecture of cellular networks sometimes creates hindrance to the optimal usage of the network resources. Due to this, a User Equipment (UE) experiencing a poor channel to the Base Station (BTS) or evolved NodeB (eNB) or any other Access Point (AP) retransmits the data. In such scenarios, Device-to-Device (D2D) communication and offload/relay underlying the cellular networks or the access networks provides a unique solution where the affected UE can find a close proximity offloader UE to relay its data to eNB. Delay Tolerant Networks (DTN) is another framework which has potential usage in low-connectivity zones like cell edge and/or remote locations in cellular networks. This chapter investigates various possibilities where D2D and DTN can be jointly used to improve teledensity as well delayed but guaranteed services to poor or no connectivity areas.

Chapter 10

Eirini Eleni Tsiropoulou, University of Texas at Dallas, USA
Panagiotis Vamvakas, National Technical University of Athens, Greece
Symeon Papavassiliou, National Technical University of Athens, Greece

The increasing demand in mobile data traffic, data hungry services and high QoS prerequisites have led to the design of advanced multi-tier heterogeneous cellular networks. In this chapter, a multi-tier heterogeneous wireless network is examined consisting of the macrocell, multiple femtocells and multiple Visible Light Communication (VLC) cells. Distributed resource allocation approaches in two-tier femtocells are presented focusing on (a) power allocation and interference management, (b) joint power and rate allocation, and (c) resource allocation and pricing policies. Similarly, the most prominent resource allocation approaches in two-tier VLC cells are examined, including (a) user association and adaptive bandwidth allocation, (b) joint bandwidth and power allocation, and (c) interference bounded resource blocks allocation and power control. The resource allocation problem in the two-tier heterogeneous environment where both femtocells and VLC-LANs are simultaneously present is also discussed. Finally, detailed future directions and comprehensive conclusions are provided.

Chapter 11

The emergence of software-defined networking (SDN) raises a set of fundamental questions, including architectural issues like whether control should be centralized or distributed, and whether control and data planes should be separated. Several open problems exist in SDN space, ranging from architectural questions that are fundamental to how networks scale and evolve to implementation issues such as how we build distributed "logically centralized" control planes. Moreover, since SDN is still in its early stage, there is an opportunity to make fault tracking framework a more integral part of the overall design process. Although SDN's goal is to simplify the management of networks, the challenge is that the SDN software stack itself is a complex distributed system, operating in asynchronous, heterogeneous, and failure-prone environments. In this chapter we will focus on three key areas: 1) SDN architecture, 2) scalable SDN systems to understand which pieces of control plane can be run logically centralized fashions, and 3) fault tracking framework to track down the failures in SDN.

The mobility management architecture in current generation LTE networks results in high signaling traffic. In this chapter, we present an Evolved Packet Core (EPC) architecture based on Software Defined Networking (SDN) concepts. The proposed EPC architecture centralizes the control plane functionality of the EPC thereby eliminating the use of mobility management protocols and reducing mobility related signaling overheads. The architecture utilizes the global network knowledge with SDN for mobility management. The proposed architecture has been implemented in the ns-3 simulator. A prototype testbed has also been implemented using the Floodlight SDN controller, a Software Defined Radio platform and relevant software.

Foreword

From the period of my graduate studies during which I was so ecstatic to have acquired a 2.4 Kbaud modem such that I could submit computing tasks from home via the client-server paradigm to the envisioned emerging 100Gbps broadband access in the very near future, I have witnessed tremendous advances in telecommunications technologies for a period of more than three decades. Evolution of Broadband Wireless Access Networks (BWAN) over the past decade has been driven by the exponential increase in mobile data traffic. The advent of newer wireless technologies, data intensive multimedia services, and heterogeneous user equipment, necessitate the development of efficient techniques for resource allocation and management in wireless access networks. The next generation BWAN aims to achieve increased capacity, improved Quality of Service (QoS)/ Quality of Experience (QoE), enhanced spectral efficiency, and high energy efficiency. A few of the unique features that help in attaining these goals are: mobile-to- mobile communications, data offloading, cross-layer optimization, cognitive spectrum allocation, interference management, novel technologies for last-meter access, and network virtualization.

The book content is nicely organized into four thematic parts. The first part containing two chapters addresses application, user context, and physical layer dependent limitations, and the potential context-aware solutions for QoE delivery. The second part of the book consists of three chapters, which look into fine granular physical layer solutions from resource allocation efficiency, throughput, and fairness perspectives, without invoking the application-specific uniqueness. The five chapters in the third part present QoS/QoE-aware solutions, in particular, fourth generation (4G) and fifth generation (5G) technology specific system level solutions for broadband content transmission over heterogeneous networks (HetNets). While the primary focus of state-of-the-art solutions has so far been at the access level, the two chapters in the fourth part unveil the state of the art and future directions on mesh routing and forwarding solutions at the core network level in handling broadband traffic, including reconfigurable architecture and fault tolerance in software defined networks.

Overall, this book discusses the emerging technologies (5G and beyond), features, constraints, and efficient schemes for heterogeneous BWANs. The architectural and component innovation has been detailed in energy-efficient information and communication technology (ICT) solutions that aims to increase network capacity, improve spectrum efficiency, and enhance network coverage. Eminent BWAN frameworks have been discussed that meet stringent QoS requirements of multimedia applications in an energy-efficient manner using 5G and beyond network technology features.

The challenges in resource allocation for next generation heterogeneous BWAN are both difficult and interesting. The researchers and technology developers have been working on them with enthusiasm, tenacity, and dedication to evolve new methods and provide solutions to keep up with the ever-increasing data and service demands. In this new age of global seamless mobile connectivity, massive information exchange, and network interdependence, it is necessary to provide technology practitioners, both professionals and students, with state-of-the-art knowledge on the efficient resource allocation and management techniques for next-generation BWAN. To this end, this book is an appropriate step in that direction by covering the timely and relevant topics.

Nirwan Ansari
New Jersey Institute of Technology (NJIT), USA

Nirwan Ansari *received the B.S.E.E. (summa cum laude, with a perfect gpa) from NJIT, Newark, the M.S.E.E. from University of Michigan, Ann Arbor, and the Ph.D. degree from Purdue University, West Lafayette, IN, respectively. He is Distinguished Professor of Electrical and Computer Engineering at NJIT, where he joined in 1988. He has also assumed various administrative positions including the NJIT Newark College of Engineering's Associate Dean for Research and Graduate Studies. He was a Visiting (Chair) Professor at the Chinese University of Hong Kong, Tohoku University, National Cheng Kung University, and Beijing University of Posts and Telecommunications, respectively. His current research focuses on green communications and networking, cloud computing, and various aspects of broadband networks and multimedia communications. He has (co-)authored three books and more than 500 technical publications, over 200 in widely cited refereed journals/magazines. For example, one of his works was the sixth most cited article published in the IEEE Transactions on Parallel and Distributed Systems, as indicated in the February 2010 EIC's notes. He has guest edited a number of special issues, covering various emerging topics in communications and networking. He frequently delivers keynote addresses, distinguished lectures, tutorials, and invited talks. Some of his recognitions include IEEE Fellow, several Excellence in Teaching Awards, a few Best Paper Awards, the NCE Excellence in Research Award, the ComSoc AHSN TC Outstanding Service Recognition Award, the NJ Inventors Hall of Fame Inventor of the Year Award, the Thomas Alva Edison Patent Award, Purdue University Outstanding Electrical and Computer Engineer Award, and designation as a COMSOC Distinguished Lecturer. He has also been awarded more than thirty US patents.*

Preface

OVERVIEW

Over the recent years, broadband wireless access network (BWAN) has emerged as a popular alternative to the wire-line access infrastructure. This is primarily associated with steady increase in data rate support and has the inherent advantages, such as, easy scalability, ease of use in the end system, and low deployment and maintenance cost. The 5th generation (5G) BWAN, which targets data rate over 10 Gbps, is expected to be ready for launch by 2020. According to the data published by Ericson and Cisco, over the recent years, the mobile broadband data traffic has been increasing exponentially every year. Traffic forecast update projects a 13-fold increase in global mobile data traffic and a 7-fold increase in network connection speeds by 2017. It is also suggested that value-added services (based on end-user information and user identification) and industry "cooperation" (simultaneous cooperation and competition between service providers) are feasible solutions for the predicted mobile data explosion. Mobile data offloading (such as Wi-Fi offloading is a cost-effective solution for delivering cellular network data that eases network congestion, provides seamless connectivity, and offers higher bandwidth to end-users.

The prominent need to enhance network capacity, throughput and users' quality of service (QoS) has led to the advent of heterogeneous next generation networks, comprising of different RAN (radio access networks) connected to a single core network. Rapidly increasing data demands and massive growth in multimedia traffic over cellular networks necessitates an in-depth and holistic study of the upcoming technologies (5G and beyond), their features, constraints, and solutions, that help in meeting the requirements of next generation mobile networks. The advent of heterogeneous BWANs has increased network capacity, improved spectrum efficiency, and enhanced network coverage. Implementing these networks, while ensuring high data rates in the wireless environment, poses certain resource allocation challenges such as: positioning the base station (BS) transceiver, efficient spectrum usage, handovers, network selection, energy efficiency, etc.

The future – 5G and beyond – heterogeneous networks would efficiently and effectively integrate the prevailing heterogeneities, such as: communication modalities, channel types, technology generations, protocol types, and QoS requirements. To address dynamic, distributed, and unpredictable nature of these networks, they need to have self-organization properties that range from self-configuration during startup, to self-adaptation to dynamic changes in operating environment, to self-healing in presence of failures and losses. Among the standardization groups in this domain, are next generation mobile networks (NGMN) alliance that aims to bring affordable mobile broadband services to the LTE and LTE-A end users and Small Cell Forum/Femto Forum that works towards adoption of small cell technologies to improve coverage, capacity, and services delivered by mobile networks.

FOCUS AND KEY FEATURES

This book will help students, researchers, scholars, practitioners, and professionals to study the features, constraints, architectures, and solutions pertaining to the next generation wireless networks, that includes 5G and beyond technologies. It is the need of the hour to have such a book that discusses the next generation heterogeneous networks from the perspective of multimedia services, its QoS constraints, and the unique constraints and demands at the user-ends – especially when 5G is expected to arrive over the next few years. Since the book comprises of the latest research in the field along with the proposed solutions for the identified issues, it has a direct impact on the future research in this area by enabling the interested people in understanding the state-of-the-art, implementing the discussed schemes practically, and planning further extensions.

Distinguishing aspects of this book are:

- In-depth and holistic study of the upcoming technologies (5G and beyond), features, constraints, and solutions that help in meeting the requirements of next generation mobile networks.
- Discusses schemes for heterogeneous broadband wireless access networks (BWANs) that increases network capacity, improved spectrum efficiency, and enhanced network coverage.
- Discusses the implementation details (i.e., architecture and network components), issues associated with heterogeneous BWANs (i.e., handovers, network selection, and base station placement), various resource allocation schemes (such as, shared resource allocation, software defined and self-organizing networks), and energy-efficient green ICT (information and communication technology) solutions.
- Illustrates eminent BWAN frameworks that meet stringent QoS requirements of multimedia applications in an energy-efficient manner using 5G and beyond network features.

TARGET AUDIENCE

The target audience for the proposed publication would be the graduate and post-graduate students that are studying wireless networks as well as those pursuing research in next generation networks, heterogeneous broadband wireless access, and mobile networks. This book will be very useful for the academicians, researchers, students, professionals, and practitioners, to study the advances in mobile networking, advent of latest wireless technologies, novel solutions for network integration, and innovative architectures in next generation broadband wireless access networks.

ORGANIZATION OF THE BOOK

The book is organized into 12 chapters. A brief description of each of the chapters follows:

Chapter 1 gives an overall picture of various multimedia services in the next-generation wireless networks, identifies the pertinent quality measures, and suggests application-aware different cross-layer solutions. The adaptive techniques consist of video streaming optimization using MPEG-DASH, video caching schemes, quality aware video transcoding, web optimization of multimedia services, and user-centric cross-layer optimization.

Chapter 2 looks at the resource constraints from the physical bandwidth perspectives that are the bottlenecks for next generation broadband service support. It then suggests cognitive spectrum mapping, prediction, and dynamic spectrum access solutions that could enable ubiquitous broadband service support. The chapter discusses the application of different interpolation and statistical techniques to create Radio Environment Map (REMs) of a region that helps in predicting channel performance metrics like channel capacity, spectral efficiency, and secondary network throughput.

Chapter 3 addresses the multicarrier resource application in a multiuser scenario, where it proposes strategies for efficient and fair usage of channel resource. The resource allocation problem is discussed from the subcarrier's perspective. Besides the conventional user-based scheme, a recent subcarrier-based shared resource allocation scheme is presented that selects the best user(s) for each subcarrier and assigns the subcarrier either to a single user or more than one user on time-shared basis according to their current signal-to-noise ratios (SNRs).

Chapter 4 presents the simulation and measurement results for direct and single hop device-to-device (D2D) communication protocols. A testbed (Multi-carrier) was developed using Software Defined radio which incorporates the concept of Spectrum Sharing through static sub-carrier allocation to D2D user by cellular system which will eventually enhance the performance of cellular as well as D2D communication system.

Chapter 5 discusses two power transfer policies; dual-source and single fixed-source, two bidirectional relaying protocols; multiple access and time division broadcast, and two relay receiver structures; time switching and power splitting, are considered to derive closed-form expressions for the outage and throughput of the network in the context of delay-limited transmission.

Chapter 6 discusses energy consumption issues in LTE and LTE-Advanced technology based broadband wireless access systems. It then presents energy-efficient solutions via intelligent traffic shaping and scheduling techniques. This chapter discusses three link level techniques that attempt to reduce the energy consumption of a LTE-A cell with intelligent MAC layer algorithms.

Chapter 7 addresses the interference management aspects for broadband quality of service support in wireless networks involving contemporary as well as upcoming technologies, such as, LTE-Advanced and beyond. This chapter discusses a method to help choose which intercell interference coordination scheme to use in order to maximize the users' data rate satisfaction ratios. It further discusses the challenges in cooperation among heterogeneous networks (HetNets).

Chapter 8 focuses on the network under utilization during low traffic periods (e.g., night zone), which enables the Mobile Network Operators (MNOs) to save energy by having their traffic served by third-party Small Cells (SCs). In this chapter, a novel market approach is proposed to foster the opportunistic utilization of unexploited SCs capacity, where the MNOs lease the resources of third-party SCs and deactivate their BSs. A multiobjective framework is formulated and a greedy auction algorithm is given to provide an energy efficient solution for the resource allocation problem within polynomial time.

Chapter 9 investigates various possibilities where D2D and delay tolerant network (DTN) can be jointly used to improve teledensity as well delayed but guaranteed services to poor or no connectivity areas. It outlines an innovative, easy to deploy framework which can be used for data offloading and to improve teledensity in poor or no coverage areas.

Chapter 10 examines a multi-tier heterogeneous wireless network consisting of the macrocell, multiple femtocells and multiple Visible Light Communication (VLC) cells. Distributed resource allocation approaches in two-tier femtocells are presented focusing on (a) power allocation and interference management, (b) joint power and rate allocation and (c) resource allocation and pricing policies. Similarly, the most prominent resource allocation approaches in two-tier VLC cells are examined, including (a) user association and adaptive bandwidth allocation, (b) joint bandwidth and power allocation and (c) interference bounded resource blocks allocation and power control.

Chapter 11 first gives an overview of network virtualization and the Software Defined Networking (SDN) architecture. Subsequently, it addresses fault instances in such networks and fault mitigation techniques. This chapter focuses on three key areas: 1) SDN architecture, 2) scalable SDN systems to understand which pieces of control plane can be run logically centralized fashions, and 3) fault tracking framework to track down the failures in SDN.

Chapter 12 addresses the challenges involved with mobility management in LTE-based broadband wireless access networks. It then proposes a solution via evolved packet core architecture based on SDN concepts. Further, performance of the proposed architectural solution is demonstrated via software simulation as well as hardware testbed emulation.

CONCLUSION

Overall, this book presents the implementation details (i.e., architecture and network components), fundamental issues associated with heterogeneous BWANs (i.e., handovers, network selection and cooperation, traffic shaping, scheduling, and interference mitigation), various resource allocation schemes (such as, shared resource allocation, software defined and self-organizing networks), and energy-efficient green ICT solutions. Furthermore, this book also discusses the eminent BWAN frameworks and solutions that meet stringent QoS and QoE (quality of user experience) requirements of multimedia applications in an energy-efficient manner using 5G and beyond network features.

Chetna Singhal
Indian Institute of Technology Kharagpur, India

Swades De
Indian Institute of Technology Delhi, India

Acknowledgment

The editors would like to acknowledge the help of all the people involved in this project, specifically, to the authors and the reviewers who took part in the technical review process, and the editorial board members for their willingness to share their expertise. Without their support, this book would not have become a reality.

First, the editors would like to thank each one of the authors for their technical contributions in this book project. The editors extend their sincere appreciation to the chapter authors for meticulously following through the updates of the chapter content to address the review comments and to meet the chapter guidelines. Second, the editors wish to acknowledge the valuable contributions of the reviewers who have added tremendous value to this book project by providing pertinent and detailed suggestions to improve quality, coherence, and content presentation of the chapters. The editors highly appreciate the reviewers' timely suggestions that helped select the right set of book chapters and improve coherence of the book by suggesting numerous updates on the selected chapters. Many of the authors also served as referees; the editors highly appreciate their double task. Finally, the authors are grateful to the editorial board members for agreeing to share their expert views on technical contents.

This book has been supported by the Department of Science and Technology under Grant nos. SB/S3/EECE/0248/2014 and DST/INSPIRE/04/2015/000793.

Chetna Singhal
Indian Institute of Technology Kharagpur, India

Swades De
Indian Institute of Technology Delhi, India

Chapter 1
Adaptive Multimedia Services in Next-Generation Broadband Wireless Access Network

Chetna Singhal
Indian Institute of Technology Kharagpur, India

Pradip Kumar Barik
Indian Institute of Technology Kharagpur, India

ABSTRACT

There is a massive upsurge in data traffic over the Internet due to multimedia services. The upcoming heterogeneous broadband wireless access networks (BWANs) provide higher data rates, increased capacity, and enhanced network coverage. Since the smart phone usage and multimedia service demand is increasing at a much faster pace as compared to the capacity and resources of the underlying network technology, adaptive multimedia services are essential to provide satisfactory quality of experience (QoE). The focus of this chapter is to discuss the adaptive techniques to provide better multimedia services to heterogeneous users in next-generation networks. These techniques consist of video streaming optimization using MPEG-DASH, video caching schemes, quality aware video transcoding, web optimization of multimedia services, and user-centric cross-layer optimization.

INTRODUCTION

More than 66% of the data traffic over internet is consumed by video streaming, according to Begen et al. (2011). According to Cisco, video streaming will constitute 72% of Global mobile data traffic by 2019. Video streaming unlike the other web applications largely depend on the streaming rates. Wireless service providers are offering an increasing number of video streaming services to the users. The diversity in wireless network infrastructure and user equipment specification has introduced new challenges for service providers to deliver acceptable quality of experience (QoE) to users. Enhancing the QoE for the users that are accessing multimedia services over wireless networks, is a topic of interest in recent

DOI: 10.4018/978-1-5225-2023-8.ch001

research. The challenge for the network operators include network resource optimization for popular multimedia content delivery, while ensuring uninterrupted service over wireless.

Multimedia services in next generation wireless networks will be able to ensure an improved QoE by employing the following optimization techniques that have been discussed at length in this chapter.

1. **Video Streaming Optimization Using MPEG-DASH:** In this module, we emphasize on the adaptive multimedia services using MPEG-DASH over the next generation broadband wireless network that promises high quality of service (QoS) with improved user experience. The basis architecture of MPEG-DASH and different ways of estimating the channel throughput are described.
2. **Video Caching for Efficient Utilization of Network Resources:** Two main applications of video caching for efficient utilization of network resources are examined in this study, one is Hierarchical web caching in Internet-based vehicular ad hoc networks (IVANET) and other is on Collaborative web caching through resource auctions among two or more wireless service providers (WSPs).
3. **Quality Aware Video Transcoding:** Video transcoding is a process of scaling the video either spatially or temporarily. Two methods of video transcoding for efficient delivery of multimedia content over wireless network are discussed namely Dependency aware distributed video transcoding in cloud and Optimal H.264/AVC video transcoding system.
4. **Web Optimization of Multimedia Services:** In this module, we differentiate mobile web browsing from PC web browsing. The architecture of mobile web browser and its limitations are discussed. Two main optimization techniques namely client side optimization and cloud based optimization is studied. The concept of mobile accelerator is described.
5. **User-Centric Cross-Layer Optimization:** Different user-centric adaptation techniques based on wireless channel condition are explained. The simulation results show the applicability of the techniques for LTE network. The user-centric feedback model is presented in this module. The performance of the proposed method is validated using simulation result.

VIDEO STREAMING OPTIMIZATION USING MPEG-DASH

Multimedia content is effectively delivered in a cost-effective manner using HTTP streaming (Begen et al., 2011). Dynamic Adaptive Streaming over HTTP (DASH) is a new standard developed in this regard, by Motion Picture Experts group (MPEG) and Third Generation Partnership Project (3GPP). Conventionally streaming is based on a client-server model that uses real time streaming protocol (RTSP). The server keeps a track of the connected client state till the session completes or the client disconnects. The media is transmitted from the server as a continuous stream of packets using transmission control protocol (TCP) or user datagram protocol (UDP).

The conventional streaming uses progressive download technique that has the following disadvantages:

1. Wastage of bandwidth if the user discontinues watching the content (or switches to other content) after the progressive download has started.
2. Bitrate is not adaptive.
3. It does not support live multimedia services.

Adaptive streaming meets the need of current day heterogeneous communication networks. For instance, HTTP streaming using TCP suffers from throughput fluctuations. In such a system, the client maintains the quality of service (QoS) by using rich signaling metadata to take content delivery decisions on the fly. A system can provide multiple alternatives (bitrate/resolution) of each audio-video component (with signaling metadata) in order to enable the client to dynamically fetch based on the available bandwidth in the network.

A client maintains a buffer to cope with mismatches in estimated and actual throughput, as well as specified and actual video bit rate in the system. Initial buffering delays adversely affects QoE during live streaming (Lohmar et al., 2011). Accurate throughput and video bitrate information is necessary to maintain a stable buffer level for a streaming client.

Multi-Bitrate Encoding

Each multimedia content is divided into smaller segments. The multi-bitrate encoding provides different bitrate versions of each video segment that can be dynamically fetched from the content delivery network (CDNs). CDN switching takes place if the available bandwidth in the network is less than the lowest bitrate supported by the CDN.

Figure 1. Multi-Bitrate encoding and representation shifting

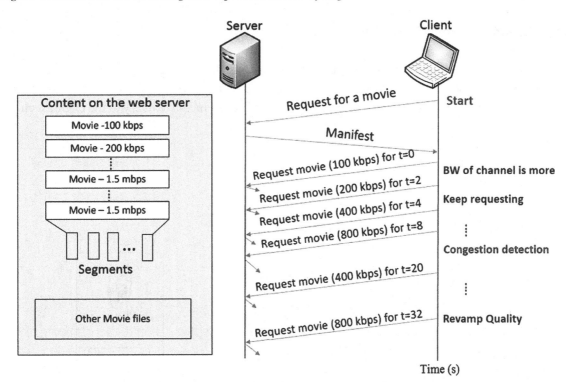

A step-wise movie streaming process in a client-server architecture is shown in Figure 1. The steps are given as follows:

1. The client sends a request for a movie to the web server.
2. The server sends the manifest with the metadata corresponding to the requested movie.
3. The client sends a request for the lowest bitrate version of the movie to have less initial buffering delay.
4. The client requests for a higher bitrate version of the movie if the supported network throughput over the wireless link is more than the bitrate of the last segment received. Client calculates the available bandwidth of the wireless link after receiving the segment from the server. If this bandwidth is more than the segment bitrate, then same process continues. Hence, the client gets the highest quality of the video from the server that the network can support.
5. In case of congestion or packet loss, then the client requests for a lower bitrate version of the video segments, to continue the streaming.
6. Smooth playback of the movie with different bitrate segments is ensured with the help of video buffer.

Adaptive Bitrate Protocol (ABR) uses multi-bitrate encoding to cater to heterogeneous user equipment (UE) with various screen resolutions e.g. mobile handsets, Laptop screen or HD-TV. Depending on the screen resolution, ABR adaptively selects the suitable manifest to be sent to the client from the web server resulting in a high QoE for each user (Akhshabi et al., 2011)

HTTP Streaming and DASH Standard

Figure 2 shows the Adaptive HTTP streaming architecture, based on Thang et al. (2012). The metadata (semantics and physical level information) about the content is provided by the content annotation module. The media preparation module provides tools for efficient media delivery to the client, such as:

*   Adaptation/Transcoding,
*   Packetization, and
*   Encapsulation.

Figure 2. Adaptive HTTP streaming architecture

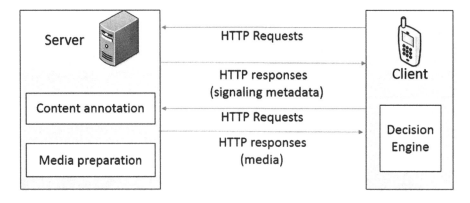

The decision engine at the client decides which version of media segment should be downloaded based on the network condition or UE screen resolution. MPEG DASH essentially specifies the metadata and media formats that are exchanged between clients and servers.

According to MPEG DASH, the metadata is called Media Presentation Description (MPD). Conventional streaming uses different protocols for signaling metadata and media delivery (e.g. by RTSP for metadata and RTP for media data), Wu, et al. (2001). HTTP streaming, on the other hand, delivers both signaling metadata and media by HTTP protocol itself.

Media Presentation Description

The hierarchy of signaling metadata is shown in Figure 3, based on Thang et al. (2012). The signaling metadata of DASH or MPD is categorized as follows:

1. **Content-Level Information:** Includes content description, such as available time, duration, minimum initial buffering, etc.
2. **Period-Level Information:** Includes the common description of a period, such as start time, duration, unique identifier, etc.
3. **Adaptation Information:** Describes the characteristics of representations and representation groups (called adaptation sets in DASH), such as bitrate, resolution, quality. Based on the information of alternatives, the client will select a segment of appropriate alternative based on terminal and network constraints.
4. **Mapping Information:** Describes the locations to retrieve actual media data. In DASH, location information is available in MPD and media segment format.

In MPEG DASH, a content comprises of multiple components (video, audio) that can be broken into smaller periods (temporal units/fragments), as shown in Figure 3 and 4. Each alternative representation of a content component can be divided into media segments. The client requests appropriate segments for a period after processing the metadata of that period. The process of receiving metadata of subsequent periods and requesting suitable segments continues. HTTP request-response exchanges between the client and server forms the basis of media delivery. The detailed content overview of MPD is shown in Figure 4.

Figure 3. Hierarchy of content division and levels of metadata

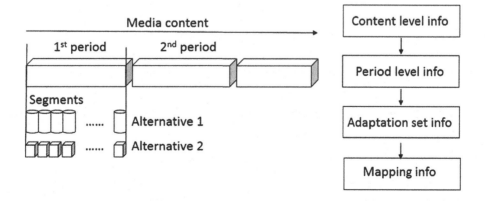

Figure 4. MPD data model and various representation

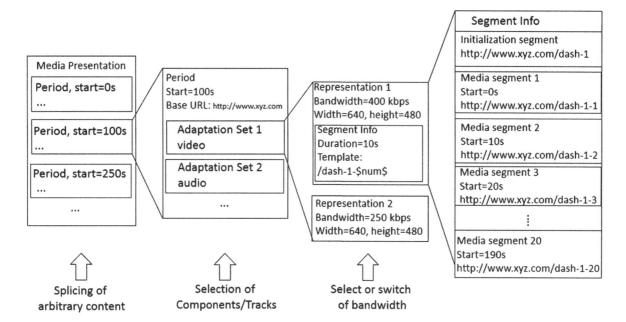

Throughput Estimation for Bitrate Adaptation

The bitrate adaptivity can be formulated by an optimization problem, as suggested by Thang et al. (2012). To adapt N components $\left\{A_n, 1 \leq n \leq N\right\}$, in a given span of time with bitrate constraint R_b^C where each alternative A_n^* of each component n has a bitrate R_n and quality Q_n, the optimization problem is to find A_n^* for each A_n so that the overall quality OQ is maximized.

$\max OQ$,

$$OQ = f\left(Q_1, Q_2, \ldots, Q_n\right),$$

and satisfy $\sum_{n=1}^{N} R_n \leq R_b^c$.

To solve the problem, the following two important aspects are considered:

- Estimation of throughput for each component of the media, which is used to find bitrate constraint R_b^C
- Support for additional metadata related to video quality in order to enable optimal selection of alternatives.

In HTTP request-response transaction, the segment throughput $T_S(i)$ for segment i is calculated as request-response duration, which is from the instant of sending the request to the instant of receiving the last byte of the response. There are different techniques to find the estimated throughput. A priori knowledge of this is required before sending a segment.

One of the method of throughput estimation is to consider the last segment throughput (Romero, 2011). $T_e(i) = T_s(i-1)$. However the estimated throughput $T_e(i)$, will cause frequent fluctuation in media quality if the channel throughput fluctuates rapidly. This situation may occur in an environment where a high mobility is associated with the device.

Another straight forward method is to apply "Smoothed" throughput which results in a stable estimation of throughput over time, Gouache, et al. (2011). The estimation is carried out in the following manner.

$$T_s(i) = \frac{Bytes \times 8}{elapsed}$$

where, *Bytes* is the number of bytes received over the duration *elapsed* .

$$T_{avg}(i+1) = (1-\alpha)T_{avg}(i) + \alpha T_s(i)$$

where $T_s(i)$ is the measured bit rate, $T_{avg}(i)$ is the average bit rate for the current iteration and α is the weight given to the current bit rate measurement.

The bit rate variance is calculated as

$$Var_{i+1} = (1-\beta)Var_i + \beta \cdot \sigma_i$$

where,

$$\sigma_i = \left| T_s(i) - T_{avg}(i) \right|$$

σ_i is the difference between the measured bit rate and the average bit rate for the current iteration, Var_i is the variance computed for the current iteration and β is the weight given to the current variance measurement.

$$T_e(i) = T_{avg}(i) - c \cdot Var_i$$

where c is a constant to provide weight for the variance.

The disadvantage of smoothed throughput estimation is that it causes late reaction of the client to large decrease in throughput.

Figure 5. Throughput estimation framework based on feature extraction

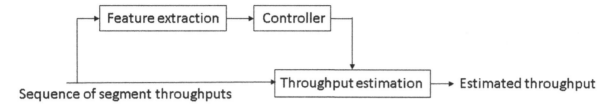

A very effective technique is shown in Figure 5, proposed by Thang et al. (2012), where the throughput estimation is obtained by considering feature extraction of the previous segment throughput. This technique is effective for short term as well as long term throughput fluctuation. The feature extraction block provides one or more properties of the previous sequence of segment throughput. Based on the extracted features, the controller changes the parameters of the throughput estimation block.

To obtain the estimated throughput for segment i, running average technique is used as follows

$$T_e(i) = \begin{cases} (1-\delta)T_e(i-2) + \delta \cdot T_s(i-1), & i > 0 \\ T_s(i-1), & i = 1, 2 \end{cases}$$

δ is a parameter which can be dynamically controlled so that the estimated throughput is free from short-term fluctuation as well as provides quick response for sudden large change in throughput. The requested bitrate for the segment $i = 0$ is the lowest bitrate available in the manifest file.

The efficiency of this technique depends on MPD content, quick response to the sudden change of channel bandwidth, database management system implemented at the server, efficient indexing of the alternatives, switching of CDNs etc. Some disadvantages of DASH are:

1. Small file size and block size segments are difficult to store and maintain,
2. Number of objects are huge,
3. Number of log entries are very large,
4. Provides stateless delivery which means loss of session reporting and loss of concurrent streams reporting,
5. Does not provide QoS in the cost of QoE,
6. Overloading network,
7. Content and network providers don't prefer DASH as it will increase the maintenance and hardware cost drastically.

VIDEO CACHING FOR EFFICIENT UTILIZATION OF NETWORK RESOURCES

Video caching provides good viewer experience by placing the caching servers in the network path. A number of video servers like Netflix, Youtube and Googleplay have their own cache servers placed at different locations across the world. Caching server placement and algorithms controlling the caching operation after cache miss etc. are addressed and designed by various researchers. Two main applications of video caching for efficient utilization of network resources are examined in this study, one is Hierarchical web caching in Internet-based vehicular ad hoc networks (IVANET) and other is on Collaborative web caching through resource auctions among two or more wireless service providers (WSPs).

Hierarchical Web Caching in Internet-Based Vehicular Ad Hoc Networks (IVANET)

IVANET opens a new area of technological advances with various applications such as Internet access from moving vehicles, online video streaming etc. (Zeadally et al., 2012). In IVANET applications, frequent disconnections from the web server while the nodes are mobile, creates low QoE. For uninterrupted voice-over-IP and video-on-demand services, the moving vehicle should be able to handle frequent disconnections of multimedia streaming sessions to offer good QoS and QoE. Solution to this can be achieved by web caching. The generalized architecture for web caching in IVANET is given by Kumar et al. (2015). The cache is placed at different levels namely Road Side Unit (RSUs), the gateway or inside moving vehicles as shown in Figure 6. By positioning the cache at different levels, the availability of the media content is increased while the vehicles are in motion. A large delay is encountered by the vehicles when it tries to access the video content from level1. Many researchers have proposed techniques to optimize the selection of resources and routes for video transmissions by sharing the traffic load between the layers. The minimization of the congestion without affecting the overall quality of multimedia content needs dynamic rate allocation in each link through which multimedia content are being streamed. A novel Quality-of-service (Qos) aware hierarchical web caching (QHWC) is proposed by Kumar et al. (2015) which overcomes the shortcomings of earlier dynamic web caching schemes such as dynamic service, weighted segment, and machine learning based. Two matrices named as load utilization ratio (LUR) and query to connectivity ratio (QCR) is used for performance measurement with respect to query delay and QoE.

Figure 6. Generalized architecture of web caching in IVANETs for video streaming applications

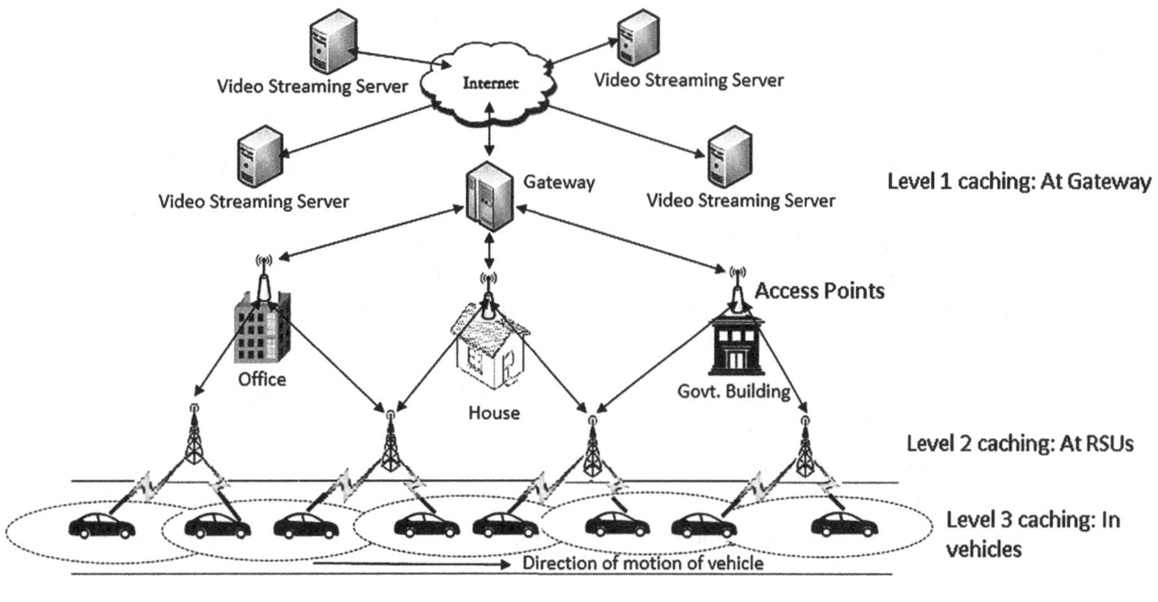

Web Caching Schemes

The model shown in Figure 6 have the following considerations:

1. Vehicles are moving in a particular direction with uniform velocity.
2. The vehicles are connected to RSUs which are placed at the side of the road.
3. The access points are located on houses, offices or government buildings. The RSUs are connected to those access points (APs) via high speed wire or wireless connectivity.
4. If any vehicle is outside the coverage area of APs or RSUs, then they can send their data through some of the other nodes (vehicles) in the network.

For efficient utilization of network resources, priority based multimedia content delivery may be considered. Here users provide an input by rating the video content, so that priority of the multimedia traffic can be increased or decreased based on the user's choice. The initial priority of the video content is set to zero.

Collaborative Web Caching through Resource Auctions among Multiple Wireless Service Providers (WSPS)

High Quality (HQ) on-demand video streaming in a wireless network needs high bandwidth of the channel. Recent advancement of wireless network such as WLAN (802.11 ac & ad), LTE-A, and advent of 5G, has made it possible.

In conventional caching namely independent caching, the caching mechanism deployed at each WSP is used to improve the overall system performance providing faster and better quality streaming delivery to mobile users (Zhang et al., 2004). The resources are always allocated to local users within the coverage area or domain of the access point.

Recently WSPs are offering high quality video streaming with proxy caching being used to locate video content closer to the end users. This makes accessibility of the video content faster, resulting in higher QoE for the end users as well as reduced load on the server. The challenge in proxy caching is that users join and leave streaming sessions frequently leading to unpredictable load on cache server. Recent deployment of wireless access points ensures that mobile users are often covered by multiple WSPs in the same area. This makes collaboration among WSPs possible, where different WSPs can assist one another in terms of bandwidth and storage resources in order to stream video content to end users.

Generally all WSPs are inherently selfish and autonomous in nature. Collaboration of multiple WSPs using resource auctions, proposed by Dai et al. (2012), solves the selfish nature of the WSPs. The cache servers, owned by different WSPs, truthfully cooperate with each other. This leads to profit maximization for individual WSPs. Collaboration through video caching exchange offers a win-win situation for all WSPs. The objectives are achieved by using Vickrey-Clarke-Groves (VCG) auctions proposed by Nisan et al. (2007), where all the decisions are taken in such a manner that truthfulness is maintained. Here each cache server acts as a bidder or sheller.

In wireless multimedia proxy caching, cost based cache replacement algorithm or server selection algorithm is used for single and multiple cache server scenario. Collaborating cache is extensively used in Internet Protocol Television (IPTV) and many other applications such as ISP based P2P network etc.

The cache servers, distributed in multiple domains (coverage area of one access point) can spontaneously cooperate with each other under some regulations to maximize the traffic volume server from each cache.

In collaborative caching, shown in Figure 7, WSPs X, Y and Z have their own cache servers deployed inside Mobile Switching Centers (MSCs) which are connected to base stations (BSs) through Radio Network Controller (RNC). The servers in individual WSPs have limited storage capacity. Without collaborative caching, if cache miss occurs in any of the domains, then the content will be requested from remote server. As the remote server is connected to multiple cache servers, frequent cache misses can create a huge load on the remote server. However, this problem can be solved using collaborative caching. Domain X can request the missing content from all neighboring WSPs and if the content is available in domain Y, it can allocate bandwidth to those requests from the mobile users of domain X. This is indicated by arrow 1 in Figure 7. Due to dynamics of the system, the efficient utilization of bandwidth resources across cache servers is a critical challenge in collaborative caching.

The practical implementation challenges in collaborating cache, due to selfishness among the deployed cache servers, are

1. Need of incentive mechanism for collaboration of different WSPs. This is required because all WSPs are mainly concerned with their individual potential benefits.
2. All WSPs should be honest to other WSPs in terms of resource sharing. There is a need of mechanism that ensures that truthfulness of the WSPs will benefit them.

Figure 7. An example of collaborative caching

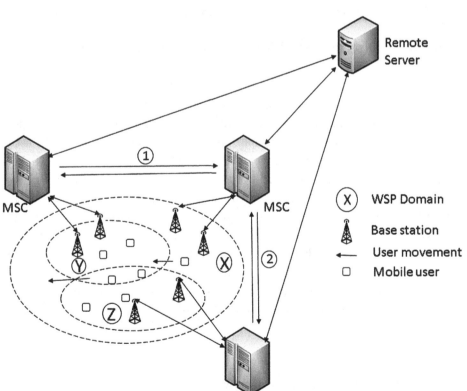

3.   A centralized coordination is required using software defined network (SDN) so that the resource sharing will be centrally controlled by a centralized controller in a given area of coverage.

QUALITY AWARE VIDEO TRANSCODING

Transcoding is a direct analog-to-analog or digital-to-digital conversion of one encoding format to another. Transcoding is usually performed in cases where a target device (or workflow) does not support the format or has limited storage capacity that mandates a reduced file size or to convert incompatible data to a better-supported format. The process of transcoding is irreversible where losses are introduced while conversion. To improve the quality of experience of video streaming services, the content providers needs to prepare multiple quality or bitrate levels appropriate to the network infrastructure and device hardware specifications. The transcoding may be performed by spatially (resolution reduction), temporally (frame rate reduction) or by using higher quantization parameters while encoding. For the best utilization of the network resources, an optimal adaptation framework for streaming multiple video objects was presented by Lim et al. (2008) where both network bandwidth and cost of transcoding are considered for transcoding of the video objects. A general framework, called utility-based video adaptation is proposed by Wang et al. (2007).

The authors discuss two methods of video transcoding for efficient delivery of multimedia content over network namely:

1.   Dependency aware distributed video transcoding in cloud proposed by Zakerinasab et al. (2015).
2.   Optimal H.264/AVC video transcoding system proposed by Al-Abri et al. (2011).

Dependency Aware Distributed Video Transcoding in Cloud (D-DVC)

In Cloud based video transcoding, a fixed number of consecutive frames in a video or group of pictures (GOP) are grouped into video chunk. The chunks are distributed to virtual machines in cloud using scalable video coding (SVC) for parallel processing. Due to inter-dependency between video frames, the GOPs are grouped to different video chunks. For example, GOPs that are very similar may be assigned to one video chunk and GOPs with high dissimilarity can be assigned to two video chunks. Highly dependent GOPs can be encoded together as the enclosed frames are very similar. The use of variable size video chunk, reduces the bitrate and transcoding time, up to three times than fixed-size chunk video encoding.

As suggested by many researchers, video transcoding in cloud is utilized for customized transcoding to mobile devices and for energy conservation on mobile devices. The performance gain of conventional video transcoding using cloud is mostly due to efficient utilization of cloud resources and parallel processing. This technique does not consider the dependency information of GOPs. Dependency-aware distributed video transcoding, proposed by Zakerinasab et al. (2015), reduces bitrate and transcoding time as well as ensures faster delivery and decoding of video for the end users.

Workflow

The generalized architecture of distributed video transcoding in the cloud is shown in Figure 8. The media files are downloaded from the server using HTTP request-response mechanism. The web server takes the request from the client and passes it to the streaming server. The streaming server, upon receiving the request from the web server instructs the transcoding controller to prepare the video appropriate to the channel bandwidth. The transcoding controller takes the raw video from the video content repository and prepare the Video chunk by grouping the GOPs. The video chunks are sent to the appropriate transcoding server where proper encoding of the video is performed parallely. The encoded individual video chunks are merged together using a video merger. At last, the transcoded video is delivered to the end user and the transcoded video is stored to the video database, if required.

The performance of the distributed video coding depends on minimization of transcoding delay, number of transcoding machines needed, energy consumption, and transcoding cost in the cloud. There is a trade-off between coding efficiency and transcoding time. Adaptive algorithm are used to determine proper chunk size based on similarities among frames in consecutive GOPs.

Scalable Video Coding

In scalable Video Coding (SVC), a layer video coding structure proposed by Schwarz et al. (2007) is used to encode video in different temporal, spatial resolution, and video qualities, inside one video stream. In H.264 standard, a SVC video consists of sequence of GOPs where each GOP starts with a key frame (I frame) followed by hierarchical temporal prediction frames. SVC supports three modes of scalability: temporal (D), spatial (T) and quality (Q). The DTQ metric defines the layer of scalability. For example DTQ= (0, 0, 0) defines the base layer with lowest quality playback of video. In SVC each frame is divided into distinct slices and further into a mesh of 16x16 macroblocks. The slices inside I, P and B frames are named as I-slice, P-slice, and B-slice respectively. The prediction order and required slices for prediction depends on the encoder. For quality scalability, SVC specifies different quantization parameters (QP).

Figure 8. Generalized architecture of distributed video transcoding in the cloud

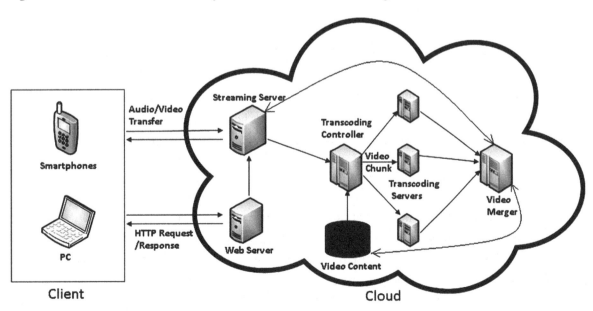

Dependency Aware Video Transcoding

To avoid coding inefficiency due to fixed-sized video chunking, dependency aware video transcoding is employed. Considering the fact that a group of n dependent GOPs can be encoded faster than n independent GOPs, a GOP-dependency model is employed which exploits the visual similarities. It clusters GOPs into video chunks according to their inter-dependency. GOP dependency is determined at the time of generating a coded version of the video from its raw version. Coded video reflects the visual similarity and greatly determines the coding complexity. The transcoding controller, shown in Figure 8, segments the video into proper chunks of video for further processing.

GOP Dependency Graph

The GOP dependency graph is derived from layer structure of SVC. Utilization of macroblocks and sub-macroblocks to model the dependency helps in better coding efficiency. The GOP dependency graph is derived in two steps.

Step 1: Generation of Macroblock Dependency Graph.

A dependency graph G_m is created based on two consecutive GOPs where each G_m is a weighted directed acyclic graph (DAG) $G_m = (V_m, N_m)$. Each node $k_i \in V_m$ represents a macroblock belonging to the key or non-key frames. The graph is formed by extracting the dependency between all the macroblocks M_i in frame F_X and M_j in F_Y. An independent macroblock is added as a new node to the graph as shown in Figure 9. The direction of the graph is from reference macroblock to the dependent macroblock. A detailed formulation of the graph has been discussed by Zakerinasab et al. (2015).

Step 2: Creating the GOP-Dependency Graph.

The G_m prepared in the previous step is used for modelling inter-GOP prediction dependency. It is then converted into a frame-dependency graph G_f, by merging nodes from the same frame into a single node. The weight of the individual arcs being merged. Next, the G_f is converted to a directed GOP-dependency graph G_g by merging nodes representing frames belonging to the same GOP into one node. The dependency between the GOPs is converted to a distance metric for the GOP clustering algorithm.

Preparing Variable-Size Video Chunks

Using the GOP-dependency graph G_g, variable sized video chunks are created using a GOP clustering algorithm. For real time transcoding of a video without apriori knowledge, OPTICS (Ordering Points to Identify the Clustering Structure) is used to cluster nodes in GOP-dependency graph G_g. OPTICS has two parameters: ε - the maximum distance among nodes in a cluster, and MinPts – the minimum number of nodes in a cluster. MinPts is set to be one by default, meaning that if there is no GOP with a strong visual similarity with a GOP, then the GOP can be processed alone as a video chunk. The com-

Figure 9. Prediction dependency links and macroblock dependency graph for inter-GOP prediction. The number inside each frame represents the encoding order inside respective spatial layer of SVC

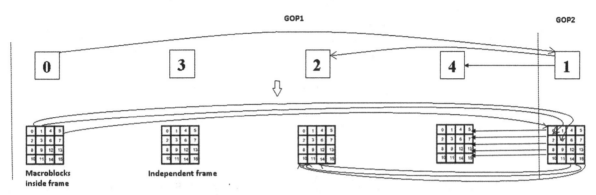

putational complexity of OPTICS depends on the complexity of ε -neighbourhood query function which is invoked exactly once for each GOP.

Dispatching Video Chunks for Distributed Transcoding in the Cloud

The transcoding controller prepares the video chunks based on their inter-dependency. Then it dispatches the variable-sized video chunks to virtual machines in the cloud for transcoding. Optimization of the dispatching algorithm for transcoding delay, number of virtual machines, or the energy consumed in the cloud, is a challenging task. The transcoding time depends on the type of video. For real-time streaming, video chunks must be transcoded with respect to their playback deadline. A simple FIFO dispatching algorithm is suitable, since it preserves the time order of video chunks. (Zakerinasab et al., 2015)

An optimal transcoding algorithm is described in the next section.

Optimal H.264/AVC Video Transcoding

The optimal transcoding of video should meet the following requirements

1.   Lower transcoder complexity in terms of computational power and memory space requirement.
2.   High quality output within the target bit rate satisfying the user QoE.
3.   Lower transcoding time requirement.

So adaptive selection of transcoding scheme is a challenging task for heterogeneous broadband wireless network as the channel bandwidth fluctuates extensively with time. The parameters for the selection of transcoding mode are available system resources, such as: memory and power, coding information of the encoded bit stream, channel bandwidth, and PSNR requirement from client. Figure 10 shows a framework for optimal video transcoding system.

Three well-known transcoding methods used for transcoding of video are Open Loop (OL) translator, Fast-Pixel domain (FP) translator, and Cascaded Pixel-domain (CP) translator, suggested by Notebaert et al. (2007). Table 1 shows a list of different combinations of the applied transcoding methods for the frame type I, P/I, P/P, B/I, and B/B.

Figure 10. Framework for optimal or adaptive transcoding system

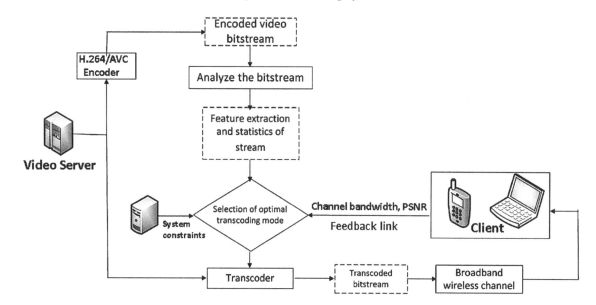

WEB OPTIMIZATION OF MULTIMEDIA SERVICES

With the development of wireless telecommunication network and the mobile phone technology, the mobile phones have become the primary means of the Internet access. Since most of the content on the Internet is designed for the PC users and the inherent limitation of mobile browsers is in terms of the processing power, network bandwidth cumulatively causes a low Web Performance. To improve the Web Performance a number of Web Optimization techniques are being followed and have been proposed by researchers over a period of time e.g. web page prefetching, speculative loading, and parallel optimization etc. The web performance can further be enhanced with the introduction of cloud computing.

Table 1. Transcoding scheme and corresponding transcoding methods

Transcoding Scheme	I	P/I	P/P	B/I	B/B
0	OL	OL	OL	OL	OL
1	-	OL	OL	OL	OL
2	FP	FP	FP	FP	FP
3	FP	OL	OL	OL	OL
4	CL	CL	CL	CL	CL
5	FP	CL	OL	CL	OL
6	FP	CL	CL	CL	OL
7	FP	CL	CL	CL	CL
8	FP	-	CL	-	CL
9	FP	OL	CL	OL	CL
10	FP	-	OL	-	OL
11	-	-	OL	-	OL

Mobile Web Browsing Architecture

The mobile web browsing architecture refers to the organization of the mobile browser, the web server, and the cloud, as well as how they interact with each other. In the cloud computing era, the cloud plays an important role in improving the performance of mobile web browsers. The cloud and the mobile browser can work together to provide a better user experience. According to the interactions among the mobile browser, the cloud, and the web server, the mobile web browsing architecture is categorized into four schemes:

1. Client-server architecture,
2. Cloud-based architecture,
3. Cloud-assisted architecture,
4. Cooperating architecture (Wang et al., 2013).

Figure 11(a) illustrates the client-server architecture, a traditional and simple architecture for mobile browsers. The mobile browser at the user-side retrieves the web contents from the remote web server using HTTP request-response mechanism. The client is responsible for all the necessary calculations to fetch the web content. In this architecture, the mobile browser is known as fat client. Examples of web browsers operating in this architecture are - Android browsers, Safari, Pocketweb etc. The advantages of this architecture are a) Easy and cost effective implementation b) More secure than architecture with external facilities. A prominent disadvantage of this architecture is that all optimization functionalities are performed at the client side which is often resource and computation-power limited.

Figure 11(b) shows the cloud-based architecture. All the messages, the browser interchanges with the server goes through the cloud agent which acts as an agent/proxy for the mobile browser. As the cloud acts as an intermediate entity, when a user accesses a web page, the mobile browser sends the request to the cloud instead of the remote web server. Some optimizations on the data, such as resizing the pictures, format change etc., are performed by the processor in the cloud after downloading all the web contents from the server. The cloud agent then sends the compressed web contents back to the user side mobile browser. The cloud agent also pre-calculates some intermediate results which are required during this process. The mobile browser acts as a thin client, in contrast to the above client-server architecture. The performance of this architecture depends on the ability of the cloud, which can reduce the network traf-

Figure 11. (a) Client-server architecture; (b) Cloud-based architecture

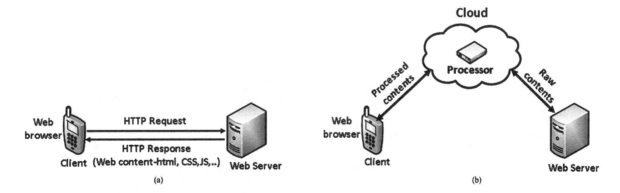

fic and local processing time, by sharing some data processing tasks. Two major disadvantages of this architecture are a) It may increase the network latency as the processing time at the cloud contributes to the end-to-end delay. b) This architecture is less secure than the client-server architecture because data path includes the cloud where data leakage may happen. Web browsers such as Opera mini, Skyfire, Amazon Silk, VMP works according to this architecture.

In the cloud-assisted architecture, the cloud and the web server act as two independent entities, which is illustrated in Figure 12(a). The client fetches the web content from the web server using the same procedure described in client-server architecture. After downloading the content, the client categorizes the content based on priority, number of critical and heavy operations etc. The content which needs heavy processing, can be offloaded to the cloud which has much higher processing power than the mobile device. In this way, the cloud offers auxiliary services to the mobile browser. This results in improved user experience. The advantages of this architecture are:

- The messages are downloaded directly by client, so chances of data leakage are very less.
- It provides faster processing.
- The power of the cloud processor can significantly increase the QoE without changing the main infrastructure.

In the cooperating architecture, a local cloud is formed by multiple mobile devices. The local cloud acts as the resource provider using device-to-device communication. The devices cooperate with each other if any device has enough resources to support other device. This collaborative nature of the mobile devices helps in downloading the web contents from the server at a faster rate, as shown in Figure 12(b). This architecture provides a faster experience. However, security challenges are present as other devices are used as intermediate entity where data leakage may occur.

Limitations of Mobile Web Browser

PC Web browser and Mobile web browser works in similar ways. Mobile web browser are more complex due to its limited computational resources, expensive network traffic, higher packet error rate, higher end-to-end delay, and limited power supply.

Figure 12. (a) Cloud-assisted architecture; (b) cooperating architecture

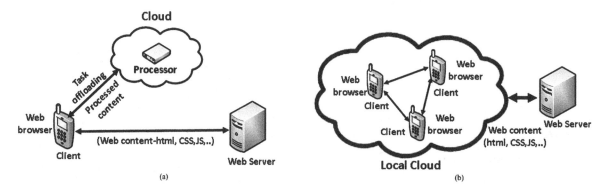

- **Computation Intensive Operation:** HTML document processing includes styles and layout calculations, execution of JavaScript, displaying the web pages, and interaction with users. CSS style sheets and layout calculations are the most computation intensive operations that accounts for maximum computation time during the web page processing.
- **Long Resource Loading Time:** To display a web page, browser needs to fetch the web content before processing it. This resource loading time is a major factor that contributes in web page loading time. The resource loading time is dependent on the network RTT (Round Trip Time). RTT depends on the size of web content and the network state (bandwidth).
- **Network Traffic:** The cost of internet over the mobile is more as compared to the internet over the PC. The amount of data being consumed in the web page is always a matter of concern for the users. Every day web pages are growing in size and getting complex, an average web page size is around 1MB now a days. This is due to different kinds of contents being added to the web pages to include new features and to make them interactive. However most of the websites doesn't have optimized mobile versions.
- **Energy Consumption:** Mobile devices have limited battery power. The applications should be optimized with minimal requirement of computational power.

Optimization Methodologies of Mobile Internet Access

The optimizations are carried out either at the mobile side or at the cloud side. These optimization techniques are proposed and validated by several researchers and have been discussed by Wang et al. (2013).

1. **Client Side Optimization:** These are the optimizations that are carried out on the mobile web browser itself. These optimization techniques are easily deployable, provides more security, and are cost effective.
   a. **Effective Caching of Web Content:** Resource loading is the biggest contributor in browser. The frequently used web resources can be stored locally in the browser cache to save RTT and bandwidth during the subsequent visits to the web page. Firstly, the cache cannot be unlimited and secondly, after some time the cache becomes redundant as the web access is dynamic i.e. it's not compulsory that the user is going to visit the same web page again. Furthermore, the web pages are also being updated frequently. So it's very important to maintain an effective cache. Traditional caching aims to reduce the resource loading time by storing raw resources –pictures, CSS files etc. The cached resource have two states: fresh and expired. If the resource can be reused without confirming with the server then it is in fresh state, whereas if the browser needs to connect to the server to confirm if the resource can be reused then it is in expired state. Now, the expired state is responsible for minimum one RTT, making the traditional caching not very effective. To overcome the shortcomings of traditional caching, smart Caching is proposed with an aim to reduce the time of computation intensive operations. Smart caching rather than storing the raw resources, focuses on storing the intermediate result of web page processing- CSS formatting results called smart style caching, and layout calculation results called layout caching. These stored results can later be applied to the identical elements in the subsequent visits to the same page. If in the previous visit, layout has been calculated for the rendered object or it has been calculated and stored in the cache, the same results can be

used. This approach not only reduces the computational effort but also saves the duplication in calculations.

b.   **Client Side Parallelization:** Web content is processed in a single thread manner so as to get the proper result. For example, Google's Chrome browser treats each tab as a separate process to increase parallelism; however the web page in each tab is still processed in a single threaded manner. Firefox uses a sequential CCS rule matching algorithm. Jones et al. (2009) analyzes the Chrome browser and discuss how parallelism of computation-intensive parts of a web browser can improve the browser to be quick responsive and energy-efficient. They describe the design and analytical model to analyze the possibility of better performance and algorithms to parallelize each browser component, including parallelizing the front-end, page layout, and scripting.

c.   **Web Page Prefetching:** According to Bouras et al. (2004), web page prefetching is the notion of predicting the web pages that the user will visit in the near future and download those web pages before actual visits. If the prediction hits, the browser can locally use the already preloaded resources. In few cases, it's possible to predict what a user is likely to click next. For example, when a user is on an online banking login page, he/she is most likely to click login. In this case, it would be great if the browser could begin loading the page before the user clicks. However, in many cases, it is difficult to know what a user is likely to access next. So, the most simple and naive way is to pre-fetch all the pages referenced by the current page. A page may have many links. But if the browser tries to fetch many links at the same time, it would cause too much traffic and most of the fetched contents may be useless.

d.   **Speculative Loading:** The idea of speculative loading was proposed by Wang et al. (2012) in order to reduce the resource loading time. This mechanism works based on prediction of resources which are linked to a web page. When a user starts accessing a web page, the browser loads the predicted useful sub resources along with the main resources, which can save the roundtrip-time to some extent. The main difference between "Speculative Loading" and "Web Prefetching" is that speculative loading predicts which resources the user may need and on the other hand, prefetching predicts which pages the user may visit. The main difficulty here is as to how accurately the browser can predict which sub-resources will be useful to the user. Wang et al.'s (2011) approach is construction of a web site's resource graph based on visiting history of the web page. Different pages of the same web site may share lots of sub resources. A revisit to a previously visited web page results in availability of the sub-resources in the resource graph. Whereas, a new visit leads to prediction of the sub-resources that may be useful according to the shared sub-resource nodes.

2.   **Cloud Based Optimization:** Mobile devices have limited resources due to its portability. Whereas the cloud can avail unlimited resources for any task. Hence cloud computing has drawn a keen interest in this generation. A device can offload its heavy task to the cloud.

a.   **Cloud Based Parallelization:** Adrenaline is a prototype system which exploits task parallelism to speed up. The system consists of Adrenaline server and a client-side browser. The browser fetches web content from the Adrenaline server which in turn fetches the content from the web server, optimizes it and decomposes the web pages into mini pages. Adrenaline server replies to the browser with all the mini pages which it has to aggregate into a single web page. The challenges faced while implicating this is web semantics and how to decompose web page into mini pages.

b. **Cloud Based Pre-Processing:** In this method, the cloud decides what needs to be processed by it and what isn't because all the data goes through the cloud. The cloud acts as an agent to a client browser and traffic between web servers. It stores requests by other users which could be later used by a new user. The cloud also performs optimization on the pictures by resizing based on device resolution. It compresses data before sending to the browser to reduce traffic bandwidth.

c. **Computation Offloading:** It's different from cloud-based pre-processing as the client browser decides when and what processes need to be offloaded to the cloud. The client can offload tiresome JavaScript code to the cloud and multimedia processing tasks too as well as merge remote display with mobile browser interface. It helps to improve the mobile browser's responsiveness and energy efficiency. However, there exists additional latency issue due to computation offloading. The user can decide whether to offload or not based on QoS requirement of the application.

d. **Cooperating with P2P Mobile Cloud:** The different mobile devices are networked with each other to form a peer-to-peer mobile cloud. The devices cooperatively downloading web contents can increase the capacity virtually of cellular link and reduce resource loading time. The resource loading is divided into two processes: web page processing and components downloading. In web page processing, the browser searches sub-resources from contents of URL and ranks them according to size. The sub-resources are further divided into sub-lists. In downloading phase, each device now downloads its sub-list resources and sends the resources to whichever device that has a user visiting the page.

TCP Optimization for Mobile Data Network

The performance of TCP for mobile data networks such as 3G/HSDPA or LTE/LTE-A is not optimal because it fails to utilize the bandwidth available in the mobile network. This is due to the fact that the mobile network deals with frequent link layer retransmission, significantly longer and load-dependent round-trip-time (RTT), bandwidth fluctuation, and non-congestion-related packet loss.

Many authors have proposed various techniques for data connectivity in mobile network such as TCP Westwood, TCP Jersey and TCP Veno etc. The challenges in developing optimized TCP for mobile network are:

- A complete redesign of TCP will have difficulties in practical deployment.
- TCP protocols are implemented as a part of the OS. Thus it calls for modification of the TCP implementation in wide variety of OS like open-source implementations (e.g., Linux and its many variants) to proprietary implementations (e.g., Microsoft Windows).
- Protocol upgradation in both server and client sides takes a long time, given the number of deployed devices are very large.
- Many servers serve both wired and non-wired users. This protocol must work well for both.

A novel approach proposed by Liu et al. (2011) uses a network layer device called *Mobile Accelerator* between internet and mobile data network. This protocol optimization technique has three major parts in implementation:

1. **Opportunistic Transmission:** This takes care of the large BDP (bandwidth delay product) problem without enlarging the client TCP buffer size. The received packets are quickly processed even before the next packet arrives, leaving the TCP buffer empty. The accelerator is wired to the internet server and has abundant memory storage. The internet server sends packets to the accelerator and it sends back an ACK signal. The receiver window size reported by the ACK is determined by the accelerator and is larger than the mobile client. The mobile accelerator then forwards the TCP packets to the receiver using Transmission Rate Control method.

2. **Transmission Rate Control:** This adaptively changes the transmission rate so that the available bandwidth is fully utilized. The accelerator starts transmission at a rate no less than the maximum channel capacity. This ensures full bandwidth utilization at start. After receiving the first ACK the transmission rate is controlled by this phase depending upon the available bandwidth using a sliding window.

   a. Time is divided into fixed small intervals. The first ACK from the receiver marks the start of the first interval.

   b. A sliding window mechanism of size M is used for bandwidth estimation where the transmitter uses the ACK data from receiver for previous M intervals to find the throughput of the channel. The accuracy of estimation depends on the selection of M based on the nature of throughput variation of the channel.

   c. The transmission rate is controlled depending upon available bandwidth.

3. **Packet Loss Recovery:** This is performed in two steps:

   a. **Step 1 (Between TCP Sender and Accelerator):** Using conventional TCP i.e. using duplicate ACKs, when packet loss occurs or previous ACK is lost.

   b. **Step 2 (Between Accelerator and Receiver):** The mobile accelerator maintains a list of unacknowledged TCP segments from receiver. When three duplicate ACKs are received, the accelerator retransmits the lost TCP segment to receiver and does not forward it back to the TCP sender, if the requested lost TCP segment is available in the accelerator. If not available, then duplicate ACKs will be forwarded to sender for retransmission.

All these are implemented inside the mobile accelerator device. The structure of the mobile accelerator is shown in Figure 13.

Figure 13. Mobile accelerator and its components

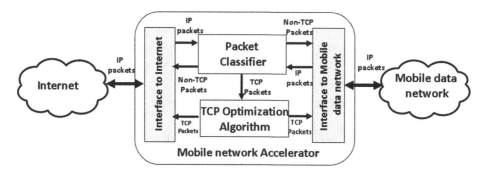

USER-CENTRIC CROSS-LAYER OPTIMIZATION

In a heterogeneous mobile network, user-centric multimedia service adapts the encoding rate using SVC or modulation and coding scheme (MCS) for uninterrupted video playback with better QoE. The feedback from UE helps the service provider to optimize the resources adaptively in order to improve QoE. Recent deployment of heterogeneous UEs with varied display capabilities, varying channel condition, and limited battery capacity demands user-centric optimization at the transmitter. There is a trade-off between energy saving and QoE. There are some constraints involved at different stages of communication and needs to be considered while designing practical systems.

Wireless Channel Characteristics

The channel condition can be defined in terms of bit error rate (BER), signal-to-noise ratio (SNR), Frame error rate (FER), or throughput in terms of delay calculation. The type of channel depends on the area whether it is a rural, sub-urban, or urban area. There are various channel model available for wireless radio access networks, such as Rayleigh fading channel, Suzuki fading channel, Nakagami channel etc. which are considered for performance evaluation in terms of capacity and BER of the wireless link. Cross layer adaptive technique proposed by Banerjee et al. (2012) have considered BER and Suzuki fading model.

Wireless channel is characterized by three different types of amplitude fluctuations, namely, very slow fading, slow fading, and fast fading. There are various path loss models available in literature to find the average received power in different environments. Constructive and destructive multipath components lead to fast changes in the channel characteristics. The nature of fading also depends on line-of-sight and non-line-of-sight connectivity of the device with the network access point.

Adaptation Techniques

Adaptation in video streaming can be introduced in two layers of ISO-OSI model viz. change of either video encoding rate at the application layer or modulation and coding scheme at the link layer. Lowering the encoding rate reduces the transmission bandwidth requirement and results in low BER. Adjusting the encoding rate is a computationally expensive operation that also consumes more power and hardware resources. One method of solving this issue may be by pre-encoding the video and storing in database at different levels of data rate by changing it spatially and temporally (used in MPEG-DASH). It helps to reduce the processing power and delay of encoding process. However, pre-encoding technique doesn't work well for live video transmissions as it introduces more delay.

The frame size (Width × Height) of different resolution are i) HD-1280×720 ii) SVGA-800×600 iii) VGA-640×480 iv) CIF-352×288 v) HQVGA-240×160 vi) QCIF-176×144. Figure 14(a) and Fig-

Table 2. The constraints at different stages of wireless communication

Multimedia Server	Service Provider	User Equipment
• Adaptive encoding scheme • Video processing power • Storage	• Earn revenue • Transmit power • Resource allocation • Deliver better QoE	• Device display resolution • Limited battery • Channel condition • Price sensitivity

ure 14(b) show the plot of data rate vs. frame rate and data rate vs. video resolution respectively of a MPEG-4 encoded video.

If the reported channel bandwidth by the receiver is 'B' then the transmitter selects the best alternative video having data rate just equal or less than 'B'. The transmitter can choose either frame rate reduction or resolution reduction to achieve the required data rate suitable for channel.

Reducing data rate also helps in the usage of robust MCS where the transmission rate is decreased by reducing the order of the modulation scheme and increasing the forward error correction overhead during bad channel condition. For example, the physical layer throughput for LTE is calculated based on allocated MCS and is given by

$$T = TBS \times N_{TB} \times N_{sf} \, bits \, / \, \sec$$

where, TBS is transport block size per subframe, N_{TB} denotes the number of transport blocks per subframe and N_{sf} is the number of subframes that are transmitted through channel per second.

Table 3 shows a set of MCS and corresponding TBS values that meet the modulation scheme and code rate requirement based on the reported channel quality indicator (CQI) from UE (3GPP TS 36.213 R10, 2011).

Figure 15 shows the CQI versus channel throughput for three different values of resource block allocation. The MCS indexes are given as example (depending on hardware specification) which are used to find the corresponding TBS index and TBS values. It is observed that the throughput decreases when the reported CQI index value is small. If 20 resource blocks are allocated and reported then CQI value is 6, the achievable throughput is 1.3 Mbps. HD video with 20 fps requires 1 Mbps data rate (from Figure 14(a)) which can be sent through the channel. The selected video has a PSNR value of 57 dB which is quite high for providing satisfactory QoE. So, even with lower value of CQI, the user can get a satisfactory QoE.

Figure 14. (a) Data rate vs. frame rate; (b) data rate vs. video resolution

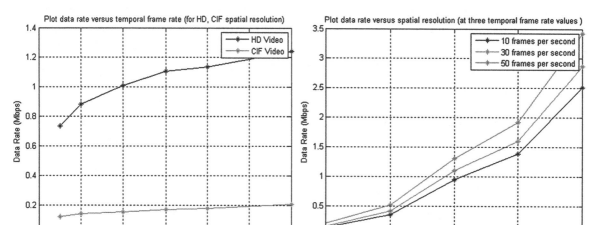

Table 3. Transport block size for different channel quality indication and corresponding MCS for N_RB=10 in LTE network

CQI	Modulation	Code rate	Bits/Symbol	MCS Index	TBS
1	QPSK	0.101449	2	0	256
2	QPSK	0.101449	2	0	256
3	QPSK	0.162319	2	2	424
4	QPSK	0.318841	2	5	696
5	QPSK	0.442210	2	7	1032
6	QPSK	0.568116	2	9	1384
7	16QAM	0.365217	4	12	2024
8	16QAM	0.469565	4	14	2536
9	16QAM	0.563768	4	16	3112
10	64QAM	0.484058	6	20	4008
11	64QAM	0.600000	6	23	4968
12	64QAM	0.692754	6	25	5736
13	64QAM	0.760870	6	27	6200
14	64QAM	0.888406	6	28	7480
15	64QAM	0.888406	6	28	7480

Figure 15. CQI vs. throughput for LTE for different values of resource blocks allocation

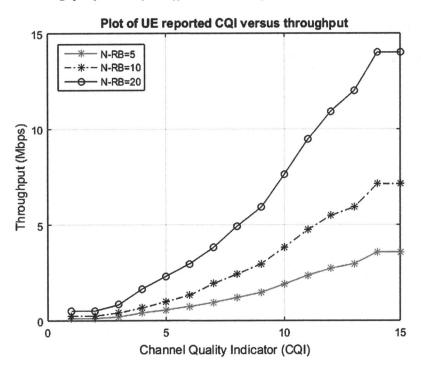

The Video quality can be measured in terms of PSNR of the original video. Lower frame rate or lower resolution encoding results in loss of information or decrease in PSNR. Figure 16 shows the plots of video PSNR vs. frame rate and PSNR vs. screen resolution. It is observed that decrease of data rate does not decrease the PSNR below the acceptable level. (Good quality video have PSNR 30 to 50 dB whereas acceptable PSNR for wireless media is 25 dB to maintain good QoE)

It is experimentally proved that without rate adaptation the receiver buffer underflows, causing pauses during playback of video.

Reducing the data rate and keeping a higher transmission rate results in stability in the buffer state. However, a high transmission rate causes video frame corruption. Keeping same data rate and reducing the transmission rate results in delay of receiving GOPs at the receiver which creates buffer underflow or freezes in video playback (Banerjee et al., 2012). So depending on the fading situation i.e. either slow or fast fading, the transmission rate or encoding rate can be varied, respectively. This optimizes the usage of processing power, stabilizes the buffer state, and ensures a smooth playback of video.

A user-centric feedback based channel adaptation model is shown in Figure 17, where the channel condition (in terms of BER), device screen resolution, receiver buffer state, and battery backup can be used as feedback parameters to the sender.

The stored or live video content from video source is encoded using MPEG-2 or MPEG-4 encoder. The packetized data is stored in the transmit buffer for caching. The modulated and coded data is transmitted through the unpredictable wireless medium. The received data with the actual data reference is used for SINR calculation and is sent as feedback to the transmitter periodically along with receiver buffer status and client screen resolution. The switching module implements the rate adaptation algorithm and chooses proper encoding rate for the encoder and MCS index for adaptation purpose.

Figure 16. (a) PSNR vs. frame rate; (b) PSNR vs. video resolution at 5 fps

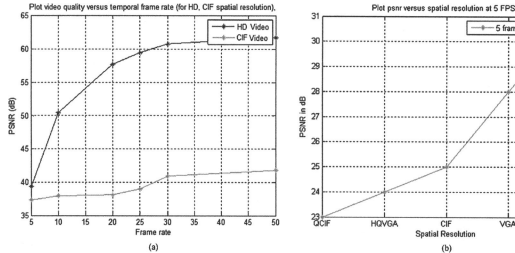

Figure 17. User-centric feedback based model for adaptive video transfer

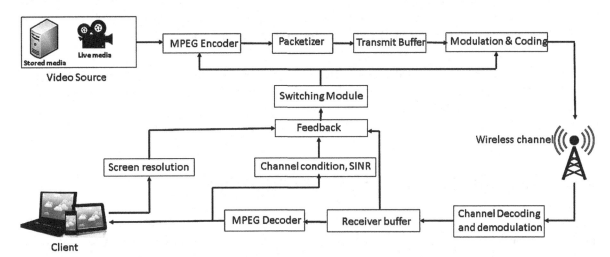

Performance Modeling and Optimization

The performance of the user-centric optimization techniques are evaluated based on the following considerations:

1. **Grouping of Users:** User Equipment (UE) capability is determined at the time of service subscription i.e. particular SVC layer number that the UE wants to receive. User grouping based on UE screen resolution and receiver SNR is done at the BS. As the distance of UE from BS increases the BS automatically puts the UE in the specific group based on periodic feedback from the UE.
2. **Time Slicing as an Energy Saving Measure:** Time slicing allows discontinuous reception at the UEs. UEs are able to save the battery by turning off their radio receiver when not receiving any data burst. Energy saving (ES) is calculated as the ratio of the radio turn-off time to the total time of reception. Apriori knowledge of the multiprotocol encapsulation-forward error correcting code (MPE-FEC) frame allows the UE to safely skip the bursts containing the layers which are irrelevant to it, thereby saving battery. (Singhal et al., 2014)
3. **Offloading in a Heterogeneous Wireless Network as QoE Measure:** In a heterogeneous network, a user is free to choose the best alternative wireless network for data communication. This provides energy efficiency and enhanced quality of user experience. If a femtocell or picocell is in range of a user device then it can choose it instead of cellular macrocell for improved multimedia service. In this way, the user can get better QoS.
4. **Adaptive Modulation and Coding Scheme:** Besides user-and channel aware SVC rate optimization at the application layer and time slicing at the link layer, at the physical layer adaptive modulation and coding scheme (MCS) can be applied. Adaptive MCS can be optimized in the given system for enhanced energy efficiency and network capacity. Clearly, this adaptation is a function of the heterogeneous user's composition in a cell and the dynamic physical channel rate constraint. Physical channel dynamics are accounted for at a slow (shadow fading) rate in order to avoid high bandwidth overhead of frequent channel state feedback. The computation of optimized MCS can be performed at the BS as well as the video server.

5. **Application Based Resource Allocation:** In today's world, different mobile application needs different amount of data rate or QoS requirement. Grouping users based on requested data rate and QoS requirement of different applications helps in efficient utilization of resources.

Thus the use of above mentioned user-centric cross layer optimization techniques helps to achieve better performance by balancing energy efficiency and QoE constraints. The adaptive feedback mechanism takes care of the channel condition and by selecting suitable encoding rate, the packet drop through the channel can be minimized.

CONCLUSION AND FUTURE RESEARCH DIRECTIONS

The upcoming wireless networks such as WLAN (802.11 ac/ad), LTE-A etc. promise a very high throughput with minimum latency to the users. Furthermore, multiple wireless technologies coexist and operate in a convergent manner as heterogeneous networks to meet the ever-increasing data-rate demands. Next generation networks are based on these heterogeneous networks with heterogeneity in terms of communication modalities, channel types, technology generations, protocol types, and QoS requirements. Due to heterogeneous nature of the mobile network and unpredictable channel condition, adaptivity and optimization in terms of resources and technology are essential to meet the user satisfaction. This chapter has discussed various optimization techniques for multimedia services for next generation broadband access network which ensures an improved QoE.

Although, several aspects of next-generation heterogeneous networks have been studied by researchers in the recent times and are discussed in this chapter. However, still there are a few additional issues in heterogeneous wireless access networks that still needs to be focused upon, like faithful collaboration among different wireless service providers with maximum revenue for each service providers. High quality multimedia services for Internet-of-things (IoT), device-to-device or machine-to-machine communication systems is still under research phase. MapReduce programming model proposed by Dean et al. (2008) can be used to obtain result by generating large data set.

REFERENCES

Akhshabi, S., Begen, A. C., & Dovrolis, C. (2011). An experimental evaluation of rate-adaptation algorithms in adaptive streaming over HTTP. ACM MMSys2011.

Al-Abri, F., Edirisingh, E., De Cock, J., Notebaert, S., & Van de Walle, R. (2011). Optimal H.264/AVC video transcoding system. *IEEE International Conference on Consumer Electronics (ICCE)*. doi:10.1109/ICCE.2011.5722613

Banerjee, N., De, S., De, P., & Dhamale, K. (2012). Dynamic Source and Channel Rate Adaptation for Video Streaming over Wireless Fading Channels. *IEEE 14th International Conference on High Performance Computing and Communications, 734 - 739.*

Begen, A. C., Akgul, T., & Baugher, M. (2011). Watching video over the Web, Part I: Streaming protocols. *IEEE Internet Computing, 15*(2), 54–63. doi:10.1109/MIC.2010.155

Bouras, C., Konidaris, A., & Kostoulas, D. (2004). Predictive prefetching on the web and its potential impact in the wide area. *World Wide Web (Bussum), 7*(2), 143–179. doi:10.1023/B:WWWJ.0000017208.87570.7a

Dai, J., Liu, F., Li, B., Li, B., & Liu, J. (2012). Collaborative caching in wireless video streaming through resource auctions. *IEEE Journal on Selected Areas in Communications, 30*(2), 458–466. doi:10.1109/JSAC.2012.120226

Dean, J., & Ghemawat, S. (2008). MapReduce: Simplified Data Processing on Large Clusters. *Communications of the ACM, 52*(1), 107–113. doi:10.1145/1327452.1327492

Gouache, S., Bichot, G., Bsila, A., & Howson, C. (2011). Distributed & adaptive HTTP streaming. *IEEE International Conference on Multimedia and Expo (ICME)*.

3GPP TS 36.213. (2011). *Version 10.1.0 R10: Evolved Universal Terrestrial Radio Access (E-UTRA); Physical layer procedures.*

Jones, C. G., Liu, R., Meyerovich, L., Asanovic, K., & Bod'ık, R. (2009). Parallelizing the web browser. *First USENIX Workshop on Hot Topics in Parallelism (HotPar '09)*.

Kumar, N., Zeadally, S., & Rodrigues, J. J. P. C. (2015). QoS-aware hierarchical web caching scheme for online video streaming applications in internet based vehicular ad hoc networks. *IEEE Transactions on Industrial Electronics, 62*(12), 7892–7900. doi:10.1109/TIE.2015.2425364

Lim, J., & Kim, M. (2008). An Optimal Adaptation Framework for Streaming Multiple Video Objects. *IEEE Transactions on Circuits and Systems for Video Technology, 18*(5), 699–703. doi:10.1109/TCSVT.2008.918847

Liu, K., & Lee, J. (2015). On Improving TCP Performance Over Mobile Data Networks. *IEEE Transactions on Mobile Computing*, (9), 1-14.

Liu, K., & Lee, J. Y. B. (2011). Mobile accelerator: A new approach to improve TCP performance in mobile data networks. *IEEE 7th International Wireless Communications and Mobile Computing Conference*.

Lohmar, T., Einarsson, T., Frojdh, P., Gabin, F., & Kampmann, M. (2011). Dynamic adaptive HTTP streaming of live content. *IEEE International Symposium on WoWMoM*. doi:10.1109/WoWMoM.2011.5986186

Nisan, N., & Ronen, A. (2007). Computationally Feasible VCG Mechanisms. *Journal of Artificial Intelligence Research, 29*(1), 19–47.

Notebaert, S., De Cock, J., Beheydt, S., De Lameillieure, J., & Van de Walle, R. (2009). *Mixed architectures for H.264/AVC digital video translating*. Multimedia Tools and Application.

Romero, L. R. (2011). *A dynamic adaptive HTTP streaming video service for Google Android* (M.S. Thesis). Royal Institute of Technology (KTH), Stockholm, Sweden.

Schwarz, H., Marpe, D., & Wiegand, T. (2007). Overview of the Scalable Video Coding Extension of the H. 264/AVC Standard. *IEEE Transactions on Circuits and Systems for Video Technology, 17*(9), 1103–1120. doi:10.1109/TCSVT.2007.905532

Singhal, C., De, S., Trestian, R., & Muntean, G.-M. (2014). Joint Optimization of User-Experience and Energy-Efficiency in Wireless Multimedia Broadcast. *IEEE Transactions on Mobile Computing*, *13*(7), 1522–1535. doi:10.1109/TMC.2013.138

Stockhammer, T. (2011). Dynamic adaptive streaming over HTTP – standards and design principles. ACM MMSys.

Thang, T. C., Ho, Q.-D., Kang, J. W., & Pham, A. T. (2012). Adaptive streaming of audiovisual content using MPEG DASH. *IEEE Transactions on Consumer Electronics*, *58*(1), 78–85. doi:10.1109/TCE.2012.6170058

Thang, T. C., Le, H. T., Nguyen, H. X., Pham, A. T., Kang, J. W., & Ro, Y. M. (2013). Adaptive video streaming over HTTP with dynamic resource estimation. *Journal of Communication and Networks*, *15*(6), 635–644. doi:10.1109/JCN.2013.000112

Wang, H., Kong, J., Guo, Y., & Chen, X. (2013). Mobile Web Browser Optimizations in the Cloud Era: A Survey. *IEEE 7th International Symposium on Service Oriented System Engineering (SOSE)*.

Wang, Y., Kim, J.-G., Chang, S.-F., & Kim, H.-M. (2007). Utility-Based Vid Adaptation for Universal Multimedia Access (UMA) and Content-Based Utility Function Prediction for Real-Time Video Transcoding. *IEEE Transactions on Multimedia*, *9*(2), 213–220. doi:10.1109/TMM.2006.886253

Wang, Z., Lin, F. X., Zhong, L., & Chishtie, M. (2011). Why are web browsers slow on smartphones?*Proceedings of the 12th Workshop on Mobile Computing Systems and Applications (HotMobile '11)*, 91–96. doi:10.1145/2184489.2184508

Wang, Z., Lin, F. X., Zhong, L., & Chishtie, M. (2012). How far can client-only solutions go for mobile browser speed?*Proceedings of the 21st international conference on World Wide Web (WWW '12)*, 31–40. doi:10.1145/2187836.2187842

Wu, D., Hou, Y. T., Zhu, W., Zhang, Y.-Q., & Peha, J. M. (2001). Streaming video over the Internet: Approaches and directions. *IEEE Transactions on Circuits and Systems for Video Technology*, *11*(3), 282–300. doi:10.1109/76.911156

Zakerinasab, M. R., & Wang, M. (2015). Dependency-Aware Distributed Video Transcoding in the Cloud. *IEEE Annual Conference on Local Computer Network*.

Zeadally, S., Hunt, R., Chen, Y., Irwin, A., & Hassan, A. (2012). Vehicular ad hoc networks (VANETs): Status, results, and challenges. *Telecommunication Systems*, *50*(4), 217–241. doi:10.1007/s11235-010-9400-5

Zhang, Q., Xiang, Z., Zhu, W., & Gao, L. (2004). Cost-Based Cache replacement and Server Selection for Multimedia Proxy across Wireless Internet. *IEEE Transactions on Multimedia*, *6*(4), 587–598. doi:10.1109/TMM.2004.830816

KEY TERMS AND DEFINITIONS

Broadband Wireless Access Networks (BWANs): Wireless broadband is high-speed Internet and data service delivered through a wireless local area network (WLAN), Cellular network (LTE, LTE-A) or wide area network (WWAN).

CDN: A content delivery network (CDN) is a system of distributed servers (network) that deliver webpages and other Web content to a user based on the geographic locations of the user, the origin of the webpage and a content delivery server.

Internet-of-Things (IoT): The internet of things (IoT) is the network of physical objects—devices, vehicles, buildings and other items—embedded with electronics, software, sensors, and network connectivity that enables these objects to collect and exchange data.

IVANET: Internet based Vehicular Ad Hoc Network (IVANET) is a highly mobile self-organizing network based on Vehicle-to-Vehicle (V2V), Vehicle-to-Infrastructure (V2I) and hybrid architecture.

MPD: The MPEG-DASH Media Presentation Description (MPD) is an XML document containing information about media segments, their relationships and information necessary to choose between them, and other metadata that may be needed by clients.

MPEG-DASH: An application level adaptive bitrate multimedia streaming that enables streaming of media content over the Internet delivered from conventional HTTP web servers with different levels of data rate support.

RTP: The Real-Time Transport Protocol (RTP) is an Internet protocol standard that specifies a way for programs to manage the real-time transmission of multimedia data over either unicast or multicast network services.

Scalable Video Coding (SVC): SVC is the name for the Annex G extension of the H.264/MPEG-4 AVC video compression standard. SVC standardizes the encoding of a high-quality video bitstream that also contains one or more subset bitstreams. This technique includes multi-layered encoding of video.

Chapter 2
Radio Environment Maps and Its Utility in Resource Management for Dynamic Spectrum Access Networks

Saptarshi Debroy
Hunter College, City University of New York, USA

Mainak Chatterjee
University of Central Florida, USA

ABSTRACT

Recent measurements on radio spectrum usage have revealed the abundance of under-utilized bands of spectrum that belong to licensed users. This necessitated the paradigm shift from static to dynamic spectrum access (DSA). Researchers argue that prior knowledge about occupancy of such bands, such as, Radio Environment Maps (REM) can potentially help secondary networks to devise effective strategies to improve utilization. In the chapter, we discuss how different interpolation and statistical techniques are applied to create REMs of a region, i.e., an estimate of primary spectrum usage at any arbitrary location in a secondary DSA network. We demonstrate how such REMs can help in predicting channel performance metrics like channel capacity, spectral efficiency, and secondary network throughput. We show how REMs can help to attain near perfect channel allocation in a centralized secondary network. Finally, we show how the REM can be used to perform multi-channel multi-hop routing in a distributed DSA network.

INTRODUCTION

Radio spectrum allocation and management have traditionally followed a 'command-and-control' approach where chunks of spectrum are allocated for specific services under restrictive licenses. The restrictions specify the technologies to be used and the services to be provided, thereby constraining the ability to make use of new technologies and the ability to redistribute the spectrum to higher valued users. Over

DOI: 10.4018/978-1-5225-2023-8.ch002

the past years, traditional approaches to spectrum management have been challenged by new insights into the actual use of spectrum. In most countries, all frequencies have been completely allocated to specific uses and spectrum appears to be a scarce resource within the current regulatory framework. Moreover, recent experimental studies have revealed that spectrum utilization is time and space dependent and that most parts of radio spectrum are highly underutilized (Shared Spectrum Company, 2007; Buddhikot, M., 2005; F. communications commission, 2004).

Such limitations have motivated a paradigm shift from static spectrum allocation towards a notion of dynamic spectrum management where secondary networks/users (non-license holders) can 'borrow' idle spectrum from those who primary networks/users (license holders) without causing harmful interference to the latter. Dynamic Spectrum Access (DSA) networks that utilize such unused spectrum holes within the licensed band have been proposed as a possible solution to the spectrum crisis. The idea is to detect times when a particular licensed band is unused and use it for transmission without causing interference to the licensed user. Secondary users equipped with cognitive radio enabled devices will facilitate such DSA where the cognitive radios continuously monitor the presence of primary users and opportunistically access the unused or under-utilized licensed bands (Akyildiz, I. F, 2006). However, the most important regulatory aspect of these networks is that the secondary nodes must not interfere with primary transmissions. Thus, when secondary nodes detect transmissions from primaries, they are mandated to relinquish those interfering channels immediately and switch to other non-interfering channels.

Due to the temporal and spatial fleetingness of spectrum occupancy, such reactive nature of secondary networks is insufficient for desired utilization of under-used licensed spectrum. Researchers have argued that a prior knowledge of the possible transmission activities of the primaries can allow the secondary nodes to effectively access the available resource and predict the expected radio and network performances for quality of service (QoS) provisioning in secondary networks. Such prior knowledge would also help the secondary networks in finding better routes from a source to a destination where route existence and quality are ever changing with primary activity. Thus, there is a need to proactively estimate the spectrum usage at any arbitrary location and then extend that for predicting the nature of spectrum utilization in a region of interest. The recent ruling by FCC (FCC, 2007) also necessitates the need for secondary networks to create, manage and refer to spectrum usage databases for secondary access opening new discussions on design, implementation techniques, and capabilities of such spectrum usage databases.

Spectrum databases are usually manifested either through mandating primary transmitters to report their transmission activities to a central authority, or through building spectrum usage or radio environment maps (REMs), e.g., TV whitespace database (Google, 2015), often called spectrum cartography. Such REMs provide signal strength values from primary transmitters on different channels in a particular geographical region, i.e., multiple 3D plots with one for each channel. The stringent policy enforcement of reporting spectrum activities has had some roadblocks in terms of the underlying legal and policy issues, which are suspected to pose a barrier for wide-adoption of dynamic spectrum access technologies. Thus, primary usage prediction schemes and models have garnered much traction in recent times. Such schemes vary from modeling spectrum utilization using statistical models (Riihijarvi, J., 2008) to real-world measurement data based prediction models (Li, Y., 2009). Some of these techniques are specific to primary network types (such as, TV, cellular etc.) and some are more extensible for any generic primary networks.

This book chapter seeks to introduce concepts of Radio Environment Maps and its utility in efficient resource provisioning in DSA networks. First Section II presents the approaches and consideration for effective and accurate REM construction. Section III discusses how such REMs can be used to predict secondary channel performance metrics that can ensure optimal resource allocation. Subsequently, Section IV discusses how such REM-aided performance metrics prediction can be used for effective and near-optimal resource allocation in terms of channel allocation in a centralized secondary network and multi-channel multi-hop route selection in a distributed secondary network. Finally, conclusions are drawn in the last section.

RADIO ENVIRONMENT MAPS: APPROACHES AND CONSIDERATIONS

In this section, we describe the most popular REM construction approaches and the key considerations needed to make them accurate, i.e., representative of real life primary usage scenario.

Radio Environment Map Construction Approaches

Direct Interpolation Based Methods

The direct method based on the interpolation approaches estimate the primary spectrum usage at any arbitrary location. Such REMs are most often constructed by first fusing measurements from different sensor locations at a centralized or distributed node(s) using cooperative (Ganesan, G., 2007) or collaborative sensing (Ghasemi, A., 2005; Visotsky, E., 2005); and then by applying geostatistical and variational interpolation methods to predict spectrum usage at different location on a geographic plane. The most widely adopted direct interpolation methods for REM construction are: inverse distance weighted (IDW) methods (Denkovski, D., 2012), nearest neighbor (NN) methods (Alaya-Feki 2012), spline methods (Mateos, G., 2009), Kriging methods (Phillips, C., 2012), and modified Shepard's (MS) methods (Debroy, S., 2016). Among these, IDW, NN methods consider mostly local spatial data for interpolation, whereas spline, and Kriging methods use global measurements for primary usage estimation. In IDW based methods, it is assumed that signal spatial samples which are close to each other, are more alike than those which are farther apart. Thus more weightage are given to sensor measurement data close to the interpolating point than further. In NN methods, the sensor measurement with the minimum Euclidean distance from the interpolating point is adopted for the estimated usage at the interpolating point. Spline methods use thin-plate splines based on radial basis functions for interpolation and performs well even in the absence of precise channel frequency and bandwidth information; however suffer from computational complexity issues. The Kriging methods apply a weighted average interpolation technique that takes into account both the distances and the degree of influence between the sensor measurements when estimating the signal level at any arbitrary point.

In one of our earlier works (Debroy, S., 2016)., we presented a modified version of well known Shepard's interpolation function that takes into consideration the locations, number, and relative orientation of the sensor measurement points that constructs a continuously differentiable distribution function. The function estimates the spectrum utilization at any arbitrary location. Our proposed scheme borrows the essence of cooperative spectrum sensing by allowing participating secondary sensor nodes to share their measured spectrum data periodically with a fusion node. However, unlike conventional cooperative spectrum sensing where the devices share decision vectors (representing occupancy of channels), the sensors share their raw spectrum data which are later fused to estimate spectrum usage at unknown points. The proposed scheme is independent of the outdoor fading and shadowing environment; only the sampling and reporting frequencies may vary depending on the environment. Figure 1(a) and Figure1(b) show the power spectral density of primary channel usage for a channel of bandwidth 100 KHz using modified Shepard's interpolation method and with 40 and 80 sensor measurement points respectively. The experiment was performed for a 100x100 sq. km. region with real-world spectrum data archive of 2.4 GHz ISM band in Germany from RWTH Mobnets (Riihijarvi, J., 2008). Locations of the sensor measurement points are shown explicitly. The surface plots become increasingly accurate as the number of data points increases. However, there is a trade-off between the accuracy of estimation and computation complexity with is dependent on other physical and environmental factors such as type of primary network (threshold signal strength to operate, probability of primary activity), accuracy of sensors involved in detecting signals, location of the sensors, physical environment in terms of terrain affecting fading and shadowing (Faint, S., 2010; Wei, Z., 2013).

Indirect Location Based Methods

The indirect REM construction methods make use of known parameters of the transmitter and radio propagation modeling to estimate primary occupancy. One of the notable works (Yilmaz, H. B., 2015) in this area proposes a transmitter location estimation based REM construction where the location and transmission power of the primary transmitter is estimated and subsequently REM is constructed taking into account the propagation channel properties. In a similar SNR-aided method (Sun, G., 2010), a low-cost, high-precision localization method for REM construction technique is proposed without any prior knowledge of the interference source other than the transmitter power. Finally in (Meshkova, E., 2011), an indoor REM is constructed by studying the characterization and modeling of the radio indoor environment based on spectrum measurements from heterogeneous spectrum sensors.

Considerations for Radio Environment Map Construction Accuracy

Selection of Spectrum Sensing Locations

The accuracy of REM construction is dependent on the gathered spectrum usage data, and thus such accuracy can be greatly improved by fusing sensed data from strategic locations. Be it centralized or distributed secondary networks, and either with a central repository or multiple fusion centers, strategically placing the sensing locations (pre-deployment) or relying more on data from strategic locations (post-deployment) that in turn depends on the primary transmitter locations have been found to profoundly impact the accuracy of the constructed REM. Research has shown (Debroy, S., 2016) that *iterative clustering* technique using tree structured vector quantization (TSVQ) is one such intelligent strategy for sensing location selection. *Vector quantization* (VQ) is a powerful data compression technique where an ordered set of real numbers is quantized. The idea of such quantization is to find $|\Delta|$ representation points (distinct vectors) from a large set of vectors so that the average distortion is minimized. With iterative clustering, the size of the representation points grows from 1 to the desired value, $|\Delta|$. Thus, for DSA networks, given a set of primary transmitter locations, their centroid (say S_1) is the ideal representation point when $|\Delta|=1$, as the sum of the Euclidean distances to all the primary transmitters is minimum at the centroid.

Figure 1. Radio environment map construction example with different number of sensor measurements used for interpolation: (a) REM with 40 sensor measurements; (b) REM with 80 sensor measurements

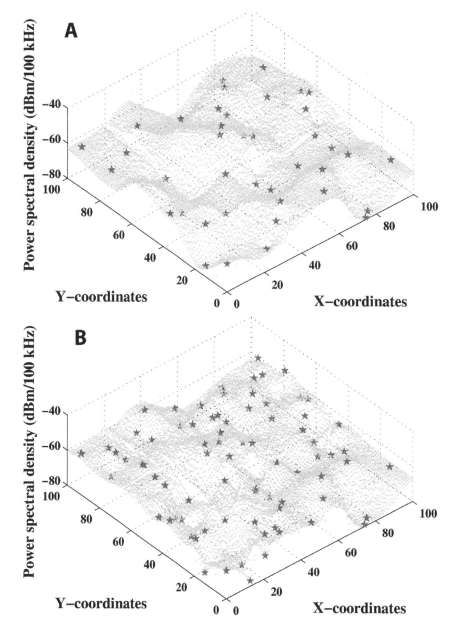

With further iterations, can be split into two points, S_1 and $S_1 + \varepsilon$, where ε is a small Euclidean distance. Each of the primary transmitter locations is grouped on to the closer of the two representation points thereby creating two clusters with two representation points. Again, the new centroids of these two newly formed clusters are determined and the old representation points, S_1 and $S_1 + \varepsilon$, are updated with the new centroids' position creating new representation points S_1 and S_2. Similar iterative clustering is performed until the desired size of $|\Delta|$ is achieved. The utility of iterative clustering based sensing location selection over random and deterministic sensing location selection is demonstrated in Figure 2 in a simulated environment representing a centralized DSA network. The utility is measurement in terms of mismatches in estimating primary occupancy using REM constructed through measurement interpolation using the sensing locations selected by three completing techniques. In deterministic selection, locations are chosen uniformly in a grid-like orientation to cover the entire region without considering the locations of the primaries with random selection choosing locations randomly. The performance comparison is made for low primary activity of value 0.3. The figure illustrates that iterative clustering performs better than random and deterministic selections in terms of average mismatches for any number of selected sensing locations for interpolation.

Spectrum Data Falsification in Cooperative Sensing and Sharing

Cooperative spectrum sensing and sharing for REM construction can be vulnerable when multiple malicious nodes share false local sensing reports. As a result, the fused decision may be altered, hence jeopardizing the reliability of REM. Such phenomenon where local sensing result is manipulated is known as Spectrum Sensing Data Falsification (SSDF) or Byzantine attack (Bhattacharjee, S., 2013). A malicious node can either advertise 'occupied' channels as 'available' and vice versa inducing errors or can alter primary spectrum usage data enough to impact interpolation outcome, and such attacks can be collaborative when attackers plan and attack together, or non-collaborative. Hence researchers proposed methods for secondary node-centric trust/reputation evaluation techniques in DSA networks and trust-aware spectrum usage information fusion schemes to preserve the correctness of primary oc-

Figure 2. Utility of iterative clustering based sensing location selection technique in terms of mismatches in estimating primary occupancy using REM constructed through measurement interpolation

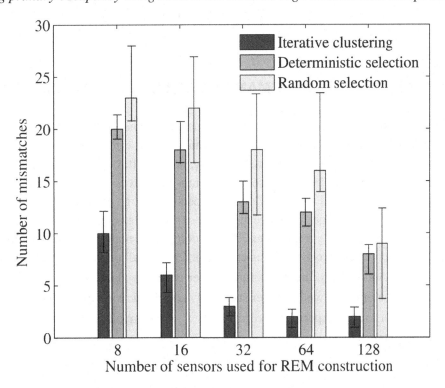

cupancy estimation. Among them, works such as (] Chen, R., 2008; Rawat, A. S., 2011) are notable for centralized DSA networks. In (] Chen, R., 2008), the authors propose a reputation aware malicious node isolation scheme in a centralized DSA network and argue that for any practical scenario majority of the nodes cannot be malicious. Hence, the fusion center uses a majority voting rule to arrive at a global inference on primary occupancy. In (Rawat, A. S., 2011), the authors propose a Kullback-Leibler (KL) divergence based method for cooperative spectrum sensing and sharing under low density collaborative SSDF attacks in a centralized DSA network. The authors observe that below a certain fraction of malicious nodes (50% of all secondary nodes in the networks), their method is able to accurately predict primary occupancy and thus proving to be useful for REM generation.

In our previous works (Bhattacharjee, S., 2011; Bhattacharjee, S., 2013), we proposed trust based fusion techniques for distributed DSA networks under SSDF attacks to improve the integrity of cooperative spectrum sensing and sharing for more accurate REM construction. The proposed monitoring technique gathers trust evidences that could indicate the presence of anomalies in spectrum sensed data for multiple channels shared by other nodes. The anomaly monitoring technique takes into account the relative spatio-spectral orientation of the nodes and isolates potentially malicious nodes using either:

- An optimistic Beta expectation based trust model for low intensity of attacks.
- A conservative Dirichlet distribution inspired trust model for aggressive attacks.

Based on the secondary nodes' trust values, a trust based fusion is adopted that excludes the spectrum sensed data of an untrustworthy node from participating the fusion to generate REM. Figure 3(a) and Figure 3(b) demonstrate the utility of such trust based fusion for REM generation for a simulated distributed DSA network environment. The utility is measured in terms of number of mismatches between estimated and actual number of primary occupied channels. The figures show that for any probability and type (collaborative and non-collaborative) of attacks, the total number of mismatches for a trust based fusion is much less than that for blind fusion, thus proving to be more useful for accurate REM construction.

SECONDARY CHANNEL PERFORMANCE METRICS PREDICTION USING REMS

The REM of a geographical region helps the secondary network to not only estimate or predict the primary spectrum usage of that region, but such usage estimate can be effectively used to predict channel performance metrics, such as, available channel capacity, network throughput, and spectral efficiency for any secondary communication between a secondary transmitter-receiver pair and also the secondary network as a whole. Below we will show how primary spectrum usage information from REMs can be used to predict secondary channel performance metrics. For this, we assume a scenario where K secondary nodes are exposed to M primary transmitters. And to complicate matters, we also assume secondary channel reuse, i.e., a secondary receiver is interfered by potentially all primary and secondary transmitters on all possible channels. Thus, the interference experienced by a secondary receiver at (x_t, y_t) is due to the primary transmitters as well as other secondary communication using the same channel. Let us suppose that the interference experienced receiver at (x_t, y_t) from all primary transmitters is which is available from the latest REM.

Figure 3. Comparison in terms of number of mismatches between the estimated and actual primary occupancy between trust based and blind fusion techniques of sensed data for REM construction: (a) non-collaborative attack; b) collaborative attack

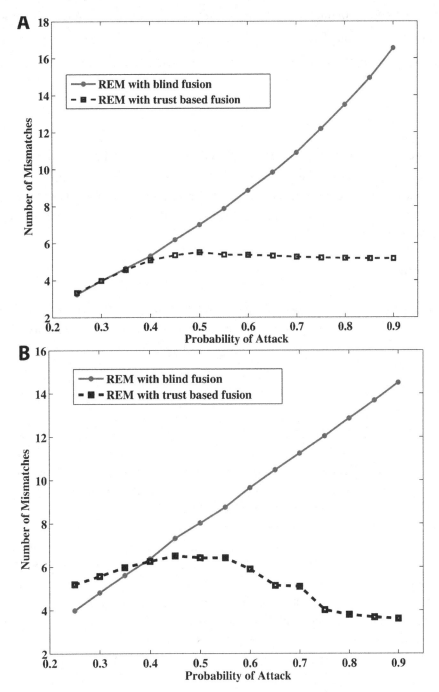

Now the secondary network (i.e., a base station for centralized networks, and a stand-alone node for distributed networks) can easily predict received signal strength at (x_t, y_t) as $P\left|h_q^t\right|^2$, where P is the transmit power of the corresponding secondary transmitter and h_q^t is the channel gain between the secondary transmitter-receiver pair. Thus, if I_q^t is the estimated co-channel interference at receiver (x_t, y_t) experienced from another secondary communication using same channel ch_q, then:

$$I_q^t = \sum_{\forall j \in K^q} P\left|h_q^t\right|^2 \qquad (1)$$

where K^q is the set of all other secondary pairs using channel ch_q, a parameter known by the secondary network. Now, with the above parameters, the secondary network can easily calculate critical channel performance metrics, such as, channel capacity, spectral efficiency, and secondary throughput in order to optimize the overall secondary communication before or during the channel resource allocation process to secondary nodes.

Channel Capacity

Using Shannon-Hartley's capacity model for a band-limited channel with additive white Gaussian noise (AWGN) (Shannon, C. E., 2001), the theoretical maximum secondary channel capacity C_q^t for the channel ch_q used by K^q set of secondary pairs can be estimated as:

$$C_q^t = B \log_2\left(1 + \frac{P\left|h_q^t\right|^2}{\varphi_q^t + I_q^t}\right) \qquad (2)$$

where B is the channel bandwidth. In Figure 4(a), we show the predicted secondary channel capacity characteristics for an arbitrary secondary receiver location calculated using Equation 2. The figure shows different channel capacity values for 1000 channels of 100KHz each in the primary spectrum of 2.4 GHz ISM band. Such representation of channel capacity can be exploited by a particular transmitter-receiver pair for selecting best channel/s in terms of maximum achievable capacity when multiple such free channels are available for communication. Through another 3D representation shown in Figure 4(b), we present the estimated channel capacity values (calculated using Equation 2) of a particular channel for multiple potential receiver locations to a particular transmitter. Such representation can be further exploited for: a) optimal allocation of a particular channel to the best contending secondary nodes, and b) optimal location selection of a secondary node (in cases where secondary node installation is pre-planned) for statistically empty channels. Both approaches shown in Figure 4(a) and Figure 4(b) are highly effective for better overall secondary utilization.

Figure 4. Predicted channel capacity characteristics with REM: (a) channel capacity for different chan-nels; (b) channel capacity of a region for same channel

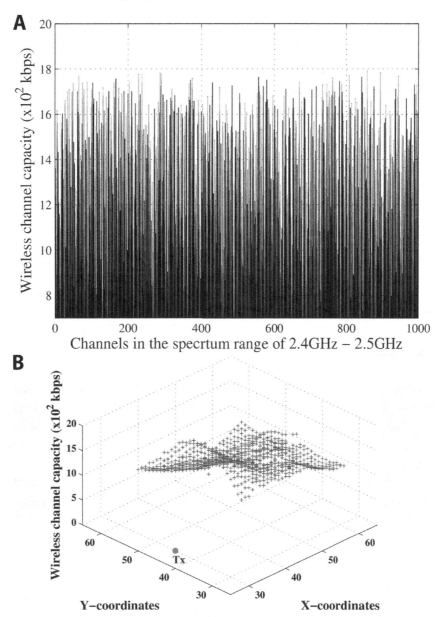

Secondary Network Throughput

The secondary network throughput depends on the number of secondary pairs in a network using the same channel. When a secondary transmitter transmits with power P to a receiver at (x_t, y_t) on a channel ch_q, then the predicted transmission rate considering all other secondary communication using the same channel is given by:

$$\pi_q^t = \log\left(1 + \frac{P\left|h_q^t\right|^2}{\varphi_q^t + I_q^t + \sigma^2}\right) \tag{3}$$

where the received signals are corrupted by zero-mean additive white Gaussian noise of power σ^2. To predict the network throughput for channel ch_q, summation of the transmission rates of all the secondary pairs using ch_q is taken (Jeon, S.-W., 2011):

$$\Pi_q = \sum_{\forall j \in K^q} \pi_q^t = \sum_{\forall j \in K^q} \log\left(1 + \frac{P\left|h_q^t\right|^2}{\varphi_q^t + I_q^t + \sigma^2}\right) \tag{4}$$

In Figure 5(a) and Figure 5(b), we show the system throughput and per-pair throughput in kbps for the simulation scenario discussed previously. The nature of system throughput is similar to a conventional wireless network saturating after a certain point. Per-pair throughput characteristic shows convexity where there exists a optimal number of secondary pairs using a particular channel that yields maximum per-pair throughput.

Spectral Efficiency

Secondary spectral efficiency provides an indication of how efficiently a bandwidth-limited frequency spectrum can be used. Spectral efficiency measured in bits/sec/Hz can be represented in two ways: link spectral efficiency and system spectral efficiency. The former is defined as the net bit-rate that can be achieved by a link per channel bandwidth (Hz). Similarly, system spectral efficiency is defined as the maximum throughput, summed over all nodes, divided by the channel bandwidth. It quantifies the number of secondary nodes that can be simultaneously supported by the available spectrum in a geographic area. Thus, link spectral efficiency for ch_q between a secondary transmitter-receiver pair can be predicted as:

$$\xi_q^t = \frac{1}{B}\log\left(1 + \frac{P\left|h_q^t\right|^2}{\varphi_q^t + I_q^t} + \sigma^2\right) \tag{5}$$

Similarly, the system spectral efficiency is obtained as:

$$\Xi_q = \sum_{\forall j \in K^q} \xi_q^t = \sum_{\forall j \in K^q} \frac{1}{B}\log\left(1 + \frac{P\left|h_q^t\right|^2}{\varphi_q^t + I_q^t} + \sigma^2\right) \tag{6}$$

Figure 5. Predicted throughput characteristics with REMs: (a) system throughput; (b) per-pair throughput

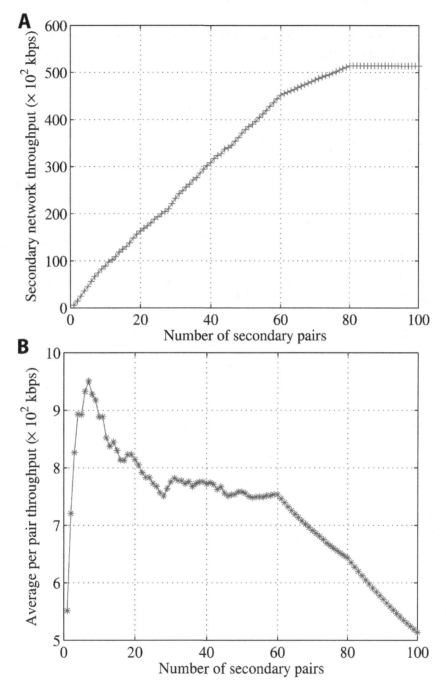

Thus, we see that just by estimating the primary signal strength φ_q^t on a channel ch_q from the REM, multiple key secondary channel performance metrics can be predicted for better utilization of the available spectrum and sustainable and effective secondary communication.

RESOURCE ALLOCATION USING REMS

In this section, we demonstrate how REM-aided performance metrics prediction can be used for effective and near-optimal resource allocation for:

1. Channel allocation in a centralized secondary network.
2. Multi-channel multi-hop route selection in a distributed secondary network.

Channel Allocation in Centralized DSA Networks

The utility of REMs for channel resource allocation can be easily understood for a secondary network within TV white space (TVWS) primary environment. The TVWS (sub-900 MHz TV band) is one of the first primary networks to be mandated by FCC for secondary communication and IEEE has already proposed an initial draft standard (IEEE 802.22 WRAN) (IEEE 802.22, 2011) for secondary communication to exploit such unused bands. The core components of an IEEE 802.22 WRAN are base stations (BS) and consumer premise equipments (CPE) as shown in Figure 6. Secondary nodes (BSs and CPEs) opportunistically access unused or underutilized TV bands when not in use.

Primary and Secondary Networks in IEEE 802.22 WRAN

The primary network consists of TV transmitters, TV receivers and wireless microphones with the latter taking only a small amount of band space. The TV transmitters are deployed depending on population density in a geographic region with an urban area having denser transmitters than rural regions. The secondary IEEE 802.22 WRANs are centralized networks divided into cells, each having one BS. The

Figure 6. Architecture of an IEEE 802.22 Wireless Regional Area Network

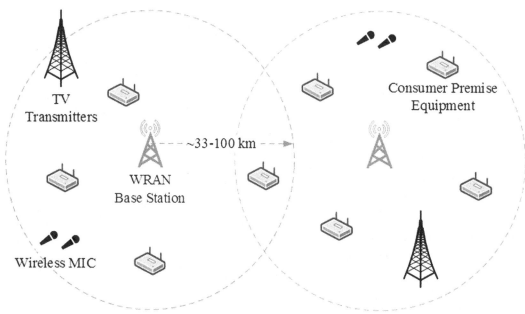

BS communicates with the CPEs in its cell as well as with neighboring BSs. The BS is aware of the location of all the CPEs under it. The existence of pre-defined control channels are not mandated, i.e., BS and the CPEs may need to communicate with only the free channels that are currently not being used by the primary users.

Resource Allocation Problem

The two major challenges in allocating channels to the CPEs are: a) the absence of pre-defined control channels between the BS and the CPEs, and b) inability of the BS to view a global spectrum availability of its cell using traditional spectrum sensing approaches. The ability of the BS to assign the optimal channels to the CPEs depends on not only how well the BS is able to capture the availability of all channels at a particular CPE location, but also finding out the occupancy of a particular channel at all CPE locations. Since the BS cannot perform sensing at locations other than itself, it has to rely upon the sensed spectrum reports shared by the CPEs. If all the CPEs were to continuously share their spectrum usage reports, the BS would have the most accurate information. However, the communication overhead becomes a bottleneck as sharing of data has to be done on the same channels that the BS is supposed to allocate. Thus, channel assignment to CPEs becomes a challenge which can be address using REMs.

In our earlier paper (Debroy, S., 2016), we designed an on-demand channel allocation scheme for IEEE 802.22 WRANs using REMs. In our scheme, the CPEs work as data points and feed their spectrum usage data to the BS for it to create the map. The map enables the WRAN to achieve an efficient channel resource allocation in two aspects. First, the map is used for quicker communication with a candidate CPE and increases the probability of rendezvous between the CPE and the BS. Such communication allows the BS to acquire the actual spectrum usage at the CPE and evaluate different performance metrics. Secondly, such proactive performance analysis not only identifies the best candidate channel for a CPE but also indicates the best possible CPE among candidate CPEs for a particular channel. Channel allocation scheme thus adopted increases the overall network throughput and achieves close to optimal secondary spectrum usage.

Improving Rendezvous Probability Using Maps

The means of initial communication between the BS and a CPE looking for channels is the beacons sent by the BS and subsequent handshaking process. The latest IEEE 802.22 based WRAN specifications (IEEE P802.22a/D2, 2013) mandate the MAC layer to be able to adapt dynamically to changes in the environment by sensing the spectrum. Although the MAC layer is mandated to consist of specific data structures, details about the mechanism and involved channels (i.e., dedicated common control channel or dynamic channel rendezvous) for such rendezvous are not specified. However, in the absence of any control channel, this communication is probabilistic, i.e., the BS can send beacons with the specific data structures on the available channels and hope that the CPEs respond. Although viable, this traditional technique is ineffective and probability of rendezvous between the BS and a CPE is low. With the help of a REM, the beacon broadcast scheme can be made intelligent that can minimize the number of channels where beacons are sent and thus increasing the probability of dynamic rendezvous with the CPEs. This obviates the need for any control channel between the BS and the CPEs making the secondary communication completely opportunistic.

For the REM-aided intelligent beacon broadcasting scheme, the beacons are sent only on selected channels depending on the requirement of idle CPEs. These selected channels are those that belong to the common set of the available channels at the BS and the set of channels which are estimated to be available for the idle CPEs (from the map). The BS sends beacons in each of this common pool of channels and waits for channel allocation request from any node and after a stipulated time moves to the next channel. In case of successful reception of a channel allocation request, the BS logs the request before moving to next channel. At the end of the beacon cycle, the BS proceeds to allocate channels to the nodes whose channel allocation requests were successfully received during the beacon broadcast cycle. Such prediction of channel usage at CPE and sending beacons only on the potential free channels also reduces harmful interference to primaries.

Intelligent Channel Allocation

The allocation process by the BS is initiated by the reception of a channel allocation request from any CPE (as a reply to BS beacon) on any of the free channels. Such allocation reply is accompanied with raw spectrum usage at the CPE location which in turn helps the BS to create the REM. The BS predicts the set of available channels at the CPE locations. In order to ensure no co-channel interference, the BS can estimate from the map all channels that can be allocated to a CPE without causing secondary co-channel interference to other CPEs, and also estimate all the CPEs that can be allocated the same channels without interference. Enabled by such predictions, the BS can also estimate the expected channel performance metrics (as discussed in Section III) for all the allocable (without causing interference to other CPEs) free channels at a CPE location. Such REM-aided greedy channel allocation ensures close to optimal overall secondary utilization. Although more optimized channel allocation schemes can be designed using the primary usage information from REMs, the utility of such maps in achieving near optimal allocation cannot be denied.

We demonstrated the utility of REM in improving the rendezvous probability and in ensuring close to optimal channel allocation by designing an experimental set-up with locations of TV stations being simulated in a 500×500 sq. miles grid using TV station location distribution (Riihijarvi, J., 2008) The total number of channels is varied from 50-400 with corresponding bandwidth of 6 MHz-750 kHz. The power-profile of the TV stations ranges between 10kW-1MW. We identified different regions with dense and sparse primary densities (mimicking big cities and small towns) and deployed IEEE 802.22 WRAN cells. Locations of different types of nodes and transmission patterns are kept different for different scenarios while total number of CPEs, and density are kept the same. Figure 7(a) compares the performance of the map-aided intelligent beacon broadcast against conventional probabilistic rendezvous technique in terms of expected number of successful handshakes in a beacon period. It is evident that for any number of unallocated CPEs, the map assisted beacon broadcast technique performs better than conventional beacon broadcast. In Figure 7(b), we compare the performances of channel allocation with and without using REM for different number of free channels in terms of normalized supported data rate. We define normalized aggregate data rate as the aggregate bit rate supported by the allocated channels to the total achievable capacity of the free channels. We see that except for very low number of free channels, the REM-assisted allocation overall achieves better utilization. For very low number of available channels, if there are more idle CPEs, it creates more collision during beacon broadcast phase resulting less utilization.

Figure 7. REM-aided resource allocation performance in terms of intelligent beacon broadcast and near-optimal channel allocation among candidate CPEs: (a) benefits of intelligent beacon broadcast with REM in terms of expected number of successful handshakes; (b) normalized supported data rate improvement for different number of idle CPEs using REM

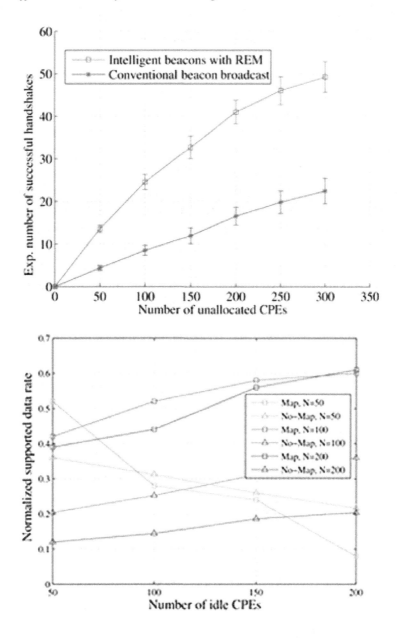

Multichannel Multihop Routing in Distributed DSA Networks

Since in a DSA network, the spectrum availability is space and time variant, selection of the best channel between a given pair of transmitter and receiver is very crucial. When some information has to be routed over multiple hops, sophisticated routing algorithms are needed that can not only find the best route but also find the best channel to use at every hop.

Routing Challenges in DSA Networks

The main challenges for multi-hop routing in a distributed DSA network over conventional ad-hoc networks are:

1. Spatio-temporal spectrum-awareness in terms of finding unoccupied channels in a region and at a particular time.
2. Protecting licensed primary receivers and other ongoing secondary communication from harmful interference.

Figure 8 shows one such scenario where a suboptimal route from source (SU_1) to destination (SU_6) yields harmful interference to primary receivers (RX_1 and RX_2) with an alternate route ($SU_1 \rightarrow SU_7 \rightarrow SU_8 \rightarrow SU_9 \rightarrow SU_6$) being available, assuming all the users are using the same channel. The figure also shows that such suboptimal routing leading to interference to other existing secondary communication (SU_3) due to hidden/exposed terminal problem. It is interesting to note that such interference could have been avoided by intelligently choosing different channels for communication for different hops. Thus, designing efficient routing solutions for multi-hop DSA networks requires a tight coupling between the routing module and the component responsible for managing spectrum availability such that the routing module can be continuously aware of the surrounding physical environment.

Figure 8. Inefficient routing interfering primary receivers and other hidden/exposed secondary nodes

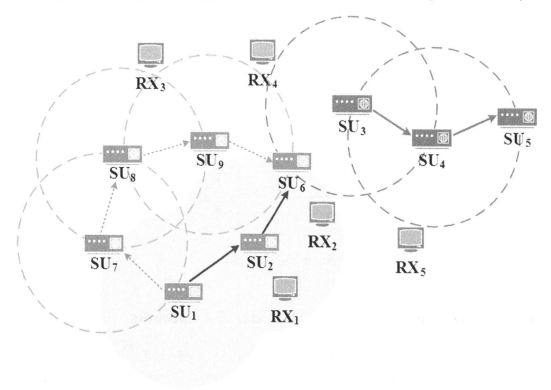

Traditionally, there are two different ways to achieve such competence:

1. Spectrum database or REMs.
2. Distributed sensing mechanisms at secondary locations.

The recent trend is more towards 'query and use' which is especially facilitated through REMs (Li, Y., 2009; Debroy, S., 2016; Harrold, T., 2011), that effectively ensures:

*   Low cost secondary nodes with sensing capability de-coupled from devices can use the map to find vacant channels, and
*   The primary receivers are protected from any kind of harmful interference caused by such secondary communications.

Reference from a map helps building a routing scheme which can couple the legacy ways of assessing the route quality with novel measures on path stability, spectrum availability. A REM aided routing also helps in finding the alternate routes in case of unpredictable route failures due to sudden appearance of primary transmissions. The sudden appearance of primary renders a given channel unusable in a given area, thus resulting in unpredictable route failures, which requires frequent path re-routing either in terms of users or used channels. In such scenarios, effective signaling procedures aided by REMs are useful to restore broken paths with minimal effect on the perceived quality. Furthermore, protecting such primary transmission from secondary communications is made more effective by the use of maps since the spectrum usage scenario of a region is made known to the routing entities.

Notable REM Aided Secondary Routing

Notable works on routing protocols with spectrum knowledge or map include (Cheng, G., 2007; Chowdhury, K. R., 2011; Lin, S. C., 2014). Distributed algorithms are presented in (Cheng, G., 2007; Chowdhury, K. R., 2011) performs multi-hop multi-channel routing DSA networks with partial or complete spectrum knowledge and being aware of channel properties. As one of first comprehensive REM-aided secondary routing techniques, authors in (Lin, S. C., 2014) propose a opportunistic routing protocol for regular and large-scale DSA networks with wireless fading channels, employing a cooperative networking scheme to enable multipath transmissions. In our earlier work (Debroy, S. 2014), we proposed a multi-hop multi-channel secondary routing using our interpolation based REM (Debroy, S., 2016). In our scheme, the secondary network has two components: intelligent sensors in the control plane and unintelligent secondary nodes in the data plane. The sensors are deployed in the area of interest either at strategic locations or randomly depending on the technique used for the construction of the map. The sensors' responsibilities are broadly two-fold: spectrum map creation and route discovery. These secondary nodes have no sensing capability and are instructed by the sensors to use a particular channel intended for a particular destination. Secondary nodes under the purview of a single sensor are called non-edge nodes while nodes lying in the overlapping regions are called edge nodes as shown in Figure 9(a) and Figure 9(b).

Intra-Domain Routing

Discovery of a route is initiated when a secondary node sends a route request (RREQ) to its associated sensor on the control channel. A route from source to destination can be of two kinds depending on their relative locations: intra-domain and inter-domain. When the source and destination are under the purview of the same sensor then it is called intra-domain and for such routing, a sensor upon receiving the RREQ checks whether the destination is associated with it. If so, then for each source node, the sensor consults the most recent map and eliminates all the channels which are occupied. For all the available channels in the spectrum, using the current map the sensor calculates a power value which is the upper bound on secondary transmission power for a particular channel so that no primary receivers are interfered on that channel. Such upper bound generates connected edges among secondary nodes that can sustain communication (with sustainable capacity values as weights). Thus, all such edges eventually create a connectivity graph within a domain for the most current map. Finally, by employing any well-known shortest path algorithm, the sensor determines the shortest path between the source and destination within its domain.

Inter-Domain Routing

For inter-domain routing, RREQ is flooded to the neighboring domains. Therefore once the sensor determines the need of inter-domain routing, it finds the shortest route from the source to each of the edge nodes currently covered under it. The edge nodes, upon the reception of a RREQ where the edge node itself is not the final destination, try to connect to the other sensor/s and initiate a RREQ. Once the neighboring sensor receives the RREQ, it follows the same recursive process of finding a route to the destination or to the edge nodes until the final destination is found. The route discovery scheme employs a selective flooding mechanism where a sensor does not cater to the same RREQ request through its domain as shown in Figure 9(a). When RREQ reaches the intended receiver, route reply (RREP) packet is sent from the destination to the source along the same path which does not involve any sensors, but only the secondary nodes as shown in Figure 9(b).

CONCLUSION

The chapter discussed how different interpolation and statistical techniques are applied to create Radio Environment Maps of a region, i.e., an estimate of primary spectrum usage at any arbitrary location in a secondary DSA network. We demonstrated how such REMs can help in predicting channel performance metrics like channel capacity, spectral efficiency, and secondary network throughput. We showed how REMs can help to attain near perfect channel allocation in a centralized secondary network (i.e., IEEE 802.22 WRAN) by improving the channel rendezvous probability and guaranteeing allocation of best candidate channel. Finally, we showed how the REM can be used to perform multi-channel multi-hop routing in a distributed DSA network. We demonstrated how REMs in such act as reference to find the best channels along a route that not only maximize channel capacity but also protects primary receivers through secondary power control.

Figure 9. Efficient inter-domain route discovery mechanism with the help of local REMs construction: (a) RREQ forwarding through selective flooding; (b) Unicast RREP propagation

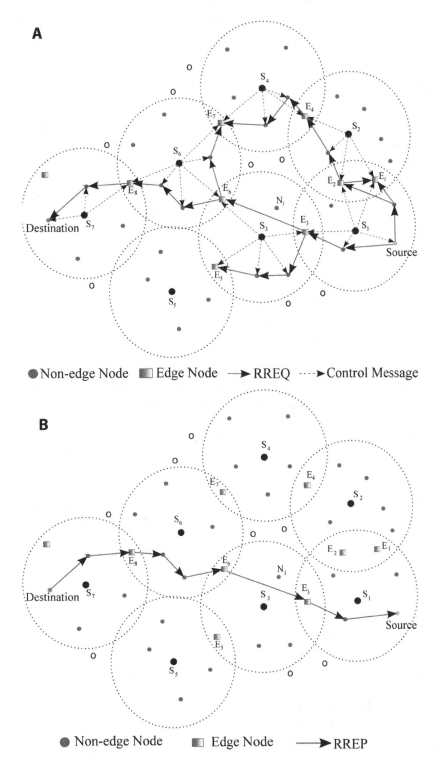

Overall, the chapter seeks to introduce the readership towards a new direction of resource allocation in next generation networks where the secondary access is proactive rather than legacy reactive 'sense and use' techniques. The chapter also tries to shed light on the possible implications of such paradigm shift by introducing cross-layer channel allocation techniques that use REMs.

REFERENCES

Akyildiz, I. F., Lee, W.-Y., Vuran, M. C., & Mohanty, S. (2006). Next generation/dynamic spectrum access/cognitive radio wireless networks: A survey. *Computer Networks*, *50*(13). 2127–2159. doi:10.1016/j.comnet.2006.05.001

Alaya-Feki, A. B. H., Jemaa, S. B., Sayrac, B., Houze, P., & Moulines, E. (2008). Informed spectrum usage in cognitive radio networks: Interference cartography. *IEEE 19th International Symposium on Personal, Indoor and Mobile Radio Communications*, 1–5.

Bhattacharjee, S., Debroy, S., & Chatterjee, M. (2011) Trust computation through anomaly monitoring in distributed cognitive radio networks. *IEEE 22nd International Symposium on Personal, Indoor and Mobile Radio Communications*, 593–597.

Bhattacharjee, S., & Kwiat, K. (2013). Utilizing misleading information for cooperative spectrum sensing in cognitive radio networks.*IEEE International Conference on Communications (ICC)*.2612–2616. doi:10.1109/ICC.2013.6654929

Bhattacharjee, S., Sengupta, S., & Chatterjee, M. (2013). Vulnerabilities in cognitive radio networks: A survey. *Computer Communications*, *36*(13). 1387–1398. doi:10.1016/j.comcom.2013.06.003

Buddhikot, M., Kolodzy, P., Miller, S.,Ryan, K., and Evans, J., (2005). Dimsumnet: new directions in wireless networking using coordinated dynamic spectrum. Proceedings from *World of Wireless Mobile and Multimedia Networks, WoWMoM*, 78–85.

Chen, R., Park, J. M., & Bian, K. (2008). Robust distributed spectrum sensing in cognitive radio networks. *The 27th Conference on Computer Communications. IEEE, INFOCOM*.

Cheng, G., Liu, W., Li, Y., & Cheng, W. (2007). Spectrum aware on-demand routing in cognitive radio networks.*2nd IEEE International Symposium on New Frontiers in Dynamic Spectrum Access Networks, DySPAN*, 571–574. doi:10.1109/DYSPAN.2007.80

Chowdhury, K. R., & Akyildiz, I. F. (2011). Crp: A routing protocol for cognitive radio ad hoc networks. *IEEE Journal on Selected Areas in Communications*, *29*(4). 794–804. doi:10.1109/JSAC.2011.110411

Debroy, S.,Bhattacharjee,S.,& Chatterjee,M.(2016).*Spectrum map and its application in resource management in cognitive radio networks. IEEE Transactions on Cognitive Communications and Networking*.

Debroy, S., & Chatterjee, M. (2014). Spectrum map aided multi-channel multi-hop routing in distributed cognitive radio networks. *IEEE 25th Annual International Symposium on Personal, Indoor, and Mobile Radio Communication (PIMRC)*. 947–952.

Denkovski, D., Atanasovski, V., Gavrilovska, L., Riihijrvi, J., & Mhnen, P. (2012). Reliability of a radio environment map: Case of spatial interpolation techniques.*7th International ICST Conference on Cognitive Radio Oriented Wireless Networks and Communications (CROWNCOM).*248–253. doi:10.4108/icst.crowncom.2012.248452

Faint, S., Reten, O., & Willink, T. (2010). Impact of the number of sensors on the network cost and accuracy of the radio environment map.*23rd Canadian Conference on Electrical and Computer Engineering (CCECE).*1–5. doi:10.1109/CCECE.2010.5575188

FCC. (2007). *FCC adopts rule for unlicensed use of television white spaces.* Retrieved from: http://www.fcc.gov/

Federal Communications Commission (FCC). (2004). *Notice of proposed rule making.* eT Docket no. 04113. FCC.

Ganesan, G., & Li, Y. (2007). Cooperative spectrum sensing in cognitive radio, part I: Two user networks. *IEEE Transactions on Wireless Communications, 6*(6). 2204–2213. doi:10.1109/TWC.2007.05775

Ghasemi, A., & Sousa, E. (2005). Collaborative spectrum sensing for opportunistic access in fading environments.*IEEE International Symposium on New Frontiers in Dynamic Spectrum Access Networks, DySPAN,* 131–136. doi:10.1109/DYSPAN.2005.1542627

Google. (2015). *Google spectrum database.* Retrieved from: https://www.google.com/get/spectrumdatabase/

Harrold, T., Cepeda, R., & Beach, M. (2011). Long-term measurements of spectrum occupancy characteristics.*IEEE Symposium on New Frontiers in Dynamic Spectrum Access Networks, DySPAN,* 83–89.

IEEE 802.22. (2011). *IEEE 802.22, working group on wireless regional area networks (WRAN).* Retrieved from: http://grouper.ieee.org/groups/802/22

IEEE P802.22a/D2. (2013). *IEEE draft standard for wireless regional area networks part 22: Cognitive wireless ran medium access control (MAC) and physical layer (PHY) specifications: Policies and procedures for operation in the TV bands - Amendment: Management and control plane interfaces and procedures and enhancement to the management information base (MIB).* IEEE.

Jeon, S.-W., Devroye, N., Vu, M., Chung, S.-Y., & Tarokh, V. (2011). Cognitive networks achieve throughput scaling of a homogeneous network. *IEEE Transactions on Information Theory, 57*(8). 5103–5115. doi:10.1109/TIT.2011.2158874

Li, Y., Quang, T. T., Kawahara, Y., Asami, T., & Kusunoki, M. (2009). Building a spectrum map for future cognitive radio technology. *Proceedings of ACM workshop Cognitive radio networks,* 1–6. doi:10.1145/1614235.1614237

Lin, S. C., & Chen, K. C. (2014). Spectrum-map-empowered opportunistic routing for cognitive radio ad hoc networks. *IEEE Transactions on Vehicular Technology, 63*(6). 2848–2861. doi:10.1109/TVT.2013.2296597

Mateos, G., Bazerque, J. A., & Giannakis, G. B. (2009). Spline-based spectrum cartography for cognitive radios.*Conference Record of the Forty-Third Asilomar Conference on Signals, Systems and Computers*, 1025– 1029.

Meshkova, E., Ansari, J., Denkovski, D., Riihijarvi, J., Nasreddine, J., Pavloski, M., & Mhnen, P. et al. (2011). Experimental spectrum sensor testbed for constructing indoor radio environmental maps.*IEEE Symposium on New Frontiers in Dynamic Spectrum Access Networks (DySPAN)*.603–607. doi:10.1109/DYSPAN.2011.5936253

Phillips, C., Ton, M., Sicker, D., & Grunwald, D. (2012). Practical radio environment mapping with geostatistics.*IEEE International Symposium on Dynamic Spectrum Access Networks (DYSPAN)*.422–433. doi:10.1109/DYSPAN.2012.6478166

Rawat, A. S., Anand, P., Chen, H., & Varshney, P. K. (2011). Collaborative spectrum sensing in the presence of byzantine attacks in cognitive radio networks. *IEEE Transactions on Signal Processing*, *59*(2). 774–786. doi:10.1109/TSP.2010.2091277

Riihijarvi, J., & Mahonen, P. (2008). Exploiting spatial statistics of primary and secondary users towards improved cognitive radio networks. *Cognitive Radio Oriented Wireless Networks and Communications, CrownCom*, 1 –7.

Riihijarvi, J., Mahonen, P., Wellens, M., & Gordziel, M. (2008). Characterization and modelling of spectrum for dynamic spectrum access with spatial statistics and random fields.*IEEE19th International Symposium on Personal, Indoor and Mobile Radio Communications, PIMRC*, 1 –6. doi:10.1109/PIMRC.2008.4699912

Shannon, C. E. (2001). A mathematical theory of communication. *SIGMOBILE Mob. Comput. Commun.*, *5*(1). 3–55. doi:10.1145/584091.584093

Shared Spectrum Company. (2007). *Spectrum Occupancy Measurements Loring Commerce Centre Limestone, Maine*. Retrieved from: http://www.sharedspectrum.com/papers/spectrum-reports/

Sun, G., & Van de Beek, J. (2010). Simple distributed interference source localization for radio environment mapping. *Wireless Days (WD)*. 1–5.

Visotsky, E., Kuffner, S., & Peterson, R. (2005). On collaborative detection of tv transmissions in support of dynamic spectrum sharing.*IEEE International Symposium on New Frontiers in Dynamic Spectrum Access Networks, DySPAN*, 338–345. doi:10.1109/DYSPAN.2005.1542650

Wei, Z., Zhang, Q., Feng, Z., Li, W., & Gulliver, T. A. (2013). On the construction of radio environment maps for cognitive radio networks.*IEEE Wireless Communications and Networking Conference (WCNC)*.4504–4509. doi:10.1109/WCNC.2013.6555304

Yilmaz, H. B., & Tugcu, T. (2015). Location estimation-based radio environment map construction in fading channels. *Wirel. Commun. Mob. Comput.*, *15*(3). 561–570. doi:10.1002/wcm.2367

Chapter 3
Fulfilling the Rate Demands:
Subcarrier–Based Shared Resource Allocation

Ravikant Saini
Indian Institute of Technology Delhi, India

Swades De
Indian Institute of Technology Delhi, India

ABSTRACT

Mobile connectivity these days is no more a privilege but a basic necessity. This has led to exponentially-increasing data rate demands over the network, causing tremendous pressure to the access network service planners. Orthogonal frequency division multiple access (OFDMA) is being considered for resource allocation in higher generation communication networks, where spectrum efficiency improvement while fulfilling the users' data rate demands is a key aspect of interest. Normally resource allocation is considered from the viewpoint of users, with the users selecting their best available subcarriers. In this chapter, the resource allocation problem is approached from the subcarrier's perspective. Besides the conventional user-based scheme, a recent subcarrier-based shared resource allocation scheme is presented that selects the best user(s) for each subcarrier and assigns the subcarrier either to a single user or more than one user on time-shared basis according to their current SNRs. Unlike the user-based schemes, in the proposed scheme each user can contend for any subcarrier.

INTRODUCTION

With the increasing overlap of users' active mobile time and their awake time, mobile connectivity is expected to be always present anytime, anywhere. Users find it hard to wait for any time lag in connection setup due to the requirement of remaining connected on social applications, be it early morning or just before they are off to bed. Thus, mobile connectivity these days is no more a desire, but it is appearing as a basic need of the user. But the requirement of instant connectivity raises immense pressure on the wireless infrastructure planners, as this is the last-mile which is the bottleneck. The flexibility

DOI: 10.4018/978-1-5225-2023-8.ch003

of access network has taken a great leap following the transition from wired (e.g., dial-up connection, Digital Subscriber Line (DSL)) to broadband wireless (e.g., Long-Term Evolution – Advanced (LTE-A), Worldwide Interoperability for Microwave Access (WiMAX)) for the last-mile connectivity. Yet, the current generations of wireless access network protocols find it hard to cater to the ever-increasing data rate demands of the mobile users. These days, a mobile devices is no longer a calling facility but a data hungry demon with a day-by-day increasing appetite. With the social networking platforms, such as, Facebook and YouTube, as common information sharing avenues, and powerful smart phones in every pocket, it is quite formidable to satisfy a user with anything less than the prefect quality video on the move. One strong physical layer technology is required to cater to the data rate demands of mobile users and stand hard against the impairments of wireless channel. Orthogonal frequency division multiple access (OFDMA) which divides a wide band channel into multiple narrow band channels, appears as a robust technology against the multipath fading effect of wireless channel. Next section provides a brief overview of resource allocation schemes in OFDMA.

Background on OFDMA

OFDMA which is being considered as a potential physical layer technology for next generation communication networks such as LTE-A and WiMAX, offers multiuser diversity along with time and frequency diversity. Resource allocation in OFDMA includes subcarrier allocation among users, and bit and power allocation over subcarriers. OFDMA has gathered considerable attentions in the research community as well as communication systems industry. The overall resource optimization problem being NP hard (Afolabi, 2013; Liu, 2014), several approaches have been suggested to solve it in parts. In a class of algorithms, one starts with minimizing the overall required transmitter power under minimum user rate constraints; such algorithms are termed as margin adaptive algorithms (Wong, 1999; Kivanc, 2003; Zhang, 2004; De, 2014). In another class, the objective is maximizing the overall capacity under power constraints; such algorithms are called as rate adaptive algorithms (Rhee 2000; Jang 2003; Shen, 2005; Mohanram, 2005; Song, 2003, 2005(1), 2005(2); Bin-Shimol, 2006; Biagioni, 2009; Gao, 2011; Zhu, 2009, 2012; Sharma, 2014).

For multimedia applications, rate adaptive algorithms are of more interest compared to margin adaptive techniques due to their open objective of capacity maximization. Rhee and Cioffi (2000) proposed a rate adaptive algorithm in a landmark paper suggesting that each subcarrier should be assigned to a user that has a good channel gain over it. But, for fair allocation, the algorithm initially allocates the best subcarrier to the set of users and then keep on selecting the least served user and allocating the best subcarrier to it. Jang and Lee (2003) gave analytical proof of the assertions made by Rhee (2000) that, in OFDMA systems, capacity maximization is achieved by allocating each subcarrier to a user having the best channel gain on that subcarrier.

Some other approaches offered suboptimal solution to the optimization problem, either by considering flat power distribution and performing subcarrier allocation, or subcarrier and power allocations were done in two steps. Shen et al. (2005) divided the problem in two parts. Initially subcarriers are distributed assuming flat power distribution, and then power is distributed over the subcarriers optimally by root finding method. Mohanram and Bhashyam (2005) proposed a suboptimal algorithm that switches between subcarrier allocation and power allocation for every subcarrier.

To reduce the signaling load of channel state information (CSI) feedback, a direction of research considered collecting subcarriers in sub-channels and OFDM symbols in time slots. Along this line, resource allocation was considered as a two-dimensional mapping by Ben-Shimol et al. (2006), where they proposed raster scan based algorithms for allocation of slots on the time-frequency plane to the users, but a user was constrained to use the same modulation scheme on all the slots. Biagioni et al. (2009) proposed that the users be allowed to use modulation techniques based on one's average signal-to-noise ratio (SNR) in the slot, and based on (Rhee, 2000), they proposed two modified algorithms to improve efficiency and fairness. Zhu and Wang (2009, 2013) considered collection of subcarriers in chunks and allocation was done per OFDM symbol rather than over a collection of symbols. Zhu (2009) analyzed throughput performance of chunk resource allocation, and Zhu (2012) presented a chunk based bit and power allocation algorithm. De et al. (2014) proposed and evaluated optimum subcarrier allocation and power control policies in OFDM system for source-aware applications. Gao and Wang (2011) presented optimal chunk allocation strategy for various power control policies. Sharma et al. (2014) studied optimum and suboptimum source coding adaptation solutions for block-coded content transmission over OFDM fading channels respectively with and without CSI feedback.

During resource allocation, most of the fairness-constrained algorithms select a user according to least served data rate in order to maintain fairness, and for each chosen user, the best subcarrier is selected according to its channel gain, i.e., received signal-to-noise ratio (SNR), to maximize the total data rate (Rhee, 2000; Shen, 2005; Biagioni, 2009; Wong, 2004; Ma, 2008; Shen, 2003; Sadr, 2009). These algorithms are classified as user-based resource allocation (UBRA), as these algorithms are designed by looking at the problem from users' perspective. In this chapter another perspective of resource allocation is introduced, i.e., resource allocation from the viewpoint of subcarriers. For each subcarrier, the algorithm identifies how many users are equally capable in using a subcarrier, and then if required, the subcarrier is time shared between them. First of all, a generic OFDMA system model is outlined, before the issues with user based resource allocation algorithm are discussed in detail.

SYSTEM MODEL

Let us consider an OFDMA system with single base station and M mobile users uniformly spread in the coverage area. The total system bandwidth is W, and N is the total number of subcarriers in the system. A time division duplex (TDD) frame structure containing O OFDM symbols is considered. For simplicity of exposition the frame duration is taken $T_o = OT_s$, where T_s is the symbol duration – considered to be equal to the inverse of subcarrier spacing, i.e., $T_s = \dfrac{N}{W}$.

The channel capacity of a single subcarrier in OFDMA system is given by:

$$C_0 = \frac{W}{N} \log_2 \left(1 + \gamma_0\right) \text{(bits/s)}$$

where γ_0 is the effective SNR received on the subcarrier, including the effect of SNR gap that takes care of the bit error rate (BER) requirement of the user.

It is assumed that resources on the frequency-time plane are shared among the users in the form of slots, where each slot contains D contiguous subcarriers on the frequency axis and E contiguous OFDM symbols on the time axis. Let $F = N/D$ and $G = O/E$ denote respectively the numbers of frequency and time slots. Then, the capacity of a slot can be simplified as (Biagioni, 2009):

$$C_{slot} = DE \log_2 \left(1 + \alpha_{slot}^2\right) \text{(bits/slot)}$$

where α_{slot} is the average multi-path channel coefficient in the slot, defined as:

$$\alpha_{slot} = \frac{\sum_{d=1}^{D} \sum_{e=1}^{E} \alpha_{d,e}}{DE}$$

Here $\alpha_{d,e}$ is the multi-path channel coefficient of the d th subcarrier on the e th OFDM symbol in the slot. Perfect CSI is assumed to be available at both receiver and transmitter, which is used by the resource allocation algorithm for sharing the resources. Based on the CSI value, capacity achievable by a user-i on a particular slot $\left(j, k\right)$ is given as:

$$C_{j,k}^i = DE \log_2 \left(1 + \gamma_{j,k}^i\right) \text{(bits/slot)}$$

where $\gamma_{j,k}^i$ is the SNR of the i th user on the $\left(j, k\right)$ th slot. With $x_{j,k}^i$ as the allocation identifier, the problem of capacity maximization is formulated as:

$$\max_{x_{j,k}^i} \left\{ DE \sum_{i=1}^{M} \sum_{j=1}^{F} \sum_{k=1}^{G} x_{j,k}^i \log_2 \left(1 + \gamma_{j,k}^i\right) \right\}$$

subject to:

$$\sum_{i=1}^{M} x_{j,k}^i = 1 \forall j, k \tag{1}$$

The objective of a resource allocation algorithm is to find out the allocation matrix $X = \left[x_{j,k}^i\right]$ so as to maximize the overall capacity of the system.

Uniqueness of the Existing Policy and Motivation for Improved Alternatives

The existing OFDMA resource allocation policy is classified as UBRA. From Equation 1, it can be noted that, UBRA scheme does not allow slot sharing, thus $x_{j,k}^i$ takes only binary values, given as:

$$x_{j,k}^{i} = \begin{cases} 1 & \textit{if user-i is allotted} \left(j,k\right) \textit{th slot} \\ 0 & \textit{otherwise} \end{cases}$$

While the UBRA may be fair on capacity allocation in the long run, by letting a user choose the best subcarrier or slot during resource allocation at a given time, the other potentially better scenarios may be overlooked where a different user could use the resource better. Thus, it is anticipated that the above class of allocation may be suboptimal in terms of system capacity. In the current proposal authors re-look at the resource allocation problem from the other perspective of finding the best user(s) for a subcarrier, rather than a user finding the best subcarrier. Wong et al. (1999) introduced the concept of time sharing a subcarrier, through a sharing factor taking value within interval {0,1}. The optimum solution gives the optimal value of the sharing factor for each subcarrier. However, each subcarrier is assigned to a single user having the largest sharing factor over that subcarrier.

Since the time, Jang and Lee (2003) formally proved that a subcarrier should be allocated to only one user, it became a thumb rule to allocate a subcarrier or a slot to a single user. Alternatively, the resource allocation problem in OFDMA systems can be addressed from a different angle, where the aim is to have a naturally fair resource allocation to the users, irrespective of the time-scale of usage by a user, while pushing up the achievable system capacity limit. For this purpose, the option of sharing a subcarrier in time dimension is investigated and a resource allocation algorithm based on subcarrier sharing is proposed (Saini, 2014). A new category of allocation called subcarrier-based shared resource allocation (SBSRA) is defined, where for each subcarrier the algorithm decides whether to allocate it to an individual user or time share it among the users. Thus, for each subcarrier a fair contention among the users is maintained, which offers an extra degree of freedom.

Referring to Equation 1, SBSRA scheme enables slot sharing among the users and allows fractional value of the variable $x_{j,k}^{i}$, which is in general from the set $\left\{0, 1/E, 2/E, \cdots, 1\right\}$. Allowing fractional values gives an extra degree of freedom to SBSRA which is expected to improve capacity and fairness.

USER-BASED VS. SUBCARRIER-BASED RESOURCE ALLOCATION

The algorithm presented in (Rhee, 2000) is considered as benchmark for the class of algorithms providing constrained fairness solution to the optimization problem, Equation 1, and is considered as representative for the UBRA class. The slotted version of UBRA, which was proposed and studied in (Biagioni, 2009), is considered for performance comparison with respect to the proposed SBSRA scheme.

User-Based Resource Allocation (UBRA)

The resource allocation algorithm presented in (Rhee, 2000) works in two steps. In the first step there is a *'for loop'* in which the algorithm allocates one best subcarrier (according to maximum SNR) to each user. In the second step there is a *'while loop'* where the algorithm picks a least rate user and then allocates a best subcarrier to this user. This process continues until all the subcarriers are allocated. The resulting fairness in this strategy is based on the basic assumption that the number of subcarriers is much larger compared to the number of users. In the slotted version of the algorithm, slots on the time-frequency plane are allocated to the users (Biagioni, 2009).

Subcarrier-Based Shared Resource Allocation (SBSRA)

As an alternative strategy, in SBSRA it is proposed to time share the resources among equally capable users. Consider a simplified OFDMA system with one subcarrier per frequency slot and E symbols per time slot. Suppose over a subcarrier a user having maximum SNR is able to support a data rate R_{max} according to some discrete rate adaptation criterion. Then, if there are $(m-1)$ other users $(m \leq M)$ that too can support the same data rate on that subcarrier, then there are three options:

1. Allocate the subcarrier to the user having maximum SNR for the entire time slot. This scheme, termed as 'no sharing' scheme, has been a conventional approach proposed in (Wong, 1999; Rhee, 2000; Jang, 2003). This option is considered for comparison with the proposed approaches described below.
2. Time-share the subcarrier among m users by dividing OFDM symbols among them equally. This is one of the proposed schemes, which is called 'equal sharing' scheme. This approach is considered for theoretical discussion but it has practical limitations.
3. Time-share the subcarrier among, say, $\min(m, E)$ users by dividing OFDM symbols among them uniformly. This modified proposed scheme is identified as 'uniform sharing scheme'. This is a practical approach, which is also studied further in the paper.

The proposition below provides the basis for gain in fairness while retaining the capacity.

Proposition 1: The OFDMA systems implementing the three different schemes of subcarrier allocation, i.e., allocating a subcarrier to single best user, equally sharing the subcarrier among m users, and uniformly sharing the subcarrier among $\min(m, E)$ users, offer the same capacity.
Proof: See Appendix.

Thus, by increasing the granularity of resource allocation from time slot level to OFDM symbol level, i.e., by allowing sharing of the OFDM symbols within a slot among the competitive users, a higher short-term fairness without any loss of capacity can be achieved. Based on this concept, proposed 'uniform sharing' algorithm that works at the level of supported data rates has been outlined below.

Pseudocode

Let the data rate supported by a user-i on a subcarrier-j be denoted as R_j^i.

```
                    for every subcarrier j do
find  R_max = max{R_j^i} ∀i
find the set of users  U_j = {i : R_j^i = R_max} if |U_j| = 1 then
allocate all the OFDM symbols to the only user in the set  U_j
else
allocate OFDM symbols among  min(E,|U_j|) users in the set  U_j uniformly
end if
end for
```

The above algorithm can be easily extended for allocation of slots on the frequency-time plane in OFDMA systems. In that case, each slot is considered independently for allocation on time-shared basis among the competitive users. The slotted version of SBSRA has also been considered for comparative performance study with the slotted UBRA (Biagioni, 2009).

Complexity Analysis

Before analyzing the capacity and fairness performance of the two algorithms, their computation complexities are investigated.

Lemma 1: Complexity of the UBRA algorithm in an M users N subcarriers system is $\mathcal{O}(N^2)$, while for SBSRA it is $\mathcal{O}(MN)$.

Proof: In UBRA, the first *for loop* selects the best subcarrier for each user. For the first user the maximum SNR is searched over all N subcarriers. For each subsequent user the search space reduces by one. Thus, the searches involved in the *for loop* is $MN - M(M-1)/2$. Rest of the $N - M$ subcarriers are allocated in the *while loop*, where the algorithm continue to select the least served user and allocate the best available subcarrier. Finding the least served user involves a search over M users. Picking the best available subcarrier involves a search over the leftover subcarrier space, which keep reducing from $(N - M)$ to 1 with each subcarrier allocation. So the search associated with the *while loop* is $(N - M)(N + M + 1)/2$. Considering $N \gg M$, the overall complexity of UBRA algorithm is $\mathcal{O}(N^2)$.

In SBSRA, for each subcarrier, first the algorithm finds the data rates offered to different users based on their respective SNRs, which involves M calculations. In the second step the algorithm finds the user offering the best data rate on the subcarrier, which involves a search over M users. Then algorithm finds if there are any other users that can achieve the same (maximum) data rate, which again involves comparison over M users. Finally the algorithm picks E users uniformly for symbol allocation. Thus, each subcarrier allocation involves computations on the order of $(3M + E)$. The overall complexity of the SBSRA algorithm is $\mathcal{O}(MN)$.

On the similar lines, complexity of the slotted version of UBRA algorithm for an M users OFDMA system with $K = FG$ slots over frequency-time plane can be proved to be $\mathcal{O}(K^2)$, while that for SBSRA it can be proved to be $\mathcal{O}(MK)$.

In the following section, the capacity and fairness analysis of UBRA and SBSRA are presented, and thereby the stage is set for their relative performance evaluation.

CAPACITY AND FAIRNESS ANALYSIS

This section characterizes the capacity and fairness performance of UBRA and the proposed SBSRA schemes. The channel is considered to experience frequency selective Rayleigh fading. For simplicity of capturing the basic performance gain, capacity of the system is measured in terms of bits per subcarrier and fairness is measured by Jain's fairness index (Jain, 1984). It can be trivially proved that capacity of an OFDMA system in bits per subcarrier is the same as the standard measure of capacity in bits/s/Hz.

2-Users 2-Subcarriers Case

First the capacity analysis of 2 users 2 subcarriers case is considered as a proof of concept.

Let the received SNR matrix be denoted as:

$$\underline{\Gamma} = \begin{pmatrix} \gamma_1^1 & \gamma_2^1 \\ \gamma_1^2 & \gamma_2^2 \end{pmatrix}$$

where γ_j^i is the SNR of user-i on jth subcarrier. In Rayleigh fading channel with average received SNR $\bar{\gamma}$, the SNR [3] is exponentially distributed with probability density function given by: $f_{\Gamma}(\gamma) = \frac{1}{\bar{\gamma}} e^{-\frac{\gamma}{\bar{\gamma}}}$.

For the time being, two level adaptive modulation scheme is assumed, i.e., if the received SNR is above a threshold γ_{th}, the supported data rate is b, otherwise it is 0.

UBRA

Since the number of users is equal to the number of subcarriers, resource allocation to all the users is finished in the *for loop* itself. In this case, if $\gamma_1^1 > \gamma_2^1$, user-1 uses subcarrier-1, otherwise user-1 uses subcarrier-2. Note that user-2 has no other option but to go with the leftover subcarrier.

Consider the case when $\gamma_1^1 > \gamma_2^1$. There are three possible sub-cases:

1. $\gamma_{th} > \gamma_1^1$;
2. $\gamma_1^1 > \gamma_{th} > \gamma_2^1$;
3. $\gamma_2^1 > \gamma_{th}$.

User-1 can use subcarrier-1 in case 2 and 3 only. Hence the capacity assigned to user-1 is given by: $C_{u_1} = b(1 - e^{-\beta}/2)e^{-\beta}$, where $\beta = \gamma_{th}/\bar{\gamma}$. Correspondingly, the capacity assigned to user-2 on subcarrier-2 is $C_{u_2} = be^{-\beta}/2$.

Capacity assigned to both the users in the other case (when $\gamma_1^1 < \gamma_2^1$) is the same as above.

Thus, the overall capacities of the two users are $C_{u_1} = 2b\left(1 - e^{-\beta}/2\right)e^{-\beta}$ and $C_{u_2} = be^{-\beta}$.

$$C_{ubra} = 2b\left(1 - e^{-\beta}/2\right)e^{-\beta} + be^{-\beta} = b\left(1 - \left(1 - e^{-\beta}\right)^2\right) + b\left(1 - \left(1 - e^{-\beta}\right)\right) \tag{2}$$

SBSRA

SBSRA allocates each subcarrier independently to either one user or shares among more than one user. Considering 'equal sharing' scheme, algorithm compares γ_1^1 and γ_1^2 with γ_{th} for allocation of subcarrier-1. There exist four cases:

1. $\gamma_1^1 > \gamma_{th}$ and $\gamma_1^2 > \gamma_{th}$: Subcarrier has to be time-shared between the two users. Considering equal sharing, their respective capacities are $C_{u_1} = C_{u_2} = be^{-\beta} / 2$.

2. $\gamma_1^1 > \gamma_{th}$ and $\gamma_1^2 < \gamma_{th}$: Subcarrier is used by user-1 and the capacity is $C_{u_1} = b\left(1 - e^{-\beta}\right)e^{-\beta}$

3. $\gamma_1^1 < \gamma_{th}$ and $\gamma_1^2 > \gamma_{th}$: Subcarrier is used by user-2 and the capacity is $C_{u_2} = b\left(1 - e^{-\beta}\right)e^{-\beta}$

4. $\gamma_1^1 < \gamma_{th}$ and $\gamma_1^2 < \gamma_{th}$: In this case subcarrier is not at all usable.

Thus, each user's capacity over a single subcarrier is given by: $C_{u_1} = C_{u_2} = b(1 - e^{-\beta} / 2)e^{-\beta}$.

Since all subcarriers are independent, the overall capacity in SBSRA scheme is obtained as:

$$C_{sbra} = 2b\left[1 - \left(1 - e^{-\beta}\right)^2\right] \tag{3}$$

Capacity Improvement of SBSRA over UBRA

The capacity gain can be obtained as:

$$C_{gain} = C_{sbsra} - C_{ubra} = b\left(1 - e^{-\beta}\right)e^{-\beta},$$

which has a peak at average SNR $\bar{\gamma}_{max} = \gamma_{th} / \ln(2)$.

As observed from Equation 2 and Equation 3, assigned capacities to the users are different in UBRA, while they are the same in SBSRA. Further, accounting the gain, this simple case of 2 users 2 subcarriers demonstrates the capacity gain and fairness improvement by SBSRA. In the subsequent developments, more generalized cases of UBRA and SBSRA capacity and fairness performance are discussed.

M-Users *M*-Subcarriers Case

The above 2 users 2 subcarriers scenario can be simply extended to M users and M subcarriers case in UBRA and SBSRA, respectively.

UBRA

Each user's capacity in this case is obtained as:

$$C_{u_i} = b\left(1 - \left(1 - e^{-\beta}\right)^{M+1-i}\right),$$

where $i = 1,2,....M,$ is the order of the users in the *for loop* of the UBRA scheme. Hence the total capacity of the UBRA scheme is given by:

$$C_{ubra} = b\sum_{i=1}^{M}\left(1 - \left(1 - e^{-\beta}\right)^{M+1-i}\right)$$

SBSRA

In this case, the capacity of each user on each subcarrier remains the same and is obtained as: $C_{u_i} = b\left[1 - \left(1 - e^{-\beta}\right)^M\right] / M$. The overall capacity of SBSRA is given by:

$$C_{sbsra} = Mb\left[1 - \left(1 - e^{-\beta}\right)^M\right]$$

Comparing C_{ubra} and C_{sbsra}, SBSRA has the inherent capability of achieving nearly perfect fairness along with improved capacity. A more generalized scenario is presented below.

M-Users *N*-Subcarriers Case, When *N>M*

Normally the number of subcarriers are more compared to the number of users in an OFDMA system, hence, only *N>M* is considered.

UBRA

The exact capacity of UBRA scheme in *M* users *N* subcarriers case cannot be obtained by simple extension of *M* users *M* subcarriers case. In the general case with *N>M* after first *M* subcarriers' allocation to *M* users in the *for loop*, users are picked up in *while loop* according to their latest total served data rate in ascending order for the subsequent allocations.

Thus, the order of the users being picked in the *while loop* does not follow a fixed pattern. The proposition below asserts that the order of user selection in UBRA affects its capacity, and there is a special case of UBRA which serves as an upper bound to the original UBRA.

Proposition 1: In the original UBRA algorithm, the order of user selection in the *while loop* affects the achievable capacity. The capacity is maximum if in the subsequent subcarrier allocations *(while loop)* the users are chosen in the same order as in the first iteration *(for loop)*.

Proof: In order to show that user selection in the *while loop* affects the achieved capacity in UBRA, a 2 users 3 subcarriers OFDMA system is considered. Let the SNR matrix be:

$$\underline{\Gamma} = \begin{pmatrix} \gamma_1^1 & \gamma_2^1 & \gamma_3^1 \\ \gamma_1^2 & \gamma_2^2 & \gamma_3^2 \end{pmatrix}$$

where γ_j^i is the SNR of user-*i* on *j* th subcarrier. The capacity assigned to user-1 in the for loop is b times the probability that $\max(\gamma_1^1, \gamma_2^1, \gamma_3^1) > \gamma_{th}$. Probability that user-1 selects subcarrier-1, i.e., $\gamma_1^1 > (\gamma_2^1, \gamma_3^1)$, is 1/3. Thus, the capacity assigned to user-1 on subcarrier-1 is $C_{u_1}^1 = b\left[1 - \left(1 - e^{-\beta}\right)^3\right] / 3$.

Considering all other possible cases, i.e., γ_2^1 and γ_3^1 as maximum SNRs, the overall capacity assigned to user-1 in the for loop is:

$$C_{u_1}(f) = b\left[1 - \left(1 - e^{-\beta}\right)^3\right].$$

User-2 has two options γ_2^2 and γ_3^2 and the probability that $\gamma_2^2 > \gamma_3^2$ is 1/2. Thus the capacity assigned to user-2 on subcarrier-2 is $C_{u_2}^2 = b\left[1 - \left(1 - e^{-\beta}\right)^2\right]/2$. Considering the other possible case of user-2 picking subcarrier-3, overall capacity assigned to user-2 in the for loop is:

$$C_{u_2}(f) = b\left[1 - \left(1 - e^{-\beta}\right)^2\right].$$

Now the algorithm enters in the *while loop* where it selects the user having the least data rate and allocates it the next subcarrier. As the capacity assigned to user-2 is lower than the capacity assigned to user-1, original UBRA algorithm will select user-2 and allocate it the next subcarrier.

If user-2 is selected then it selects the only leftover subcarrier-3. The capacity assigned to user-2 is equal to b times the probability that $\gamma_2^2 > \gamma_3^2 > \gamma_{th}$, which is equal to $C_{u_2}^3 = be^{-2\beta}/2$. Considering the other possible case, capacity assigned to user-2 in the while loop is: $C_{u_2}(w) = be^{-2\beta}$. Thus the over-all capacity assigned to user-1 is: $C_{u_1} = b\left[1 - \left(1 - e^{-\beta}\right)^3\right]$.

And the capacity assigned to user-2 is:

$$C_{u_2} = C_{u_2}(f) + C_{u_2}(w) = b\left[1 - \left(1 - e^{-\beta}\right)^2\right] + be^{-2\beta}.$$

In the other scenario when user-1 is considered again for subcarrier allocation in *while loop*. User-1 has already selected subcarrier-1 with probability 1/3. Now the capacity assigned to user-1 shall be b times the probability that $\gamma_1^1 > \gamma_3^1 > \gamma_{th}$. Three distinct cases arise for calculation of the above probability: $\gamma_1^1 > \gamma_3^1 > \gamma_{th} > \gamma_2^1$, $\gamma_1^1 > \gamma_3^1 > \gamma_2^1 > \gamma_{th}$, and $\gamma_1^1 > \gamma_2^1 > \gamma_3^1 > \gamma_{th}$. Respective capacities assigned in these three cases are $be^{-2\beta}(1 - e^{-\beta})/2$, $be^{-3\beta}/6$, and $be^{-3\beta}/6$. The capacity assigned to user-1 on subcarrier-3 is $C_{u_1}^3 = b\left(3e^{-2\beta} - e^{-3\beta}\right)/6$. Considering all other possible cases (γ_2^1 and γ_3^1 as maximum SNRs), the overall capacity assigned to user-1 in the while loop is: $C_{u_1}(w) = b\left(3e^{-2\beta} - e^{-3\beta}\right)/2$.

Thus the overall capacity assigned to user-1 is:

$$C_{u_1} = C_{u_1}(f) + C_{u_1}(w) = b\left[1 - \left(1 - e^{-\beta}\right)^3\right] + \frac{b}{2}\left(3e^{-2\beta} - e^{-3\beta}\right)$$

And the capacity assigned to user-2 is:

$$C_{u_2} = b\left[1 - \left(1 - e^{-\beta}\right)^2\right]$$

Comparing $C_{u_2}(w)$ and $C_{u_1}(w)$, it is noted that $C_{u_1}(w) > C_{u_2}(w)$, i.e., capacity assigned to user-1 is higher then the capacity assigned to user-2 in the while loop. In fact the capacity difference is $C_{diff} = be^{-2\beta}\left(1-e^{-\beta}\right)/2$. User-1 achieves higher capacity because it has higher number of options (3 in this case) compared to user-2 (2 options), to choose from. Thus, choosing user-1 as the first user in the *while loop* maximizes the capacity achieved by UBRA.

Extension of this argument further for the general case of *M* users *N* subcarriers system is as follows. An iteration is defined as serving *M* subcarriers to *M* users. There are $\left\lceil \dfrac{N}{M} \right\rceil$ iterations to be performed.

In the first iteration ($I = 1$ i.e., for loop), as the users keep on picking their best available subcarriers, the number of leftover subcarriers ($n' = N + 1 - u_i$) that a subsequent user finds, keep on reducing with index $u_i = \{1, 2, \cdots, M\}$. The capacity assigned to a user-u_i in the first iteration ($I = 1$) can be easily obtained by simply extending the analysis of *M* users *M* subcarriers system. Capacity assigned to a user is b times the probability that the maximum available SNR from the leftover subcarriers is above the threshold, and is obtained as:

$$C_{u_i}(1) = b\left(1 - \left(1 - e^{-\beta}\right)^{N+1-u_i}\right)$$

As observed from above equation, the capacity assigned to the users diminishes with user index u_i. So the last user $u_i = M$, achieving the least capacity, will be picked by the algorithm for allocation in while loop. In contrast, if the users are allowed to continue in the same order, 1 to *M*, then the first user $u_i = 1$, who had the highest rate allocated in the first iteration, will get higher capacity because it gets to choose from the highest number of leftover subcarriers and the probability of finding next higher SNR to be above threshold is higher for $u_i = 1$. Thus, if the users are chosen in the same order for successive blocks of M subcarriers allocation, the achieved capacity will be higher than the original UBRA algorithm's capacity, though its offered fairness will be poorer. Hence the capacity achieved in the special case of UBRA is an upper bound to what can be achieved in the original UBRA algorithm.

A new notion of effective subcarriers is introduced for further discussion on capacity analysis of UBRA bound. In the first iteration, for each user u_i, the number of effective subcarriers is the same as the number of leftover subcarriers ($n' = N + 1 - u_i$), which are the number of subcarriers that a user gets to choose from. In subsequent iterations, the number of effective subcarriers keep on reducing by *M*, as *M* subcarriers are allocated to *M* users in each iteration.

In the second iteration each user picks up a subcarrier (with maximum SNR) from the set of $(n' - M)$ effective subcarriers. Each user has $(M - 1)$ unused SNRs which cannot be used by the user as they have been used by other users; these are designated as free locations, when SNRs are arranged in descending order. Thus, the required SNR which is to be picked up in this iteration can be placed at any of the *M* places ($(M - 1)$ free locations and its original location). In order to find the capacity assigned to a user, for each possible location of the required SNR (referred to as required location in further discussion), permutations of filling the higher order SNR locations and combinations of all the lower order

SNR locations are calculated and multiplied with the probability of picking that required location. In second iteration $(I = 2)$ the permutations and combinations for a user u_i are $p = P_{i_2}^{M-1}$ and $c = (N - 1 - u_i - i_2)!$, where $i_2 = 0, 1, \cdots, M - 1$ is the index of required location.

The probability of picking the required location is considered next. For each user, the probabilities of an ordered set of SNR locations is computed beforehand and then the probability required for any required location in the ordered set is obtained by summing the probabilities of all the lower order SNR locations with respect to the required location. Probabilities of the ordered set can be calculated by using binomial expansion. Probability of an ordered location $o = 0, 1, \cdots, n'$ for a user u_i is:

$$\Pr(u_i, o) = \frac{1}{n'!} C_o^{n'} e^{-(n'-o)\beta} e^{-o\beta}$$

where $C_k^n = \dfrac{n!}{k! \, n - k!}$. Along with the ordered probability, an additional factor, which is referred as pre-factor, should be multiplied. The pre-factor in the first iteration is equal to the effective number of subcarriers n' for each user. In each subsequent iteration I it is computed for each user u_i as follows:

$$p_f(I, u_i) = \prod_{i_t=1}^{I} \left(N - u_i + 1 - (i_t - 1)M \right)$$

Thus, the capacity assigned to a user u_i in iteration $I = 2$ is obtained as:

$$C_{u_i}(I) = p_f(I, u_i) \sum_{i_2=0}^{M-1} P_{i_2}^{M-1} (n' - I - i_2)! \left[1 - \sum_{h=1}^{I+i_2} \Pr(u_i, h) \right]$$

where h is the index of already allocated higher SNR locations in the ordered set with respect to the required location i_2. Note that, permutations are the same for all users in an iteration, while combinations, pre-factor, and probability of picking a location are different for each user u_i.

In every subsequent iteration, free locations keep increasing due to allocations in previous iterations, while the number of combinations keep reducing with the reducing number of effective SNRs. In the third iteration the number of free locations increases to $2(M - 1)$ and further sub-cases should be considered while considering the permutations. The permutations and combinations for the third iteration $I = 3$ are: $p = P_{i_2}^{M-1} P_{i_3}^{2(M-1)-i_2}$ and $c = (n' - I - i_2 - i_3)!$ where $i_3 = 0, 1, \cdots, 2(M - 1)$.

The capacity assigned to a user u_i in the iteration $I = 3$ is found as:

$$C_{u_i}(I) = p_f(I, u_i) \sum_{i_2=0}^{M-1} P_{i_2}^{M-1} \sum_{i_3=0}^{2(M-1)-i_2} P_{i_3}^{2(M-1)-i_2} \cdot (n' - I - i_2 - i_3)! \left[1 - \sum_{h=1}^{I+i_2+i_3} \Pr(u_i, h) \right]$$

Extending to the general case, the capacity assigned to a user u_i in an iteration I is given by:

$$C_{u_i}(I) = p_f(I, u_i) \sum_{i_2=0}^{M-1} P_{i_2}^{M-1} \sum_{i_3=0}^{2(M-1)-i_2} P_{i_3}^{2(M-1)-i_2} \cdot \sum_{i_4=0}^{3(M-1)-i_2-i_3} P_{i_4}^{3(M-1)-i_2-i_3} \cdots$$

$$x\left(n' - I - i_2 - i_3 - i_4 \cdots\right)! \left[1 - \sum_{h=1}^{I+i_2+i_3+i_4 \cdots} \Pr\left(u_i, h\right)\right] \tag{4}$$

Capacity of all except the last subcarrier is obtained by the above method. For the last subcarrier the reason for different computation is its last position. In this case, the possible combinations are the same for each required location. This can be achieved in the above analysis by removing the dependency of permutations and combinations on the current iteration variable, i.e., i_I. The overall system capacity bound is obtained by summing up all the capacities assigned to the users in the successive iterations.

SBSRA

The capacity of SBSRA scheme can be found by simple extension from previous section, since the average rate offered by each subcarrier is the same. Thus, the general M users N subcarriers capacity for the SBSRA scheme is given by:

$$C_{sbsra} = Nb\left[1 - \left(1 - e^{-\beta}\right)^M\right]$$

M-Users *N*-Subcarriers *L*-Thresholds Case

Till now, just 2 level adaptive modulation offering binary rates {b, 0} has been considered. This analysis can be extended by considering multilevel adaptive modulation. The received SNR γ is now compared with respect to *(L+1)* SNR regions $\{S_l\}$, where $l = 0, 1, \cdots L$. SNR region S_l is bounded by the SNR thresholds γ_l and γ_{l+1}. Assuming $\gamma_0 = 0$ and $\gamma_{L+1} = \infty$. Squared M QAM supports $2l$ bits in the SNR region S_l that offers a chosen minimum bit error rate (BER) guarantee.

UBRA

In UBRA, with M users M subcarriers, denoting $\beta_l = \dfrac{\gamma_l}{\bar{\gamma}}$, each users' capacity is given as:

$$C_{u_i} = \sum_{l=1}^{L} (2l)\left[\left(1 - e^{-\beta_{l+1}}\right)^{M+1-u_i} - \left(1 - e^{-\beta_l}\right)^{M+1-u_i}\right]$$

Thus, the overall capacity in UBRA is

$$C_{ubra} = \sum_{u_i=1}^{M} \sum_{l=1}^{L} (2l) \left[\left(1 - e^{-\beta_{l+1}}\right)^{M+1-u_i} - \left(1 - e^{-\beta_l}\right)^{M+1-u_i} \right]$$

Since exact analysis of capacity in UBRA with *M* users *N* subcarriers *(N>M)* is difficult to achieve. The extension of capacity bound analysis with *L* thresholds is achieved by changing the way the probabilities are calculated. Now each SNR can lie in any of the *(L+1)* SNR regions. Accordingly, the probabilities of all possible combinations of ordered SNRs in various SNR regions are calculated. The equation governing the probabilities of ordered SNRs in various SNR regions is given as

$$\Pr(u_i) = \frac{1}{n'} C_{l_1}^{n'} \left(e^{-\beta_L}\right)^{n'-l_1} \cdot C_{l_2}^{l_1} \left(e^{-\beta_{L-1}} - e^{\beta_L}\right)^{l_1-l_2} \cdot C_{l_3}^{l_2} \left(e^{-\beta_{L-2}} - e^{\beta_{L-1}}\right)^{l_2-l_3} \cdots \left(1 - e^{\beta_1}\right)^{l_L}$$

where $l_1 = 0,1,\cdots n'$, $l_2 = 0,1,\cdots l_1$, $l_3 = 0,1,\cdots l_2$., etc., with each l_a representing the number of SNRs that are shifted from higher order SNR region S_{L-a+1} to immediately lower order SNR region S_{L-a}. For example, $l_2 = 1$ means, out of l_1 SNRs in SNR region S_{L-1}, one SNR is in the lower SNR region S_{L-2}. These probabilities are stored in an array with running index calculated as $\sum_{n=1}^{L} l_n$. Once this set of probabilities is known, probability for a required location is obtained by considering all the possible cases of placing the required location in various SNR regions. By plugging in these new probabilities in Equation 4, the overall UBRA capacity bound can be calculated for multiple threshold case.

SBSRA

In SBSRA, the capacity for *M* users *M* subcarriers case can be written as:

$$C_{sbsra} = M \sum_{l=1}^{L} (2l) \left[\left(1 - e^{-\beta_{l+1}}\right)^{M} - \left(1 - e^{-\beta_l}\right)^{M} \right]$$

Similarly, the capacity for *M* users *N* subcarriers case can be written as

$$C_{sbsra} = N \sum_{l=1}^{L} (2l) \left[\left(1 - e^{-\beta_{l+1}}\right)^{M} - \left(1 - e^{-\beta_l}\right)^{M} \right]$$

RESULTS AND DISCUSSION

In this Section MATLAB based computer simulation results are presented which verifies the analysis and claims of performance improvement. First, the results for validation of analytical formulation are presented, followed by the results showing the capacity and fairness improvements achieved by the proposed SBSRA scheme.

Downlink of an OFDMA system is considered. The number of users and number of subcarriers are varied to compare the performance of resource allocation schemes with different parameters. All the users are assumed to experience same average received SNR, but their instantaneous SNR values dynamically differ due to multi-path fading effects (Zhu, 2009). This condition can be achieved by a suitable power control strategy at the base station (Biagioni, 2009). All subcarriers are assumed to experience quasi static Rayleigh fading which remains constant for a frame duration but varies from one frame to another. Performance of the OFDMA system is characterized in terms of average number of bits that can be supported per subcarrier and evaluated as a function of average received SNR observed by the users. Four-level adaptive modulation scheme has been considered, which uses squared constellation M-QAM as 4-, 16-, 64-QAM with a target BER of 10^{-3}.

Performance of SBSRA Variants

First the simulation results to verify the proposition on 'no sharing', 'equal sharing', and 'uniform sharing' allocation schemes in SBSRA are presented.

Figure 1(a) shows capacity and long-term fairness performance, while Figure 1(b) shows short-term fairness performance. As observed from the plots, all three schemes show the same capacity and long-term fairness performance, which validates the theoretical proof presented in Appendix. In order to capture short-term fairness, the numbers of frames have been varied from 10 to 300. As seen in Figure 1(b) short-term fairness of 'equal sharing' approach is the highest and also marginally higher than that of the 'uniform sharing' scheme, and both of them offer a better short-term fairness compared to the 'no sharing' scheme. This validates the intuitive assertion of achieving short-term fairness which can be exploited in resource allocation for rate constrained applications.

Figure 1. Capacity and fairness comparison of various SBSRA schemes for a 16 users 16 subcarriers OFDMA system

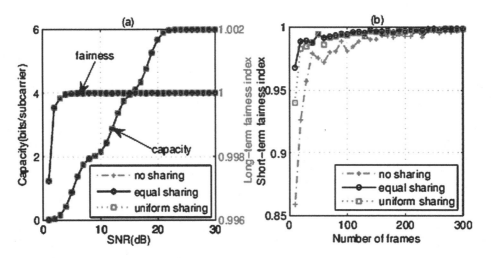

Validation of Analytical Performance of UBRA and SBSRA

In this section the numerical and simulation-based results on capacity and fairness performance of UBRA and SBSRA algorithms are presented. Since in SBSRA all the three variants ('no sharing', 'equal sharing', 'uniform sharing') show the same capacity and fairness, 'equal sharing' variant is considered in the subsequent SBSRA results.

M Users M Subcarriers Case

Figure 2 presents the capacity and fairness comparison of the two algorithms.

The simulation-based and numerical plots closely match, validating the presented analytical model for both the algorithms for the *M* users *M* subcarrier OFDMA system. As observed from the plots the capacity and fairness performance of the proposed SBSRA scheme is better than the UBRA scheme because of the inherent imbalance created by the UBRA algorithm, particularly because the number of users are equal to the number of subcarriers.

M Users N Subcarriers Case

A more practical scenario is considered where the number of subcarriers is larger than the number of users. Figure 3 presents the capacity and fairness comparison of SBSRA, UBRA, and UBRA bound.

Due to complexity involved in numerical UBRA bound calculations, this result has been obtained for a 4 users 16 subcarriers OFDMA system and simulation performance has been averaged over 10^5 frames. It is clear from Figure 3(a) that the capacity achieved by UBRA bound offers the ceiling to what can be achieved by the UBRA scheme, which validates the proof of proposition 2. Figure 3(b) shows that,

Figure 2. Capacity and fairness comparison of UBRA and SBSRA in a 16 users 16 subcarriers OFDMA system

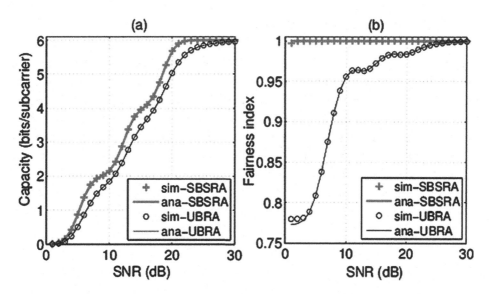

Figure 3. Capacity comparison of SBSRA, UBRA, and UBRA bound in a 4 users 16 subcarriers OFDMA system

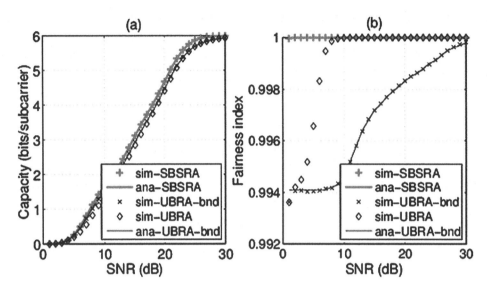

UBRA bound shows poor fairness performance compared to UBRA, which is due to the fixed order of user's selection. Fairness of SBSRA scheme is nearly perfect at all SNRs, as it caters to different users while allocating the resource per subcarrier.

Capacity Gains of SBSRA

Capacity and fairness improvement in SBSRA scheme compared to UBRA scheme are now studied further. Particularly, the utilization of multiuser and spectral diversity and variation of the performance with coherence time and coherence bandwidth are analyzed.

Improvement with Variable Received SNR

In Figure 4, the capacity and fairness performance of SBSRA and UBRA are presented for a 32 users OFDMA system with number of subcarriers as parameter at different average received SNRs.

Performance of SBSRA is independent of the number of subcarriers as argued earlier. So the SBSRA result is shown without any distinction of number of subcarriers. With increasing number of subcarriers, UBRA capacity improves as it starts gaining from spectral diversity. Figure 4(b) shows the relative fairness performance of SBSRA. Even in terms of long-term fairness the percentage improvement is as high as 31% in a 32 users 32 subcarriers system. With higher number of subcarriers UBRA performance improves in terms of fairness.

Figure 4. SBSRA and UBRA capacity and fairness versus received SNR, with number of subcarriers as parameter in a 32 users OFDMA system

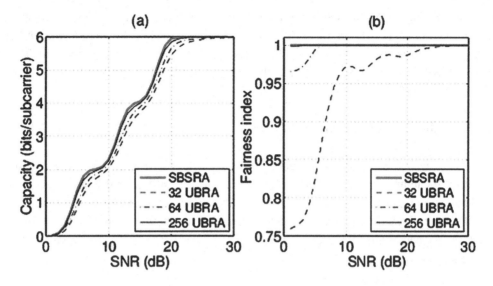

Improvement with Variable Number of Subcarriers

The performance of UBRA and SBSRA in a 32 users OFDMA system with varying number of subcarriers is presented here. This performance comparison exhibits the utilization of spectral diversity by the two algorithms.

The straight lines in the Figure 5(a) gives simulation-based proof of the claim that the capacity obtained by SBSRA algorithm remains the same at varying number of subcarriers. Plot shows that SBSRA

Figure 5. SBSRA and UBRA capacity and fairness at variable number of subcarriers with average received SNR as parameter in a 32 users OFDMA system

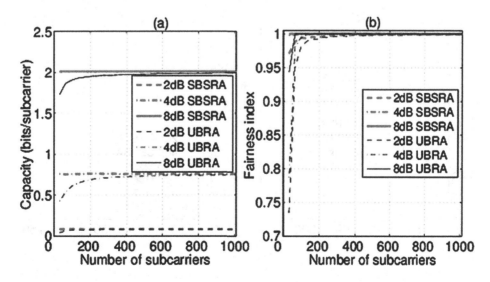

already operates at the optimum capacity level, while UBRA tries to achieve this saturation capacity at a very large number of subcarriers compared to the number of users. For example, UBRA achieves capacity within 5% range of SBSRA saturation capacity, when the number of subcarriers is more than 10 times the number of users in the SNR range 2-6 dB. With increasing average received SNR, percentage capacity gain reduces, as at higher SNRs both the algorithms performs equally well. The fairness performance of UBRA (Figure 5(b)) also similarly improves with increased number of subcarriers and increased received SNR.

Improvement with Variable Number of Users

Figure 6 presents the SBSRA and UBRA capacity and fairness performances for a 256 subcarriers OFDMA system. It captures how efficiently these two algorithms utilize multiuser diversity.

As observed in Figure 6(a), compared to UBRA, SBSRA utilizes multiuser diversity more efficiently. Capacity in SBSRA follows the exponential relation described in Section: Capacity and Fairness Analysis. Note that, the capacity gain achieved by SBSRA is as high as 140% at 4 dB received SNR when the number of users in the system is 56.

Improvement with Variable Number of Symbols and Variable Number of Subcarriers per Slot

Figure 7 presents the SBSRA and UBRA capacity and fairness performance for an OFDMA system with varying number of OFDM symbols per slot. A 32 users, 256 subcarriers OFDMA system having 12 OFDM symbols per frame is considered. In practical OFDMA systems, number of OFDM symbols per slot depends on the coherence time. So these plots capture the performance of the two algorithms at varying channel coherence time.

Figure 6. SBSRA and UBRA capacity and fairness at variable number of users with average received SNR as parameter in a 256 subcarriers OFDMA system

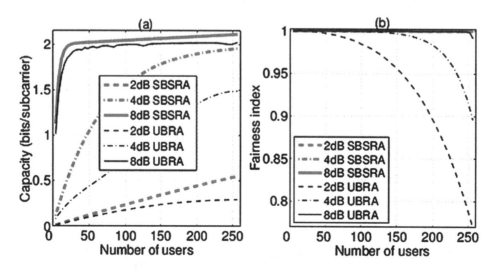

Figure 7. SBSRA and UBRA capacity and fairness at variable number of symbols with average received SNR as parameter in a 32 users OFDMA system

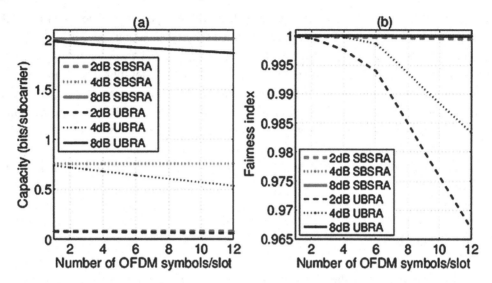

Four subcarriers per frequency slot is considered, and number of OFDM symbols is varied as 1, 2, 3, 4, 6, and 12 symbols per slot. As observed in Figure 7(a), capacity achieved by SBSRA remains constant with the increment in the number of OFDM symbols, while the capacity of UBRA degrades almost linearly. This decay can be attributed to the amount of imbalance that UBRA creates which increases linearly with increasing number of OFDM symbols per slot.

Performance of SBSRA remains unaffected by the change in number of subcarriers per frequency slot, which depends on coherence bandwidth in practical OFDMA systems. UBRA performance shows linear decay with the increased number of subcarriers per frequency slot. Thus, capacity gain increases with increment in number of subcarriers as well as number of OFDM symbols per slot.

Maximum gain is achieved when there are 12 OFDM symbols and 8 subcarriers per slot. As observed form the table, the capacity gain is significantly high in the moderate SNR values, i.e., 2-6 dB. At very high average SNR, the order of subcarrier and user selection does not make significant difference, because the effect of variability of a subcarrier's quality is very little to the different users, and hence both algorithms perform nearly equally well.

FUTURE RESEARCH DIRECTIONS

Resource allocation problems in multiuser OFDMA communication systems are hard to tackle because of their combinatorial nature. This chapter proposes a novel view of resource allocation by looking at the possibility of finding the best user(s) for a subcarrier. The current scheme which assumes availability of perfect CSI can be further extended for the cases of imperfect or partial CSI. The average received SNR of all the users is assumed to be same, it would be interesting to find out a resource allocation algorithm when such an assumption is no longer valid. The physical layer resource allocation assumes all time availability of data to be transmitted. But for a bursty traffic scenario such as voice and video, this is not true. Optimizing physical layer resources based on the type of the data and ensuring good quality of service (QoS) would be an interesting cross layer optimization challenge.

CONCLUSION

This chapter proposes to utilize the system resources from the perspective of the resources rather than the users of the resources. A proof of concept is presented which states that there is an improvement in computation complexity, system capacity, as well as user-level fairness by considering the resource allocation problem from the subcarrier's perspective (called SBSRA) rather than user's perspective (called UBRA). Analytical upper bound on the UBRA capacity and the exact expression of capacity achieved by the SBSRA scheme are presented. In spite of using slot level CSI, SBSRA scheme achieves the granularity of OFDM symbol level in resource allocation and this increased degree of freedom results in improved capacity and fairness. SBSRA utilizes multiuser diversity and spectral diversity optimally and its performance is fairly independent of the coherence properties of the fading channel in time and frequency dimensions.

ACKNOWLEDGMENT

This work has been supported by the Department of Science and Technology 598 (DST) under Grant SB/S3/EECE/0248/2014.

REFERENCES

Afolabi, R. O., Dadlani, A., & Kiseon, K. (2013). Multicast scheduling and resource allocation algorithms for OFDMA-based systems: A survey. *IEEE Communications Surveys and Tutorials*, *15*(1), 240–254. doi:10.1109/SURV.2012.013012.00074

Ben-Shimol, Y., Kitroser, I., & Dinitz, Y. (n.d.). Two-dimensional mapping for wireless OFDMA system. *IEEE Transactions on Broadcasting*, *32*(3), 388–396.

Biagioni, A., Fantacci, R., Marabissi, D., & Tarchi, D. (2009). Adaptive subcarrier allocation schemes for wireless OFDMA systems in WiMAX networks. *IEEE Journal on Selected Areas in Communications*, *27*(2), 217–225. doi:10.1109/JSAC.2009.090212

De, S., Saini, R., & Sharma, A. (2014, October). Source-aware adaptive power allocation in OFDM systems for rate constrained applications. *IEEE Communications Letters*, *18*(10), 1855–1858. doi:10.1109/LCOMM.2014.2358648

Gao, N., & Wang, X. (2011). Optimal subcarrier-chunk scheduling for wireless OFDMA systems. *IEEE Transactions on Wireless Communications*, *10*(7), 2116–2123. doi:10.1109/TWC.2011.050511.100458

Jain, R., Chiu, D. M., & Hawe, W. R. (1984). *A quantitative measure of fairness and discrimination for resource allocation in shared computer system. Eastern Res. Lab*. Digital Equipment Corp.

Jang, J., & Lee, K. B. (2003). Transmit power adaptation for multiuser OFDM systems. *IEEE Journal on Selected Areas in Communications*, *21*(2), 171–178. doi:10.1109/JSAC.2002.807348

Kivanc, D., Li, G., & Liu, H. (2003). Computationally efficient bandwidth allocation and power control for OFDMA. *IEEE Transactions on Wireless Communications*, *2*(6), 1150–1158. doi:10.1109/TWC.2003.819016

Liu, Y., & Dai, Y. (2014). On the complexity of joint subcarrier and power allocation for multi-user OFDMA systems. *IEEE Transactions on Signal Processing*, *62*(3), 583–596. doi:10.1109/TSP.2013.2293130

Ma, Y. (2008). Rate maximization for downlink OFDMA systems. *IEEE Transactions on Vehicular Technology*, *57*(5), 3267–3274. doi:10.1109/TVT.2007.914054

Mohanram, C., & Bhashyam, S. (2005). A sub-optimal joint subcarrier and power allocation algorithm for multiuser OFDM. *IEEE Communications Letters*, *9*(8), 685–687. doi:10.1109/LCOMM.2005.1496582

Rhee, W., & Cioffi, J. M. (2000). Increase in capacity of multiuser OFDM system using dynamic subchannel allocation. *Proc. IEEE VTC 2000-Spring*, *2*, 1085–1089. doi:10.1109/VETECS.2000.851292

Sadr, S., Anpalagan, A., & Raahemifar, K. (2009). Suboptimal rate adaptive resource allocation for downlink OFDMA systems. *International Journal of Vehicular Technology*, *2009*, 1–10. doi:10.1155/2009/891367

Saini, R., & De, S. (2014). Subcarrier based resource allocation. *Proc. Nat. Conf. Commun.*, 1-6.

Sharma, A., De, S., Gupta, H. M., & Gangopadhyay, R. (2014). Multiple description transform coded transmission over OFDM broadcast channels. *Elsevier Physical Commun.*, *12*, 79–92. doi:10.1016/j.phycom.2014.05.001

Shen, Z., Andrews, J. G., & Evans, B. L. (2005). Adaptive resource allocation in multiuser OFDM systems with proportional rate constraints. *IEEE Transactions on Wireless Communications*, *4*(6), 2726–2736. doi:10.1109/TWC.2005.858010

Shen, Z. J., Andrews, G., & Evans, B. L. (2003). Optimal power allocation in multiuser OFDM systems. *Proc. IEEE Globecom*, 337–341.

Song, G., & Li, Y. G. (2003). Adaptive subcarrier and power allocation in OFDM based on maximizing utility. *Proc. IEEE VTC 2003-Spring*, *2*, 905–909.

Song, G., & Li, Y. G. (2005). Cross-layer optimization for OFDM wireless networks, Part I: Theoretical framework. *IEEE Transactions on Wireless Communications*, *4*(2), 614–624. doi:10.1109/TWC.2004.843065

Song, G., & Li, Y. G. (2005). Cross-layer optimization for OFDM wireless networks, Part II: Algorithm development. *IEEE Transactions on Wireless Communications*, *4*(2), 625–634. doi:10.1109/TWC.2004.843067

Wong, C. Y., Cheng, R. S., Letaief, K. B., & Murch, R. D. (1999). Multiuser OFDM with adaptive subcarrier, bit, and power allocation. *IEEE Journal on Selected Areas in Communications*, *17*(10), 1747–1758. doi:10.1109/49.793310

Wong, I. C., Shen, Z., Evans, B. L., & Andrews, J. G. (2004). A low complexity algorithm for proportional resource allocation in OFDMA systems. *Proc. IEEE Wksp. Sig. Proc. Sys. Design and Implementation*. doi:10.1109/SIPS.2004.1363015

Zhang, Y. J., & Letaief, K. B. (2004). Multiuser adaptive subcarrier-and-bit allocation with adaptive cell selection for OFDM systems. *IEEE Transactions on Wireless Communications*, *3*(5), 1566–1175. doi:10.1109/TWC.2004.833501

Zhu, H., & Wang, J. (2009). Chunk-based resource allocation in OFDMA systems Part I: Chunk allocation. *IEEE Transactions on Communications*, *57*(9), 2734–2744. doi:10.1109/TCOMM.2009.09.080067

Zhu, H., & Wang, J. (2012, February). (2112) Chunk-based resource allocation in OFDMA systems Part II: Joint chunk, power and bit allocation. *IEEE Transactions on Communications*, *60*(2), 499–509. doi:10.1109/TCOMM.2011.112811.110036

KEY TERMS AND DEFINITIONS

CSI: Channel state information.
DSL: Digital subscriber line.
LTE: Long term evolution.
OFDMA: Orthogonal frequency division multiple access.
SBSRA: Subcarrier based shared resource allocation i.e., resource allocation from the perspective of subcarriers allowing sharing of a subcarrier among users.
UBRA: User based resource allocation i.e., resource allocation from the perspective of users.
WiMAX: Worldwide interoperability for microwave access.

APPENDIX

In an M user system, there are M users contending for a single subcarrier. Also consider two level adaptive modulation scheme where, if the received SNR is greater than a SNR threshold γ_{th} then the subcarrier can support b bits, otherwise the subcarrier is not used at all.

Capacity of 'No Sharing' Allocation Scheme

Since all users are assumed to have the same average received SNR, probability that user-i has the maximum SNR is $1/M$. Probability that the maximum SNR is above threshold is given by $P = 1 - \left(1 - e^{-\beta}\right)^M$. Correspondingly, the capacity assigned to each user is $C_{u_i} = \dfrac{b}{M}\left(1 - \left(1 - e^{-\beta}\right)^M\right)$ and the overall capacity is obtained as $C_{nos} = b\left(1 - \left(1 - e^{-\beta}\right)^M\right)$.

Capacity of 'Equal Sharing' Allocation Scheme

Probability that m users' SNRs are above threshold is: $P = C_m^M \left(e^{-\beta}\right)^m \left(1 - e^{-\beta}\right)^{M-m}$. When resources are shared equally, the capacity assigned to each of the users in the set of m users is given by: $C_{u_i} = \dfrac{b}{m} C_m^M \left(e^{-\beta}\right)^m \left(1 - e^{-\beta}\right)^{M-m}$. Probability of any user getting selected in the above m users' group is m/M. Hence, average capacity assigned to each of the user in the set of M users is obtained as:

$$C_{u_i} = \frac{b}{M} C_m^M \left(e^{-\beta}\right)^m \left(1 - e^{-\beta}\right)^{M-m}.$$

The total capacity of each user is obtained by averaging over all the possible values of m: $C_{u_i} = \dfrac{b}{M}\left(1 - \left(1 - e^{-\beta}\right)^M\right)$. Thus, the overall capacity of the equal sharing scheme is $C_{eqs} = b\left(1 - \left(1 - e^{-\beta}\right)^M\right)$.

Capacity of 'Uniform Sharing' Scheme

Assuming that there are $E < M$ OFDM symbols in a slot, that are to be shared uniformly among the users. Probability that there are m users having their SNRs above threshold is given by:

$$P = C_m^M \left(e^{-\beta}\right)^m \left(1 - \left(e^{-\beta}\right)\right)^{M-m}.$$ Till $m \leq E$, the capacity assigned to each user is: $C_{u_i} = \dfrac{b}{M} C_m^M \left(e^{-\beta}\right)^m \left(1 - \left(e^{-\beta}\right)\right)^{M-m}$. For $m > E$, the contending users are more in number compared to the available OFDM symbols, available resources are to be shared among E users by a factor of $1/E$. Probability of picking E users uniformly out of m users is E/m and probability of picking m users, hav-

ing the same high SNR, among the total M users is m/M. Thus, the capacity of each user is given by $C_{u_i} = \dfrac{b}{M} C_m^M \left(e^{-\beta}\right)^m \left(1 - \left(e^{-\beta}\right)\right)^{M-m}$, which is the same as the capacity achieved when $m \leq E$. Thus, the total capacity of each user is given by:

$$C_{u_i} = \sum_{m=1}^{M} \frac{b}{M} C_m^M \left(e^{-\beta}\right)^m \left(1 - \left(e^{-\beta}\right)\right)^{M-m} = \frac{b}{M} \left(1 - \left(1 - e^{-\beta}\right)^M\right)$$

and the overall capacity of the uniform sharing case is $C_{ufs} = b \left(1 - \left(1 - e^{-\beta}\right)^M\right)$.

Since the capacity achieved on a single subcarrier is same for all the three schemes, the overall OFDMA capacity achieved by all the three schemes will be the same.

Chapter 4
Design and Measurement Results for Cooperative Device to Device Communication

Naveen Gupta
Indraprastha Institute of Information Technology Delhi, India

Vivek Ashok Bohara
Indraprastha Institute of Information Technology Delhi, India

Vibhutesh Kumar Singh
Indraprastha Institute of Information Technology Delhi, India

ABSTRACT

In this chapter, the authors present the simulation and measurement results for direct and single hop device-to-device (D2D) communication protocols. The measurement results will further argument the development of D2D communication and will also help in understanding some of the intricate design issues which were overlooked during theoretical or computer simulations. The measurements were taken on a proof-of-concept experimental testbed by emulating a cellular scenario in which a Base station (BS) and many D2D enabled devices coordinate and communicate with each other to select an optimum communication range, transmit parameters, etc. A testbed (Multi-carrier) was developed using Software Defined radio which incorporates the concept of Spectrum Sharing through static sub-carrier allocation to D2D user by cellular system which will eventually enhance the performance of cellular as well as D2D communication system. Our purposed and deployed protocol have shown significant improvement in received Signal to Noise Ratio (SNR) as compared to conventional direct transmission schemes.

INTRODUCTION

Every natural calamity reminds us of our heavy dependence on infrastructure for information dissemination, and the lack of easily deployable low cost emergency communication services. In any catastrophic natural calamity, such as earthquake, flood, Tsunami etc., communication services are plagued by last

DOI: 10.4018/978-1-5225-2023-8.ch004

mile connectivity issues and destruction of cellular infrastructure. For instance, after Nepal earthquake in 2015 (Denolle, M. A., 2015) and Siachun earthquake in China (Gupta, H. et.al, 2008), most of the cellular infrastructure such as base station (BS) and switching centers were inoperable within minutes of the earthquake. Even if some of these remains functional they are usually plagued by the acute demand of data and voice traffic during the time of disaster rendering the use of mobile devices.

The above motivates the use of a cellular service that is minimally dependent on network infrastructure. Device-to-device (D2D) communication can be visualized as one such service in which devices have minimal dependency on network infrastructure (Babun L., 2015). In a typical D2D cellular communication scenario, the users who are within the D2D range set up a direct radio link instead of routing through the network control authority (NCA) or BS. The communication can occur in two modes, in the first mode data and control signals are transmitted in the same channel which is also allocated to cellular users whereas in the second mode control signals and data are transmitted on channels which are orthogonal to cellular users (Babun L., 2015). Since, the user equipment (UE) exchange data directly through the D2D link circumventing the BS, it can achieve a higher data rate as compared to conventional cellular services. D2D reduces the load on the network and provides robustness against infrastructure failures (Babun L., 2015). Further, it is also low power consuming and spectrally more efficient, since transmit power and required spectrum for a given coverage area is reduced considerably.

The performance of D2D communication can be further enhanced by taking advantage of proximity to other devices by using a cooperative (a.k.a relay) mode of communication (Babun L., 2015). Inclusion of mobile relays and relay assisted D2D communications can increase the achievable transmission capacity, and also improve the coverage of networks (Singh, V. K., et.al., 2016). Relay transmission improves the coverage area, which will be really useful in case of emergency scenarios. However relay selection and energy efficient resource allocations need to be done in optimize way to enhance the capacity and reliability of D2D communications. A multiuser relay assisted D2D network is given in (Hasan, M., et.al., 2014), which formulated a robust optimization problem for relay selection under channel uncertainties. A power efficient relay selection algorithm has been proposed in (Li., P. et.al., 2013). However algorithm focuses on reducing the complexity involved in relay selection and thus solution is non optimal. In addition to the problem of relay selection, energy efficiency and resource allocation, security is also an essential aspect for the success of D2D communication. Security architecture of D2D communication under 3GPP LTE framework has been analyzed in (Wang., M., et.al., 2015). It analyzes the existing security solutions that can be applied to secure the D2D communication and evaluate the performance based on security requirements.

In this work we have obtained proof-of-concept measurement results for low cost, readily deployable D2D communication prototype testbed. The implemented D2D testbed emulates a portable BS and duplex transceivers which are capable of acting as relays as and when required. The portability of this system enables it to be readily deployed in any emergency scenario in order to have immediate access to communication services.

Figure 1 and Figure 2 depict two generic communication scenarios in which D2D communication is useful. In the line with conventional cellular infrastructure, we assume that the BS is still responsible for connection establishment, synchronization, resource allocation and resource release by control signals. Figure 1 shows a cellular environment in which there are two UEs and one BS. Since the two UEs are in close proximity to each other they can be designated as a D2D pair. This scenario represents a general D2D scenario in which two D2D enabled devices within a cell will be allocated channel resource on request by the BS, which can be used by the users for D2D communication.

Figure 1. A direct D2D communication scenario

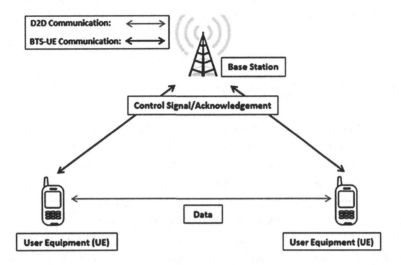

Figure 2 illustrates a scenario when two D2D enabled devices within a cell cannot communicate directly as a D2D pair (due to distance, unfavorable channel conditions etc.). In this case the BS will request some other node/nodes to act as a relay, which will relay the data from one device to another. For instance, BS is interested in communicating with a user near the cell boundary, BS may utilize the

Figure 2. A cooperative D2D communication scenario

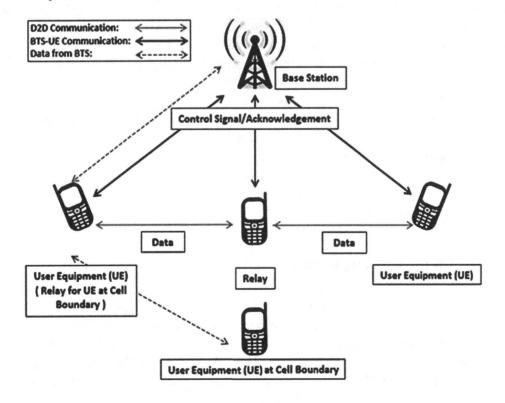

assistance of relay device which is in proximity to both BS and UE. This will benefit both users and BS, as the user at the cell boundary can achieve required SNR, and the BS does not need to transmit signal with high power in order to serve this user.

BACKGROUND AND RELATED WORK

Majority of the prior research work like, Babun L., (2015) and Holland, M. M., Aures, R. G., & Heinzelman, W. B. (2006), that evaluate the performance of D2D communication protocols are often limited to theoretical frameworks or computer simulations. In such cases, practical significance of D2D communication has often been overlooked. Few of the previous hardware implementations of D2D communication, for instance, FlashLinQ by Wu, X., et.al., (2013), utilizes the licensed spectrum. The system was implemented on the FPGA board (Vertex-4), alongside a DSP Chip, TMSC64x. Through the experimental results, various concepts of D2D communication were demonstrated. Other existing implementations include work done by, Karvounas, D., et.al., (2014), in which a testbed was developed using a DSP development board, based on TMS320C6670/6678. Using this board authors have implemented the UE and evolved-NodeB (eNB). In addition the work done by, Karvounas, D., et.al., (2014), incorporated three D2D services, i.e., open discovery, restricted discovery and communication capability. A D2D test-bed implementation and testing was described in the work done by Baron, L. et.al., (2015), where each node is powered by Intel Atom D510 and 4Gb RAM. Baron, L. et.al., (2015), uses unlicensed Wi-Fi band for communication. In the work done by, Asadi, A. et.al., (2013), Wi-Fi direct links of android devices are used to emulate a D2D scenario. However, it increases the power consumption. Most of the previous experimental testbeds for D2D communication utilized off the shelf hardware and were primarily based on direct D2D communication. In this work we have designed and implemented a D2D experimental testbed for two different framework. In the first framework, we implemented a generic D2D communication where there is direct communication between UEs (a.k.a D2D users). In second framework, we incorporated a cooperative relaying wherein the communication between two UEs takes place via a relay.

Cooperative relaying represents a new class of wireless communication technique, in which one or more relays are used to improve the performance of a system via spatial diversity. Relay can be based on amplify and forward (AF) or decode and forward (DF). Cooperative relaying has been incorporated for D2D communication in, Gündüz, D. et.al., (2013). Specifically in, Gündüz, D. et.al., (2013), authors proposed a cooperative relaying scenario to do D2D communication in cellular network. Specifically, an UE which acts as a relay can help to achieve the target rate of a cellular user. In return it can get access of the cellular user spectrum to do its own communication.

COOPERATIVE D2D FRAMEWORK

In this section, we present a scheme to facilitate cooperative D2D communication in cellular networks. In the present context, mobile user equipment (UE) in a cellular link is denoted by cellular user (CU), and DT denotes D2D transmitter whereas, DR denotes D2D receiver. A BS is centered in a cell in the cellular network which operates on licensed frequency band. We assume that through orthogonal frequency division multiple access (OFDMA), allocated spectrum is divided into number of orthogonal subcarriers

Figure 3. D2D system model with cooperation

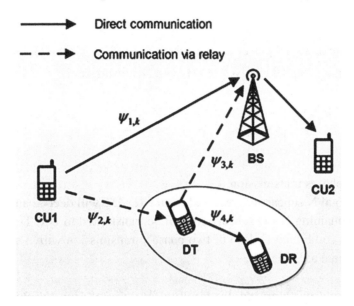

with equal bandwidth. Each cellular link has number of preassigned subcarriers for its communication. The proposed scheme is schematically depicted in Figure 3.

According to the proposed scheme, total transmission is divided into two time phases. In Phase 1, CU broadcasts its data over N allocated subcarriers to BS which is overheard by DT. In Phase II, DT forwards few successfully decoded (D) subcarriers to BS while remaining (N - D) subcarriers can be used by DT for D2D communication with DR. Hence while working as a relay for cellular uplink, a D2D user can get access to cellular spectrum in exchange for fulfilling the target rate requirement of cellular user. However, if DT is not able to decode cellular subcarrier in Phase 1, then outage will occur and no retransmission of cellular signal would be possible in Phase 2, albeit particular subcarrier can be used by DT for D2D communication. In our experimental setup D (number of subcarrier forwarded by DT to BS in Phase II) has been set to N/2.

Rate and Outage Probability for Cooperative D2D

The channels over the nodes are modeled as frequency nonselective Rayleigh block fading with $\Psi_{i,k} \sim CN(0, \varsigma_i^{-l})$, $i = 1, 2, 3, 4$, where ζ is the distance between transmitter and receiver, and l is path loss exponent. The instantaneous channel gain for each subcarrier is defined as, $\gamma_{i,k} = \left|\Psi_{i,k}\right|^2$, and the additive white Gaussian noise (AWGN) at each receiver is denoted by σ^2. The cellular and D2D signal are denoted as $s_{cu,k}$ and $s_{dt,k}$ respectively with zero mean and $E\left\{s_{cu,k}s_{cu,k}^*\right\} = E\left\{s_{dt,k}s_{dt,k}^*\right\} = 1$.

Cellular Rate and Outage Probability

In first phase CU broadcasts N subcarriers to BS which is overheard by DT. Signal received by DT in phase I is,

$$\gamma_k^{DT,1} = \sqrt{p_{cu,k}}\,\Psi_{2,k} s_{cu,k} + n_{2,k}; 1 \leq k \leq N \tag{1}$$

where, $p_{cu,k}$ denotes cellular signal power for kth subcarrier and $n_{2,k}$ is AWGN noise at DT.

The instantaneous rate of signal received at DT with N subcarriers is,

$$R_N^{cu-dt} = \frac{1}{2} \sum_{k=1}^{N} \log_2\left(1 + \frac{p_{cu,k}\gamma_{2,k}}{\sigma^2}\right), \tag{2}$$

where ½ is due to two phases transmission.

In Phase II, out of total N subcarriers received from CU_1, DT will decode and forward only D subcarriers to BS while remaining N - D subcarriers will be transmitted to DR. The instantaneous rate at BS after maximal ratio combining (MRC) of two phase's transmission with a condition of successful decoding of cellular signal at DT is,

$$R_{cu}^{coop} = \frac{1}{2} \sum_{k=1}^{N} \log_2\left(1 + \frac{p_{cu,k}\gamma_{2,k}}{\sigma_1^2} + \frac{p_{dt,k}\gamma_{3,k}}{\sigma_1^2}\right) + \frac{1}{2} \sum_{k=1}^{N-D} \log_2\left(1 + \frac{p_{cu,k}\gamma_{1,k}}{\sigma_1^2}\right) \tag{3}$$

When DT is unable to decode the cellular signal received in Phase I of transmission then there will be no transmission from DT to BS in Phase II. However, BS would still be able to receive the cellular signal from CU-BS link. Thus the cellular outage probability with cooperation is,

$$p_{cu,out}^{coop} = \Pr(R_N^{cu-dt} > R_{th}^c)\Pr(R_{cu}^{coop} < R_{th}^c) + \Pr(R_N^{cu-dt} < R_{th}^c)\Pr\left(\frac{1}{2}R_N < R_{th}^c\right) \tag{4}$$

where,

$$R_N = \sum_{k=1}^{N} \log_2\left(1 + \frac{p_{cu,k}\gamma_{1,k}}{\sigma_2^2}\right). \tag{5}$$

R_N denotes the instantaneous rate when CU transmits all N subcarriers to BS.

When, $p_{cu,k} = p_{cu}, \forall k; p_{dt,k} = p_{dt}, \forall k$ and $\gamma_{1,k} = \gamma_1, \forall k; \gamma_{2,k} = \gamma_2, \forall k; \gamma_{3,k} = \gamma_3$ solving (4), we will get,

$$p_{cu,out}^{coop} = e^{\frac{\zeta_2^l \sigma^2}{p_{cu}}\rho_1(1-e^{-\zeta_1^l a}-\zeta_1^l \Upsilon_1)} + \left(1 - e^{\frac{\zeta_2^l \sigma^2}{p_{cu}}\rho_1}\right)\left(1 - e^{\frac{\zeta_1^l \sigma^2}{p_{cu}}\rho_1}\right) \tag{6}$$

where,

$$\Upsilon_1 = \int_{\gamma_1=0}^{a} e^{\left(\delta_2\gamma_1 - \frac{\delta_1}{\gamma_1^{\frac{N}{D}-1}} \right)} d\gamma_1, \delta_1 = \frac{\zeta_3^l \Lambda^{\frac{1}{D}}}{p_{dt} p_{cu}^{\frac{N}{D}-1}}, \delta_2 = \frac{\zeta_3^l p_{cu}}{p_{dt}} - \zeta_1^l.$$

D2D Rate and Outage Probability

Signal received by DR in Phase II is,

$$\phi_k^{DR,2} = (p_{dt,k})^{\frac{1}{2}} \Psi_{4,k} s_{dt,k} + n_{4,k}. \tag{7}$$

The instantaneous rate at DR is given as,

$$R_{d2d}^{coop} = \frac{1}{2} \sum_{k=1}^{N-D} \log_2 \left(1 + \frac{p_{dt,k} \gamma_{4,k}}{\sigma_4^2} \right). \tag{8}$$

If the target rate for D2D communication is defined as R_{th}^d, then the outage will occur when $\Pr(R_{d2d}^{coop} < R_{th}^d)$. For $p_{dt,k} = p_{dt}, \forall k$ and $\gamma_{4,k} = \gamma_4, \forall k$,

$$\Pr\left(\gamma_4 < \frac{\rho_2 \sigma^2}{p_{dt}} \right) = 1 - e^{\frac{\zeta_4^l \sigma^2}{p_{dt}} \rho_2}, \tag{9}$$

where, $\gamma_4 \sim \exp(\zeta_4^l)$ and $\rho_2 = 2^{\frac{2R_{th}^d}{(N-D)}} - 1$.

SIMULATION RESULTS

In the simulation model, the nodes CU, DT, DR, and BS are considered to be co-linear. Distance between CU and BS is set to 500 meters. DT and DR lie in between CU and BS and distance between DT-DR is fixed to 100 meters. We have chosen target rate for both cellular and D2D link as 32 bits/sec/Hz and N=32 denotes total number of subcarriers preassigned by BS to CU. The cellular and D2D subcarrier power has been set to 100 mW, whereas noise variance is 120 dBm, and the path loss exponent has been set to 4 (considering urban area).

Figure 4 shows the outage probability of cellular and D2D system vs number of subcarriers required for cooperation. From Figure 4, we can observe that as number of forwarded subcarriers 'D' from DT to BS increases, outage probability decreases. With this given power and target rate profile, for $\zeta_2 = 300$ m, if DT forwards only 5 subcarriers to BS then outage performance of cellular system with cooperation is better than the outage performance without cooperation. For higher values of D, it is quite obvious

Figure 4. Cellular and D2D outage probability

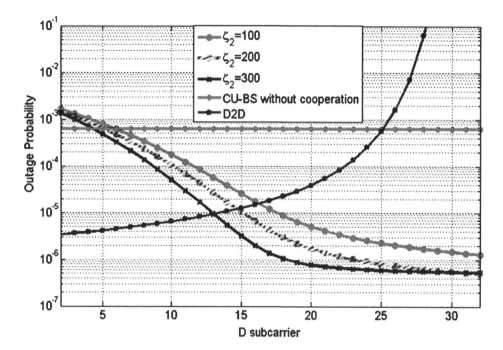

that the outage probability decreases, as more subcarriers are relaying to BS. However, for D > 23, the outage probability reduces slowly or is almost stagnant. This is due to the fact that, when D approaches its maximum value, the successful decoding of cellular signal at DT becomes the limiting factor for outage probability. Suppose there is some acceptable outage probability constraint for cellular user i.e. 10^{-3}. We can see that for a particular distance, number of subcarriers D to achieve the above constraint is 4. Hence, in this proposed scheme, enormous number of subcarriers are available for D2D communication. In contrast, D2D outage probability decreases with increase in number of subcarriers D. It is quite obvious that if D increases, number of subcarriers available for D2D communication (N – D) decreases, consequently outage probability increases.

EXPERIMENTAL SETUP

This section discusses the experimental setup used for obtaining measurement results. The set-up was tested in an open environment on a normal working day within our institute campus. The experimental set-up has been depicted in Figure 5. Signaling and synchronization between all the nodes are done through the BS.

The experimental setup consisted of three UE devices (which can also capable of acting as a relay), and a BS. The BS decides one of the following on the basis of received signal strength indication (RSSI):

- Whether D2D communication is feasible.
- If (a) is true, then communication should take place through a direct link or through a relay.

Figure 5. Experimental test-bed

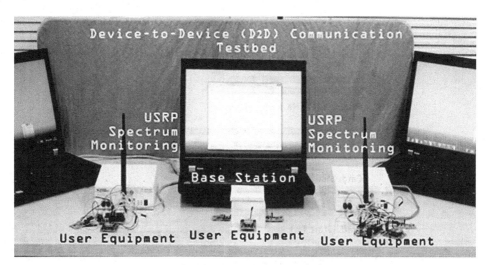

To test the BS-UE link we have transmitted 1000 packets from various distances and we have recorded the RSSI for each packet received. D2D link was tested by transmitting 500 packets at various possible distances and the packet drop count was measured to determine the threshold distance for communication. The experiments have been further divided into various setups, which are discussed in detail below.

Setup 1: Direct D2D Communication

Setup 1 has been shown in Figure 1 and illustrated through the flow graph in Figure 6. In this setup, BS through the RSSI value of the last received packet, estimates the distance between itself and the nodes, and thus is aware of the radial distance between the devices. To initiate the process, one of the devices will request the BS to allow a connection to another device which is in the same cell. The BS based on the localization information of the devices in the cell will decide whether it is going to be a normal cellular communication (data being relayed through BS) or a D2D communication. Once acknowledged for D2D communication, receiving device will be instructed by the BS to be in receiving mode and transmitting device will be instructed to start the transmission. At the end of transmission, both will send a data transfer success notification to BS. The connection will be closed and allocated resources are released.

Setup 2: Cooperative D2D Communication

Setup 2 has been shown in Figure 2 and can be illustrated through the flow graph in Figure 7. In this setup, we have deployed a BS, two duplex and one relay device. In addition, all the devices are capable of acting as a relay. The BS can estimate their location inside the cell through RSSI values of packets received from devices. To initiate the process, one of the device will request BS to allow a connection to another device within the cell.

The BS based on RSSI information infers that the requesting devices are out of range for a direct D2D communication. Apart from this, BS also knows that there is another device in proximity, capable of acting as a relay to both the devices which want to communicate. The data packets will first arrive

Figure 6. Inter-communication between devices during D2D communication

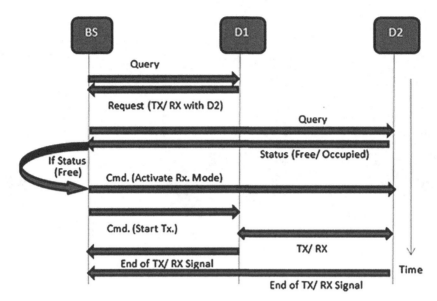

Figure 7. Communication between devices during single hop D2D communication and data multicasting

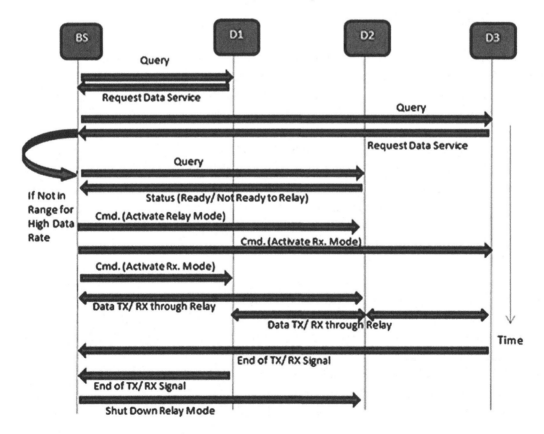

at the relay and then forwarded to the destination. Both transmitting and receiving devices send a data transfer success notification to BS and the connection will be closed.

MEASUREMENT RESULTS AND ANALYSIS

This section presents the measurement results and analysis of given D2D testbed. To test the BS-UE link, we have transmitted 1000 packets from different distances and have accounted the RSSI value of each packet, which gives us an estimate of the communication range and efficiency of the link.

RSSI vs. Distance Relation

Here we have transmitted 1000 data packets from BS to UE at various distances. The average RSSI of 1000 packets at each distance was also calculated and plotted. Following observations can be made from Figure 8:

- As the distance between the BS and UE increases, instantaneous and average value of the RSSI decreases as shown in Figure 8. It is due to the path loss and fading in the wireless channel.
- The variance of the RSSI of received packets also increases with the increase in the distance between the BS and UE. The RSSI value is used to estimate the approximate distance between BS and a device within the cell. Based on this model, the BS is also able to predict the possibility of D2D communication between different devices by setting a threshold RSSI value. RSSI based localization (Sugano, M. et.al. 2006) is an established method to localize various objects within a locality and could be accurately used to estimate the radial distances.

Figure 8. RSSI vs. distance plot; the distance is taken from the BS as reference.

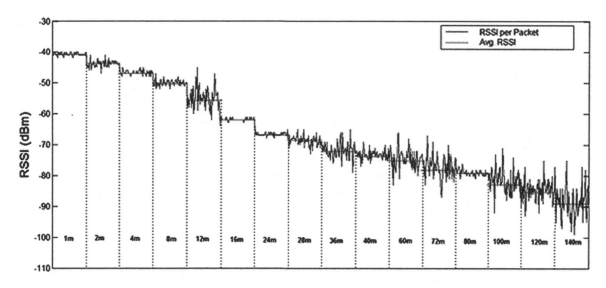

Estimating Cellular Parameters

Figure 9 shows the variation of packet efficiency with respect to the RSSI of the data packet received. Here, *Packet efficiency is (number of packets received correctly/ number of packets transmitted) *100.* From Figure 9, it is quite obvious that if the average RSSI of the packets is above a threshold, then there would be virtually no packet drop (<15%) out of 1000 packets transmitted and the efficiency of the communication will be nearly >85%. However, when RSSI decreases, there is an increase in packet drops as shown in Figure 10. It has also been validated by experimental work done by, Holland, M. M., Aures, R. G., & Heinzelman, W. B. (2006). From Figure 10, we can also gauge the distance threshold needed for estimating the cell radius. From the experimental data collected, we have observed that our BS has a range of about 120m with an efficiency threshold of 85%.

The radius of the cell is 120m and thus a BS can cater to an area of about 0.045 Km². The range can be extended to a radius of more than 1 Km by high power amplifiers. Circular symmetry of the cell was decided through the radiation pattern of the antenna uses by the testbed.

Here, *Packet efficiency is (number of packets received correctly/ number of packets transmitted) *100.*

Analysis of D2D Communication Measurement Results

For D2D measurements the efficiency threshold was set to 90% and 500 packets were transmitted from one device to another with varying distances. With these parameters the D2D communication range was estimated to be 30m as shown in Figure 10. Beyond this distance, relay needs to be incorporated between the devices. The distance was varied for both the devices, taking the reference point as relay and it was found that the range with relay was extended slightly more than twice of the range with direct communication. We also observed that there is a steeper drop in packet efficiency in the test case without relay as compared to the case in which the relay was used. From Figure 10, we conclude that the D2D maximum range with a relay device is 62 m, whereas the efficiency threshold has been set to 90%.

Experimental setup for multicarrier cooperative D2D communication, is shown in Figure 11.

Figure 9. Variation of packet efficiency with RSSI of BS

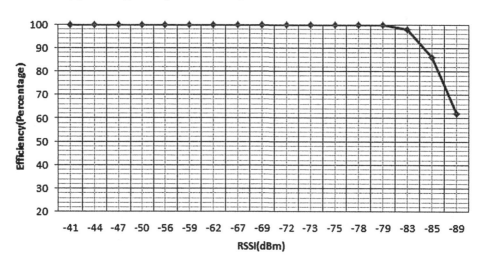

Figure 10. Variation of packet efficiency with distance from BS

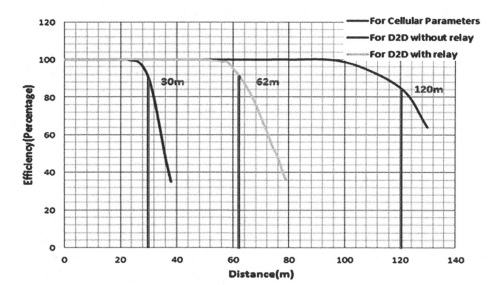

Table 1. Parameters used for experiment

No. of packets transmitted	1000
Data length	48
Pilots	4
Cyclic prefix	12
Modulation scheme	QPSK
Channel coding scheme	Convolution (1/2)
Relayed subcarriers (N/2)	32
Cooperative relay protocol	DF
No. of subcarriers (N)	64

Figure 11. Actual experimental setup for multicarrier cooperative D2D communication

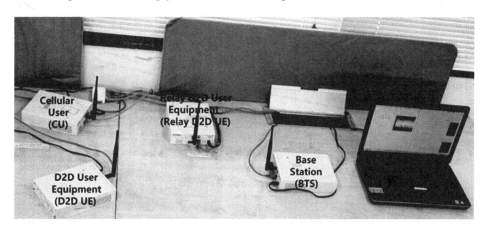

In this experimental set-up, total time is divided into two phases. The parameters used in this experiments are listed in Table 1. In Phase 1, total of 1000 packets are transmitted from CU to BS and which is also overheard by DT. In Phase II, 1000 packets which were overheard by DT is decoded and superimposed with the data that needed to be transmitted by DT to DR for D2D Communication. BS applies MRC to combine the signal received in two time phases. Results have been plotted for different CU-BS distance. Point to be noted that, in Phase 1, N=64 subcarriers carry CU-BS data transmitted by CU to BS, which is received by BS and DT. In Phase-II, out of total N subcarriers available, only N/2 successfully decoded subcarriers forwarded by DT to BS whereas remaining N/2 subcarriers will be used for DT-DR communication.

Signal to Noise Ratio (SNR) Measurement Result

Figure 12 shows received SNR with respect to transmitter gain for different CU-BS distances. Here we compare the received SNR of direct CU-BS communication i.e. without MRC with communication via relay, in which DT acts as a relay and forward CU data in exchange of spectrum access (with MRC). From Figure 12, we can see that the received SNR with proposed scheme (with MRC) is always better than without MRC (i.e. communication without relay). In Figure 12, d denotes the distance between CU-BS. As d increases received SNR at BS decreases. A relay (DT) is placed in the center of CU-BS, whereas DT-DR distance is same as CU-DT distance. For instance, d=2m CU-DT will be 1m. Hence given analytical model given in previous section is validated by experiment.

Figure 13 shows received SNR with respect to transmitter gain for DT-DR communication. From Figure 13, we can see that received SNR increases with respect to transmit gain of DT. Here d denotes the radial distance between DT-DR. We can observe from the figure that as transmit gain increases received SNR with proposed scheme increases.

Figure 12. Comparison of transmit gain vs. SNR for CU-BS link with and without MRC

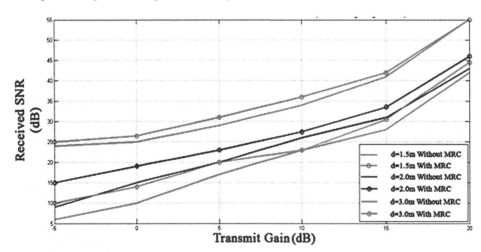

Figure 13. Comparison of transmit gain vs. SNR for DT-DR link

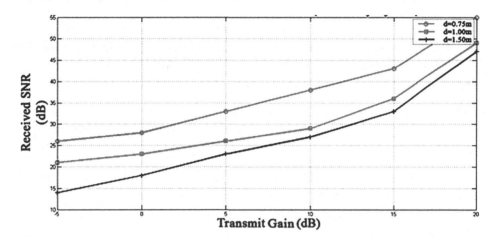

CONCLUSION

Simulation and measurement results as a proof-of-concept for device to device communication in cellular networks have been presented. An experimental setup is performed by emulating a cellular scenario in which a Base station (BS) and many D2D enabled devices coordinate and communicate with each other to select an optimal communication parameters. Using software defined radio, a multicarrier testbed was also developed, which incorporates the cooperative subcarrier sharing in cellular network. Measurement and simulation results with proposed scheme show significant improvement in received signal to noise ratio (SNR) and outage probability as compared to conventional direct communication.

REFERENCES

Asadi, A., & Mancuso, V. (2013, November). WiFi Direct and LTE D2D in action. In Wireless Days (WD). 2013 IEEE IFIP, 1-8.

Babun, L. (2015). Extended Coverage for Public Safety and Critical Communications Using Multi-hop and D2D Communications. *FIU Electronics thesis and dissertation, 2015.*

Baron, L., Boubekeur, F., Klacza, R., Rahman, M. Y., Scognamiglio, C., Kurose, N., & Fdida, S. (2015, September). Demo: OneLab: Major Computer Networking Testbeds for IoT and Wireless Experimentation.*Proceedings of the 21st Annual International Conference on Mobile Computing and Networking*, 199-200. doi:10.1145/2789168.2789180

Denolle, M. A., Fan, W., & Shearer, P. M. (2015). Dynamics of the 2015 M7. 8 Nepal earthquake. *Geophysical Research Letters*, *42*(18), 7467–7475. doi:10.1002/2015GL065336

Gündüz, D., Yener, A., Goldsmith, A., & Poor, H. V. (2013). The multiway relay channel. *IEEE Transactions on Information Theory*, *59*(1), 51–63. doi:10.1109/TIT.2012.2219156

Gupta, H., Rao, N. P., Shashidhar, D., & Mallika, K. (2008). The Disastrous M 7.9 Sichuan Earthquake of 12 May 2008. *Journal of the Geological Society of India, 72*, 325–330.

Hasan, M., Hossain, E., & Kim, D. I. (2014). Resource Allocation Under Channel Uncertainties for Relay-Aided Device-to-Device Communication Underlaying LTE-A Cellular Networks. *IEEE Transactions on Wireless Communications, 13*(4), 2322–2338. doi:10.1109/TWC.2014.031314.131651

Holland, M. M., Aures, R. G., & Heinzelman, W. B. (2006, September). Experimental investigation of radio performance in wireless sensor networks. In Wireless Mesh Networks. *WiMesh 2006. 2nd IEEE Workshop on,* 140-150.

Karvounas, D., Georgakopoulos, A., Tsagkaris, K., Stavroulaki, V., & Demestichas, P. (2014). Smart management of D2D constructs: An experiment-based approach. *IEEE Communications Magazine, 52*(4), 82–89. doi:10.1109/MCOM.2014.6807950

Li, P., Guo, S., Cheng, Z., & Vasilakos, A. V. (2013). Joint relay assignment and channel allocation for energy-efficient cooperative communications. Proceedings IEEE Wireless Communications and Networking Conference (WCNC), 626-630. doi:10.1109/WCNC.2013.6554636

Singh, V. K., Chawla, H., & Bohara, V. A. (2016). *A Proof-of-Concept Device-to-Device Communication Testbed.* arXiv preprint arXiv:1601.01398

Sugano, M., Kawazoe, T., Ohta, Y., & Murata, M. (2006). Indoor localization system using RSSI measurement of wireless sensor network based on ZigBee standard. *Target, 538, 050.*

Wang, M., & Yan, Z. (2015). Security in D2D Communications: A Review. Trustcom/BigDataSE/ISPA, 2015 IEEE, 1199-1204.

Wu, X., Tavildar, S., Shakkottai, S., Richardson, T., Li, J., Laroia, R., & Jovicic, A. (2013). FlashLinQ: A synchronous distributed scheduler for peer-to-peer ad hoc networks. *IEEE/ACM Transactions on Networking, 21*(4), 1215–1228. doi:10.1109/TNET.2013.2264633

KEY TERMS AND DEFINITIONS

AF: Amplify & Forward.
AWGN: Additive White Gaussian Noise.
BS: Base Station.
Cooperative Relay: Cooperative relaying is a novel technique for wireless communications promising high gains in throughput and energy efficiency.
CU: Cellular User.
D2D: Device-to-Device.
Device-to-Device Communication: In Device-to-Device communication two or more devices communicate with each other, without or with a minimal dependence of a network mediator or network control authority (NCA).
DF: Decode & Forward.
DR: D2D Receiver.

DT: D2D Transmitter.

eNB: evolved Node-B.

FPGA: Field Programmable Gate Array.

Localization: A technique to estimate the location of device.

MRC: Maximal Ratio Combining.

NCA: Network Control Authority.

OFDMA: Orthogonal Frequency-Division Multiple Access.

Outage Probability: Outage probability is a measurement for performance. It is defined as the probability when mutual information is less than the given threshold. The importance of outage probability is that when outage occurs, there is more likely to have decoding failure. In other words, it is a typical error.

RSSI: Received Signal Strength Indicator.

SDR: Software Defined Radio.

SNR: Signal-to-Noise Ratio.

Spectrum Sharing: The same spectrum is being shared by multiple devices.

UE: User Equipment.

USRP (Universal Software Radio Peripheral): Universal Software Radio Peripheral (USRP) is a range of software-defined radios designed and sold by Ettus Research and its parent company, National Instruments.

Chapter 5

Green Cognitive Relay Communications with Hardware Impairments for Future Wireless Networks

Nalin Dushantha Kumara Jayakody
National Research Tomsk Polytechnic University, Russia

Dang Khoa Nguyen
Aalborg University, Japan

ABSTRACT

Wireless Power Transfer is a promising solution to increase the lifetime of wireless nodes and hence alleviate the energy bottleneck of energy constrained wireless networks. In this Chapter, we discuss two power transfer policies; dual-source and single fixed-source, two bidirectional relaying protocols; multiple access and time division broadcast, and two relay receiver structures; time switching and power splitting, are considered to derive closed-form expressions for the outage and throughput of the network in the context of delay-limited transmission. This framework assists the reader not only to quantify the degradation of outage probability and throughput of the networks due to the impairments of realistic transceiver but also to provide realistic insight into the effect of power transfer policies, relaying protocols and receiver structures on outage and throughput of the networks.

INTRODUCTION

All living and machine objects rely on both information and power for their existence. Although these two entities are in harmony in nature, in traditional engineering design, information and power are handled by separate systems with limited interaction. While wireless power transfer (WPT) through radio waves has already been employed in various applications (e.g., the radio-frequency identification (RFID) technology, healthcare monitoring, etc.), radio wave-based information transfer and power transfer have largely been designed separately. Many forthcoming applications could benefit from a joint consideration of

DOI: 10.4018/978-1-5225-2023-8.ch005

information and power transfer. For example, wireless implants can be charged and calibrated concurrently with the same signal, wireless sensor nodes can be charged with the control signals received from the access points, and mobile phones can download emails while being wirelessly charged. Initial efforts on WPT have focused on long-distance and high-power applications. However, both the low efficiency of the transmission process and the health concerns for such high-power applications prevented their further development. With sensors and wireless transceivers getting ever smaller and more power- efficient, we envision that radio waves will not only become a major source of power for operating these devices, but also their information and power transmission aspects will be unified. A design that jointly takes into account both information and power can provide significant engineering breakthroughs and lead to potential new applications and services for next-generation sustainable societies.

Two common methods to design co-located receiver architecture for EH are time- switching based (TSB) and power-splitting based (PSB). In TS, the receiver switches in time between energy harvesting and information decoding, while in PSB the receiver splits the received signal into two streams of different power for energy harvesting and information decoding. EH has to be realized by properly allocating the available resources and sharing them among both information transfer and energy transfer. Designing TSB/PSB EH receivers in a point-to- point wireless environment to achieve various trade-offs between wireless information transfer and energy harvesting is considered in (Ng, Lo, & Schober, pp. 635–6370, 2013; Shi, Liu, Xu & Zhang, pp. 3269–3280, 2014).

As a sustainable remedy to strengthening the lifetime of energy constrained wireless devices, EH technique has received considerable attention since it meets the requirements of green communications. Besides to the traditional renewable energy sources such as solar and wind, radio frequency (RF) signals radiated by ambient transmitters can be identified as a viable new intuition for EH. In (Paradiso & Starner, pp. 18–27, 2005; Le & Fiez, pp. 1287-1302, 2008), wireless nodes gather energy of RF signals in the surrounding environment to self-power the transmission. Recently, some critical advances of WPT have largely increased the feasibility of EH in practical wireless applications (Suh & Chang, pp. 1784-1789, 2002; Huang & Lau, pp. 902-912, 2014). With concurrent development in the antenna technology and EH circuit designs, wireless energy transfer is recognized as a valuable candidate for future networks.

Cognitive radio is emerging as a means to improve the wireless spectrum utilization (Hunter & Sanayei, pp. 375--391, 2006). In cognitive radio, secondary users (SUs) are allowed to transmit wireless signals in the same frequency bands that are officially allocated to primary users (PUs). In order to maintain quality-of-service of primary transmission links, the transmit power of SUs should be limited to the maximum interference allowance of PUs. Consequently, this power constraint limits the performance of SUs. In order to tackle the transmit power limitation in cognitive networks, the concept of two-way cognitive relay (TWCR) networks has been proposed in (Yang, Alouini & Qaraqe, pp. 1240-1243, 2012; Kim, Duong, Elkashlan, Yeoh & Nallanathan, pp. 992-997, 2013) among others. TWCR networks exploit the advantages of two-way relaying protocols and cognitive radios. Also, they are able to overcome transmit power limitations and boost the system performance.

In the previous literature, the TWCR networks analyzed using the outage probability (OP) and throughput of the systems under perfect transceiver hardware assumption, however this is far from the reality. In (Yang et al., 2012), a tight approximation of the OP for amplify-and-forward TWCR networks was provided. Closed-form expressions for the OP of TWCR network, in the presence of multiple primary users, were derived in (Kim et al., 2013). However, transceivers in wireless communication system suffer from several types of impairments such as, in-phase/quadrature imbalance (Zou, Valkama & Renfors, pp. 2496-2508, 2008; Li, Matthaiou & Svensson, pp. 2271-2285, 2014), and high power amplifier non-linearities (Qi & Aissa, pp. 876-887, 2012). Undoubtedly, transceiver impairments degrade the system performance, especially when the power budget is high (Bjornson, Matthaiou & Debbah, pp. 4512-4525, 2013).

An energy harvesting cognitive radio scenario is considered in (Hoang, Niyato, Wang & Kim, pp. 2039-2052, 2014; Usman & Koo, pp. 3164-3173, 2014) where a secondary user (SU) with finite battery capacity opportunistically accesses the primary user (PU) channels. PU is powered by various wireless energy harvesting technology. In (Hoang, Liang, Wong, Zeng & Zhang, 1206-1211, 2009), spectrum sensing policies are studied for energy-constrained CR taking into account the dynamics of the primary network in a POMDP framework. Energy harvesting CR which optimizes its sensing and transmit energies is analyzed in (Sultan, pp. 500-503, 2012) for a single-user single-channel setting in the presence of sensing errors.

Sensor networks consist of multiple sensors enabling measurements of various physical quantities, like for example accelerations, temperatures, pressures etc. The choice of sensor types depends on the application area of the network. In most cases, sensor networks can be connected with the main control (network coordinator) unit using wires, however in some special cases, this is not the most beneficial solution. The examples are aerospace applications, where weight is a very important factor, and extreme conditions applications, like for example nuclear power plants. As an example, the total weight of all cables used in the Ariane 5 launcher is about 70% of the total mass of rocket's avionics. In these cases, a Wireless Sensor Networks can be used to limit the number of cables. Work in (Huang & Zhou, pp. 86-93, 2015; Seah, Eu & Tan, pp. 1-5, 2009) tackles the problem of energy consumption by incorporating the technique of radio frequency (RF) energy harvesting in the sensor nodes. Not only does a RF signal carry information but energy too, so information transmission and power transfer can occur simultaneously. Various distributed and stateless forwarding strategies for wireless sensor networks proposed in (Huang, pp. 3121-3125, 2013), which aim at maximizing the network lifetime while achieving a high forwarding success rate. This energy efficient strategy can be further enhance using wireless energy assisted scheme as proposed in this chapter and has also done in that paper.

In (Huang & Lau, pp. 902-912, 2014; Cover & Gamal, pp. 572-584, 1979), wireless relaying networks has been mentioned as an effective method of extending the network coverage or providing the diversity gain using existing infrastructure. In practice, this is often achieved by using idle nodes in the network as relays to forward the signals from the source to the destination. One of the main problems of current relaying protocols is that the relaying node has to consume its own energy to perform such operations, which discourages idle nodes from taking part in relaying, especially when they have limited battery life. Energy harvesting relaying can solve this problem by allowing the relaying node to harvest wireless energy from the source and to use the harvested energy for relaying.

There are significant number of articles investigated the resource allocation scheme for cooperative networks. The power allocation, frequency allocation and joint allocation of both in a single orthogonal frequency division multiple access (OFDMA) cell are discussed in literature (Shen, Andrews & Evans, pp. 2726-2737, 2005). The Soft Frequency Reuse (SFR) in two-hop networks is presented in (Guan, Zhang, Li, Liu & Zhang, pp. 1446-1450, 2007), in order to advance the spectral efficiency. To improve the cell-edge MSs' Quality of service (QoS) and to increase system throughput, (Singhal, Kumar, De, Panwar & Tonde, pp. 48-60, 2014) give their solution respectively.

In today's developing wireless networks, the issues linked to handoff are not treated as an independent physical layer issue. The protocol end points that are located in the BS are needed to be moved from the source BS to the target BS. This relocation can be performed in the following ways:

- Transfer from the source BS to the target BS.
- Initialization after the handoff.

In LTE networks, the moving is take place using an amalgam approach, where the downlink protocol is transferred from the source BS to target BS. In (Shen, Andrews & Evans, pp. 2726-2737, 2005), in order to increase the capacity while improving the QoS performance of the active cell-edge users, authors present a new handoff scheme, which they call split handoff, in an OFDMA cellular network.

In specific applications, such as wireless sensor networks in remote areas, where the power supply unit is difficult to recharge, a self-powered relay node is much preferable. Among various resources that can be converted to power, radio frequency energy is a preferred method in wireless networks. Hence, the relay nodes are able to be powered by the radio signals. However, the relevant research on the OP and throughput of radio frequency energy harvesting (EH) relaying has also assumed perfect hardware (see e.g., (Nasir, Zhou, Durrani & Kennedy, pp. 3622-3636, 2013; Medepally & Mehta, pp. 3543-3553, 2010; and references therein).

In this work, we present a detailed performance analysis of an energy harvesting (EH) based decode-and-forward (DF) TWCR network (EH-TWCR) in the presence of transceiver imperfections by utilizing the generalized impairment model of (Schenk, 2008). The main contributions of this Chapter are twofold:

1. We portray the self-powered EH-TWCR networks with two energy transfer policies, two relaying protocols, and two relay receiver structures while keeping the limited transmit power levels. To further explore the benefit on network throughput, we propose four data frame structures for the network with various combinations of energy transfer policies, relaying protocols, and relay receiver architecture possible network cases with respect to the balanced comparison.

2. We provide new closed-form expressions for the OP and throughout of the considered networks under the impact of transceiver imperfection. Also, the influence of configuration parameters on network throughput is accounted. Our analysis set useful design guidelines for implementing a suitable protocol for EH-TWCR networks. Based on these results, network designers will be able to predict the maximum level of hardware imperfections that can be tolerated to achieve a predetermined performance.

In this Chapter, we consider a half-duplex TWCR network as illustrated in Figure 1. Herein, we assume that the effects of transmitter of the primary network are neglected, whereas a receiver (*Rx*) is considered as a primary user. The secondary users consist of two communication nodes *A*, *B* and one relay node *R*. Each node is equipped with a single antenna. Hence, the quality-of-service of primary network can be ensured if the transmit power at the secondary network is limited to a maximum tolerance interference power I_p. Also, secondary transmitters are managed with carrier sense multiple access with collision avoidance (CSMA/CA) protocol. In other words, primary receiver can detect primary received signal properly when secondary users transmit signals with power lower than I_p.

All channels of the cognitive relay network are assumed to be reciprocal and experience quasi-static block Rayleigh fading, whose coefficients are constant over the communication cycle T (Medepally, Mehta, pp. 3543-3553, 2010), (Zhou, Zhang, Ho, pp. 4754-4767, 2013) - (Luo, Zhang, Lim, pp. 1196-1207, 2013). The channel coefficients of the wireless communication links $A \rightarrow R$, $R \rightarrow B$, $A \rightarrow Rx$, $B \rightarrow Rx$ and $R \rightarrow Rx$ are denoted as h_m and g_n, where $m \in \{1, 2\}$ and $n \in \{1, 2, 3\}$ are complex Gaussian distributed random variables with zero mean and variances $\frac{1}{\lambda_m}$ and $\frac{1}{\omega_n}$ respectively. The additive noise terms η_i, $i \in \{A, B, R\}$, have zero mean and variance N_0, $\eta_i \sim CN(0, N_0)$. Moreover, it is assumed that there is no line-of-sight transmission link from A to B.

In addition, the channel state information of all wireless channels of the two hop information links are assumed to be known at the respective transmitter and receiver, which, for instance, could be obtained through feedback from a given node. In order to protect the primary receiver (Rx) from the secondary user interface signals, the peak transmit power is $P_i = \frac{I_P}{|g_n|^2}$. Where $i \in \{A, B, R\}$ and $n \in \{1, 2, 3\}$.

For our analysis, we determine the exponentially distributed random variables $\rho_m = |h_m|^2$ and $v_n = |g_n|^2$ for $m \in \{1, 2\}$ and $n \in \{1, 2, 3\}$, whose means are $\frac{1}{\lambda_m}$ and $\frac{1}{\omega_n}$, respectively. Finally, following the discussion in previous section, the aggregate impairment level during the information processing (IP) phase is represented by κ^2 where $i \in \{A, B, R\}$.

Hardware Impairments' Model

We have modified the transceiver hardware impairments model originally proposed in (Schenk, 2008) to cater for the proposed scheme. It is assumed that the source transmits a signal $x \in C$ with power P_x over the wireless channel with fading coefficient h to the receiver. The signal experiences AWGN η. The practical transceiver impairments at the source distort signal x before it is emitted, whilst the imperfect transceiver hardware of the receiver distorts received signal during the reception phase. Each source of distortion can be represented by a different model. Yet, let τ_1, τ_2 be the *aggregate distortion* affecting the source and destination, respectively. The received signal can be succinctly expressed as

$$y = h\left(x + \tau_1\right) + \tau_1 + \eta. \tag{1}$$

Figure 1. An energy harvesting two-way cognitive relay network

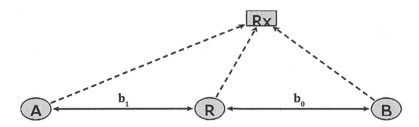

As in (Matthaiou, Papadogiannis, Bjornson & Debbah, pp. 1136-1139, 2013; Nguyen, Matthaiou, Duong & Ochi, pp. 1970-1975, 2015), $\tau_1 \sim CN\left(0, hk_1^2 P_x\right)$ and $\tau_2 \sim CN\left(0, hk_2^2 P_x\right)$ where k_1, k_2 are the *impairment levels* at the source and destination transceivers, respectively. Following (Matthaiou, Papadogiannis, Bjornson & Debbah, pp. 1136-1139, 2013), the distortion powers caused by transceiver impairments at the source and destination can be, more compactly, represented by an aggregate distortion power at the receiver, such that $\tau \sim CN\left(0, hk^2 P_x\right)$, where $k \triangleq \sqrt{k_1^2 + k_2^2}$ is the aggregate impairment level. Then, Equation 1 can be written as,

$$h\left(x + \tau\right) + \eta . \tag{2}$$

DF-TWCR NETWORKS WITH ENERGY HARVESTING

We describe an EH-TWRC network, where the information exchanged from two source nodes A and B is assisted by a self-powered intermediate node R. The relay R harvests energy from wireless signals that transmitted from A (and B) in the EH phase. Exchanged data from A and B are transmitted to R during the broadcast (BC) phase, and then this data is decoded and re-encoded with a suitable network coding operation before we forward to B and A in the relaying (RL) phase. In this framework, we configure the EH-TWCR network with two EH policies dual-source (DS) and single-fixed-source (SFS) policy, two relaying protocols time division broadcast (TDBC) and multiple access broadcast (MABC) protocol, and two relay receiver structures time switching based (TSB) and power splitting based (PSB) architecture.

We propose a paradigm that duration of the EH, and RL phase are fixed over the network configurations as $2t$, and t [*sec*], respectively, whereas, the duration of BC phase varies due to the network configuration (length $2t$ or t). Depending on the network configurations, the EH, BC and RL phase are contributed to form a transmission cycle, T. Thereby, the duration T varies corresponding to the network configuration. This Chapter presents the benefit of each network configuration and offer the balanced comparison on the performance between all possible network configurations. For the sake of convenience, we shorten the description of specific network configuration, for example, the network that is configured with DS energy transfer policy, TDBC relaying protocol, and TSB relay receiver architecture is denominated by DS-TDBC-TSB network. All possible network configurations are explained and analysed in the later parts of this Chapter.

Energy Transfer Policy

During the EH phase, R harvests energy from the RF signals which are transmitted from other nodes in TWCR network. We assume that the transmit powers at A and (or) B to R in the EH phase satisfy the maximum allowable interference1 I_P, hence $P_A^{EH} = P_B^{EH} = \tilde{I}_p < \min\left(\dfrac{I_P}{v_1}, \dfrac{I_P}{v_3}\right)$. The collected energy at R is utilized to decode and re-encode data in BC phase and also transmit signal in the RL phase. The amount of harvested power depends on energy transfer policy, the power conversion efficiency of the rectification circuit and the receiver architecture of relay node. The power conversion efficiency is denoted as μ ($0 < \mu \leq 1$) (Zhou, Zhang & Ho, pp. 4754-4767, 2013). Note that hardware impairments are not taken into account during the EH phase as:

- The hardware used for harvesting energy is different from that used in transmitting/receiving data.
- Any type of hardware imperfections in the EH circuitry is eventually captured by μ.

Two energy transfer policies, i.e., DS and SFS policy, are described in the following section:

- **DS Energy Transfer Policy:** In the DS energy transfer policy, the relay harvests power from the signals that are transmitted from both A and B during the EH phase.
- **SFS Energy Transfer Policy:** In this policy, the relay harvests power from the transmitted signal either A or B which is predetermined before transmission take place. Without loss of generality, the received signal in EH phase at R for the SFS policy is assumed to be transmitted from the fixed node A.

Relaying Protocol

In this section, we describe two relaying protocols: the TDBC and MABC. The relay protocols consist of two data transmission phases, i.e., BC and RL phase. The frame structure of the BC phase determines the category of relaying protocol. Note that the decoders and encoders of each node in TWCR network are assumed to be flawless.

- **TDBC Protocol:** In the TDBC protocol, the duration of BC phase is divided into two equal time slots (length of durations are equal to half of the BC phase). In the first time slot, A transmits signal to R, whereas B transmits to R in the second time slot. The received data at R is decoded and re-encoded, then it is combined with XOR operation (network coding) before forwarded to B and A in the RL phase.
- **MABC Protocol:** In the MABC protocol, R concurrently receives data from both node A and node B via two orthogonal channels in the BC phase. The received data at R is also decoded, re-encoded then combined with XOR operation (network coding) before forwarded to B and A in the RL phase.

Relay Receiver Architecture

The architecture of relay receiver determines the strategy that data received from antenna of the relay is feed to its energy harvesting block and data processing block in chronology or concurrence. Therefore, the receiver architecture affects the frame structure and the length of T. In this Chapter, we consider two structures of relay receiver namely, TSB and PSB architectures (Zhou, Zhang & Ho, pp. 4754-4767, 2013).

TSB Architecture

The TSB architecture is depicted in the Figure 2. The receiver antenna of the relay is successively connected to the energy harvesting block and the data processing block over time. The incoming data to these blocks is controlled by the timing mechanism. Hence, the EH phase and the BC phase occur in two separated time slots.

Figure 2. Relay receiver with TSB architecture

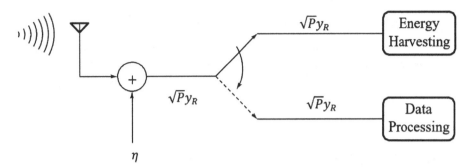

PSB Architecture

The PSB architecture is depicted in the Figure 3. The receive antenna of the relay is connected to both energy harvesting block and data processing block. Therefore, the received data at the relay antenna is shared with these blocks. ε is defined as power sharing fraction $(0 < \varepsilon < 1)$. Due to this receiver structure, the EH phase and the BC phase may concurrently occur in a given time slot, the transmission cycle can therefore be shortened, thereof. This is a benefit offered by the PSB architecture over the TSB architecture.

PERFORMANCE ANALYSIS: TSB ARCHITECTURE

In this section, we elaborate on the impact of transceiver impairments on the *signal to noise plus distortion ratio* (SNDR), the outage performance and throughput of the EH DF TWCR networks. The relay receiver is configured with TSB architecture.

DS Policy: TDBC Protocol

In this configuration, the network utilizes the DS policy - TDBC protocol - TSB architecture. The data frame structure of the communication cycle T is shown in Figure 4. The relay R harvests energy from transmitted signals from both A and B in the EH phase. Then, R consequently receive the transmit data from A and B in the first and the second time slot of the BC phase. Later, R forwards the re-encoded

Figure 3. Relay receiver with PSB architecture

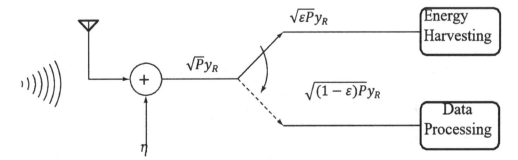

signal to both A and B in the RL phase. Thus, the duration of T is $5t$ [sec]. Defined ρ_1 and ρ_2 are the amplitude of channel h_1 and h_2, respectively, the acquired energy at R is parameterized as

$$E_H = \mu \left(P_A^{EH} \left| h_1 \right|^2 + P_B^{EH} \left| h_2 \right|^2 \right) 2t = \mu \tilde{I}_P \left(\rho_1 + \rho_2 \right) 2t . \tag{3}$$

where $\rho_A = P_A^{EH} \left| h_1 \right|^2$ and $\rho_B = P_B^{EH} \left| h_2 \right|^2$, respectively.

Transmit Power in the RL Phase

In order to determine the end-to-end SNDR, we need the information of transmit energy of the relay in the RL phase. The harvested energy in the EH phase is used for decoding, re- encoding signals in the BC phase as well as forwarding data in the RL phase. We assume that the total harvested energy at R in the EH phase is distributed equally to the total duration of the BC phase and the RL phase. Thus, from Equation, the transmit power at R in the RL phase is

$$P_R = \frac{E_H}{3t} = \frac{\mu \tilde{I}_P 2t}{3t} \left(\rho_1 + \rho_2 \right) = Y_1 \left(\rho_1 + \rho_2 \right) \tag{4}$$

where $Y_1 = \dfrac{2}{3} \mu \tilde{I}_P$

End-to-End SNDR

In the BC phase, the information transfers in different time slots from A and B to R, hence, the instantaneous SNDR at either R of the link $A \rightarrow R$ and $B \rightarrow R$ or at A (or at B) of the link $R \rightarrow A$ (or the link $R \rightarrow B$) in the RL phase, respectively, are independent and statistically similar. Without loss of generality, only the communication link $A \rightarrow R \rightarrow B$ is investigated herein. We assume that A transmits data with the peak power. Then, the SNDR at R of the $A \rightarrow R$ link is given by

$$\gamma_1 = \frac{\dfrac{I_P}{N_O} \left| h_1 \right|^2}{\dfrac{I_P}{N_O} K_R^2 \left| h_1 \right|^2 + \left| g_1 \right|^2} = \frac{\bar{\gamma} \rho_1}{\bar{\gamma}_1 K_R^2 \rho_1 + \nu_1} \tag{5}$$

Figure 4. Data frame structure of the DS-TDBC-TSB network

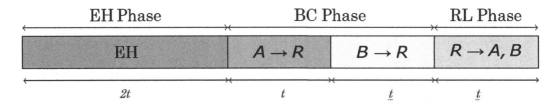

In the RL phase, R forwards the received data from the previous two time slots to A and B with the transmit power equals to given in Equation 4. Then, the SNDR at B of the link $R \to B$ is given by

$$\gamma_2 = \frac{\overline{\gamma_1}(\rho_1 + \rho_2)}{\overline{\gamma_1}K_B^2(\rho_1 + \rho_2) + \frac{\nu_2}{\nu_1}} \tag{6}$$

where $\tilde{Y}_1 = \dfrac{Y_1}{N_0}$.

Providing that the end-to-end SNDR of the wireless link $A \to R \to B$ is calculated by the minimum SNDR at R and B, we can obtain end-to-end SNDR as

$$\gamma = \min(\gamma_1, \gamma_2) \tag{7}$$

Outage Performance Analysis

Denote that $F(\cdot)$ and $f(\cdot)$ are the cumulative distributed function (CDF) and the probability distributed fucntion (PDF) of a random variable (RV), respectively. In Equation 5 and Equation 6, ρ_1 appears as a common RV in both γ_1 and γ_2, therefore the CDF of γ, $F_\gamma(\gamma)$, in Equation 7 can be expressed as

$$F_\gamma(\gamma) = \int_0^\infty \left[F_{\gamma_1}\Big|_{\rho_1}(\gamma) + F_{\gamma2}\Big|_{\rho_2}(\gamma) - F_{\gamma_1}\Big|_{\rho_1}(\gamma)F_{\gamma2}\Big|_{\rho_1}(\gamma) \right] f_{\rho_1}(x)dx \tag{8}$$

The following propositions will enable us to analytically evaluate Equation 8:

Proposition 1: The CDF of γ_1 conditioned on ρ_1 is given by

$$F_{\gamma_1}\Big|_{\rho_1}(\gamma) = \exp\left(-\frac{\overline{\gamma}(1 - k_R^2\gamma)}{\omega_1\gamma}\rho_1 \right) \tag{9}$$

Proof: From the definition of the CDF of a RV, we have

$$F_{,1\big|_{\rho_1}}(\gamma) = Pr\left[\frac{\gamma\rho_1}{\gamma\rho_1 k_R^2 + v_1} \leq \gamma \right] = 1 - F_{v1}\left(\frac{\gamma\left(1 - k_R^2\gamma\right)\rho_1}{\gamma} \right)$$

This result leads directly to Equation 9.

Proposition 2: The CDF of γ_2 conditioned on ρ_1 is given by

$$F_{\gamma 2}\Big|_{\rho_1}(\gamma) = \frac{\omega_2}{\lambda_2^2 C_1} \exp\left(\frac{\rho_1}{\lambda_2}\right) \exp\left(\frac{\omega_2}{\lambda_2^2 C_1}\right) E_1\left(\frac{\omega_2}{\lambda_2^2 C_1}\right) \tag{10}$$

where $C_1 \triangleq \dfrac{\tilde{Y}_1\left(1 - k_B^2 \gamma\right)}{\gamma}$ and $E_1(x) = \displaystyle\int_0^\infty \frac{e^{-t}}{t}\, dt$ is the exponential integral function.

Proof: By the definition of CDF of a RV, we have

$$F_{\gamma 2}\big|_{\rho 1}(\gamma) = \Pr\left[\frac{\overline{\gamma}_1(\rho_1 + \rho_2)}{\overline{\gamma}_1 K_B^2(\rho_1 + \rho_2) + \dfrac{\nu_2}{\nu_1}} \leq \gamma\right] \tag{11}$$

$$= 1 - \int_0^\infty F_X(C_1 y) f_Y\big|_{\rho 1}(y)\, dy$$

where $X \triangleq \dfrac{\upsilon_2}{\rho_2}$ and $Y \triangleq \rho_1 + \rho_2$. It is apparent that $F_X(x) = 1 - \dfrac{\omega_2}{x\lambda_2 + \omega_2}$ and

$$f_Y\big|_{\rho_1}(y) = \frac{1}{\lambda_2} \exp\left(-\frac{y - \rho_1}{\lambda_2}\right).$$

Substituting these results into Equation 11, we obtain

$$F_{\gamma 2}\big|_{\rho 1}(\gamma) = \int_0^\infty \left(\frac{\omega_2}{\omega_2 + \lambda_2 y}\right) \frac{1}{\lambda_2} \exp\left(-\frac{y - \rho_1}{\lambda_2}\right) dy \tag{12}$$

After some algebraic manipulations, we can obtain the result shown in Equation 10. Using the previous theorems, Equation 8 is recast as

$$F_\gamma(\gamma) = I_1 + I_2 - |\, I_3 \tag{13}$$

where we can define from Proposition 1 and Proposition 2:

$$I_1 = \frac{\omega_1 \gamma}{\omega_1 \gamma + \lambda_1 \bar{\gamma}(1 - k_R^2 \gamma)}$$

$$I_2 = C_2 \frac{\lambda_2}{\lambda_1 + \lambda_2}, \quad C_2 \triangleq \frac{\omega_2}{\lambda_2^2 C_1} \exp\left(\frac{\rho_1}{\lambda_2}\right) \exp\left(\frac{\omega_2}{\lambda_2^2 C_1}\right) E_1\left(\frac{\omega_2}{\lambda_2^2 C_1}\right)$$

$$I_3 = C_3 \frac{\lambda_2 \omega_1}{\lambda_1 \lambda_2 \bar{\gamma}\left(1 - k_R^2 \gamma\right) + \omega_1 \gamma \left(\lambda_1 + \lambda_2\right)}$$

Gathering the previous results together, the OP at nodes A and B at a specific SNDR threshold (γ_t) of the networks is given in Equation 14 and Equation 15, respectively.

$$OP_A(\gamma_t) = \frac{\omega_3 \gamma_t}{\omega_3 \gamma_t + \lambda_2 \bar{\gamma}(1 - k_R^2 \gamma_t)}$$
$$+ \frac{\omega_2}{\lambda_1^2 C_1} \exp\left(\frac{\omega_2}{\lambda_1^2 C_1}\right) E_1\left(\frac{\omega_2}{\lambda_1^2 C_1}\right)\left[\frac{\lambda_1}{\lambda_2 + \lambda_1} - \frac{\lambda_1 \omega_3}{\lambda_2 \lambda_1 \bar{\gamma}(1 - k_R^2 \gamma) + \omega_3 \gamma_t (\lambda_1 + \lambda_2)}\right] \quad (14)$$

$$OP_B(\gamma_t) = \frac{\omega_1 \gamma_t}{\omega_1 \gamma_t + \lambda_2 \bar{\gamma}(1 - k_R^2 \gamma_t)}$$
$$+ \frac{\omega_2}{\lambda_2^2 C_1} \exp\left(\frac{\omega_2}{\lambda_2^2 C_1}\right) E_1\left(\frac{\omega_2}{\lambda_2^2 C_1}\right)\left[\frac{\lambda_1}{\lambda_1 + \lambda_2} - \frac{\lambda_2 \omega_1}{\lambda_1 \lambda_2 \bar{\gamma}(1 - k_R^2 \gamma) + \omega_1 \gamma_t (\lambda_1 + \lambda_2)}\right] \quad (15)$$

Outage probability of the DS-TDBC-TSB networks is the sum of the OP of the link $A \to R \to B$ and the OP of the link $B \to R \to A$. It is obtained as

$$OP(\gamma_t) = OP_A(\gamma_t) + OP_B(\gamma_t) \quad (16)$$

where $OP_A(\gamma_t)$ and $OP_B(\gamma_t)$ are the OP at A and B, given in 14 and 15, respectively.

Throughput Analysis

We assume that the sources transmit information to the destinations at a fixed communication rate. We can now analyze the network throughput in the context of delay-limited transmission. The transmission rates at A and B of the TWCR networks are given as $R_A = \log_2(1 + \gamma_A)$ and $R_B = \log_2(1 + \gamma_B)$ [bits/s/Hz], respectively, where γ_A and γ_B are the corresponding threshold SNDRs. The network throughput is measured as the sum of the throughput of each wireless link at a given transmit rate. Hence, the network throughput, T, in this network configuration is determined as

$$\tau = \frac{t}{5}\left[R_A\left(1 - OP_A(\gamma_A)\right) + R_B\left(1 - OP_B(\gamma_B)\right)\right] \quad (17)$$

where $OP_A(\gamma_A)$ and $OP_B(\gamma_B)$ are the OPs at A and B, respectively. By substituting the OPs at A and B from Equation 14 and Equation 15 into Equation 17, the exact expression of the network throughput is obtained.

SFS Policy: TDBC Protocol

In this subsection, the network is configured with SFS policy, TDBC protocol, and utilizes TSB receiver architecture. The data frame structure of the transmission cycle T is similar to the one of DS-TDBC-TSB network that was shown in Figure 4. The only different is R harvests energy from the signal that is transmitted from A only.

The energy harvested at R is then given by

$$E_H = \mu P_A^{EH} \left| h_1 \right|^2 2t = \mu \bar{I}_P \rho_1 2t \tag{18}$$

Transmit Power in the RL Phase

Similarly, we assume that the entire harvested energy at R in the EH phase is distributed equally to the total duration of BC phase and RL phase. Thus, from Equation 18, the transmit power at R in the RL phase equals to

$$P_R \frac{E_H}{3t} = \frac{\mu \bar{I}_P 2t}{3t} \rho_1 = \gamma \rho_1 \tag{19}$$

End-to-End SNDR

As the transmit power at R is harvested from A, the SNDR of the link A $\rightarrow$ R $\rightarrow$ B is different from the SNDR of the link B $\rightarrow$ R $\rightarrow$ A. Similarly, we assumed that A and B transmit data with peak power respectively. The transmit power at R in the RL phase equals to. P_R is the harvested energy at R that is given in Equation 19. The SNDRs at R and B of the link A $\rightarrow$ R $\rightarrow$ B are given respectively by

$$\gamma_{1,ARB} = \frac{\overline{\gamma} \rho_1}{\gamma k_R^2 \rho_1 + \nu_1} \tag{20}$$

$$\gamma_{2,ARB} = \frac{\overline{\gamma}_1 \rho_1 \rho_2}{\gamma_1 k_R^2 \rho_1 \rho_2 + \nu_2} \tag{21}$$

Therefore, the end-to-end SNDR at B can be obtained as

$$\gamma_B = \min(\gamma_{1,ARB}, \gamma_{2,ARB}) \tag{22}$$

$$\gamma_{1,ARB} = \frac{\bar{\gamma} \rho_2}{\bar{\gamma}_1 k_R^2 \rho_2 + \nu_3} \tag{23}$$

$$\gamma_{2,ARB} = \frac{\overline{\gamma}_1 \rho_1}{\overline{\gamma}_1 k_R^2 \rho_1 + \dfrac{\nu_2}{\rho_1}} \tag{24}$$

Likewise, the end-to-end SNDR at A is calculated as

$$\gamma_A = \min\left(\gamma_{1,BRA}, \gamma_{2,BRA}\right) \tag{25}$$

Outage Performance Analysis

It can be seen that ρ_1 appears a common RV in both $\gamma_{1,ARB}$ and $\gamma_{2,ARB}$ as given in Equation 20 and Equation 21, respectively. Hence, the end-to-end CDF γ_B needs to be computed as follows:

$$F_{\gamma B}(\gamma) = \int_0^\infty \left[F_{\gamma 1,ARB}\Big|_{\rho_1}(\gamma) + F_{\gamma 2,ARB}\Big|_{\rho_1}(\gamma) \right] - \left[F_{\gamma 1,ARB}\Big|_{-\rho_1}(\gamma) F_{\gamma,ARB}\Big|_{\rho_1}(\gamma) \right] f_{\rho 1}(x) dx \tag{26}$$

The following proposition will enable us to evaluate Equation 26:

Proposition 3: The CDF of $^3{}_{2,ARB}$ conditioned on ρ_1 is given by

$$F_{\gamma 2,ARB}\Big|_{\rho_1}(\gamma) = \frac{\omega_2 \gamma}{\omega_2 \gamma + (1 - k_B^2 \gamma)\overline{\gamma}_1 \lambda_2 \rho_1} \tag{27}$$

Proof: From the definition of the CDF of a RV, we have

$$F_{\gamma 2,ARB}\Big|_{\rho_1}(\gamma) = \Pr\left[\frac{\overline{\gamma}_1 \rho_1 \rho_2}{\overline{\gamma}_1 k_B^2 \rho_1 \rho_2 + \nu_2} \langle \gamma \right] = 1 - \int_0^\infty F_{\nu_2}\left(\frac{\overline{\gamma}_1(1 - k_B^2 \gamma)\rho_1 x}{\gamma} \right) f_{P2}(x) dx$$

By substituting CDF and PDF of the exponential RV ρ_2 into the above equation, the CDF of $^3{}_{2,ARB}$ conditioned on ρ_1 can be obtained as in Equation 27.

The CDF of $\gamma_{1,ARB}$ conditioned on ρ_1 can be obtained with the help of Proposition 1. We can readily show that

$$F_{\gamma 1,ARB}\Big|_{\rho_1}(\gamma) = \exp\left(-\frac{\overline{\gamma}(1 - k_B^2 \gamma)\rho_1}{\omega_1 \gamma} \right) \tag{28}$$

The end-to-end CDF of γ_B is derived by substituting Equation 26 with Equation 27 and Equation 28, hence CDF of $F_{\gamma B}(\gamma)$ can be obtained as

$$F_{\gamma B}(\gamma) = \frac{1}{\lambda_1 C_3} + \frac{1}{\lambda_1 C_1}\exp\left(\frac{1}{\lambda_1 C_1}\right)E_1\left(\frac{1}{\lambda_1 C_1}\right)\frac{1}{\lambda_1 C_1}\exp\left(\frac{C_3}{\lambda_1 C_1}\right)E_1\left(\frac{C_3}{\lambda_1 C_1}\right) \tag{29}$$

where $C_3 \triangleq \dfrac{\tilde{\gamma}\lambda_1\left(1-k_R^2\gamma\right)+\omega_1\gamma}{\lambda_1\omega_1\gamma}$. Now we derive the CDF of γ_A as provided in Equation 25. We first notice that $\gamma_{1,BRA}$ and $\gamma_{2,BRA}$ are two mutually independent RVs as shown in Equation 23 and Equation 24, respectively. Thus, the CDF of γ_A can be expressed as

$$F_{\gamma A}(\gamma) = F_{\gamma 1,BRA}(\gamma) + F_{\gamma 2,BRA}(\gamma) - F_{\gamma 1,BRA}(\gamma)F_{\gamma 2,BRA}(\gamma) \tag{30}$$

The CDF of $\gamma_{1,BRA}$ is found based on Proposition 3, while the CDF of $\gamma_{2,BRA}$ is derived with the help of Proposition 2. In particular, we have

$$F_{\gamma 1,BRA}(\gamma) = \frac{\gamma\omega_3}{\gamma\omega_3 + \overline{\gamma}\lambda_2(1-k_R^2\gamma)} \tag{31}$$

$$F_{\gamma 2,BRA}(\gamma) = \frac{\omega_2}{\lambda_1^2 C_4}\exp\frac{\omega_2}{\lambda_1^2 C_4}E_1\left(\frac{\omega_2}{\lambda_1^2 C_4}\right) \tag{32}$$

where $C_4 \triangleq \dfrac{\tilde{\gamma}_1\left(1-k_A^2\gamma\right)}{\gamma}$. The CDF of γ_A is obtained by inserting Equation 31 and Equation 32 into Equation 30. Consequently, the OP at A and B under the specified SNDR threshold (γ_t) of the network are respectively given in Equation 33 to Equation 34.

$$OP_A(\gamma_t) = \frac{\gamma_t\omega_3}{\gamma_t\omega_3 + \overline{\gamma}\lambda_2(1-k_R^2\gamma_t)} + \frac{\omega_2}{\lambda_1^2 C_4}\exp\left(\frac{\omega_2}{\lambda_1^2 C_4}\right)\times E_1\left(\frac{\omega_2}{\lambda_1^2 C_4}\right)\left[1 - \frac{\gamma_t\omega_3}{\gamma_t\omega_3 + \overline{\gamma}\lambda_2(1-k_R^2\gamma_t)}\right] \tag{33}$$

$$OP_B(\gamma_t) = \frac{1}{\lambda_1 C_3} + \frac{1}{\lambda_1 C_1}\exp\left(\frac{1}{\lambda_1 C_1}\right)E_1\left(\frac{1}{\lambda_1 C_1}\right)\frac{1}{\lambda_1 C_1}\exp\left(\frac{C_3}{\lambda_1 C_1}\right)E_1\left(\frac{C_3}{\lambda_1 C_1}\right) \tag{34}$$

The OP of TWCR network with SFS policy, TDBC protocol and TSB architecture at a specific SNDR threshold is the sum of the OPs of the link $A \rightarrow R \rightarrow B$ and the OP of the link $B \rightarrow R \rightarrow A$, such that

$$OP(\gamma_t) = OP_A(\gamma_t) + OP_B(\gamma_t) \tag{35}$$

where $OP_A(\gamma_t)$ and $OP_B(\gamma_t)$ are the OPs at A and B given in Equation 33 and Equation 34, respectively.

Throughput Analysis

Similar to Section IV-A4, the network throughput with delay limited transmission is obtained as Equation 17, in which $OP_A(\gamma_A)$ and $OP_B(\gamma_B)$ denote the OPs at A and B corresponding to the transmission rate R_A and R_B from Equation 33 and Equation 34.

DS Policy: MABC Protocol

In this configuration, the network utilizes the DS policy and the MABC protocol while the TSB architecture is implemented in the relay receiver. The data frame structure of the transmission cycle T is shown in Figure 5.

First, R collects energy from transmitted signals from both A and B in the EH phase. Similarly, the harvested energy at R is given as in Equation 3. Then, A and B simultaneously transmit to R in the BC phase. Later, R forwards the received signals to both A and B in the RL phase. In this case, the duration of the BC phase is t [sec]. As the transmission rate from A and B is similar to the previous network configuration, therefore, it needs only t [sec] to simultaneously transmit data from A and B to R. The duration of T of this configuration is $4t$ [sec]. The transmit power at R in the RL phase is parameterized as

$$P_R = \frac{E_H}{2t} = \frac{\mu \bar{I}_P 2t}{2t}\left(\rho_1 + \rho_2\right) = \gamma_2\left(\rho_1 + \rho_2\right) \tag{36}$$

where $\gamma_2 = \mu \tilde{I}_P$. As the direct communication link between A and B is not considered in this Chapter, the SNDRs at A and B in this network configuration are statistically similar to the SNDRs of the DS-TDBC-TSB networks which derived in Section IV-A. Therefore, the OP of the DS-MABC-TSB networks can be evaluated by following a similar line of reasoning as in Section IV-A with the only difference pertaining to the replacement of $\tilde{\gamma}_1$. With $\tilde{\gamma}_2 = \dfrac{\gamma_2}{N_0}$.

Moreover, the throughput the DS-MABC-TSB networks can be calculated as in Equation 17 by appropriate scaling with $\dfrac{1}{4}$ because the length of one communication cycle of this configuration is $4t$ [s]. It is characterized as;

$$\tau = \frac{t}{4}\left[R_A\left(1 - OP_A(\gamma_A)\right) + R_B\left(1 - OP_B(\gamma_B)\right)\right] \tag{37}$$

Figure 5. Data frame structure of the DS-MABC-TSB network

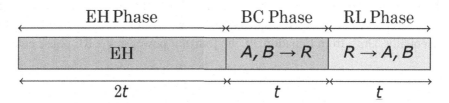

SFS Policy: MABC Protocol

In this content, the network is configured with the SFS policy, the MABC protocol while the TSB architecture is implemented in the relay receiver. The data frame structure of the transmission cycle is similar to the one was shown in Figure 5. However, the relay R only collects energy from the transmitted signal from A in the EH phase. As a result, the transmit power at the relay in the RL phase is expressed as

$$P_R = \frac{E_H}{2t} = \frac{\mu \overline{I}_P 2t}{2t} \rho_1 = \gamma_2 \rho_1 \tag{38}$$

Likewise, the end-to-end SNDRs of the SFS-MABC-TSB networks is statistically similar to those in Section IV-B2. Thus, we can derive the CDF of the end-to-end SNDRs by Equation 33 and Equation 34 with substituting Υ_2 for Υ_1. In the same manner, we can character the network OP and throughput by the similar method in Section IV-C where $OP_A(\gamma_t)$ and $OP_B(\gamma_t)$ are the OPs at A and B also given in Equation 33 and Equation 34, respectively.

PERFORMANCE ANALYSIS: PSB ARCHITECTURE

In this section, the relay receiver is implemented with the PSB architecture. In this PSB receiver architecture, the EH phase and the BC phase occur simultaneously, the relay always harvests energy from the wireless signals that are transmitted from both nodes A and B of the network. Therefore, only the DS energy transfer policy is consider for the network that utilizes the PSB relay receiver structure. We now elaborate the impact of transceiver impairments on the OP and throughput of the EH-TWCR networks with DS policy for different relaying protocols. We note that the power sharing fraction is ε $(0 < \varepsilon < 1)$.

DS Policy: TDBC Protocol

In this configuration, the network utilizes the DS policy and the TDBC protocol. Data frame structure of the transmission cycle is shown in Figure 6. The relay simultaneously harvests energy and collects data from the wireless signals that are transmitted form A and B consecutively in $2t$ [s] duration. Hence, duration of T is $3t$ [sec]. The acquired energy at the relay node is parametrized as

$$E_H = \varepsilon \mu \left(P_A^{EH} |h_1|^2 + P_B^{EH} |h_2|^2 \right) t = \varepsilon \mu \overline{I}_P \left(\rho_1 + \rho_1 \right) t \tag{39}$$

Transmit Power in the RL Phase

The harvested energy is used to power the relay in the current transmission cycle RL phase and the consecutive transmission cycle BC phase. Same as before, we assume that the total harvested energy at R is distributed equally. Thus, from Equation 39, the transmit power in the RL phase equals to

Figure 6. Data frame structure of the DS-TDBC-PSB network

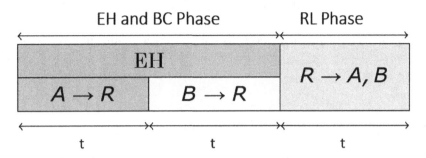

$$P_R = \frac{\varepsilon\mu\bar{I}_P(\rho_1 + \rho_2)t}{3t} = \gamma_3(\rho_1 + \rho_2) \tag{40}$$

where $Y_3 = \frac{1}{3}\varepsilon\mu\tilde{I}_P$.

End-to-End SNDR

Similar to the Section IV-A, only the end-to-end SNDR of the link $A \to R \to B$ will be considered. We assume that A transmits data with the peak power $\dfrac{I_P}{|g_1|^2}$ in the BC phase, the receiver power of the in-coming signal to the data processing block is $(1-\varepsilon)\dfrac{I_P}{|g_1|^2}$. The SNDR at R of the A→ R wireless kink in the first time slot of the BC phase is given by

$$\gamma_1 = \frac{(1-\varepsilon)\dfrac{I_P}{N_O}|h_1|^2}{(1-\varepsilon)\dfrac{I_P}{N_O}K_R^2|h_1|^2 + |g_1|^2} = \frac{\hat{\gamma}\rho_1}{\hat{\gamma}_1 K_R^2\rho_1 + \nu_1} \tag{41}$$

where $\tilde{Y} = (1-\varepsilon)\dfrac{I_P}{N_0}$ in the RL phase, R forwards the received data from the previous two time slots to A and B with the transmit power of $\dfrac{P_R}{|g_2|^2}$, where P_R is given in Equation 40. Then, the SNDR at B of the communication link R→B is given by

$$\gamma_2 = \frac{\overline{\gamma_3}(\rho_1 + \rho_2)}{\overline{\gamma_3}K_B^2(\rho_1 + \rho_2) + \dfrac{\nu_2}{\rho_2}} \tag{42}$$

where $\tilde{Y}_3 = \dfrac{Y_3}{N_0}$, The end-to-end SNDR of the wireless link $A \rightarrow R \rightarrow B$ of the cognitive DF network with DS energy transfer, TDBC protocol and PSB relay receiver architecture is then given as

$$\gamma = \min(\gamma_1, \gamma_2) \tag{43}$$

Outage Performance and Throughput Analysis

From Equation 41 and Equation 42, it implies that the end-to-end SNDRs of the networks in this case study have identical distribution with the end-to-end SNDRs of the networks in Section IV-A. Hence, the OP of the networks can be characterized as

$$OP(\gamma_t) = OP_A(\gamma_t) + OP_B(\gamma_t) \tag{44}$$

where $OP_A(\gamma_t)$ and $OP_B(\gamma_t)$ are the outage probabilities at A and B, given in Equation 14 and Equation 15, respectively, with the only difference pertaining to the replacement of $\tilde{Y}_1$ with $\tilde{Y}_3$ and $\overline{Y}$ with $\hat{Y}$. Likewise, the throughput of the networks can be obtained as

$$\tau = \frac{t}{3}\left[R_A\left(1 - OP_A(\gamma_A)\right) + R_B\left(1 - OP_B(\gamma_B)\right)\right] \tag{45}$$

DS Policy: MABC Protocol

In this configuration, the network utilizes the DS policy and the MABC protocol. The data frame structure of the transmission cycle is shown in Figure 7. We assume that the energy harvesting duration length is fixed and equal to $2t$. Therefore, R simultaneously harvests energy and collects data from the wireless signals that are transmitted in turn form A and B in $2t$ [s] duration. Hence, duration of T is $3t$ [sec]. The acquired energy at the relay node is parameterized as

$$E_H = \varepsilon\mu\left(P_A^{EH}\left|h_1\right|^2 + P_B^{EH}\left|h_2\right|^2\right)2t = \varepsilon\mu\overline{I}_P\left(\rho_1 + \rho_1\right)2t \tag{46}$$

The harvested energy is used to power the relay in the current transmission cycle RL phase and the BC phase of the next communication cycle. Thus, from Equation 46, the transmit power in the RL phase is given as

$$P_R = \frac{\varepsilon\mu\overline{I}_P\left(\rho_1 + \rho_2\right)2t}{3t} = \gamma_4\left(\rho_1 + \rho_2\right) \tag{47}$$

$$Y_3 = \frac{2}{3}\varepsilon\mu\tilde{I}_P.$$

The OP of the DF TWCR network in this configuration can be evaluated by following a similar line of reasoning as section IV-A with only difference pertaining to the replacement of $\tilde{Y}_1$ with $\tilde{Y}_4 = \dfrac{Y_4}{N_0}$ and $\overline{Y}$ with $\hat{Y}$.

Moreover, the network throughput of the DS policy, MABC protocol, TSB architecture network can be calculated as in Equation 45.

NUMERICAL RESULTS AND DISCUSSION

In this section, a set of numerical results for the OP and throughput of the DF TWCR networks with different energy transfer policies, relaying protocols and receiver architectures are presented. The network nodes are arranged in Cartesian coordinates where node A is located at the origin. We consider the case where coordinates of relay R, node B and Rx are (0.4, 0), (1, 0) and (0.8, 0.8), respectively. The relation between transmitted and received power with distance d is given by the decaying path loss model d^{-2}. The fixed transmission rates R_A and R_B are chosen to be 2 [bits/s/Hz] to acquire the OP and delay-limited network throughput. Furthermore, the hardware impairment in the range [0, 0.175] are examined, which resemble the maximum tolerable error vector magnitudes (EVMs) of 3GPP LTE requirements. For the sake of clarity, we assume that $k_A^2 = k_B^2 = k_R^2 = k^2$, the energy conversion efficiency is taken as $\mu = 0.8$ and the power sharing fraction is set to $\varepsilon = 0.5$, unless otherwise stated. We note that all the equation in this Chapter are also applicable for the ideal transceiver, $k^2 = 0$.

Corroboration of Analytical OP Results

In this subsection, the analysis results of network OP and throughput provided in Section IV and V are verified. First, the analytical results of the OP in the network with TSB relay receiver architecture are plotted. Figure 8 and Figure 9 respectively show the OP at terminal nodes A and B of the DF TWCR networks with TSB receiver architecture with respect to $\dfrac{I_P}{N_0} \epsilon \left[0, 40\right]$ (dB).

It can be seen that the analysis and simulation results are identical in all cases of the TSB network when different energy transfer policies and relaying protocols are employed. Accordingly, our analysis of OP at node A and B as given in Equation 14, Equation 15, Equation 33 and Equation 34 are verified. As anticipated, the OP at node A and B in Figure 8 of the network with DS energy transfer policy are

Figure 7. Data frame structure of the DS-MABC-PSB network

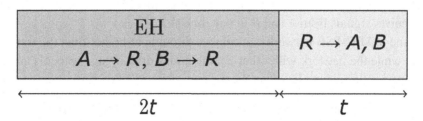

similar for the same transmission protocol. However, Figure 9 shows that the OP at A in the SFS energy transfer policy is much higher compared to the OP at B; in fact, the OP at A is higher than the OP at B due to the difference of distribution in two random variables $Y_{2,ARB}$ and $Y_{2,BRA}$, This indicates that the node chosen to transfer energy to the relay has the highest OP. Impact of transceiver imperfections is clearly shown by the increment of OP when the ideal transceiver ($k^2 = 0$) is replaced by the impairment transceiver ($k^2 = 0.175$).

Figure 10 illustrates the OP of EH-TWCR network with respect to $\frac{I_P}{N_0} \epsilon [0,40]$ (dB) where the relay utilizes TSB receiver architecture. As shown in the figure, network OP in analysis and simulation of the TSB relay receiver network match for all possible cases of energy transfer policies and relaying protocols under either ideal ($\kappa^2 = 0$) or impairment transceiver ($\kappa^2 = 0.175$). With the same level of hardware impairments, the DS-TDBC network achieves the best OP performance whereas the SFS-MABC network provides the worst among four networks configurations. More specifically, the networks with DS policy outperform the networks with SFS policy. This can be explained by the fact that transmit power in DS policy is higher than in SFS policy. We also observe that the TDBC networks provides the OP less than the network with MABC in term of OP due to the benefit of serial transmission in the TDBC protocol. When we consider the impact of transceiver impairment, we experience an approximate 2.5 dB loss in the SNR while maintaining the OP at nodes A and B when the impairment level κ^2 increases from 0 to 0.175 for the TSB network with all scenarios of energy transfer policies and relaying protocols.

The corroboration of OP analytical results of the PSB network with the SFS energy transfer policy and the TDBC/MABC relaying protocol can be obtained similarly. However, those results are not be plotted to avoid duplication and to maintain the clarity.

Achieved Throughput

Figure 11 illustrates throughput of DF TWCR network with respect to $\frac{I_P}{N_0} \epsilon [0,40]$ (dB) for six configurations of the networks with different energy transfer policies, relaying protocols and relay receiver structures that are considered in this work. The obtained results corresponding to the specific hardware impairment level, $k^2 = 0.1275$.

It can be seen that the DS-MABC-PSB networks is offered highest throughput among all other network configurations. On the other end, the SFS-TDBC-TSB networks provides the smallest throughput. This phenomenon can be attributed to the fact that DS policy provides more energy to transmit data in the RL phase than the SFS policy, and also the transmission cycle in the MABC-PSB network is the shortest whereas it is the longest in TDBC-TSB network. The networks utilizes MABC protocol and PSB receiver architecture outperform the TDBC- TSB networks in term of throughput because the benefit of data frame structure duration. However, MABC relaying protocol is more sophisticated to implement since the relay receives signals from A and B in one time slot.

Interestingly, the MABC-PSB network can achieve throughput higher than the transmission rate of each source node while the network with other combinations of relaying protocols and receiver architecture can only provide throughput less than the transmission rate of each source node. In the low SNR regime, $\frac{I_P}{N_o} < 10$ [dB], throughput of the DS-TDBC-PSB networks outperform only the SFC-TDBC-TSB

Figure 8. OP at A (or at B) of DS-TSB network with respect to I_P/N_0

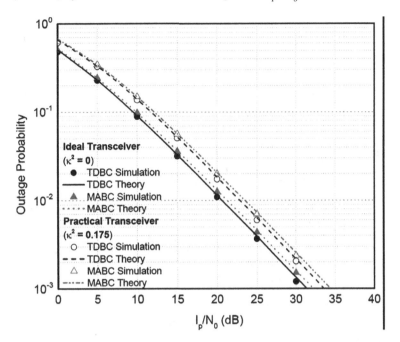

networks. In the high $\dfrac{I_P}{N_o} > 35$ [dB] regime where system OP approaches to zero, the upper bound throughputs of each combined policies, protocols, and receiver architecture are established. In our simulation scenario with the fixed transmission rate $R_A = R_B = 2$ [bits/s/Hz], the upper bound throughput of the MABC-PSB network and the TDBC-TSB networks are 2.67 and 0.8 [bits/s/Hz], respectively. This fact can be explained by the advantages of transmit power and the length of transmission data frame as above and a notation of the reception rate at the relay is sum of the transmission rate of two source nodes.

The Impact of Transceiver Impairments (κ^2)

Figure 12 illustrates the throughput of network with respects to hardware impairment levels, $\kappa^2 \in [0, 0.175]$. As shown in Figure 12, the throughput decreases as κ^2 increases from 0 to 0.18 for the network with TSB receiver structure. This trend is observed for the networks with all possible configurations. In the context of delay limit transmission, the decrement in throughput for the network with MABC protocol is more noticeable than the network with TDBC protocol. The impact of hardware impairment on throughput of network with the SFS policy is more remarkable than the network with DS policy. These observations suggest that the network utilizing MABC protocol or the SFS policy is more sensitive to transceiver' quality than the TDBC protocol or the DS policy. Therefore, the combination of DS policy and TDBC protocol for the EH-TWCR network provides the highest level of limiting factor impact of transceiver hardware impairment on the network throughput. A similar conclusion is made for the throughput of network with PSB relay receiver structure as in Figure 13.

Figure 9. OP at A of SFS-TSB network with respect to I_P/N_0

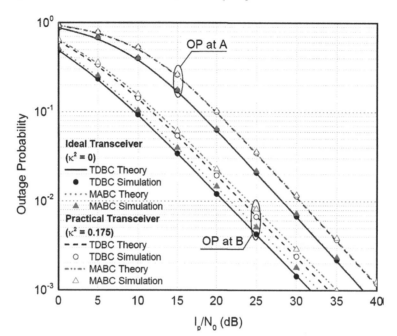

Figure 10. TSB network OP with respect to I_P/N_0

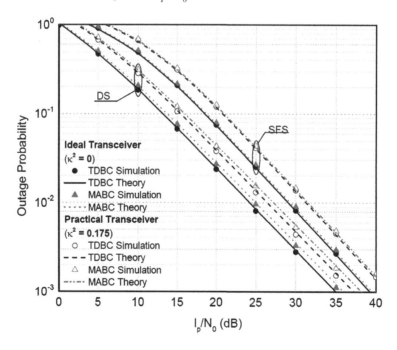

Figure 11. Throughput respect to policies, protocols and receiver architecture

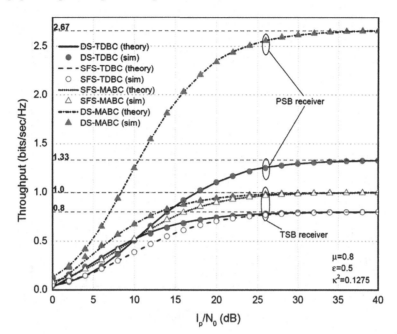

Figure 12. Throughput with respect to κ^2 for the TSB receiver

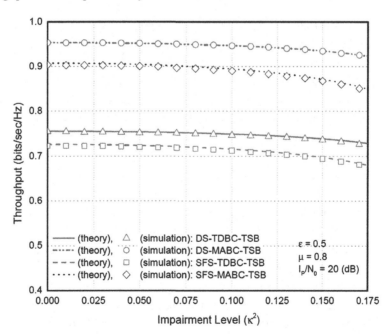

Figure 13. Throughput with respect to κ^2 for the PSB receiver

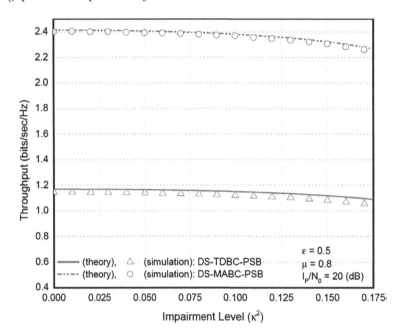

The Effect of Energy Conversion Efficiency (μ)

Figure 14 and Figure 15 illustrate the delay limit throughput respects to the energy conversion efficiency, $\mu \in [0, 1]$ for different network configurations. It can be seen that the throughput increases from 0 to upper bound throughput as μ increases from 0 to 1 for all cases. The throughput of SFS networks approaches to the upper bound throughput as μ increases slower than the network with DS protocol. This is because the transmit power in the RL phase of the SFS networks is smaller than that of the DS networks, therefore the low quality EH circuitry impact the throughput of networks with the SFS policy more than the networks with DS policy.

The Effect of Power Sharing Factor (ε)

Figure 16 shows the effect of power sharing factor ε to the network throughput of the PSB network. The throughput increase as ε rises from 0 to the optimal value of ε, but it decreases as ε increases from the optimal value to 1. It can be explained based on the harvested power in the EH phase and the power of received signal in the BC phase. When ε is smaller than the optimal value, the harvested power increase while the received signal power is decreased as ε increases. The received signal powers at the data processing block still higher than the level that is required to decode the signal correctly. Thus, the network throughput increases. However, when ε is larger than the optimum value, the harvested energy still increases but the power of incoming signal to the data processing is lower than the required level, hence, the transmit signal is recovered improperly at the relay. Eventually, the throughput of the network decreases.

Figure 14. Throughput with respect to μ for the TSB receiver

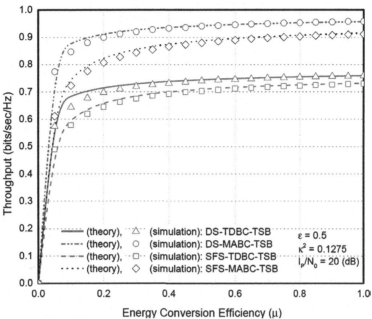

Figure 15. Throughput with respect to μ for the PSB receiver

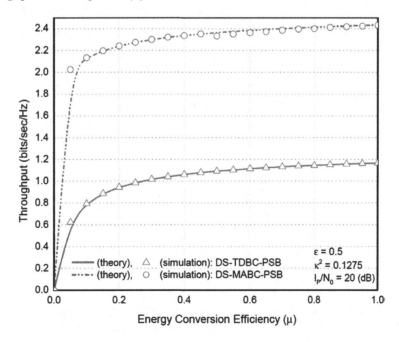

Figure 16. Throughput with respect to ε for the PSB receiver architecture

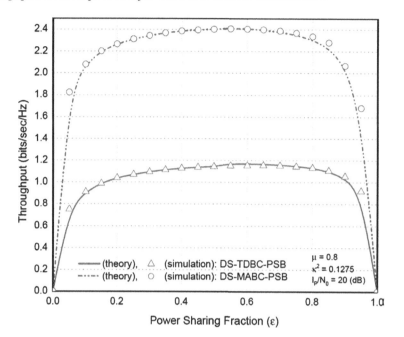

CONCLUSION AND FUTURE WORK

The proposed work can be used in the practical wireless sensor networks. Also, there are some applications in the vehicular and cellular applications. The proposed work take in to account the hardware impairment and that provides a good practical gauge on what level the system performances can be used unlike most of other reported works. In the future works, we look in to the best cooperative mechanism (BCM) for wireless energy harvesting and spectrum sharing in 5G networks. We will formulate an optimization problem using BCM with an objective to maximize throughput of PUs and SUs with constraints on data rate and energy harvest save ratios. Also, interesting researchers may look in to novel energy modulation schemes which maximizes energy transfer rates.

Physical transceivers have hardware impairments that introduce distortions which damage the performance of communication systems. The massive amount of technical contributions in the area of cooperative cognitive relaying neglect hardware impairments and, thus, adopts ideal hardware. Such estimates make sense in low-rate systems, but can results in high misleading consequences when analyzing future high-rate systems. In the future works, a similar analysis for the ergodic capacity will also be pursued, resulting in new upper bound using independent but non-identically distributed Nakagami-m fading.

This chapter investigated the OP and throughput of EH-TWCR networks. Our analysis provided insight and understanding into self-powered TWCR relaying scheme based on DF. For instance, it was found that DS-MABC- PSB provides the best throughput albeit at the expense of implementation complexity, whereas SFS-TDBC-TSB offers a simpler solution with a lower throughput. On the other hand, a network with the SFS policy and MABC protocol is more sensitive to hardware impairments than with DS policy and TDBC protocol. In addition, we also confirmed that the transceiver impairments substantially deteriorate the OP and throughput. The system performance degradation has been quantified as a function of the level of hardware impairments. Ideally, these results can be used to select hardware of appropriate quality to meet the predetermined OP and throughput requirements for future EH-TWCR networks.

ACKNOWLEDGMENT

This work is supported (in part) by the Ministry of Education and Science (federal budget) of the Russian Federation grant No. 3942 and performed in accordance with Russian Government Resolutions No. 2014/226 of 2016. The work was done in part while the D. N. K. Jayakody was with the Institute of Computer Science, University of Tartu, and was supported in part by the Norwegian-Estonian Research Cooperation Programme through the grant EMP133 and by the Estonian Research Council through the research grants PUT405.

REFERENCES

Bi, S., Ho, C., & Zhang, R. (2015). Wireless powered communication: Opportunities and challenges. *IEEE Communications Magazine*, *53*(4), 117–125. doi:10.1109/MCOM.2015.7081084

Bjornson, E., Matthaiou, M., & Debbah, M. (2013). A new look at dual-hop relaying: Performance limits with hardware impairments. *IEEE Transactions on Communications*, *61*(11), 4512–4525. doi:10.1109/TCOMM.2013.100913.130282

Björnson, E., Zetterberg, P., & Bengtsson, M. (2012, December). Optimal coordinated beamforming in the multicell downlink with transceiver impairments. In *Global Communications Conference (GLOBECOM)*, (pp. 4775-4780). IEEE. doi:10.1109/GLOCOM.2012.6503874

Cover, T., & Gamal, A. E. (1979). Capacity theorems for the relay channel. *IEEE Transactions on Information Theory*, *25*(5), 572–584. doi:10.1109/TIT.1979.1056084

Gollakota, S., Reynolds, M. S., Smith, J. R., & Wetherall, D. J. (2014). The emergence of RF-powered computing. *Computer*, *47*(1), 32–39. doi:10.1109/MC.2013.404

Guan, L., Zhang, J., Li, J., Liu, G., & Zhang, P. (2007, September). Spectral efficient frequency allocation scheme in multihop cellular network. In *2007 IEEE 66th Vehicular Technology Conference* (pp. 1446-1450). IEEE. doi:10.1109/VETECF.2007.308

Guo, Y., Kang, G., Zhang, N., Zhou, W., & Zhang, P. (2010). Outage performance of relay-assisted cognitive-radio system under spectrum-sharing constraints. *Electronics Letters*, *46*(2), 182–184. doi:10.1049/el.2010.2159

Hoang, A. T., Liang, Y. C., Wong, D. T. C., Zeng, Y., & Zhang, R. (2009). Opportunistic spectrum access for energy-constrained cognitive radios. *IEEE Transactions on Wireless Communications*, *8*(3), 1206–1211. doi:10.1109/TWC.2009.080763

Hoang, D. T., Niyato, D., Wang, P., & Kim, D. I. (2014). Opportunistic channel access and RF energy harvesting in cognitive radio networks. *IEEE Journal on Selected Areas in Communications, 32*(11), 2039–2052. doi:10.1109/JSAC.2014.141108

Huang, K. (2013, June). Mobile ad hoc networks powered by energy harvesting: Battery-level dynamics and spatial throughput. In *2013 IEEE International Conference on Communications (ICC)* (pp. 3121-3125). IEEE.

Huang, K., & Lau, V. K. (2014). Enabling wireless power transfer in cellular networks: Architecture, modeling and deployment. *IEEE Transactions on Wireless Communications, 13*(2), 902–912. doi:10.1109/TWC.2013.122313.130727

Huang, K., & Zhou, X. (2015). Cutting the last wires for mobile communications by microwave power transfer. *IEEE Communications Magazine, 53*(6), 86–93. doi:10.1109/MCOM.2015.7120022

Hunter, T. E., Sanayei, S., & Nosratinia, A. (2006). Outage analysis of coded cooperation. *IEEE Transactions on Information Theory, 52*(2), 375–391. doi:10.1109/TIT.2005.862084

Jeffrey, A., & Zwillinger, D. (Eds.). (2007). *Table of integrals, series, and products.* Academic Press.

Kim, K. J., Duong, T. Q., Elkashlan, M., Yeoh, P. L., & Nallanathan, A. (2013, December). Two-way cognitive relay networks with multiple licensed users. In *2013 IEEE Global Communications Conference (GLOBECOM)* (pp. 992-997). IEEE.

Le, T., Mayaram, K., & Fiez, T. (2008). Efficient far-field radio frequency energy harvesting for passively powered sensor networks. *IEEE Journal of Solid-State Circuits, 43*(5), 1287–1302. doi:10.1109/JSSC.2008.920318

Lee, S., & Zhang, R. (2015). Cognitive wireless powered network: Spectrum sharing models and throughput maximization. *IEEE Transactions on Cognitive Communications and Networking, 1*(3), 335–346. doi:10.1109/TCCN.2015.2508028

Letaief, K. B., & Zhang, W. (2009). Cooperative communications for cognitive radio networks. *Proceedings of the IEEE, 97*(5), 878–893. doi:10.1109/JPROC.2009.2015716

Li, J., Matthaiou, M., & Svensson, T. (2014). I/Q imbalance in two-way AF relaying. *IEEE Transactions on Communications, 62*(7), 2271–2285. doi:10.1109/TCOMM.2014.2325036

Luo, S., Zhang, R., & Lim, T. J. (2013). Optimal save-then-transmit protocol for energy harvesting wireless transmitters. *IEEE Transactions on Wireless Communications, 12*(3), 1196–1207. doi:10.1109/TWC.2013.012413.120488

Matthaiou, M., Papadogiannis, A., Bjornson, E., & Debbah, M. (2013). Two-way relaying under the presence of relay transceiver hardware impairments. *IEEE Communications Letters, 17*(6), 1136–1139. doi:10.1109/LCOMM.2013.042313.130191

Medepally, B., & Mehta, N. B. (2010). Voluntary energy harvesting relays and selection in cooperative wireless networks. *IEEE Transactions on Wireless Communications, 9*(11), 3543–3553. doi:10.1109/TWC.2010.091510.100447

Nasir, A. A., Zhou, X., Durrani, S., & Kennedy, R. A. (2013). Relaying protocols for wireless energy harvesting and information processing. *IEEE Transactions on Wireless Communications, 12*(7), 3622–3636. doi:10.1109/TWC.2013.062413.122042

Ng, D. W. K., Lo, E. S., & Schober, R. (2013). Wireless information and power transfer: Energy efficiency optimization in OFDMA systems. *IEEE Transactions on Wireless Communications, 12*(12), 6352–6370. doi:10.1109/TWC.2013.103113.130470

Nguyen, D. K., Matthaiou, M., Duong, T. Q., & Ochi, H. (2015, June). RF energy harvesting two-way cognitive DF relaying with transceiver impairments. In *2015 IEEE International Conference on Communication Workshop (ICCW)* (pp. 1970-1975). IEEE. doi:10.1109/ICCW.2015.7247469

Panigrahi, B., Sharma, A., & De, S. (2012). Interference aware power controlled forwarding for lifetime maximisation of wireless ad hoc networks. *IET Wireless Sensor Systems, 2*(1), 22-30.

Paradiso, J. A., & Starner, T. (2005). Energy scavenging for mobile and wireless electronics. *IEEE Pervasive Computing / IEEE Computer Society [and] IEEE Communications Society, 4*(1), 18–27. doi:10.1109/MPRV.2005.9

Qi, J., & Aissa, S. (2012). On the power amplifier nonlinearity in MIMO transmit beamforming systems. *IEEE Transactions on Communications, 60*(3), 876–887. doi:10.1109/TCOMM.2012.021712.110006

Qi, J., Aissa, S., & Alouini, M. S. (2012, April). Analysis and compensation of I/Q imbalance in amplify-and-forward cooperative systems. In *2012 IEEE Wireless Communications and Networking Conference (WCNC)* (pp. 215-220). IEEE. doi:10.1109/WCNC.2012.6214150

Raghunathan, V., Ganeriwal, S., & Srivastava, M. (2006). Emerging techniques for long lived wireless sensor networks. *IEEE Communications Magazine, 44*(4), 108–114. doi:10.1109/MCOM.2006.1632657

Schenk, T. (2008). *RF imperfections in high-rate wireless systems: impact and digital compensation.* Springer Science & Business Media. doi:10.1007/978-1-4020-6903-1

Seah, W. K., Eu, Z. A., & Tan, H. P. (2009, May). Wireless sensor networks powered by ambient energy harvesting (WSN-HEAP)-Survey and challenges. In *Wireless Communication, Vehicular Technology, Information Theory and Aerospace & Electronics Systems Technology, 2009. Wireless VITAE 2009. 1st International Conference on* (pp. 1-5). IEEE.

Shen, Z., Andrews, J. G., & Evans, B. L. (2005). Adaptive resource allocation in multiuser OFDM systems with proportional rate constraints. *IEEE Transactions on Wireless Communications, 4*(6), 2726–2737. doi:10.1109/TWC.2005.858010

Shi, Q., Liu, L., Xu, W., & Zhang, R. (2014). Joint transmit beamforming and receive power splitting for MISO SWIPT systems. *IEEE Transactions on Wireless Communications, 13*(6), 3269–3280. doi:10.1109/TWC.2014.041714.131688

Singhal, C., Kumar, S., De, S., Panwar, N., Tonde, R., & De, P. (2014). Class-based shared resource allocation for cell-edge users in OFDMA networks. *IEEE Transactions on Mobile Computing, 13*(1), 48–60. doi:10.1109/TMC.2012.210

Smith, J. R. (Ed.). (2013). *Wirelessly Powered Sensor Networks and Computational RFID*. Springer Science & Business Media. doi:10.1007/978-1-4419-6166-2

Sudevalayam, S., & Kulkarni, P. (2011). Energy harvesting sensor nodes: Survey and implications. *IEEE Communications Surveys and Tutorials, 13*(3), 443–461. doi:10.1109/SURV.2011.060710.00094

Suh, Y. H., & Chang, K. (2002). A high-efficiency dual-frequency rectenna for 2.45-and 5.8-GHz wireless power transmission. *IEEE Transactions on Microwave Theory and Techniques, 50*(7), 1784–1789. doi:10.1109/TMTT.2002.800430

Sultan, A. (2012). Sensing and transmit energy optimization for an energy harvesting cognitive radio. *IEEE Wireless Communications Letters, 1*(5), 500-503.

Usman, M., & Koo, I. (2014). Access strategy for hybrid underlay-overlay cognitive radios with energy harvesting. *IEEE Sensors Journal, 14*(9), 3164–3173. doi:10.1109/JSEN.2014.2324565

Yang, L., Alouini, M. S., & Qaraqe, K. (2012). On the performance of spectrum sharing systems with two-way relaying and multiuser diversity. *IEEE Communications Letters, 16*(8), 1240–1243. doi:10.1109/LCOMM.2012.052112.120746

Zhong, C., Ratnarajah, T., & Wong, K. K. (2011). Outage analysis of decode-and-forward cognitive dual-hop systems with the interference constraint in Nakagami-fading channels. *IEEE Transactions on Vehicular Technology, 60*(6), 2875–2879. doi:10.1109/TVT.2011.2159256

Zhou, X., Zhang, R., & Ho, C. K. (2013). Wireless information and power transfer: Architecture design and rate-energy tradeoff. *IEEE Transactions on Communications, 61*(11), 4754–4767. doi:10.1109/TCOMM.2013.13.120855

Zou, Y., Valkama, M., & Renfors, M. (2008). Digital compensation of I/Q imbalance effects in space-time coded transmit diversity systems. *IEEE Transactions on Signal Processing, 56*(6), 2496–2508. doi:10.1109/TSP.2007.916132

Chapter 6
Link Level Resource Allocation Strategies for Green Communications in LTE–Advanced

Prashant Kallappa Wali
International Institute of Information Technology, India

Amudheesan Aadhithan N
International Institute of Information Technology, India

Debabrata Das
International Institute of Information Technology, India

ABSTRACT

Mobile operators are showing a growing concern for energy efficiency in cellular networks in the recent past not only to maintain profitability, but also to tackle the overall environment effects. Such a trend is motivating the standardization bodies, network operators and researchers to aggressively explore techniques to reduce the energy consumption in the network. This trend has stimulated the interest of researchers in an innovative new research area called green cellular networks which is a vast research discipline that needs to cover all the layers of the protocol stack and various system architectures. Since Long Term Evolution-Advanced (LTE-A), which promises better support to richer applications, is fast emerging as the next generation cellular network standard and expected to aggravate the energy consumption problem, various techniques have been proposed and researched to improve its energy efficiency. This chapter discusses three link level techniques that attempt to reduce the energy consumption of a LTE-A cell with intelligent MAC layer algorithms.

INTRODUCTION

The last decade has not only seen a phenomenal rise in the number of cellular subscribers but also in their demand for data. Accordingly, it has resulted in an explosive expansion and growth in the cellular networks. It is estimated that there were more than 4 million base stations (BSs) serving mobile users

DOI: 10.4018/978-1-5225-2023-8.ch006

and this number is predicted to keep increasing in the years to come (Hasan, 2011). This enormous growth in the cellular industry has pushed the limits of energy consumption in wireless networks. Also, the emergence of the LTE-A promises to offer better support to richer applications through enhanced data rates is expected to act as a catalyst for the explosive growth in the number of subscribers and their demand for traffic. This will result in a substantial increase in the number of base stations and also the power they consume, further aggravating the energy consumption problem. Hence, there is an acute need to introduce power saving mechanisms in LTE-A to mitigate the energy consumption.

The breakdown of power consumption in a typical cellular network shows that the base stations (called as eNodeB in LTE-A and henceforth shall be interchangeably called as eNodeBs) consume up to 60% of the total power and the rest is divided between mobile switching centers, data centers and core transmission equipments (Hasan, 2011). Since eNodeBs have the biggest share of the energy consumption in cellular networks, it is necessary to identify the elements in the eNodeBs which contribute most to the overall energy consumption. From the power consumption point of view, there are two groups to which the elements of a eNodeB can belong to:

1. Radio frequency equipment (which includes power amplifiers and transceivers), which serve one or more sectors/cells.
2. Support system which includes alternate current/direct current (AC/DC) power conversion modules, air conditioning elements, analog and digital signal processors, battery backup, etc.

The largest energy consumer in the eNodeB is the power amplifier (PA), which has a share of around 65% of the total energy consumption (Chen, 2010). Of the other base station elements, significant energy consumers are: air conditioning (17.5%), digital signal processing (10%) and AC/DC conversion elements (7.5%) (Correia, 2010).

New research aimed at reducing energy consumption in the cellular access networks can be achieved at three levels: component, link and network (Hasan, 2011), (Lorincz, 2012). Investigations at the component level focus on improving the linearity and efficiency of the power amplifier. One way to improve the efficiency is by using a specially designed power amplifier like Doherty, or special materials for power amplifier transistors, like high-frequency materials such as Si, GaAs or GaN. Other techniques to improve efficiency include envelope tracking (Forster, 2012), or crest factor reduction, like peak windowing or amplitude scaling. A digital pre-distortion technique is used in the power amplifier for cancelling the distortion, and therefore achieving better linearity (Hirata, 2010). A reduction in the power consumption of the signal processing can be done by combining ASIC, DSP or FPGA architectures of integrated circuits to achieve better efficiency (Zoican, 2008). AC/DC conversion in eNodeBs can be improved using highly efficient converters that can increase their efficiency even in high traffic load situations. Air conditioning power consumption can be reduced by minimizing the operational temperature of base station models, or by using additional elements like heat exchangers, membrane filters and smart fans or heater modules (Roy, 2008). Component level energy savings can also be achieved by implementing distributed eNodeB architecture, where the radiofrequency equipment is placed near the antennas to minimize the losses in cables (Etoh, 2008). The possibility of deploying photovoltaic panels and wind turbines on the base station sites is also another method investigated to reduce the power consumption. Combining these two renewable energy sources can also lead to a potential reduction in the power consumption by 50% (ATIS, 2012).

The network level technique for reducing energy consumption can be enabled by dynamic management of network resources, which allows shutting down of entire eNodeBs during a low traffic load. In such a scenario, neighbouring eNodeBs provide coverage and take over the traffic load of those eNodeBs that are turned off (Correia, 2010). This can be combined with dynamic transmission power selection, antenna tilting, multihop relaying or by coordinated multipoint transmission and reception (Oh, 2011).

At the link level, the potential for energy savings is in the transmission techniques on the air interface. The link level considers possible sleep modes of some eNodeB components (micro and macro sleep), wherein they can be switched off for a certain time. The eNodeB should provide a differentiation between by scheduling traffic load in the uplink and downlink transmissions (Correia, 2010). Cell wilting and blossoming techniques can also be implemented to improve the energy efficiency provided by sleep modes of the eNodeB. These techniques, used for the design of eNodeB sleep and wake-up transients, consist of a progressive eNodeB switching off and on. These transients are shown to be very short, which allows eNodeBs to be switched off and on in a short time with no significant reduction in the energy savings obtained through sleep mode approaches (Conte, 2011). The 4G systems aim at dynamic frequency spectrum allocation depending on traffic load (Blume, 2011). The cancellation of the interference in cellular networks using distributed antenna systems and algorithms, such as linear zero forcing, minimum squared error and successive interference cancellation, also contributes to the reduction of energy consumption (Han, 2011). Another link level technique that has caught the attention of researchers is the possible sleep modes of the eNodeB components (micro and macro sleep) like Power Amplifiers (PA) through intelligent traffic scheduling (Conte, 2011).

Among the aforementioned levels, in this chapter, the focus is on power-saving mechanism at the link level through intelligent traffic scheduling that enables sleep modes of the eNodeB components resulting in reduced energy consumption.

FEASIBILITY OF SLEEP MODES

The main part of the energy that is consumed in mobile networks is mostly spent when no user is accessing that specific part of the network since the key idea with which cellular radio systems have been designed till now is to be always on. Even though it is found that no user is served in most of the cells most of the time by examining the traffic in a cellular network with a short enough time resolution, e.g. on millisecond level, on a longer time scale, e.g. few minutes, only very few cells carry no traffic. Consequently, there is a large energy saving potential for fast dynamic mechanisms that allow for a cell to switch off cell specific signaling whenever there is no user data transmitted or received in the cell (Frenger, 2011).

A well accepted model of the power consumption in a typical LTE-A eNodeB (Lorincz, 2012), (Frenger, 2011) is shown in Figure 1. The power input for a eNodeB increases linearly with the utilization of the PA (number of PRBs on which data is scheduled in the downlink). Typically, the fixed power consumption part (P_o) is in the same order as the variable power consumption part (P_v). The input power P_{in} required to transmit data on k PRBs can be computed as follows (Lorincz, 2012):

$$P_{in} = P_o + k \cdot \alpha \cdot P_{PRB} \tag{1}$$

where, $\alpha \cdot P_{PRB}$ is the amount of power required to be fed into the eNodeB to transmit a power P_{PRB} in a single PRB. Eqn. 1 indicates that irrespective of the number of PRBs used to transmit data to UEs, there is a fixed power P_o that is consumed by the PA if kept in the *ON* state. This means that even if there is no data to be transmitted ($k = 0$), the input power required to keep the PA in the *ON* state would be P_o. On the other hand, it is known that the PA can be switched to light sleep mode (Frenger, 2011) instead of keeping it in the *ON* state when there is no data to be scheduled.

In a deep sleep level the power use can be close to zero Watt. However, to wake up from this low power mode the PA may require more time. But in a light sleep mode, the inactivation and the activation of the PA is much faster, however, at the expense of somewhat reduced power savings (Lorincz, 2012), (Frenger, 2011). Even with a light sleep mode, the input power P_{in} required would only be a small fraction of the power P_o. Hence, if sleep modes are adapted for the PA whenever there is no data to be transmitted in a subframe, we can modify eqn. 1 as follows:

$$
\begin{aligned}
P_{in} &= P_o + k \cdot \alpha \cdot P_{PRB}, 0 < k \le N \\
&= P_S, k = 0
\end{aligned}
\tag{2}
$$

where, P_S is the amount of power required to hold the PA in light sleep mode.

Hence, significant power savings can be potentially enabled by putting the cell into some kind of sleep mode. However, even when no user data is communicated in the cell, the cellular standard mandates that the base stations must carry out some minimum amount of transmissions that can significantly limit the feasibility of cell discontinuous transmission (DTX). In a WCDMA system, for example, each cell needs to continuously transmit a common pilot channel (P-CPICH) and a common control channel (P-CCPCH) and therefore the PA utilization never goes below 10%, leaving no time at all for cell DTX. But the LTE standard supports cell-DTX behaviour as will be discussed next after a brief description of the LTE-A downlink frame format.

Figure 1. Power consumption model of a LTE-A eNodeB

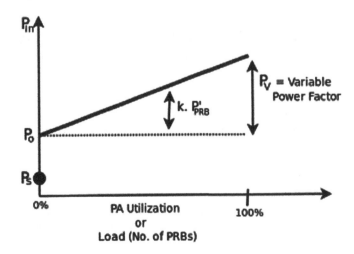

LINK LEVEL STRATEGIES FOR GREEN COMMUNICATIONS IN LTE-ADVANCED

The transmission format specified for the LTE downlink is known as orthogonal frequency division multiplexing, OFDM (Erik, 2008). Transmission by means of OFDM can be seen as a kind of multi-carrier transmission. One way to increase the overall transmission bandwidth, without suffering from increased signal corruption due to radio-channel frequency selectivity, is the use of so-called multi-carrier transmission. Multi-carrier transmission implies that, instead of transmitting a single more wideband signal, multiple more narrowband signals, often referred to as subcarriers, are frequency multiplexed and jointly transmitted over the same radio link to the same receiver. By transmitting M signals in parallel over the same radio link, the overall data rate can be increased up to M times. At the same time, the impact in terms of signal corruption due to radio-channel frequency selectivity depends on the bandwidth of each subcarrier. The basic characteristics of OFDM transmission, which distinguish it from a straightforward multi-carrier extension of a more narrowband transmission scheme is by the use of a relatively large number of narrowband subcarriers. In contrast, a straightforward multi-carrier extension would typically consist of only a few subcarriers, each with a relatively wide bandwidth. As an example, a WCDMA multi-carrier evolution to a 20 MHz overall transmission bandwidth could consist of four (sub)carriers, each with a bandwidth in the order of 5 MHz. In comparison, OFDM transmission may imply that several hundred subcarriers are transmitted over the same radio link to the same receiver. Moreover, Tight frequency-domain packing of the subcarriers with a subcarrier spacing $f = 1/T_u$, where T_u is the per-subcarrier modulation-symbol time. The subcarrier spacing is thus equal to the per-subcarrier modulation rate $1/T_u$.

Since OFDM is a multi-carrier transmission technique the physical radio resource can conceptually be described as a time-frequency grid where each resource element consists of one sub-carrier during one symbol. In LTE-A, each downlink frame is of 10 ms duration and consists of ten subframes. Each subframe is of 1 ms duration. A subframe consists of two 0.5 ms slots, with each slot containing seven OFDM symbols. In the frequency domain, the system bandwidth B is divided into several subcarriers, each with a bandwidth of 15 kHz. A set of 12 consecutive subcarriers for a duration of one slot is called a physical resource block (PRB).

Each sub-frame begins with a downlink control region spanning between 1 to 3 OFDM symbols. These first 1-3 symbols in each subframe are used to carry control channels like Physical Downlink Control Channel (PDCCH), Physical Control Format Indicator Channel (PCFICH) and so on. The rest of the symbols are used to carry transport channels like Physical Broadcast Channel (PBCH), Physical Downlink Shared Channel (PDSCH) and so on in the downlink. The total amount of available physical resources during one subframe depends on the number of subcarriers, *i.e*, the total bandwidth allocated for the LTE-A carrier. For example, 10 MHz cell bandwidth would correspond to 600 subcarriers, 50 PRBs and 10 PDCCHs in each subframe while 5 MHz cell bandwidth would correspond to 300 subcarriers, 25 PRBs and 5 PDCCHs in each subframe. PDCCH is used to carry the downlink control information and PDSCH is used to carry data in the downlink. The eNodeB includes downlink scheduling assignments in PDCCH, which are used by the UEs to know where they receive data on the PDSCH. The PDCCH also includes uplink scheduling grants, which are used to indicate the shared uplink resources (Physical Uplink Shared Channel, PUSCH) the UEs use to send data to the eNodeB (Farooq, 2009), (Erik, 2008). The primary and secondary synchronization signals (PSS and SSS, respectively) are transmitted in sub-frame 0 and 5 and the (physical) broadcast channel (PBCH) is transmitted in sub-frame 0.

In LTE-A, traffic scheduling is performed over each millisecond slot called as Transmission Time Interval (TTI). The eNodeB decides which PRB to allocate to which User Equipment (UE) based on the scheduling policy and the channel feedback from the UEs in each TTI. A key point to note is that the one PRB pair in time is the smallest block of frequency that can be allocated to a UE.

Some of the methods that have been proposed to enable link level energy efficiency in LTE-A include inserting Multi-cast and Broadcast Single Frequency Network(MBFSN) subframes within a frame when there is low/no data to be scheduled in a LTE-A cell. Another method includes shaping the downlink traffic to enable more frequent sleep modes at the eNodeB, while ensuring the Quality of Service (QoS) requirements of the application in terms of delay are successfully met. We will first introduce the two methods briefly and then describe PS-SPS that uses the idea of shaping the downlink traffic for VoLTE to enable power saving.

MBSFN SUBFRAMES INSERTION METHOD

MBSFN sub-frame insertion method to enable sleep modes for an eNodeB was proposed by Frenger, et.al, in (Frenger, 2011). Recall that one resource block pair contains 14×12 resource elements (assuming normal cyclic prefix). Within this resource block, some resource elements (OFDM symbols) are used to transmit cell specific reference signals (CRS) related to one antenna port in LTE. LTE standard supports up to four such cell specific reference signals that are used by the User Equipments (UEs) as demodulation reference, for estimating the channel quality, and also for measurements during mobility to choose the best cell to connect to. The other resource elements within the resource block pair can be filled with user specific data. Beside the normal (unicast) data subframes, LTE also provides a special type of sub-frame called multi-cast and broadcast single frequency network (MBSFN) sub-frame. These subframes are used to transmit broadcast information to all UEs in a cell when required. This type of sub-frame consists of a short control region at the beginning of the subframe, similar to the normal sub-frames, while the rest of the sub-frame may be empty. Six out of the ten sub-frames in a radio frame can be configured as such MBSFN sub-frames (1, 2, 3, 6, 7, and 8).

When the traffic load is low, in order to reduce energy consumption, a cell can be configured with up to 6 MBSFN sub-frames in a frame that are not used (Frenger, 2011). Hence, Figure 2 shows the minimum amount of signals that need to be transmitted in a cell with no traffic at all (in addition higher layer system information is required on a less frequent time scale than a radio frame, not shown in Figure 2). In contrast to e.g. WCDMA, where the cell is required to transmit continuously, there is a significant possibility to reduce energy consumption with cell DTX in LTE. When counting the actually transmitted OFDM symbols in a radio frame with 6 MBSFN sub-frames and assuming a PA wake up time of 30 s it becomes apparent that the PA can be in low power DTX mode in 74% of the time when there is no traffic in the cell. This simple calculation alone gives some indication that cell DTX is an effective method for reducing energy consumption in LTE when there is no or very little traffic.

TRAFFIC BUFFERING AND SHAPING

Another method to enable eNodeB sleep modes was proposed by Rohit Gupta, et. al, in (Rohit, 2012). In this method, it is proposed to shape the incoming downlink traffic to enable more frequent sleep

Figure 2. MBSFN subframe insertion technique

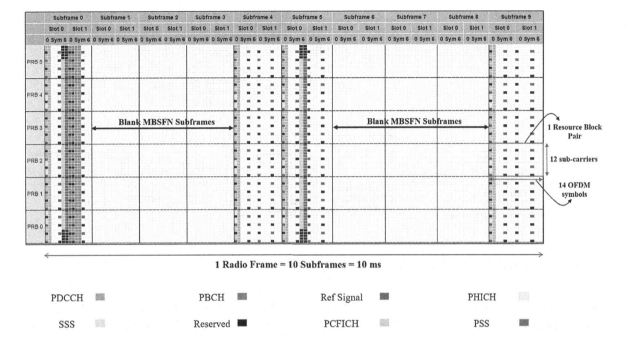

PDCCH PBCH Ref Signal PHICH

SSS Reserved PCFICH PSS

modes at the eNodeB, while ensuring the Quality of Service (QoS) requirements of the application in terms of delay are successfully met. The statistics and QoS requirements of traffic arrival depends on the application generating the traffic (Y. Chen, 2004). Traffic statistics of different applications vary greatly in terms of throughput and delay requirements. It is this delay tolerance that can be exploited in the scheduler to achieve significant system EE gains to enable DTX for Green Base Stations.

Figure 3 shows the architecture of scheduling which enables traffic shaping to introduce DTX at the Base Station. The traffic for all the users arrive at the Call Admission Control (CAC) module, which is responsible for allowing the traffic resources into the system based on user/traffic priorities, etc. The CAC module provides the estimate of the traffic characteristics (for example, aggregate throughput, delay tolerance, etc.) to the Traffic Shaping module. The Traffic Shaping module is responsible for buffering the traffic in order to not violate the QoS characteristics of the traffic, especially in terms of delay performance of the application. The Traffic Shaping module passes the shaped traffic to the scheduler, which assigns resources in terms of radio resource blocks in each TTI. The input to the scheduler is channel quality indicator (CQI) estimates, based on the current channel conditions provided by each user. The scheduler can implement any of the OFDMA based scheduling algorithms such as Max C/ I (Pokhariyal, 2006), Round Robin or Green Scheduler (Strinati, 2010). eNodeB Sleep mode manager plays the key role in enabling DTX at the eNodeB as it is responsible for putting the eNodeB components to sleep for the inactive periods of traffic. The Traffic Shaping module provides input to the eNodeB sleep mode manager regarding the duty-cycle of the time intervals of sleep modes of the eNodeB.

Figure 3. Green scheduling architecture for DTR and traffic shaping

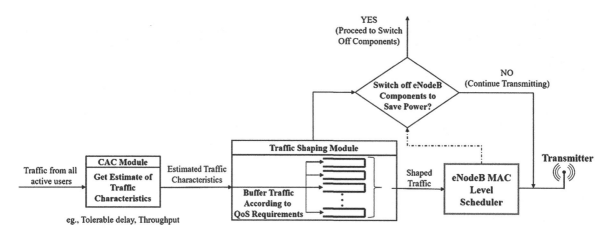

POWER SAVING SEMI PERSISTENT SCHEDULER

Power Saving-Semi Persistent Scheduling (PS-SPS) is a method proposed for VoLTE traffic in the downlink of LTE-A cell to reduce the power consumption at the link level. PS-SPS applies the buffering strategy to VoLTE traffic by considering not only its throughput and delay requirements but also exploits its traffic pattern. PS-SPS is based on an intelligent modification of the traditional SPS (called as SPS henceforth and to be explained in a later section) that results in power saving. PS-SPS enables power saving in the eNodeB and also retains the ability to support a large number of VoLTE calls like SPS.

The following reasons can be attributed to the benefits that a power saving scheduler like PS-SPS can offer:

1.   VoLTE traffic is expected to constitute a major portion of the total traffic once LTE-A is fully deployed (Farooq, 2009).
2.   VoLTE traffic gets the highest priority in each scheduling interval in LTE-A (3GPP-TS 23.401, 2008).

PS-SPS persistently and intelligently allocates physical resource blocks (PRBs) from a downlink subframe for initial transmissions of VoLTE packets to active users till all the PRBs are utilized in that subframe. This maximizes the resource utilization of each subframe in which PRBs are allocated for initial transmissions of VoLTE packets and enables more sleeping modes in the eNodeB. This results in substantial reduction in the power consumption compared to SPS.

In order to understand how PS-SPS enables more sleep modes of the eNodeB, the working of traditional SPS is explained briefly first.

Semi Persistent Scheduling (SPS)

In LTE-A, scheduling is done on a dynamic basis. This means that, each PRB in the downlink subframe gets scheduled to one of the active UEs based on their feedback of the channel estimate. The scheduler uses this information along with the QoS requirement of the applications that the UEs are running to decide which PRBs should be allocated to the UEs in each subframe. The information about which PRBs are allocated to each UE, *i.e.,* on which PRBs the data is scheduled for each UE in the current subframe is indicated through PDCCH control signal sent at the beginning of each subframe. This kind of scheduling is called dynamic scheduling. In principle, dynamic scheduling can be used for VoLTE users also, but dynamic scheduling of each VoLTE packet requires multiple of signaling. This is because, on an average, VoLTE users are one half of time in silent state and the other half in active state. When a user is in active state, a voice packet arrives every 20ms while in inactive periods an SID (Silence Insertion Descriptor) packet comes every 160ms. Additionally, these VoLTE packet sizes are small enough to fit within 1-3 PRBs when the channel conditions are moderate (Dajie, 2007). Because of the small packet size and constant inter-arrival time of VoLTE packets, dynamic scheduling results in large amount of signaling. This makes it very difficult to support large number of VoLTE calls in the system since the PDCCH signaling resources are limited in number. In order to reduce the amount of control signaling, a mechanism called persistent scheduling was proposed for VoLTE traffic (3GPP-TSG-RAN, 2006), (3GPP-TSG-RAN-WG1, 2007). In persistent scheduling, control signaling is used only once to persistently allocate a sequence of PRBs as well as a fixed modulation scheme to a VoLTE user which should also include resources required for retransmissions. Even though this mechanism reduces control signaling compared to dynamic scheduling, a major disadvantage of persistent scheduling is the mismatch between resource allocated and resource actually needed due to different Hybrid ARQ (HARQ) operation points required for retransmissions among users (Dajie, 2007).

To overcome this problem, a combining of dynamic and persistent scheduling called semipersistent scheduling (SPS) was proposed next. In this mechanism, one control signal is used to persistently allocate PRB resources for only initial transmissions of fresh VoLTE packets but not for their retransmissions in case of failures. Hence, the retransmissions are handled through dynamic scheduling only. Hence, SPS can be activated in uplink and/or downlink and includes two parts: persistent scheduling for initial transmissions and dynamic scheduling for retransmissions (Dajie, 2007). Each UE is allocated PRBs where initial transmissions can be scheduled without PDCCH signaling.

If a first transmission fails, the eNodeB tries to dynamically schedule the corresponding HARQ retransmission by using control signaling Since VoLTE packets arrive (or sent) every 20 msec for/from a UE, SPS allocation consists of dedicated PRBs for a UE every 20 msec, *i.e*, a UE is allocated a fixed number of PRBs to send and/or receive its data in every 20th subframe. There are two stages to SPS allocation of resources (3GPP-TS 23.401, 2008) as shown in Figure 4.

Figure 4. Semi-Persistent scheduling in downlink

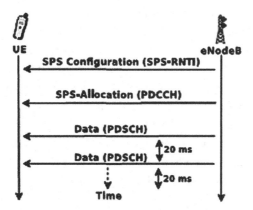

1. **Configuration Stage:** The eNodeB can configure the UE with SPS at any time but, typically this is done at the time of dedicated bearer establishment for the VoLTE service. Configuration of SPS doesn't mean that the UE can start using SPS grants/assignments.

2. **Activation Stage:** The eNodeB can activate SPS at any time using Downlink control information (DCI) in PDCCH signal which is monitored by the UE in every subframe. Once the activation is done through PDCCH, the UE starts receiving its data on the allocated PDSCH resources (PRBs) every 20 msec.

Power Saving-Semi Persistent Scheduler (PS-SPS)

PS-SPS intelligently modifies the resource allocation policy of traditional SPS for VoLTE traffic in the downlink of a LTE-A cell (Wali, 2015). It is based on the following observations that can be deduced from Eqn. 2. If k PRBs are used to transmit data in a TTI (subframe), the useful power component is $k \cdot P_{PRB}$. The power utilization factor can be defined as:

$$U = \frac{k \cdot P_{PRB}}{P_o + k \cdot \alpha \cdot P_{PRB}} \tag{3}$$

From the above Equation 3, the scheduler should maximize U in those subframes in which VoLTE packets are bound to be transmitted in order to minimize the power consumption of the eNodeB. This means that if a downlink transmission is going to happen in a subframe, then the scheduler should try to maximize the number of PRBs that are used for initial transmission of VoLTE packets. By doing so, the scheduler automatically is able to support active VoLTE calls using less number of subframes compared to SPS. This will in turn maximize the number of subframes in which the PA can be put to sleep mode. Hence, in PS-SPS, the objective is to maximize useful PRBs in those subframes in which VoLTE packets are bound to be scheduled. PS-SPS treats the downlink subframes as a sequence of cycles in time domain where each cycle consists of 20 subframes numbered 1-20 and runs the algorithm shown in flow chart 1 in Figure 5. Whenever a UE in *Voice_Listen* state (state in which the user is listening to voice from the other party) in a new call or for a UE which has returned back to *Voice_Listen* state from *Silence_Listen* state (state in which the user is hearing silence from the other party) in an ongoing call needs PRBs to be allocated in the downlink, beginning from subframe 1, the scheduler sequentially searches for the first subframe in the cycle which has free and sufficient PRBs and allocates those PRBs to the UE. This allocation is indicated to the UE through PDCCH. PS-SPS follows this rule every time PRBs have to be allocated. Because of this rule, all PRBs are allocated in a subframe before the next subframe in the cycle is considered for allocation by PS-SPS. This kind of resource allocation results in maximum PRB utilization for each subframe in which VoLTE traffic is scheduled. The scheduler handles the UEs in each subframe according to the order of states (or state transitions) as shown in the flowchart. For all states (or state transitions) except while persistently scheduling VoLTE packets to the UEs in *SPS_Allocated_Subframe* state (users who already have PRB allocations in that subframe), PDCCH is used.

Figure 6 shows an example of how SPS would dedicate PRB resources to 4 UEs in *Voice_Listen* state compared to traditional SPS and Figure 7 shows how PS-SPS would dedicate PRB resources to the same 4 UEs. It can be seen from Figure 7that PS-SPS dedicates all PRBs in the first two subframes in each cycle for the 4 UEs. For SPS, the dedicated PRBs might be spread randomly as shown in the Figure 5

Figure 5. PS-SPS algorithm

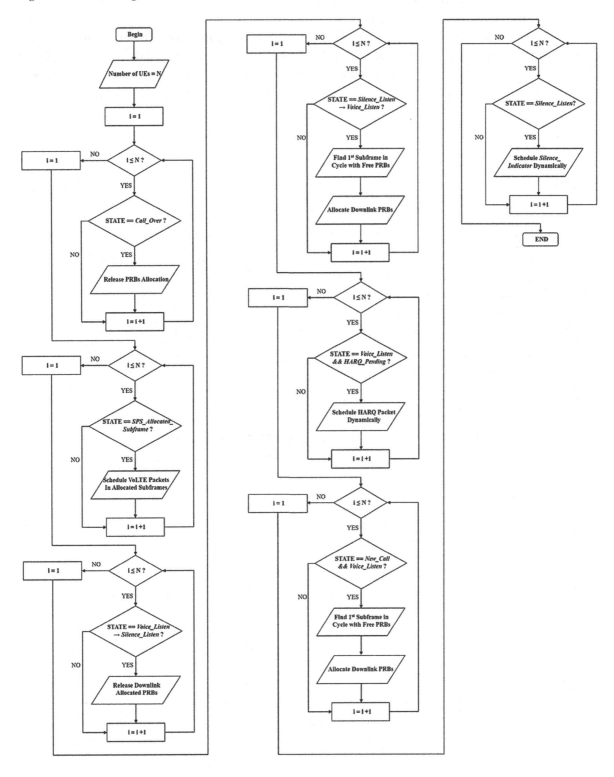

since SPS dedicates PRBs to the UEs in the first subframe in which it finds a sufficient number of them starting from the subframe in which the UEs move to *Voice_Listen* state.

The performance of PS-SPS compared to SPS can be seen in Figure 8 for a 10 MHz cell for the parameters shown in Table 1. The results are shown for 50 PRBs in the downlink for data scheduling and 4 PDCCH resources. For SPS also, the order in which the states are handled is the same as PS-SPS except while making new persistent PRB allocations. Unlike the PS-SPS, in SPS, allocations are made in the

Figure 6. SPS PRB allocation

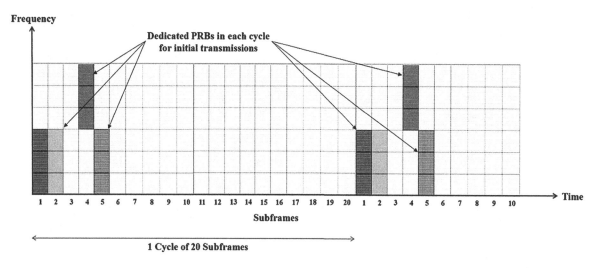

Figure 7. PS-SPS PRB allocation

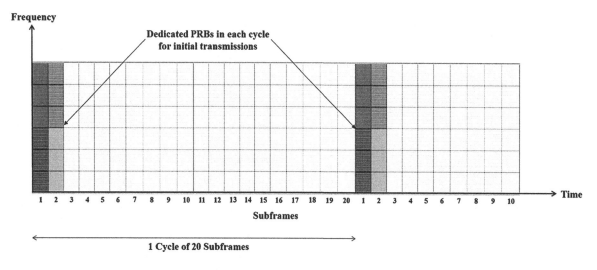

Table 1. Simulation parameters used to investigate power saving ability of PS-SPS compared to SPS

Parameter	Values
Number of Users in the cell	0-120 in steps of 20
Arrival Rates of Calls	0.1 calls/sec and 4.0 calls/sec.
Call Duration	Exponentially distributed with a mean of 30 seconds.
Voice Listen State Duration	Exponentially distributed with a mean of 2 seconds.
Silence Listen State Duration	Exponentially distributed with a mean of 2 seconds.
Size of SPS allocation	3 PRBs (40 bytes per voice packet for 12.2 kbps AMR codec).
Max. Transmissions allowed	3
Size of Silent Indicator	1 PRB
Duration of Simulation Run	10 Hours (36000000 subframes).
Power Considerations	P_o = 170 W, P_s = 10 W, P_v =275 W

current subframe if there are free PRBs available. Figure 8 shows the various results of the simulation in four plots with X-axis representing the number of VoLTE users in the cell in all the plots.

Plot 1 shows the percentage of the available PRBs that are used in both the schemes to support the VoLTE calls. It can be seen that the number of PRBs used are the same in both schemes. The PRB utilization per used subframe is shown in Plot 2. This is the average number of PRBs used per subframe for subframes in which data transmission happened. Clearly, PS-SPS provides larger values of PRB utilization compared to SPS.

Plot 3 of Figure 8 compares the percentage of subframes in which the PA could be put to sleep model. The plot shows that PS-SPS effects the PA sleep modes in a much larger fraction of the total number of subframes. In 70% of the subframes, for PS-SPS, the PA is putinto sleep mode as compared to only 20% in SPS when the arrival rate is 0.1 calls/sec with 120 VoLTE users in the cell. The gap reduces for arrival rate of 4.0 calls/sec as expected since most of the subframes start filling up with useful PRBs.

Plot 4 of Figure 8 shows the power consumption for both the schemes along the Y-axis and the percentage power saving of PS-SPS as compared to SPS for 120 VoLTE users for both call arrival rates. The power saving is calculated the ratio between the excess power consumed by SPS compared to PS-SPS and the power consumed by SPS. PS-SPS provides 60% power saving as compared to SPS for arrival rate of 0.1 calls/sec. The saving reduces from 60% to 12% for 120 VoLTE users making calls at a rate of 4.0 per second.

CONCLUSION

This chapter discussed three link level techniques that attempt to reduce the energy consumption of a LTE-A cell with intelligent MAC layer algorithms. Various network level, link level and component level techniques to reduce the energy consumption in a cellular network were discussed. After discussing the feasibility of link level techniques through sleep mode operations of the base stations, two link level techniques; MBSFN Subframes Insertion Method, Traffic Buffering and Shaping Method were presented. Finally, a power efficient resource allocation method for VoLTE traffic called as Power-

Figure 8. Performance comparison results for a 10 MHz cell

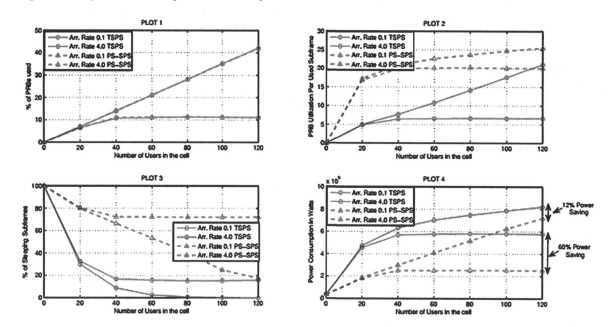

Saving Semi-Persistent Scheduler that inherits the ideas of the idea of traffic buffering and shaping was presented as a use case.

REFERENCES

Automatic Terminal Information Service (ATIS). (2012). *Report on Wireless Network Energy Efficiency*. Available online: http://www.atis.org/topsc/Docs/Deliverables/ATIS-I-0000033.pdf

Blume, O., Eckhardt, H., Klein, S., Kuehn, E., & Wajda, W. M. (2010). Energy savings in mobile networks based on adaptation to traffic statistics. *Bell Labs Tech. J.*, *15*(2), 7794. doi:10.1002/bltj.20442

Calvanese Strinati, E., & Greco, P. (2010). Green resource allocation for ofdma wireless cellular networks. In *Personal Indoor and Mobile Radio Communications (PIMRC)*. IEEE 21st International Symposium on. doi:10.1109/PIMRC.2010.5671817

Chen, T., Haesik, H., & Yang, Y. (2010). Energy efficiency metrics for green wireless communications. *Proceedings International Conference on Wireless Communications and Signal Processing (WCSP)*. doi:10.1109/WCSP.2010.5633634

Chen, Y., Farley, T., & Ye, N. (2004). Qos requirements of network applications on the internet. *Inf. Knowl. Syst. Manag.*, *4*, 5576. Available: http://portal.acm.org/citation. cfm?id=1234242.1234243

Conte, A. (2011). Cell wilting and blossoming for energy efficiency. *IEEE Wireless Communications*, *18*(5), 50-57.

Correia, L. M., Zeller, D., Blume, O., Ferling, D., Jading, Y., Godor, I., & van der Perre, L. et al. (2010). Challanges and enabling technologies for energy aware mobile radio networks. *IEEE Communications Magazine*, *48*(11), 6672. doi:10.1109/MCOM.2010.5621969

Dahlman, E. (2008). *3G evolution: HSPA and LTE for mobile broadband*. Academic Press.

Etoh, M., Ohya, T., & Nakayama, T. (2008). Energy consumption issues on mobile network systems. *Proceedings of International Symposium on Applications and the Internet (SAINT)*, 365-368. doi:10.1109/SAINT.2008.84

Forster, C., Dickie, I., Maile, G., Smith, H., & Crisp, M. (n.d.). *Understanding the Enviromental Impact of Communication Systems*. Ofcom Study Report. Available online: http://stakeholders.ofcom.org.uk/binaries/research/technology-research/environ.pdf

Frenger, P. (2011). Reducing Energy Consumption in LTE with Cell DTX. *IEEE 73rd Vehicular Technology Conference (VTC Spring)*, 1-5. doi:10.1109/VETECS.2011.5956235

3. GPP TS 23.401 V8.1.0. (2008). *General Packet Radio Service (GPRS) enhancements for Evolved Universal Terrestrial Radio Access Network (E-UTRAN) access*. 3GPP.

3. GPP TSG RAN WG1 Meeting #47, R1-063275. (2006). *Discussion on control signaling for persistent scheduling of VoIP*. Riga, Latvia: 3GPP.

3. GPP TSG RAN WG1 Meeting #47bis, R1-070098. (2007). *Discussion on control signaling for persistent scheduling of VoIP*. Sorrento, Italy: 3GPP.

Gupta & Calvanese Strinati. (2012). Base-Station Duty-Cycling and Traffic Buffering as a Means to Achieve Green Communications. *2012 IEEE Vehicular Technology Conference (VTC Fall)*.

Han, C., Harrold, T., Armour, S., Krikidis, I., Videv, S., Grant, P. M., & Hanzo, L. et al. (2011). Green radio: Radio techniques to enable energy-efficient wireless networks. *IEEE Communications Magazine*, *49*(6), 4654. doi:10.1109/MCOM.2011.5783984

Hasan, Z., Boostanimehr, H., & Bhargava, V. K. (2011, November). Green Cellular Networks, A Survey, Some Research Issuesand Challenges. *IEEE Communications Surveys and Tutorials*, *13*(4), 524–540. doi:10.1109/SURV.2011.092311.00031

Hirata, H., Totani, K., Maehata, T., Shimura, T., Take, M., Jurokawa, Y., & Hirata, Y. et al. (2010). *Development of high efficiency amplifier for cellular base stations*. SEI Tech. Rev.

Jiang, D., Wang, H., Malkamaki, E., & Tuomaala, E. (2007). Principle and Performance of Semi-Persistent Scheduling for VoIP in LTE System. *International Conference on Wireless Communications, Networking and Mobile Computing, WiCom 2007*, 2861 - 2864. doi:10.1109/WICOM.2007.710

Khan, F. (2009). *LTE for 4G Mobile Broadband Air Interface Technologies and Performance*. Cambridge University Press. doi:10.1017/CBO9780511810336

Lorincz, Garma, & Petrovic. (2012). Measurements and Modelling of Base Station Power Consumption under Real Traffic Loads. *Sensors, 12*, 4281-4310. doi:10.3390/s120404281

Oh, E., Krishnamachari, B., Liu, X., & Niu, Z. (2011). Toward dynamic energy-efficient operation of cellular network infrastructure. *IEEE Communications Magazine*, *49*(6), 5661. doi:10.1109/MCOM.2011.5783985

Pokhariyal, A., Kolding, T., & Mogensen, P. (2006). Performance of downlink frequency domain packet scheduling for the UTRAN long term evolution. *Personal, Indoor and Mobile Radio Communications, 2006 IEEE 17th International Symposium on*, 1-5. doi:10.1109/PIMRC.2006.254113

Roy, S. N. (2008). Energy logic: A road map to reducing energy consumption in telecommunications networks. In *Proceedings of Emerson Network Power*. IEEE 30th Telecommunications Energy Conference (INTELEC), San Diego, CA. doi:10.1109/INTLEC.2008.4664025

Wali, P., & Das, D. (2015). PS-SPS: Power saving-semi persistent schedulr for VoLTE in LTE-Advanced. *2015 IEEE International Conference on Electronics, Computing and Communication Technologies (CONECCT)*. doi:10.1109/CONECCT.2015.7383916

Zoican, S. (2008). The role of programmable digital signal processors (dsp) for 3 g mobile communication systems. *ACTA Tech.Napoc.*, *49*, 4956.

Chapter 7
User–Oriented Intercell Interference Coordination in Heterogeneous Networks (HetNets)

Zhi Liu
Waseda University, Japan

Xiaoyan Wang
Ibaraki University, Japan

Mianxiong Dong
Muroran Institute of Technology, Japan

Yusheng Ji
National Institute of Informatics, Japan

Hao Zhou
University of Science and Technology of China, China

Yoshiaki Tanaka
Waseda University, Japan

ABSTRACT

HetNet is a hot research topic in the next generation broadband wireless access network and mitigating the intercell interference could improve the system throughput. Users care whether their requested data rates can be satisfied or not the most. Hence a user-centric intercell interference coordination scheme (i.e. resource allocation scheme considering user request) is necessary. In this paper, at each specific subframe, when users have data requests, the corresponding base station first selects which user to serve based on each user's 'instant data rate', data rate request and capacity gained. Then given the users selected, a method is proposed to help choose which intercell interference coordination scheme to use in order to maximize the users' data rate satisfaction ratios. Intensive simulations are conducted and the results demonstrate that the proposed scheme achieves considerable gains over competing schemes in terms of the data rate satisfaction ratio and system capacity in Config.4b scenarios defined by 3GPP.

DOI: 10.4018/978-1-5225-2023-8.ch007

INTRODUCTION

Heterogeneous network (HetNet) has recently become a hot research topic of 3GPP Long Term Evolution-Advanced (LTE-A) and is one fundamental issue of the 4G and 5G cellular networks (Wang C. X., 2014) or the next generation broadband wireless access networks. HetNets are composed by deploying small cells such as picocells, femtocells, etc. besides macrocells to help offload macrocells, improve area coverage and provide high data rate transmission in 'hotspots' (Ghosh, 2010) (Lopez-Perez D. G., 2011) such as the sport center or shopping mall. Macrocell is the usual base station used in the cellular communication. A picocell is a small cellular base station that covers a small area such as offices, shopping center, metro station, etc. Femtocell is an even smaller, low-power cellular base station, which is mainly for use in home or small business office. Typically, the coverage of picocell is 200 meters or less and the coverage of femtocell is 10 meters or less.

Given multiple cells co-exist, how each user equipment (UE) selects the service cell is non-trivial. User association discusses how each UE selects the service cell, and the user association scheme can affect the system performance significantly. The cell selection is typically based on the measured reference signal received power (RSRP). And the cell, which provides the largest RSPR, will be the service cell for the corresponding user. While in HetNet, due to the transmission power difference between macrocell e-NB (i.e., base station) and picocell e-NB (10.3.0., 2011), users may connect to macrocell instead of picocell which has shorter path loss distance. To offload macrocell and mitigate uplink (UL) interference, range expansion is introduced (Okino, 2011) (Guvenc, 2011). The main idea is adding an offset to increase the picocell's coverage, hence the problems caused by power differences between cells in HetNets can be solved. Figure 1 illustrates one typical HetNet with region expansion, which is also the scenario we will discuss in this paper. Abbreviations MUE, PCUE, and PEUE denote macro user equipment, picocell center user equipment, and picocell range expanded region user equipment, respectively. In the scenario shown in Figure 1, PEUE is the user in the expanded region, and this user receives stronger signal form macro-eNB but is served by the pico-eNB. According to the different requirements, more small base stations can be added in this scenario.

Figure 1. Illustration of the HetNet with one macro-eNB and pico-eNB

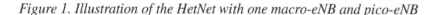

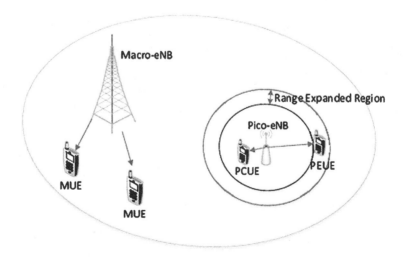

After each base station selects the users to serve, one base station's users can overhear the signals from other base stations as well, since the small cell and macrocell are operated at the same frequency. But these signals are not what they need and we call these signals the intercell interference. The intercell interference greatly degrades the overall system performance. Diminishing the intercell interference could improve the system throughput and there are related researches with the objective to reduce the intercell interference. Almost blank subframe (ABS (Wang Y. &., 2012, May)) and coordinated multipoint (CoMP (Hoydis, 2011, June) (Barbieri, 2012)) are two state-of-the-art methods for intercell interference coordination.

ABS is proposed in enhanced intercell interference coordination (eICIC) by 3GPP to handle interference in 3GPP Release 10 (Wang Y. &., 2012, May). The eICIC is an enhanced version of the traditional intercell interference coordination (ICIC). The eICIC allows macrocell to send an ABS subframe at a certain time to avoid interference in low power cells (Wang Y. &., 2012, May) (Lopez-Perez D. G., 2012). When ABS is used, macro-eNB does not send any data signals but critical system information and reference signals with very low power. Given no data signals are sent, the interference to the small cell users are avoided. Then pico-eNB users can receive data from pico-eNB during ABS subframes and receive almost nothing from macro-eNB, which means intercell interference could be regarded as zero and picocells' throughput is improved with the sacrifice of macrocells' throughput. CoMP is a popular technology applied to make different macro-eNBs cooperating in multi-cell scenarios and can be used in HetNets for intercell interference elimination (Hoydis, 2011, June) (Barbieri, 2012). Macro-eNB is always more powerful than pico-eNB and other small nodes, macro-eNB is then in charge of collecting the shared information, calculating the coordinated beamforming matrix, and sending the coordinated beamforming matrix to the cooperating nodes.

How to rely on the ABS and CoMP for the interference coordination becomes vital and there are many related researches about the intercell interference coordination. For example, (Luo, 2013) investigated both the ABS and CoMP for PEUEs, and proposed to choose ABS or CoMP for the selected users at each subframe using the capacity as the selection criteria to maximize the total system throughput, i.e. at each specific subframe, the system first selects the users to serve and then chooses to use the interference coordination method, which leads to the largest system capacity. But there are some problems with these existing schemes:

1. The intercell interference between macro-eNB and PCUEs is assumed to be small, therefore the intercell interference coordination when MUEs and PCUEs are served is usually ignored in literature.
2. Users' data rate requirements, which directly affect the quality of users' experience (QoE), are usually not considered.
3. For a specific network subframe, how to decide which users to serve based on the users' instant data rates is non-trivial since instant data rates could vary according to the interference coordination schemes selected. How this could be done has not been solved in any formal way.

Specifically, different from PEUEs, PCUEs receive stronger signal from picocell than macrocell, the intercell interference between macro-eNB and PCUEs is not that large. Then this interference is usually not considered (e.g. this interference is not considered in (Luo, 2013)), but performing the interference coordination for PCUEs and macro-eNB users can help improve the system performance as shown in (Liu Z. &., 2014). Proportional fairness is a widely used scheduling algorithm, which tries to maximize the total while at the same time allows all users enjoy at least a minimal level of service. (Luo, 2013) and (Liu Z. &., 2014) used the proportional fairness to select which users to serve, but they are proportional to the number of slots used without considering the instant data rate and users' data rate requests, hence the results could be improved. Moreover, different users have different data rate requirements, e.g. video users (Liu Z. C., Multiple description coding and recovery of free viewpoint video for wireless multi-path streaming, 2015) and the users surfing the internet pages have quite different data rate demands. The provided data rates directly affect the users' quality of experience, and users care whether their requests can be satisfied or not the most. The two state-of-the-art intercell interference coordination methods ABS and CoMP provide users with different throughput. Specifically, both pico-eNB user and MUE can receive data from the corresponding base station when CoMP is applied. If macro-eNB sends ABS subframes, pico-eNB user's capacity is larger compared with the throughput gained when macro-eNB and pico-eNB perform CoMP, but macro-eNB user receives nothing in this case. Most of the existing intercell interference coordination schemes do not take the users' data rate requirements into consideration. How to maximize the ratio of each user's data rate achieved to her/his corresponding requested data rate is not obvious. (Liu Z. &., 2014) provided a greedy algorithm to maximize the users' satisfaction ratios, and the satisfaction ratio is defined as the ratio of users' actual received data rates to their data rate requests. The satisfaction ratio is bounded by 1.

In this book chapter, we address these three mentioned problems at the same time and reallocate the network resource co-considering users' data rate requests. We select the users to serve based on their 'instant data rates' and consider the data rate requirements during all the subframes including when the picocell central users are served. Users' data rate requests are taken into consideration when the intercell interference coordination schemes are selected. We formulate this into an optimization problem, i.e. maximize the ratio of each user's achieved data rate to her/his requested data rate and propose a method to solve this problem. Intensive simulations are conducted and the results demonstrate that our proposed scheme achieves considerable gains over competing schemes in terms of the data rate satisfaction ratio in Config.4b scenarios defined by 3GPP.

The rest of this book chapter is organized as follows. Related Work section introduces the related work in the field of intercell interference coordination including the development of the ABS, CoMP, the intercell interference coordination and user centric intercell interference coordination. The HetNet system applied in this paper is introduced in the System Section and how to calculate the channel capacity in different situations is explained as well in this section. How we formulate this into an optimization problem and how to solve the optimization problem are presented in the Formulation Section. The simulation results are shown in the Results Section. This paper is concluded in the Conclusion and Future Work Section with some discussions on the future work.

RELATED WORK

This related work section is divided into three parts. The first part introduces the two state-of-the-art interference coordination schemes ABS and CoMP. The second part discusses the state-of-the-art intercell interference coordination methods and the user-centric intercell interference coordination scheme is introduced in the third part. The last part introduces the existing user centric scheduling algorithm and the difference with our paper is mentioned.

ABS and CoMP

In the next generation cellular system, better transmission capabilities are required in 'hotspots', where people gather in some area (e.g. shopping mall or sports center) during specific time. HetNet is one possible solution for this problem, since we can deploy small cells such as picocells, femtocells, etc. besides macrocells to help offload macrocells, improve area coverage and provide high data rate transmission in hotspots. This solution has already been used and is proven to be effective. Hence HetNet has recently become a hot research topic of 3GPP LTE-A and is one fundamental issue of the 4G and 5G cellular networks (Wang C. X., 2014) or the next generation broadband wireless access networks.

Given the small cells reuse the macrocell's frequency, all the users in the coverage area can overhear all the base stations' signal. But each user is supposed to receive the signal from the corresponding base station only and all the signal from other base station is noise (we name the signal as interference). These interference significantly degrades the system performance and how to eliminate these interference becomes a critical issue in HetNet researches.

There are two state-of-the-art intercell interference coordination schemes in literature: ABS and CoMP. ABS is proposed in eICIC by 3GPP to handle interference in 3GPP Release 10 (Wang Y. &., 2012, May). The eICIC is an enhanced version of the traditional ICIC. The eICIC allows macrocell to send an ABS subframe at a certain time to avoid interference in low power cells (Wang Y. &., 2012, May) (Lopez-Perez D. G., 2012). In our scenario, when ABS is used, macro-eNB does not send any data signals but critical system information and reference signals with very low power. Given no data signals are sent, the interference to the small cell users is avoided. Then pico-eNB users can receive data from pico-eNB during ABS subframes and receive almost nothing from macro-eNB, which means intercell interference could be regarded as zero and picocells' throughput is improved with the sacrifice of macrocells' throughput (who is supposed to work for most of the time since the power of the macrocell is the largest in the HetNets).

Macrocells are connected to picocells and other low power cells through an operating and management (OAM) or X2 interface (Access, 2010). The information messages are exchanged to facilitate this coordination between cells. Therefore CoMP, which is a popular technology applied to make different macro-eNBs cooperate in multi-cell scenarios, could be used in HetNets for intercell interference elimination (Hoydis, 2011, June) (Barbieri, 2012). Macro-eNB is always more powerful than pico-eNB and other small nodes, macro-eNB is then in charge of collecting the shared information, calculating the coordinated beamforming matrix, and sending the coordinated beamforming matrix to cooperating nodes. However, if the signal-to-interference-plus-noise ratio (SINR) is low, the performance of CoMP is not that good. Moreover, CoMP has large signaling overhead, high computational complexity, and the performance is highly related with the accuracy of the channel knowledge. In this book chapter, we assume the information needed for CoMP could be obtained in time.

Intercell Interference Coordination

Most of the existing work dedicate to solve how to coordinate the intercell interference during the period when small cells' edge users are served and use the system throughput as the only selection criteria, which is one important factor to evaluate the system performance (Luo, 2013) (Li Y. N., 2012) (López-Pérez, 2011) (Deb, 2014) (Kosta, 2013) (Liu A. L., 2014) (Zhou, 2015) (Moon, 2014) (Wang J. S., 2012) (Adhikary, 2015).

Specifically, (Li Y. N., 2012) provided an overview of eICIC schemes in the standardization process of LTE-A and CoMP, and introduced a novel scheme combining the dynamic CoMP and semi-static eICIC coordination under super-cell heterogeneous network deployment. Simulations were conducted and better performances were shown compared with state-of-the-art schemes. (López-Pérez, 2011) focused on the range expansion. The range expansion was introduced to increase the pico-cell's affiliated users with the objective to offload macrocell and mitigate uplink (UL) interference. A novel cooperative macro-eNB/pico-eNB scheduling approach was proposed to mitigate the macrocell downlink (DL) interference towards PEUEs. (Deb, 2014) proposed a novel algorithm to jointly determine the amount of radio resources that the macrocells should allocate to picocells, and the association rules that help decide the user association. This algorithm accounts the network topology, traffic load and the interference map between the macrocell and the picocells. This scheme provided very good performance, but CoMP was not applied in this scheme. (Kosta, 2013) overviewed the recent developments of the promising intercell interference mitigation techniques since the intercell interference significantly degrades the system performance. The intercell interference mitigation is potential to avoid the intercell interference through intercell interference coordination. The intercell interference coordination problem was formulated and solved using optimization methods in a multi-cell OFDMA-based system. Some research directions in simplifying the problem and associated challenges were given. The main trend of the intercell interference coordination techniques was introduced. The methods introduced in this paper could also be applied in any typical multi-cellular environment based on OFDMA technology. (Liu A. L., 2014) proposed a two timescale hierarchical radio resource management (RRM) scheme for HetNet with dynamic resource block (similar idea with ABS) control, including the long term controls and short term controls. The long term controls are adaptive to the large scale fading at a RRM server for co-Tier and cross-Tier interference control. The short term control (user scheduling) is adaptive to the local channel state information at each BS to exploit the multi-user diversity. The authors exploited the sparsity in the interference graph of the HetNet topology, derived structural properties for the optimal almost blank resource block control, and proposed a two timescale alternative optimization solution, which was asymptotically optimal at high SNR and with low complexity for user scheduling and almost blank resource block control. (Zhou, 2015) studied the scalable video multicast over HetNet with range expansion and ABS scheme. By resource allocation and user association, an optimization problem was raised and solved by decoupling this problem into two problems. The simulation results showed that the proposed scheme can outperform the state of the art competing schemes greatly. In (Moon, 2014), a cell selection and interference management scheme for the HetNet scenario with both the macrocell and picocell (considering the LTE-A downlink channel) was proposed. In this scheme, SINR decided the selection and the cell expansion range varied with different offset value. The intercell interference was managed using ABS in the time domain. The flexible ABS density further increased the spectrum efficiency and the simulation results showed that the proposed scheme can provide better results. (Wang J. S., 2012) studied the semi-static intercell interference coordination and dynamic intercell interference coordination methods. The joint decision and multiple feedback schemes were proposed with the aim to enhance the system performance by appropriate selection of normal/mute transmitting status and accurate scheduling for dynamic intercell interference coordination. The proposed scheme achieved better average performance at the system level and for edge users compared with the semi-static ICIC and conventional dynamic ICIC methods. (Adhikary, 2015) considered the hotspots in the heterogeneous cellular network. A large number of antennas were assumed at the macrocell (massive-MIMO), and this could help concentrate its transmission energy in the direction of hotspots it serves for the interference coordination. The authors also developed three low-complexity strategies for explicit intertier interference coordination. While the two strategies involved turning OFF small cells intelligently, the last one offloaded macrocell traffic to small cells thereby providing significant throughput gains. The analysis in this paper provided insights into where exactly the deployment of small cells provided most benefits for a given performance metric, e.g., uniform vs. cell-interior vs. cell-edge.

User-Centric Intercell Interference Coordination

Individual user's data rate requirement has not been considered in these works, but whether the user's data rate requirement can be satisfied or not directly affects the user's QoS or QoE, especially for users who are enjoying the video streaming services (Liu Z. F., 2014) (Liu Z. C., 2013) (Liu Z. C., Multiple description coding of free viewpoint video for multi-path network streaming., 2012). (Liu Z. F., 2014) (Liu Z. C., 2013) showed that the higher data rate leads to better average received video quality and the low data rate degrades the QoS and QoE. Moreover, the interference between picocell and macrocell users and the interference between macrocell and picocell central users are assumed to be small and therefore not considered, but actually the system capacity could be improved greatly when this interference is considered instead of ignored. (Liu Z. &., 2014), which is an extension of (Luo, 2013), proposed an algorithm to maximize the users' data rate satisfaction ratio in HetNet leveraging on the two existing intercell interference coordination schemes ABS and CoMP. As far as the authors understand, this is the first work on the intercell interference coordination from the standing point of optimizing users' data rate requests instead of using the total system capacity as the objective function. However, (Luo, 2013) and (Liu Z. &., 2014) chose the number of used subframes as the weight of the proportional fairness for the user selection without considering the instant data rate. Moreover, these two paper assumed there was 'full queue,' i.e. all the users were requesting data during each subframe.

Other user-oriented or user-centric approaches for the interference coordination include (Wu, 2015) (Fan, 2007) (Li C. Z., 2014) (Li C. Z., 2015). These works approach the intercell interference coordination problem considering the users' data rate requests and can better satisfy the users. Specifically, (Wu, 2015) proposed a user-centric interference nulling (IN) scheme in downlink two-tier HetNets to improve network performance by improving each user's SIR considering three parameters when the algorithm is designed: the maximum degree of freedom for IN, and the IN thresholds for the macrocell and picocell users, respectively. The performance could be observed by the analytical results. (Fan, 2007) first made sure that edge users in neighbor cells are not interfered by each other. The frequency resources were then allocated based on edge users' ratio. The rest resources can be allocated to the cell-center users with two levels of power. The simulation results showed that this proposed algorithm could improve the whole system performance, especially the throughput performance of the edge users. (Li C. Z., 2014) proposed a novel intercell interference coordination method from the users' point of view (i.e. user centric intercell interference coordination). In the discussed HetNet, the mobile user requested some neighboring BSs for interference avoidance (ABS), which was based on the relative distance between the home BS and the interfering BSs, called as the interference coordination (IC) range. Hence the most critical interfering sources for each user could be suppressed and the edge users could also enjoy high quality network channels. The simulations results showed that the proposed scheme provides a significant performance gain compared with other existing related method. (Li C. Z., 2015) is an extension of (Li C. Z., 2014). In (Li C. Z., 2015), the authors proposed an interference nulling strategy (or the user-centric interference nulling). In this scheme, the dominant interfering BS for each user was identified by comparing the interference power with the received information signal power, and this identification could help improve the performance greatly. The results showed that this scheme can achieve quite promising results. The low implementation complexity user centric approach could be easily applied to other interference management methods that were performed in the time or frequency domain.

This book chapter is an extension of (Liu Z. &., 2014), and the joint user selection (among all the users who have data transmission requirements) based on the 'instant data rate' and the data rate requests, and the intercell interference coordination (based on the ABS and CoMP) are conducted. This distinguishes this book chapter from our previous work and the state-of-the-art schemes.

User-Centric Scheduling Algorithms

The scheduling method can be classified into long-term scheduling, medium-term scheduling and short-term scheduling in terms of the scheduling period. There are also many classical scheduling algorithms such as first in first out (FIFO), earliest deadline first, shortest remaining time, fixed priority pre-emptive scheduling. Each leads to different performances and has the proper application scenario. For example, the simplest scheduling method FIFO queues the tasks in the order that they arrive at the ready queue and processes these tasks accordingly. FIFO is commonly used for a task queue.

User-centric approaches have many advantages since they can better satisfy users and provide better QoS or QoE. Hence there are many researches in this field. However, these user-centric methods mainly focus on specific area or application. These methods cannot be applied in other scenarios directly due to different constraints, utility function, etc. For example, (Xu, 2013) proposed a user-centric QoS-driven video streaming in vehicular ad hoc network and the proposed algorithm was based on the characters of the vehicular ad hoc network. This proposed method cannot be applied in the HetNet directly.

In the normal HetNet interference coordination, users are scheduled using the proportional fairness scheduling or round robin scheduler. Then the interference coordination methods are applied to the selected users' pairs as introduced in the previous subsection. This paper is different from these schemes by jointly selecting the users based on the 'instant data rate' and the data rate requests, and conducting the intercell interference coordination (based on the ABS and CoMP).

SYSTEM

In this section, we overview the system model, introduce the subframe model of ABS scheme and discuss how to calculate the capacity.

System Model

User association of HetNets decides how UEs select the service cell and user association significantly affects the overall system performance. Cell selection is typically based on the measured RSRP, i.e. each user connects to the cell which provides the largest RSRP. Due to the large difference between macro-eNB and pico-eNB's transmission power, users may connect to macrocell instead of picocell which has shorter path loss distance. Therefore the traffic load will be unevenly distributed in this scenario, thus overloading macrocells. Moreover, MUEs near pico-eNB interfere with pico-eNB in the UL and are interfered by pico-eNB in the DL. Furthermore, when data are transmitted in the UL, these macrocell users would require less power if they are served by picocell due to lower path loss. Therefore seeking to be served by the cell, which can provide the strongest DL RSRP, may not be the best strategy, and more proper solution needs to be proposed.

Range expansion is one feasible approach to solve this problem, in which an offset RE is added to pico-eNB's RSRP to increase its coverage. Specifically, pico-eNB will serve the user whose RSRP satisfies $RSRP_{macro} \leq RSRP_{pico} + RE$, where $RSRP_{macro}$ and $RSRP_{pico}$ denote macrocell and picocell's RSRP, respectively. By range expansion, users in range expanded region will be served by pico-eNB although $RSRP_{macro} > RSRP_{pico}$. This helps offload macrocells and mitigate UL interference, hence the overall network performance can be improved. The inherent problem is that the users in the expanded range suffer from the intercell interference, since they receive stronger signal from the macrocell but are served by the picocell. In another word, the users in the expanded region suffer from the low quality channels and this significantly degrades the system performance.

Figure 1 illustrates the HetNet system applied in this paper. In this discussed system, there are a total of two users, one macrocell and one picocell. MUEs, PCUEs, PEUEs are uniformly distributed within the macrocell coverage area, picocell central coverage area (excluding the expanded region), and picocell expanded coverage area, respectively. MUEs receive stronger signal from macrocell, PCUEs receive stronger signal from picocell. PEUEs receive stronger signal from macrocell and are served by the picocell. However, the density of each area can be different, e.g. the hotspots may have more users compared with other area. We use M, PC and PE to denote the user set of the macrocell users, picocell central users and picocell edge users, respectively.

ABS Frame Model

3GPP proposes the ABS to eliminate the interference between PEUEs and macro-eNB. Figure 2 shows the frame model of the ABS scheme.

As illustrated in Figure 2, the network subframes on the pico-side are divided into MUE/PCUE and PEUE subframes. The ratio of the number of PEUE subframes to the number of MUE/PCUE subframes is 1/3 (Luo, 2013) (Liu Z. &., 2014). PEUEs are scheduled and served in the PEUE subframes and PCUEs

Figure 2. Illustration of ABS frame model

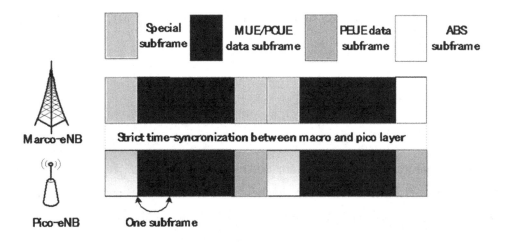

are scheduled and served in the MUE/PCUE subframes. When PEUEs are served by the picocell, macro-eNB will correspondingly transmit ABS subframes to avoid interfering PEUEs if ABS scheme is adapted.

This paper uses the same frame model, i.e. PCUEs are served in MUE/PCUE subframes and PEUEs are served in PEUE subframes. During each subframe, which macrocell user and picocell user will be selected to serve by the corresponding base station, is introduced in the FORMULATION Section.

Capacity Calculation

In this section, we introduce how to calculate the corresponding capacity when Pico-eNB serves PCUEs in MUE/PCUE subframes and PEUEs in PEUE subframes, respectively.

MUE/PCUE Subframes

When macro-eNB chooses to send ABS subframes, PCUEs can receive data from pico-eNB and receive almost nothing from macro-eNB. This means the intercell interference is mitigated and picocell's throughput is improved. However, macrocell's throughput is reduced in this case since no data is transmitted by the macro-eNB. Similarly, when pico-eNB sends ABS subframes, pico-eNB user does not receive data from the pico-eNB and MUE could be served without intercell interference. When CoMP is used, both MUE and PCUE can receive data from the corresponding base station.

If macro-eNB sends an ABS subframe to avoid interference, PCUE k's capacity could be written as follows:

$$C_k^{ABS,M} = B_{P.k} \log_2 \left(1 + \frac{P_p \left\| H_{P,P,k} \right\|_F^2}{N_0} \right)$$

where $B_{P.k}$ represents the bandwidth used in the transmission from pico-eNB to PCUE k. P_p denotes the transmission power of the pico-eNB, N_0 is the noise and $H_{P,P,k}$ stands for the channel between the pico-eNB and PCUE k. How to calculate these terms could refer to (Luo, 2013) and the Appendix. In $H_{P,P,k}$, the first P means pico-eNB and the second P indicates k is PCUE.

Similarly, if pico-eNB sends an ABS subframe, the capacity of the ith MUE could be written as follows:

$$C_i^{ABS,PC} = B_{M,i} \log_2 \left(1 + \frac{P_M \left\| H_{M,M,i} \right\|_F^2}{N_0} \right)$$

where $B_{M,i}$ denotes the transmission bandwidth used by the macro-eNB, P_M represents the transmission power of macro-eNB. $H_{M,M,i}$ represents the channel between macro-eNB and MUE i. In $H_{M,M,i}$, the first M stands for macro-eNB and the second M indicates that i is MUE.

Macro-eNB and pico-eNB cooperate and send coordinated beamforming signals to the scheduled i^{th} MUE and k^{th} PCUE if CoMP is applied. We use F to denote the coordinated beamforming matrix, and F_1, F_2 is the beamforming matrix for the scheduled MUE and scheduled PCUE, respectively. $F_{1,1}$ is part of the beamforming matrix for scheduled MUE and it is used for beamforming at the macro-eNB. The remaining $F_{1,2}$ would be used on the pico-eNB side. How to calculate F and F_1, F_2 is shown in the Appendix.

How to calculate MUE and PCUE's SINR is shown in the following equations:

$$SNIR_{M,i} = \frac{\left| \sqrt{P_M} H_{M,M,i} F_{1,1} + \sqrt{P_P} H_{P,M,i} F_{1,2} \right|_F^2}{N_0 + \left| \sqrt{P_M} H_{M,M,i} F_{2,1} + \sqrt{P_P} H_{P,M,i} F_{2,2} \right|_F^2}$$

$$SNIR_{P,k} = \frac{\left| \sqrt{P_M} H_{M,P,k} F_{2,1} + \sqrt{P_P} H_{P,p,k} F_{2,2} \right|_F^2}{N_0 + \left| \sqrt{P_M} H_{M,P,k} F_{1,1} + \sqrt{P_P} H_{P,P,k} F_{1,2} \right|_F^2}$$

In both equations, the channel between macro-eNB and PCUE k and the channel between pico-eNB and MUE i are denoted as $H_{M,P,k}$ and $H_{P,M,i}$, respectively. The system capacity gained by MUE i using CoMP is

$$C_i^{COMP} = B_{M,i} \log_2 \left(1 + SNIR_{M,i} \right)$$

The PCUE k's capacity when CoMP is used is as follows:

$$C_k^{COMP} = B_{P,k} \log_2 \left(1 + SNIR_{P,k} \right)$$

PEUE Subframes

PEUEs are served by pico-eNB during PEUE subframes. The capacities of PEUEs and MUEs could be calculated similarly as introduced in the previous section.

When macro-eNB chooses to transmit an ABS subframe to mitigate the intercell interference, the capacity of PEUE j can be calculated as follows:

$$C_j^{ABS,M} = B_{P,j} \log_2 \left(1 + \frac{P_p \left\| H_{P,P,j} \right\|_F^2}{N_0} \right)$$

Similarly, if pico-eNB transmits an ABS subframe, MUE i's capacity can be calculated as follows:

$$C_i^{ABS,PC} = B_{M,i} \log_2 \left(1 + \frac{P_M \left\| H_{M,M,i} \right\|_F^2}{N_0} \right)$$

Macro-eNB and pico-eNB cooperate and send coordinated beamforming signals to the scheduled i^{th} MUE and j^{th} PEUE when CoMP is used. Then the capacity gained by MUE i is

$$C_i^{COMP} = B_{M,i} \log_2 \left(1 + SNIR_{M,i} \right)$$

Similarly, PEUE j's capacity can be calculated as follows:

$$C_j^{COMP} = B_{P,j} \log_2 \left(1 + SNIR_{P,j} \right)$$

Please note that how to calculate $SNIR_{M,i}$ and $SNIR_{P,j}$ could be calculated the same as in MUE/PCUE subframes.

Forumulation

In this section, we first introduce how we select which users to serve based on the instant data rate and the data rate requests. Then we formulate the intercell interference coordination problem into an optimization problem addressing all these issues mentioned before. In another word, we would like to maximize each user's ratio of the data rate gained to her/his requested data rate, by taking the individual user's data rate requirement and the intercell interference when MUEs and PCUEs are served into consideration in the algorithm design. A method is proposed thereafter to help decide which intercell interference coordination scheme should be used.

This proposed method includes two steps: the first step is user selection, which helps each base station select users according to the users' instant data rate and the user's data rate request. Then after the users are selected, the interference coordination scheme is selected as introduced at the end of this section.

User Selection

Let d_i denotes user i's requested data rate, with $i \in M$ or $i \in PC$ or $i \in PE$, which means i could be a macrocell user, or picocell central user or picocell edge user. After the base station collects the data rate requests, at the MUE/PCUE subframe t, macro-eNB needs to pick up a macrocell user $i(i \in M)$ and pico-eNB needs to pick up a picocell central user $j\left(j \in PC\right)$ to serve. The way to select the user is by calculating the weight parameter as shown in the following equation and the user with the largest weight value is then selected.

$$w_i = \frac{\left(C_{i,t}^{ABC,PC}\right)^{\beta}}{d_i^{\alpha} h_{i,t}^{\gamma}}$$

In the above equation, ą, ß, and ϒ are three different constant parameters. $C_{i,t}^{ABC,PC}$ denotes the instant data rate of user i at subframe t when picocell sends an ABS subframe[1], which can be calculated as introduced in the SYSTEM Section. $h_{i,t}$ denotes the historical data volume received from the beginning to subframe t. This equation means that the user who has higher instant data rate, larger data rate request or smaller capacity gained up to that subframe will have the priority to use that network subframe. Then user i with the highest weight parameter will be selected to be served. If i is served at subframe t, we assign a label $\beta_{i,t} = 1$. This represents that during subframe t the corresponding base station will serve user i, otherwise $\beta_{i,t} = 0$. For picocell user $j\left(j \in PC\right)$, we can calculate his/her weight value w_j similarly and the user with the largest weight will then be selected.

Similarly, at MUE/PEUE subframe t, macro-eNB needs to pick up a macrocell user and pico-eNB needs to pick up a picocell edge user to serve. The way to select the users is the same as the method for the MUE/PCUE subframes, i.e. select the user who has the largest weight value. The weight calculation method is the same.

Objective Function

Assume user i's capacity gained is $c_{i,j}$ during subframe j and the window size we consider in this paper is T subframes in total. The objective is to maximize the users' average data rate satisfaction ratio. Therefore we can write the objective function as follows:

$$\max \sum_{i}^{K} \frac{\min\left(1, \frac{\sum_{t=1}^{T} \beta_{i,t} c_{i,t}}{T * d_i}\right)}{K}$$

In the above equation, $\frac{\sum_{t=1}^{T} \beta_{i,t} c_{i,t}}{T}$ calculates user 's achieved data rate, and d_i is the data rate requested. Then $\min\left(1, \frac{\sum_{t=1}^{T} \beta_{i,t} c_{i,t}}{T * d_i}\right)$ indicates user i's satisfaction ratio. Different interference coordination schemes can lead to different data rates, therefore the value of the objective function is affected and can be optimized.

Interference Coordination Scheme

We assume macrocell user $i\left(i \in M\right)$, and picocell user $j\left(j \in PC\right)$ or $j\left(j \in PE\right)$ are served. For the interference coordination, there are three possible choices: macro-eNB sends ABS subframes, pico-eNB sends ABS subframes, or macro-eNB and pico-eNB perform CoMP. Similarly with (Liu Z. &., 2014), a greedy algorithm is used to optimize the objective function, and the main idea is to select the interference coordination scheme that can contribute more to the objective.

Without loss of generality, we assume during current subframe T', MUE $i\left(i \in M\right)$ and pico-eNB user $j\left(j \in PC\right)$ or $j\left(j \in PE\right)$ are scheduled and served by the macro-eNB and pico-eNB, respectively. $\sum_{t=1}^{T'-1}\beta_{i,t}c_{i,t}$ indicates user i's total data received from the beginning to time T'. Then we compare

$$\min\left(1, \frac{\sum_{t=1}^{T'-1}\beta_{i,t}c_{i,t} + C_{i,T'}^{COMP}}{T * d_i}\right) + \min\left(1, \frac{\sum_{t=1}^{T'-1}\beta_{j,t}c_{j,t} + C_{j,T'}^{COMP}}{T * d_i}\right)$$

and

$$\min\left(1, \frac{\sum_{t=1}^{T'-1}\beta_{j,t}c_{j,t} + C_{j,T'}^{ABS,M}}{T * d_j}\right),$$

which represent the ratio increase when macro-eNB and pico-eNB perform CoMP, and the ratio increase when macro-eNB sends an ABS subframe, respectively. The corresponding intercell interference coordination scheme, which leads to larger ratio increase, will then be selected.

Since the complexity of the user selection is linear to the size of the user set and the interference coordination choices for each user pair are limited by the possible choices, the complexity of the proposed scheme is therefore trivial.

RESULTS

We introduce the simulation setup and the proposed method's performance in this section.

Simulation Setup

To evaluate the performance, the DL of a LTE-A HetNet is simulated. The spatial channel model extended (SCME), which is designed for multiple-input and multiple-output (MIMO) research in LTE-A and proposed by the 3GPP working group in 2010, is employed. The bandwidth used by macro-eNB ($B_{M,i}$), pico-eNB ($B_{P,k}, B_{P,j}$) is the same, i.e. 10MHz. The transmission period is divided into three parts; special subframes, MUE/PCUE subframes and PEUE subframes, which is the same as ABS model as shown in the SYSTEM Section. The configuration for UEs' placements used is defined by

3GPP in configuration 4b (Access, 2010). Two thirds of the UEs are distributed within a circular area as hotspot users. The center of the circular area is the pico-eNB and radius is 40 meters. We assume there is a wall 40 meters from the pico-eNB, 10dB penalty will be added to the path loss if the signal needs to cross the wall. The detailed simulation parameters are listed in Table 1. The simulation environment is built based on MATLAB, using the PC with Intel Core i5-4460 CPU and 8GB RAM.

Simulation Results

We compare our proposed scheme, which is named 'proposed', with 'user-centric' and 'capacity-centric' in the experiments. 'capacity-centric' was proposed in (Luo, 2013), and it picks up the ABS or CoMP as the intercell interference coordination scheme at each specific subframe using the system throughput as the selection criteria for PEUEs only. 'capacity-centric' does not consider the intercell interference when the PCUEs are severed. 'user-centric' is the scheme proposed in (Liu Z. &., 2014), which targets to maximize the users' satisfaction ratios. However, scheduler used in (Liu Z. &., 2014) is based on the number of subframes allocated during the window size without considering the user data rate and the instant channel quality. We run the experiments 30 times for each set of network parameters and the results are the average.

We set ą=1, ß=1, ϒ=1 and the corresponding performances in terms of the average ratios of each user' capacity to her/his data rate requirement and the total system throughput gained are shown in Figure 3 and Figure 4, respectively. The requested data rates here are assumed to follow normal distribution with mean to be 0.19 Mbps and standard deviation to be 0.1.

Table 1. Simulation parameters

Parameter	Value
System	2GHz carrier, 10 MHz bandwidth
Cellular layout	Hexagonal, 7 eNodeBs, 3 sectors per eNodeB
Duplex technique	TDD
Inter-site distance	500m
Antennas	Macro-eNB: 2 Tx; Pico-eNB: 2 Tx; UE: 2 Rx
Antenna configuration	Macro-eNB: 15 dBi antenna gain, sectorized Pico-eNB: 5 dBi antenna gain, Omni UE: 0 dBi antenna gain, Omni
Range extension offset	From 2 to 20 dB
Number of UEs	120 per cell
Placement of UEs	Configuration 4b: 2/3 clusters Configuration 1: uniform
Traffic model	Full buffer, full load
Transmitting power	Transmitting power
Transmitting power	-174 dBm/Hz
Noise figure at UE	9 dB
Channel model	SCME
Pathloss model	Macro: PL=128.1+37.6lg(R), R in km Pico: PL=140.7+36.7lg(R), R in km

Note: The full buffer, full load traffic model is used for the purpose of comparison, but our scheme also works in other cases.

In Figure 3, the x-axis stands for the range extension value RE and y-axis is the average satisfaction ratio. We could observe that the 'user-centric' performs better than the 'capacity-centric', while the latter does not take individual user' data rate request into consideration. The proposed scheme obtains the highest data rate satisfaction ratios (at least 0.04 higher than 'user-centric' in terms of the satisfaction ratio) among all the schemes evaluated, since our scheme takes the 'instant data rate' and the data rate requests into consideration when the base station selects the users to serve, compared with the 'user-centric'.

In Figure 4, the x-axis stands for the range extension value RE and y-axis is the system throughput. The 'DataR' is the sum of the users' requested data rates. The total system throughputs gained using 'proposed' and the 'user-centric' are higher than the throughput gained by the 'capacity-centric', although both schemes are dedicated to improve the users' satisfaction ratios instead of the total system capacity. The reason is that both schemes perform the intercell interference coordination for PCUEs besides PEUEs, while 'capacity-centric' only performs the intercell interference coordination when PEUEs are served. This shows the importance of performing the intercell interference coordination to all the users in HetNet instead of only performing the intercell interference in PEUE subframes. The 'user-centric' is a little bit better compared with the proposed scheme in term of the system throughput but the proposed scheme leads to larger satisfaction ratios.

We change the parameters to be ą=2, ß=1, Υ=1 and conduct the simulations. The results are shown in Figure 5. We can find that larger ą indicates that the data rate requests have larger weight, the satisfaction ratio is better compared with the case in Figure 3, in which ą=1. However, the proposed scheme still outperforms the state-of-the-art schemes greatly due to the new user selection and the intercell interference coordination methods. The gain over the 'user-centric' is at least 0.05 in terms of user satisfaction ratio.

We also test the satisfaction ratios with different average data rates requested as shown in Figure 6. In this figure, x-axis stands for the average data rate requested and y-axis is the average satisfaction ratio. In this simulation, RE=10 and the corresponding standard derivation is 0.1. We can observe that larger data rate requests lead to slightly lower average satisfaction ratios, since the total resources are limited, but the proposed scheme still outperforms the state-of-the-art schemes greatly due to the new user selection and the intercell interference coordination methods. The gain over 'user centric' is more than 0.05 in terms of the user satisfaction ratio.

Figure 3. Comparison of performance

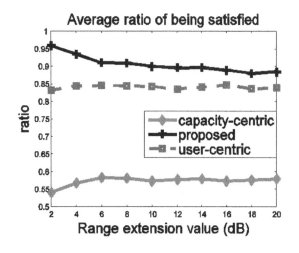

Figure 4. Comparison of system throughput

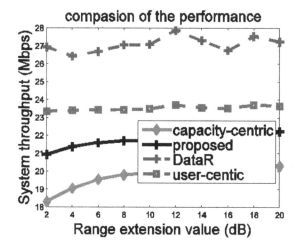

Figure 5. Comparison of the performance with a=2, β=1, γ=1

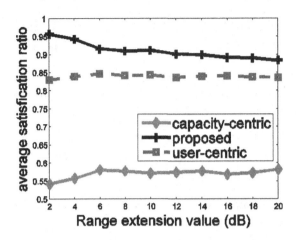

Figure 6. Comparison of the performance with varying average data rate requested

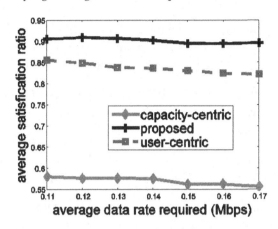

CONCLUSION AND FUTURE WORK

HetNet is a hot research topic in the next generation broadband wireless access network and the intercell interference significantly degrades the system performance. Mitigating the intercell interference can improve the system throughput and users care their requested data rates the most since whether their data rate requests can be satisfied or not directly affect the QoS or QoE. Hence a user-centric intercell interference coordination scheme for all the subframes is necessary. In this paper, at each specific subframe, when users have data requests, the corresponding base station first selects which users to serve based on each user's 'instant data rate', data rate request and the capacity gained. Then given the users selected, a method is proposed to help choose which intercell interference coordination scheme among ABS and CoMP to use in order to maximize the users' average data rate satisfaction ratio. Extensive simulations are conducted and the results demonstrate that our proposed scheme achieves considerable gains over competing schemes in terms of the data rate satisfaction ratio and the system capacity in Config.4b scenarios defined by 3GPP.

There are still many existing issues for the user centric intercell interference coordination such as how the subframes should be divided to further improve the overall performance. These are left as the future work.

ACKNOWLEDGMENT

This work is partially supported by JSPS KAKENHI Grant Number 15K21599, 16H02817 and 16K00117.

REFERENCES

10.3.   0., G. T. (2011). *Lte evolved universal terrestrial radio access (eutra) physical layer procedures (release 10)*. Author.

Access, E. U. (2010). *Further advancements for E-UTRA physical layer aspects.* 3GPP Technical Specification TR, 36, V2.

Adhikary, A. D., Dhillon, H. S., & Caire, G. (2015). Massive-MIMO meets HetNet: Interference coordination through spatial blanking. *IEEE Journal on Selected Areas in Communications, 33*(6), 1171–1186. doi:10.1109/JSAC.2015.2416986

Barbieri, A. G. (2012). Coordinated downlink multi-point communications in heterogeneous cellular networks.*Information Theory and Applications Workshop (ITA)*, 7-16. doi:10.1109/ITA.2012.6181826

Deb, S. M., Monogioudis, P., Miernik, J., & Seymour, J. P. (2014). Algorithms for enhanced inter-cell interference coordination (eICIC) in LTE HetNets. *IEEE/ACM Transactions on Networking, 22*(1), 137–150. doi:10.1109/TNET.2013.2246820

Fan, X. C. (2007). An inter-cell interference coordination technique based on users' ratio and multi-level frequency allocations.*2007 International Conference on Wireless Communications, Networking and Mobile Computing*, 799-802. doi:10.1109/WICOM.2007.206

Ghosh, A. R., Ratasuk, R., Mondal, B., Mangalvedhe, N., & Thomas, T. (2010). LTE-advanced: Next-generation wireless broadband technology. *IEEE Wireless Communications, 17*(3), 10–22. doi:10.1109/MWC.2010.5490974

Guvenc, I. (2011). Capacity and fairness analysis of heterogeneous networks with range expansion and interference coordination. *IEEE Communications Letters, 15*(10), 1084–1087. doi:10.1109/LCOMM.2011.082611.111387

Hoydis, J. K. (2011, June). Outage performance of cooperative small-cell systems under Rician fading channels. *2011 IEEE 12th international workshop on signal processing advances in wireless communications*, 551-555.

Kosta, C. H., Hunt, B., Quddus, A. U. I., & Tafazolli, R. (2013). On interference avoidance through inter-cell interference coordination (ICIC) based on OFDMA mobile systems. *IEEE Communications Surveys and Tutorials, 15*(3), 973–995. doi:10.1109/SURV.2012.121112.00037

Li, C. Z. (2014). User-centric intercell interference coordination in small cell networks.*2014 IEEE International Conference on Communication*, 5747-5752. doi:10.1109/ICC.2014.6884238

Li, C. Z., Zhang, J., Haenggi, M., & Letaief, K. B. (2015). User-centric intercell interference nulling for downlink small cell networks. *IEEE Transactions on Communications, 63*(4), 1419–1431. doi:10.1109/TCOMM.2015.2402121

Li, Y. N. (2012). *CoMP and interference coordination in heterogeneous network for LTE-advanced.* 2012 IEEE Globecom Workshops, 1107–1111. doi:10.1109/GLOCOMW.2012.6477733

Liu, A. L., Lau, V. K. N., Ruan, L., Chen, J., & Xiao, D. (2014). Hierarchical radio resource optimization for heterogeneous networks with enhanced inter-cell interference coordination (eICIC). *IEEE Transactions on Signal Processing, 62*(7), 1684–1693. doi:10.1109/TSP.2014.2302748

Liu, Z & Ji, Y(2014). Intercell Interference Coordination under Data Rate Requirement Constraint in LTE-Advanced Heterogeneous Networks. *2014 IEEE 79th Vehicular Technology Conference (VTC Spring)*. IEEE.

Liu, Z., Cheung, G., Chakareski, J. and Ji, Y., 2012, December. Multiple description coding of free viewpoint video for multi-path network streaming. In Global Communications Conference (GLOBECOM), 2012 IEEE (pp. 2150-2155). IEEE. doi:10.1109/GLOCOM.2012.6503434

Liu, Z., Cheung, G., Chakareski, J., & Ji, Y. (2015). Multiple description coding and recovery of free viewpoint video for wireless multi-path streaming. IEEE Journal of Selected Topics in Signal Processing, 9(1), 151-164. doi:10.1109/JSTSP.2014.2330332

Liu, Z., Cheung, G., & Ji, Y. (2013). Optimizing distributed source coding for interactive multiview video streaming over lossy networks. IEEE Transactions on Circuits and Systems for Video Technology, 23(10), 1781-1794. doi:10.1109/TCSVT.2013.2269019

Liu, Z. F., Feng, J., Ji, Y., & Zhang, Y. (2014). EAF: Energy-aware adaptive free viewpoint video wireless transmission. *Journal of Network and Computer Applications, 46,* 384–394. doi:10.1016/j.jnca.2014.07.010

López-Pérez, D. (2011). Inter-cell interference coordination for expanded region picocells in heterogeneous networks. *2011 20th International Conference on Computer Communications and Networks (ICCCN)*. IEEE.

Lopez-Perez, D. G., Guvenc, I., & Chu, X. (2012). Mobility management challenges in 3GPP heterogeneous networks. *IEEE Communications Magazine, 50*(12), 70–78. doi:10.1109/MCOM.2012.6384454

Lopez-Perez, D. G., Guvenc, I., de la Roche, G., Kountouris, M., Quek, T., & Zhang, J. (2011). Enhanced intercell interference coordination challenges in heterogeneous networks. *IEEE Wireless Communications, 18*(3), 22–30. doi:10.1109/MWC.2011.5876497

Luo, W. J. (2013). An adaptive ABS-CoMP scheme in LTE-Advanced heterogeneous networks. *IEEE 24th Annual International Symposium on Personal, Indoor, and Mobile Radio Communications (PIMRC),* 2769-2773.

Moon, A. M. (2014). Cell Range Expansion and Time Partitioning for Enhanced Inter-cell Interference Coordination in Heterogeneous Network. *2014 47th Hawaii International Conference on System Sciences,* 5109-5113.

Okino, K. N. (2011). Pico cell range expansion with interference mitigation toward LTE-Advanced heterogeneous networks.*2011 IEEE International Conference on Communications Workshops (ICC),* 1-5. doi:10.1109/iccw.2011.5963603

Wang, C. X., Haider, F., Gao, X., You, X.-H., Yang, Y., Yuan, D., & Hepsaydir, E. et al. (2014). Cellular architecture and key technologies for 5G wireless communication networks. *IEEE Communications Magazine, 52*(2), 122–130. doi:10.1109/MCOM.2014.6736752

Wang, J. S. (2012). Enhanced dynamic inter-cell interference coordination schemes for LTE-advanced. *2012 IEEE 75th Vehicular Technology Conference (VTC Spring),* 1-6.

Wang, Y. (2012, May). Performance analysis of enhanced inter-cell interference coordination in LTE-Advanced heterogeneous networks. *2012 IEEE 75th Vehicular Technology Conference (VTC Spring)*, 1-5.

Wu, Y. C. (2015). User-centric interference nulling in downlink multi-antenna heterogeneous networks. *2015 IEEE International Symposium on Information Theory (ISIT)*, 2817-2821. doi:10.1109/ISIT.2015.7282970

Xu, C. Z., Zhao, F., Guan, J., Zhang, H., & Muntean, G.-M. (2013). QoE-driven user-centric VoD services in urban multihomed P2P-based vehicular networks. *IEEE Transactions on Vehicular Technology*, *62*(5), 2273–2289. doi:10.1109/TVT.2012.2228682

Zhou, H. J., Ji, Y., Wang, X., & Zhao, B. (2015). Joint Resource Allocation and User Association for SVC Multicast Over Heterogeneous Cellular Networks. *IEEE Transactions on Wireless Communications*, *14*(7), 3673–3684. doi:10.1109/TWC.2015.2409834

ENDNOTE

[1]   This is chosen only when there is no Pico-eNB user to be served. Also, since MUEs can be served during all the subframes while PEUEs can only be served during MUE/PEUE subframes and the PCUEs can only be served during MUE/PCUE subframes, the case pico-eNB sending ABS subframes is not considered. This is to avoid the transmission opportunity imbalance between MUEs and pico-eNB users and provide higher capacity for Picocell users.

APPENDIX

The channel between MUE i and Macro-eNB, Pico-eNB is

$$H_1 = H_{M,i} = \left[H_{M,M,i}, H_{P,M,i} \right]$$

The channel between PEUE/PCUE j and the Macro-eNB, Pico-eNB can be written as

$$H_2 = H_{P,j} = \left[H_{M,P,j}, H_{P,P,j} \right]$$

Then the cooperative channel could be written as

$$H = \left[H_1, H_2 \right]^T$$

h_k is used to denote the aggregate interference channel observed user k. Then

$$h_k = \left[H_1^T, \ldots, H_{k-1}^T, H_{k+1}^T, \ldots, H_K^T \right]^T = \begin{cases} H_2, k = 1 \\ H_1, k = 2 \end{cases}$$

Singular value decompose h_k

$$h_k = \left[v_k^{(1)}, v_k^{(0)} \right]^H$$

where Λ is the diagonal matrix composed of elements that are singular values of h_k, $v_k^{(1)}$ is the composed of singular vectors corresponding to non-zero singular value while $v_k^{(0)}$ is composed of singular vectors corresponding to zero singular value. The columns of $v_k^{(0)}$ are candidates for kth user's beamforming matrix F_k. We continue to o singular value decompose $h_k v_k^{(0)} \left(k = 1, 2 \right)$

$$v_k^{(0)} = u \begin{bmatrix} \sum_k & 0 \\ 0 & 0 \end{bmatrix} \left[v_k'^{(1)}, v_k'^{(0)} \right]^H$$

where $v_k'^{(0)}$ is composed of singular vectors corresponding to non-zero singular value. Then the beamforming matrix of the system can be represented as

$$F = \left[F_1, F_2 \right] = \left[v_1^{(0)} v_{1,N_{R,1}}'^{(1)}, v_2^{(0)} v_{2,N_{R,2}}'^{(1)} \right]$$

$v'^{(1)}_{k,N_{R,k}}$ is the selection of the right columns $N_{R,k}$ of $v'^{(1)}_{k}$. $F_{1,1}$ is part of the beamforming matrix for scheduled MUE and it is used for beamforming at the macro-eNB. The remaining $F_{1,2}$ would be used on the pico-eNB side.

Chapter 8
Energy Efficient Resource Allocation Scheme via Auction-Based Offloading in Next-Generation Heterogeneous Networks

Alexandra Bousia
University of Thessaly, Greece

ABSTRACT

The focus of this chapter is centered on the network underutilization during low traffic periods (e.g., night zone), which enables the Mobile Network Operators (MNOs) to save energy by having their traffic served by third-party Small Cells (SCs), thus being able to switch off their Base Stations(BSs). In this chapter, a novel market approach is proposed to foster the opportunistic utilization of unexploited SCs capacity, where the MNOs lease the resources of third-party SCs and deactivate their BSs. Motivated by the conflicting interests of the MNOs and the restricted capacity of the SCs, we introduce a combinatorial auction framework. A multiobjective framework is formulated and a greedy auction algorithm is given to provide an energy efficient solution for the resource allocation problem within polynomial time. In addition, an extensive mathematical analysis is given for the calculation of the SCs cost, which is useful in the market framework. Finally, extended experimental results to estimate the potential energy and cost savings are provided.

INTRODUCTION

During the last few years, the rapid and radical evolution of mobile telecommunication services along with the emerging demand for multimedia applications due to the widespread use of laptops, tablets and smart-phones have led to a growing demand for data transmission. The traffic load is experiencing a growing increase by the factor of 10 every 5 years approximately (Global Action Plan, 2012; Cisco,

DOI: 10.4018/978-1-5225-2023-8.ch008

2015). Overall mobile data traffic is expected to reach 24.3 exabytes per month by 2019, a 13- fold increase and at a Compound Annual Growth Rate (CAGR) of 57% from 2014 to 2019 (Cisco, 2015). The mobile applications, in particular, are expected to grow in staggering rates, with mobile video showing the higher growth and getting up to 66.5%. Thus, the increasingly expanding market of web-enabled mobile devices opens the path towards a wide range of previously unimagined (data- based) applications and creates the need for ubiquitous availability of Internet (better coverage) and faster broadband connections (higher Quality of Service (QoS)) (Loozen, Murdoch, & Orr, 2013).

In order to tackle with the challenges of future mobile networks and handle the predicted increase in mobile traffic volume, operators face the need to expand their wireless infrastructure. The telecommunications companies work towards the massive deployment of their networks. At this point, it is highlighted that there were more than 8 million Base Stations (BSs) deployed and serving mobile users in 2012 (Correia et al., 2012). Let us point out here that the largest mobile telecommunications operators may maintain approximately 238000 BS sites worldwide (Vodafone Group, 2012). Moreover, the number of deployed BSs grows as the users requirements increase every year. Furthermore, Wi-Fi Access Points (APs) and third-party Small Cells (SCs), such as picocells, femtocells and mircocells, are extensively deployed in public and private areas, such as university campuses, business parks, and user homes during the last decade, introducing the trend of Heterogeneous Networks (HetNets). However, these deployments may lead to increase in energy consumption because of the extra cells that are also underutilized some hours of the day when the traffic load is low. Nevertheless, by introducing sleep mode in BSs, heterogeneous cellular networks can outperform traditional macro-cell-only networks in terms of energy efficiency.

In this chapter, motivated by the aforementioned issues and in order to foster the utilization of unexploited Internet connections, a new and open market is proposed, where a Mobile Network Operator (MNO) can lease the bandwidth made available by a third-party company through its SCs to switch off the BS and save large amounts of energy under low traffic conditions (guaranteeing the QoS constraints). Since the SCs capacity is limited, the proposal of the chapter considers the diverse predilections of each MNO. On the other hand, the third-party wants to maximize its income by leasing its capacity to the MNOs, a goal that may contradict the MNOs' tendency to save energy. Specifically, an operator is willing to lease capacity provided that its whole traffic can be offloaded, whereas the third-party may prefer to lease its resources to different MNOs, hindering the deactivation of the BSs. To that end, the offloading problem is formulated as a reverse auction. At this point, it is highlighted that the SC network cost is mathematically analyzed, as well. The main contributions of this work are summarized below:

1. A combinatorial auction is proposed and analyzed to implement an innovative market- place that enables the efficient usage of SCs resources under low traffic conditions. The mechanism is designed to provide the optimal solution that maximizes the income of the third-party and minimizes the network energy consumption, at the same time.
2. An innovative payment rule is proposed, which is based on the classical Vickrey-Clarke- Groves (VCG) scheme, and it guarantees both individual rationality and incentive compatibility (i.e., truthfulness).
3. Since the optimal auction is NP-hard, a greedy algorithm is further given to solve in polynomial time the allocation problem for large network instances.
4. Finally, the effectiveness of the proposed auction-based switching off scheme is validate and assessed. The results indicate the potential energy efficiency and cost gains in the network.

The remainder of the chapter is organized as follows. The background information concerning the state-of-the-art approaches for switching off algorithms are presented in the next section. Then, the system model and the network configuration are described. In continuation, the author introduces the auction-based resource allocation scheme for the BSs deactivation, along with the multiobjective formulation of the switching off decision. The models for the analytical calculation of the financial cost of the SCs are given next. The simulation results are provided. An extensive performance assessment is given and, finally, the chapter is concluded along with the future directions and open issues.

BACKGROUND

The greening of wireless networks has been thoroughly examined by the research community. The use of high temperature electronics, adaptive power management, new network architectures of high density, low transmit power microcells and highly efficient Power Amplifiers (PAs) are only few of the solutions that lead to energy consumption reduction. Even though, these solutions can significantly provide energy efficiency in the networks, from (Cisco, 2015; Richter, Fehske, & Fettweis, 2009; Fehske, Richter, & Fettweis, 2000), it can be concluded that the BSs still consume considerable amount of energy, even when the traffic load is significantly low, due to the power supply and PAs that are always active. More specifically, the fixed part, including air conditioning and power supply, accounts for around one fourth of total energy consumption. This amount of energy is wasted when no traffic is served by the BSs, thus, it is independent of the traffic load. Hence, the variations of the traffic and the traffic pattern play an important role on the energy consumption, since it is important to know whether or not the traffic is low for long periods during the day. The mobile traffic level throughout a way or a week varies periodically with the living pattern of mobile users. More specifically, in the daytime on weekdays, people mostly concentrate in business areas in a city and are more likely to make phone calls. At night or on weekends, most people move to residential areas. In addition, phone calls are generally less frequent at night than during the day, but larger amount of cellular data is transmitted because more data-intensive applications, such as social networking, web browsing, video streaming and video chatting are more likely to run. Given the aforementioned issues, network planning solutions can manage to save energy by monitoring the traffic load in the network and then decide whether to deactivate (or switch to sleep mode), or turn on (or switch to active mode) certain elements of the infrastructure. Thus, higher gains can be achieved by the investigation of network planning and BS switching off schemes in wireless cellular networks.

Various network planning solutions through BSs deactivation in single operator networks are investigated in (Oh, Son, & Krishnamachari, 2013; Marsan, Chiaraviglio, Ciullo, & Meo, 2009; Bousia, Antonopoulos, Alonso, & Verikoukis, C., 2012; Bousia, Kartsakli, Alonso, & Verikoukis, 2012a; Bousia, Kartsakli, Alonso, & Verikoukis, 2012b; Bousia, Kartsakli, Antonopoulos, Alonso, & Verikoukis, 2013). Moving to multi-operator environments, infrastructure sharing is exploited and novel deactivation policies are investigated in (Bousia, Kartsakli, Antonopoulos, Alonso, & Verikoukis, 2015; Bousia, Kartsakli, Antonopoulos, Alonso, & Verikoukis, 2015a; Antonopoulos, Kartsakli, Bousia, Alonso, & Verikoukis, 2015b; Bousia, Kartsakli, Antonopoulos, Alonso, & Verikoukis, 2013). The energy savings potentials are very prominent, motivating the operators to exploit the proposed solutions. The context of green networking has been extended to the HetNets, as well. The SCs are used during the day for traffic offloading, but they are most likely to remain underutilized during night, when the traffic is served by the BSs. However, even when their traffic is low, the macro BSs consume considerable energy, compared to the low-powered SCs. Hence, to achieve drastic energy savings, the opportunistic exploitation of the unused SCs capacity and the deactivation of the redundant BSs during low traffic conditions is a very promising solution.

The authors in (Richter, Fehske, & Fettweis, 2009) consider layouts featuring varying numbers of micro BSs per cell in addition to conventional macro sites. They introduce the concept of area power consumption as a system performance metric and employ simulations to evaluate potential improvements of this metric through the use of micro BSs. The same authors extend their work in (Fehske, Richter, & Fettweis, 2000), and they provide a framework to evaluate and optimize cellular network deployments with respect to the average number of micro sites per macro cell as well as the macro cell size. The SCs can be exploited to allow BSs to be switched off (Han, Safar, & Ray Liu, 2013; Bartelt, Fehske, Klessig, Fettweis, & Voigt, 2013; Soh, Quek, Kountouris, & Shin, 2013) taking into account the properties and challenges of offloading (Dong, Rallapalli, Jana, Qiu, Ramakrishnan, Razoumov, Zhang, & Won Cho, 2013; Gao, Iosifidis, Jianwei, & Tassiulas, 2013; Bao, Lin, Lee, Rimac, & Choudhury, 2013). Telecommunications companies, such as Nokia Networks (Nokia,2015), are building networks of interconnected SCs that help operators to add coverage and capacity to existing macro networks and guarantee the user service when the macro cells are turned off. An overview of existing energy efficient techniques in the literature is presented in (Alsharif, Nordin, & Ismail, 2014), highlighting the advantages and the shortcomings of the algorithms and revealing the open issues that should be further studied in the field of HetNets and operators' collaboration. In (Ashraf, Boccardi, & Ho, 2011), the application of dynamic sleep mode in BSs with pico cell deployments is studied. HetNet planning can improve the coverage of the cellular network, but will likely result in even more severe over-provisioning and thus consume more energy if the cells are unable to adapt to traffic load. The solution proposed by the authors is to introduce the dynamic sleep and wake modes in the pico cells. The result shows that the network with both macro cells and pico cells, where dynamic sleep mode algorithm is applied in pico cells, consumes less amount of energy than the network with only macro-cells. The authors in (Cai, Xiao, Yang, Wang, &. Zhou, 2013) propose an energy model for heterogeneous cellular network and a cross layer optimization method. Several pico cells (lower layer) are in the coverage area of one macro cell. The problem to solve is how to associate users to the group of macro cell and pico cells, so that energy consumption is minimized after lightly-loaded pico cells turned to sleep.

The previous works propose solutions for single-operator HetNets. However, even though the opportunistic exploitation of the unused SCs capacity and the deactivation of the redundant BSs in multi-operator HetNets can have significant, very few research works exist in the literature. The authors in (Paris, Martignon, Filippini, & Chen, 2013) propose an auction-based offloading scheme for BS switching off, where the operators submit a bidding value for the requested capacity and a third-party's income optimization approach is followed to solve the resource allocation problem. However, only a particular network configuration is considered, where the SC capacity is sufficient to serve the traffic of the whole network, allowing the switching off of all the BSs. Despite the clear benefits of the BSs switching off via offloading, shown by the authors, the proposed scheme could not be applied in real life scenarios, since the SCs may not be able to fully support the network traffic, especially when numerous MNOs are present in the same area (Marsan, & Meo, 2013). An interesting approach is presented in (Bousia, Kartsakli, Antonopoulos, Alonso, & Verikoukis, 2015 and Bousia, Kartsakli, Antonopoulos, Alonso, & Verikoukis, 2016), where an offloading mechanism, where the operators lease the capacity of an SC network owned by a third-party, in order to be able to switch off their BSs and maximize their energy efficiency, when the traffic demand is low, has been explored. The MNOs submit a set of bids to the SCs, requesting for lower capacity resources (with respect to the maximum estimated capacity requirements). On the other hand, the third-party wants to maximize its income by leasing the maximum possible amount for resources to the MNOs. The mechanism is designed based on a multiobjective framework, where the conflicting interests of the involved parties are considered, so as to provide the optimal solution that maximizes the economic profit of both the third-party and the MNOs and minimizes the network energy consumption at the same time.

In the last works, great attention is paid in the multi-MNO cooperation and HetNets sharing. It is shown that cooperation among multiple operators and third-parties accomplish greener network operation. It has been suggested that the MNOs can cooperate during low traffic periods and reduce energy consumption by deactivating the BSs of different operators through offloading their users to the SCs network. In addition, since the traffic data of each operator is sensitive information and operators may not be willing to share with their competitors, a proposal, such as an auction market, that keeps this information hidden is feasible and applicable. An auction-based offloading scheme is an appropriate mechanism for a scenario in which the operators that act as buyers and the third-party that acts as seller and none is willing to reveal information about their requirements. Thus, a collaborative scheme that does not require sharing of information is easy to be implemented in reality.

SYSTEM MODEL

The system model, depicted in Figure 1(a), considers an area served by a set of N collocated macro BSs and a set of M SCs. Each of the N BSs is owned by N different MNOs, who provide coverage through their BSs, denoted by BS_n, with $n \in N = \{1, \ldots, N\}$ characterizing the MNO. The M third-party SCs are uniformly distributed within the macro cell and the author assumes that the number of SCs is adequate to cover the service area of a BS (Andrews, 2013) (see Appendix A). Each SC is denoted by SC_m, where $m \in M = \{1, \ldots, M\}$.

In the traffic pattern, depicted in Figure 1(b), the maximum traffic per hour is expressed. The researcher focuses on the night, when the aggregated traffic per BS is relatively low (i.e., less than 25 Mbps, which corresponds to 22% of the cell's capacity, CR_{BS}). Moreover, for the sake of generality, it is assumed that the traffic volumes of different MNOs may be different, although they follow the same pattern. Hence, the author defines ρ_n (the case of $\rho_n = 1$ is illustrated in the Figure 1(b)) the percentage of each operator's traffic with respect to the maximum traffic.

PROBLEM FORMULATION

In this section, the author gives the detailed formulation and analysis of the proposed auction incentive framework. The author presents the combinatorial auction to select the MNOs that can offload all their traffic to the SCs, thus being able to switch off their BSs. The bidding strategy is provided and the Integer Linear Programming (ILP) model is formulated (Krishna, 2010). This framework provides the optimal allocation and switching off strategy. To ensure truthful bidding, the VCG payment mechanism (Krishna, 2010) is employed.

Auction for Optimal Energy Efficient Resource Allocation: The Idea

The proposed mechanism selects the subset of MNOs to offload their traffic to the SCs that have limited capacity. More specifically, an operator, acting as the buyer, is willing to lease the capacity from the third-party network to be able to switch off its traffic and attain both environmental and financial gains. On the other hand, the third-party who acts as the seller collects the bids and, through an auction, selects the subset of MNOs that can offload their traffic. The auction consists of three main steps: bidding, allocation and pricing.

Bidding Strategy

The author seeks an auction scheme to:

1. Cope with different requested resources, representing the distinct traffic requirements of the MNOs.
2. Achieve high energy efficiency, where the winners in the auction are the operators who can offload their traffic to the SCs, thereby deactivating their underutilized BSs.
3. Attain cost gains for the third-party to give the incentive for the auction participation.
4. Promote truthful bidding to prevent bidders from gaming the system, effectively discover price to ensure that the overall system is efficient, and avoid unnecessary system fluctuation due to gaming.
5. Achieve simultaneously the truthful bidding.

Each MNO $n \in N$ wants to lease specific resources $CR_{n,m}$ from SC_m (with $m \in M$) to offload their traffic, at a given price $u_{n,m}$, unknown to the other bidders. According to the auction theory (Krishna, 2010), each operator submits the bid pair $B_{n,m} = (b_{n,m}, CR_{n,m})$, representing the price, $b_{n,m} \leq u_{n,m}$, that the MNO n is willing to pay for leasing the capacity $CR_{n,m}$ from SC.

Each SC_m of the third-party (seller) is willing to lease its capacity resources CR_{SC} to a set of operators and the price paid by the winners is $p_{n,m}$.

Figure 1. Network configuration and daily traffic pattern

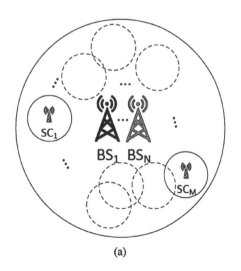
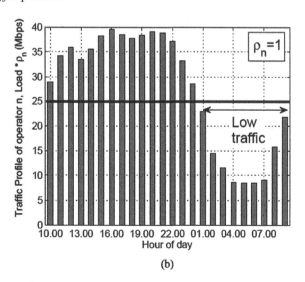

(a)   (b)

Auction Formulation

The researcher formalizes the optimal and truthful auction mechanism, presents an ILP model which provides the optimal allocation for the auction and formulates the problem of the opportunistic offloading to lead to the BSs deactivation. Each MNO $n \in N$ places the corresponding bid pair, $B_{n,m}$. Having received the bids, the third-party selects the subset of MNOs that maximizes the desired goals.

Let us define the binary variable $x_{n,m}$ as a binary decision variable that indicates whether the corresponding bidder (MNO n) is winner ($x_{n,m} = 1$) or not ($x_{n,m} = 0$) in the corresponding SC_m. Two objectives are considered:

1. **Maximization of the Third-Party Income:** The third-party wants to maximize its income. Thus, it allocates its available resources to the MNOs that offer the highest bids, so as to compensate for the SCs operational costs. We define the financial gain of the third-party, G, as:

$$G = \sum_{n \in N} \sum_{m \in M} x_{n,m} \cdot b_{n,m} - M \cdot C_{SC}, \qquad (1)$$

where C_{SC} is the SC cost, corresponding to the sum of its CapEx and OpEx. For the calculation of the cost of the SCs, the cost model is given in the next section.

2. **Minimization of the Energy Consumption:** Given the fact that BSs are the most power hungry component and are responsible for the major part of the energy in the network (Bousia, Kartsakli, Antonopoulos, Alonso, & Verikoukis, 2014), the minimization of the energy consumption is attained by reducing the number of active BSs. The network energy consumption, E[E], is defined as follows:

$$E\left[E\right] = \sum_{n \in N} E\left[E_{BS_n}\right] \cdot \left(1 - x_n\right) + M \cdot E\left[E_{SC}\right], \qquad (2)$$

with

$$x_n = \prod_{m \in M} x_{n,m}, \forall n \in N, \qquad (3)$$

while E[E_{BSn}] and E[E_{SC}] represent the BS and SC energy consumption, respectively. It is highlighted, at this point, that an operator is able to switch off its BS, if it wins in all the auctions, a condition that is represented by the product in Equation 3. The product is equal to 1 when the nth MNO wins in all the M auctions, otherwise it is 0.

The two objectives are contradictive, since the maximization of the third-party income does not imply the BSs switching off, whereas the second objective does not ensure the third-party's interests. In order to capture this tradeoff, multiobjective optimization is employed (Sawaragi, Hirotaka, & Tanino, 1985). In contrast to the state-of-the-art works (for example, the auction-based offloading in (Paris, Martignon, Filippini, & Chen, 2013)), the author incorporates in the objective function both the maximization of the third-party's income, along with the energy consumption minimization. Controversially, an auction-based switching off scheme, wherein the income of the third-party is the unique objective to be maximized is presented (Paris, Martignon, Filippini, & Chen, 2013). Thus, by taking into consideration the distinctive objectives, the ILP multiobjective optimization problem, namely P1, is formulated as follows:

$$P1 : \max \left[G, -E\left[E\right] \right],$$
(4)

s.t.

$$\sum_{n \in N} x_{n,m} \cdot CR_{n,m} \leq CR_{SC}, \forall m \in M,$$
(5)

$$x_{n,m} \in \{0,1\}, \forall n \in N, \forall m \in M.$$
(6)

Constraint Equation 5 ensures that the total number of allocated resources does not exceed its availability and constraint Equation 6 ensures the integrality of the binary variable.

The second objective of the problem, shown in Equation 2 can be transformed (Sawaragi, Hirotaka, & Tanino, 1985) to have a simpler form in the multiobjective problem. The product in Equation 3 represents the condition of whether an operator wins in all the auctions or not. Thus, in order to save higher energy, the number of switched off BSs needs to be maximized. The number of the switched off BSs is, then, calculated as:

$$N_{OFF} = \sum_{n \in N} x_n,$$
(7)

since the variable x_n is equal to 1 when the nth MNO wins in all the M auctions and switches off its BS, otherwise it is 0. Therefore, the problem is transformed as follows:

$$P2 : \max \left[G, N_{OFF} \right],$$
(8)

s.t.

$$\sum_{n \in N} x_{n,m} \cdot CR_{n,m} \leq CR_{SC}, \forall m \in M,$$
(9)

$$x_{n,m} \in \{0,1\}, \forall n \in N, \forall m \in M.$$
(10)

The objective function Equaton 8 aims at maximizing the financial gain of the third-party and maximizing the number of the switched off BSs. Constraints Equation 9 and Equation 10 are the same as constraints Equation 5 and Equation 6, respectively.

The multiobjective problem P2, representing the optimal reverse auction, is NP-hard and it has high complexity to resolve. Therefore, the third-party can hardly find a solution to efficiently allocate the resources, since the computation time necessary to solve large and real- life network instances increases very sharply.

Theorem 1 (NP-Hard Complexity of Problem P2)

The problem P2 defined in Equations 8 to 10 is NP-hard.

The proof is given in Appendix B. To this end, we use the following algorithm to solve in polynomial time the allocation problem. Algorithm 1 selects the optimal combination for the capacity allocation that at the same time maximizes the number of switched off BSs.

Algorithm 1. Optimal auction algorithm

```
                    1. Input:
                    N, M, B_{n,m},   CR_{SC}
2. Output: x_n
3. Initialize:
for n ∈ N do x_n = 0
end for
4. Allocation Phase:
for m ∈ M do
    Compute all possible combinations that do not exceed CR_{SC} C ⇐ Find _
Combinations(B_{n,m}, CR_{SC})
end for
5. Selection Phase:
for m ∈ M do for c ∈ C do
        Select the combinations with the maximum number of involved opera-
tors
 C_{max} ⇐ Select_Combinations(C)
    end for
end for
6. Switching Off Phase
for m ∈ M do
    Select the operators that are found in all the combinations
    O ⇐ Select_Operators(C_{max})
for n ∈ O do x_n  = 1
end for
end for
```

The greedy auction is summarized in Algorithm 1, and it is composed of three main phases:

1. The allocation phase, where different sets of bids are selected, until the maximum amount of data traffic generated by mobile customers can be offloaded.
2. The selection phase, where the combination of bids with the maximum number of involved MNOs is selected.
3. The switching off phase, where the corresponding BSs of the selected operators are deactivated.

Pricing Strategy

We now illustrate the payment rule, which is of crucial importance for the realization of the auction for the third-party. The VCG payment induces all the users to reveal their actual valuations for the requested bandwidth. The third-party charges the bidders (MNOs) with a price so as to compensate for the requested capacity of the different bidders. For example, an MNO who requires large bandwidth will have to pay a high price, since its request results in dissatisfying other MNOs who lose in the auction due to the limited capacity resources.

Let us denote by $p_{n,m}$ the price paid by the nth MNO to the third-party for the allocated capacity of the mth SC. Thus, the payoff function for bidder n that represents the difference between the price paid by bidder n and its true valuation is:

$$U_{n,m} = \begin{cases} u_{n,m} - p_{n,m}, & \text{if } MNOn \text{ is selected} \\ 0, & \text{otherwise} \end{cases}.$$ (11)

The payment rule for each MNO $i \in N$ can be formally defined as follows:

$$p_{i,m} = \sum_{n \in N \setminus \{i\}} \sum_{m \in M} x_{n,m}^{-i} \cdot b_{n,m} - \sum_{n \in N \setminus \{i\}} \sum_{m \in M} x_{n,m} \cdot b_{n,m}.$$ (12)

where the first term of the equation is the aggregate valuation of the allocated resources, $x_{n,m}^{-i}$, when i MNO does not participate in the auction. The second term is the aggregate valuation of the allocation, $x_{n,m}$, of MNOs other than i, when i submits its requests and hence impacts the other MNOs. In the investigated VGC auction, it holds that $b_{n,m} = u_{n,m} = p_{n,m}$.

Theorem 2 (Truthfulness of Equation 12)

The payment rule defined in Equation 12 satisfies the truthfulness property. The proof is given in Appendix C.

Theorem 3 (Individual Rationality of Equation 12)

The payment rule defined in Equation 12 satisfies the individual rationality property. The proof is given in Appendix D.

SMALL CELL COST CALCULATION MODEL

In this section, the author introduces a model to estimate the total cost of a SC deployment that is needed in the auction formulation.

The cost of a SC consists of the CapEx, for deployment and installation, and the OpEx for its operation. Chen et al. presented a detailed breakdown of the CapEx and OpEx for macrocells in (Chen, Zhang, & Xu, 2010). Following a similar approach and taking into account the typical cost of SC equipment (Small Cell Forum), the model has been adapted in order to estimate the different costs in the case of a SC.

Table 1 shows the CapEx and OpEx breakdown for SCs, whereas the respective values for the BS case (Chen, Zhang, & Xu, 2010) are also given for reference. In particular, the CapEx consists of four factors:

1. The cost for the small cell equipment.
2. The cost for deployment and installation of the SC.
3. The cost of the Radio Network Controller (RNC).
4. The cost for backhaul transmission equipment that is almost negligible in the case of SCs.
5. The OpEx, on the other hand, can be broken down to four terms:
   a. The cost of backhaul transmission, corresponding to the bandwidth needed to serve the traffic and calculated according to a simple leased line pricing.
   b. The cost for site leasing.

Table 1. CapEx and OpEx breakdown for BSs and SCs

CapEx	C_{Ca}	BS	SC
BS/SC equipment	C_{BS}^{C}, C_{SC}^{C}	c_0	$c_0/70$
Site installation and buildout	C_{Site}^{C}	$c_0/4$	$c_0/20$
RNC equipment	C_{RNC}^{C}	$3c_0/2$	$c_0/210$
Backhaul transmission equipment	C_{BT}^{C}	$c_0/4$	0
OpEx	C_{Op}	**BS**	**SC**
Backhaul and transmission lease	C_{BT}^{O}	$c_0/4$	$c_0/20$
Site lease	C_{Site}^{O}	$c_0/4$	0
Operation & Maintenance	C_{OM}^{O}	$c_0/16$	$9c_0/700$
Electric power	C_{Pw}^{O}	$c_1 E_{BS}$	$c_1 E_{SC}$

c. The cost for operation and maintenance.

d. The electric power cost that depends on the power consumption to serve the traffic $\lambda(t)$ of the SC.

In order to calculate a realistic annual SC cost, the author assumes that the CapEx estimated from Table 1 is equally distributed within 5 years. Therefore, the annual cost of a SC, C_{SC}) is the sum of the CapEx that corresponds to one year and the traffic-dependent OpEx (Chen, Zhang, & Xu, 2010) (To calculate the annual cost, the SC traffic $\lambda(t)$ must be averaged over a year):

$$C_{SC} = \frac{C_{Ca}}{5} + C_{Op}. \tag{13}$$

As shown in Table 1, the first seven cost values have been expressed with respect to the equipment cost of a macro BS c_0 measured in euros (Chen, Zhang, & Xu, 2010). The last term, i.e., the electric power, depends on the electricity charge per energy unit c_1, measured in euros/kWh, and the energy consumption of a SC E_{SC}. With these relations in mind, Equation 13 is expressed as (Chen, Zhang, & Xu, 2010):

$$C_{SC} = 0.0768 \cdot c_0 + c_1 \cdot E_{SC}. \tag{14}$$

The consumed energy E_{SC} of a SC over a specific time interval $t \in [0, T]$ can be calculated as follows:

$$E_{SC} = \int_0^T P_{SC} dt. \tag{15}$$

The relationship between the power consumption P_{SC} of the SC and the relative transmission power (P_{out}) can be formulated as a linear function. To that end, a linear approximation of the power model is adopted, given by (Auer, et al., 2011):

$$P_{SC} = P_0 + \Delta_p \cdot P_{out}, 0 < P_{out} \le P_{max}. \tag{16}$$

where P_0 is the minimum power consumption in case of no traffic in the system and Δ_p is the slope of the load-dependent power consumption.

PERFORMANCE EVALUATION

To validate the mathematical expressions and to assess the performance of the auction-based switching off algorithm, the author has developed a custom-made C simulator. In this section, the simulation setup is presented, along with the analytical and experimental results.

Simulation Scenario

In the simulations, the author considers a typical urban neighborhood where macro BSs and SCs are densely deployed. In addition, it is considered that a macro cell is served by $N = 5$ MNOs with as many BSs and $M = 15$ SCs that cover the whole cell area. Concerning the traffic model, the author assumes that the MNOs have different traffic volumes, i.e., ρ_n. Particularly, it is considered that part of the MNOs, denoted by N_{low}, have relatively low traffic with $\rho_n = 0.5$, while the remaining operators (i.e., $N - N_{low}$) are fully loaded with $\rho_n = 1.0$.

To assess the performance of the proposed scheme, the author compares the proposed energy efficient auction- based switching off strategy (referred as ESO in the rest of the paper) to two state-of-the-art approaches:

1.   An auction-based switching off scheme, where the income of the third-party is the one and only objective to be maximized (referred as ISO) (Paris, Martignon, Filippini, & Chen, 2013)
2.   A baseline scenario, where none of the BSs is switched off (referred as NSO).

The simulation parameters are summarized in Table 2.

Before proceeding to the performance analysis results, it is highlighted that the proposal and the ISO scheme do not experience any losses in terms of lost sessions. The idea behind the resource allocation strategy and the switching off decision is based on the requirement that the whole network traffic load can be served. This insight is very important, since MNOs are motivated to apply an energy efficient algorithm, if and only if the service of their users is guaranteed.

Performance Results

In Figure 2, the energy efficiency of the proposed scheme and for varying traffic loads is given. As it observed, the energy efficiency increases with the traffic load (case: $N_{low} = 1$ with higher traffic compared to the case: $N_{low} = 5$), which is a rational conclusion, while, as expected, the network energy efficiency is higher when the network traffic is lower (case: $N_{low} = 5$ with lower traffic), since fewer users implies higher number of switched off BSs. Similar observations can be concluded from the Figure 3, where the throughput is illustrated for the two different cases.

Next, the proposed algorithm (ESO) is compared to the state-of-the-art approach (ISO) in terms of the number of switched off BSs (Figure 4) and the network energy efficiency (Figure 5) for the simulation scenario presented in the previous section. More specifically, in Figure 4, it is observed that, with

Table 2. Simulation parameters

Parameter	Value
# of SCs, M	15
# of operators, N	5
Data rate, R	256 kbps
Night duration, t_{night}	9· 3600 s

Soh, Quek, Kountouris, & Shin, 2013; Marsan, & Meo, 2013.

the proposal, more BSs are switched off in the majority of the cases. The higher number of deactivated BSs is explained by the second objective that we employ in the proposed algorithm, concerning the minimization of the energy consumption. Both the ESO and the ISO schemes maximize the income gains of the third-party, since the outcome of the optimization problems leads to the allocation of the whole capacity of the SCs. However, in ISO, the BSs to be switched off are selected to increase the income of the third-party, without considering the network energy efficiency. By applying the ESO algorithm, we achieve the maximization of the third-party income, which is the first objective of the problem, along with the energy consumption minimization. Furthermore, in order to gain more insight on the network performance, we have plotted in Figure 5 the average total energy efficiency of the network for the same scenario, comparing our approach to the ISO and NSO algorithms. Our proposal always outperforms the NSO and the ISO and the energy efficiency gains are remarkable reaching up to 337%. Compared to the ISO, our proposal achieves better performance, due to the higher number of switched off BSs.

Along with the total network energy efficiency performance, it is interesting to study the individual energy efficiency gains of the different MNOs. To that end, the individual gains for the specific (but representative) cases of $N_{low} = 2$ and $N_{low} = 4$ are quantified in Table 3, where interesting conclusions can be extracted. In particular, the MNOs that switch off their BSs theoretically achieve infinite energy efficiency, as they have their traffic served at zero energy cost, whereas the active operators serve their own traffic without improving their situation. The proposed ESO offers the chance to more MNOs to switch off their BSs, providing them with extra incentives to participate in the auction. The individual gains are remarkable of our proposal for both the MNOs and the whole network.

Figure 2. Energy efficiency for varying traffic load conditions
© 2017 IEEE. Reprinted, with permission, from Bousia, A., Kartsakli, E., Antonopoulos, A., Alonso, L., & Verikoukis, C. (2014). Auction- based offloading for base station switching off in Heterogeneous Networks, Proceedings from EUCNC'16: The European Conference on Networks and Communications.

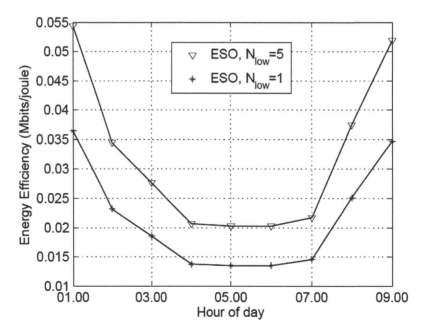

Figure 3. Throughput for varying traffic conditions

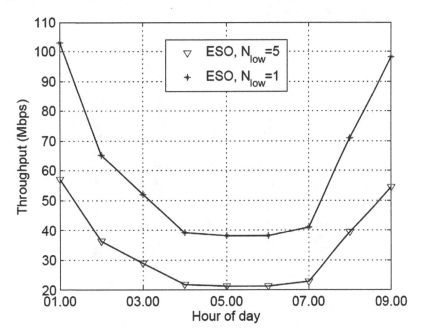

Figure 4. Number of switched off BSs for varying number of MNOs with ρ_n=0.5, N_{low}, and the rest N-N_{low} MNOs with ρ_n=1.0

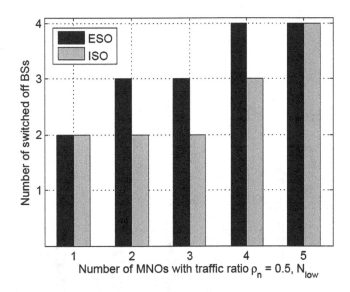

Figure 5. Network energy efficiency for varying number of MNOs with ρ_n=0.5, N_{low}, and the rest N-N_{low} MNOs with ρ_n=1.0

© *2017 IEEE. Reprinted, with permission, from Bousia, A., Kartsakli, E., Antonopoulos, A., Alonso, L., & Verikoukis, C. (2014). Auction- based offloading for base station switching off in Heterogeneous Networks, Proceedings from EUCNC'16: The European Conference on Networks and Communications.*

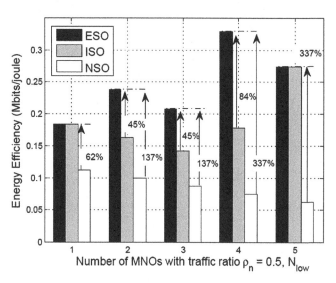

Table 3. Operator energy efficiency (x 10² Mbits/joule)

Scheme	$N_{low}=2$					$N_{low}=4$				
	Op.1	Op.2	Op.3	Op.4	Op.5	Op.1	Op.2	Op.3	Op.4	Op.5
ESO	∞	∞	∞	1.5	1.5	∞	∞	∞	∞	1.5
ISO	∞	∞	1.5	1.5	1.5	∞	∞	∞	0.7	1.5

Figure 6. Annual network cost for varying numbe of MNOs with ρ_n=0.5, N_{low}, and the rest N-N_{low} MNOs with ρ_n=1.0

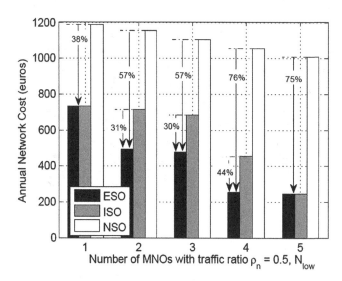

To provide further insights for our approach, the annual network cost is given in Figure 6. The total cost of the network is the sum of the average cost of all operators and the third party for the operation of all infrastructure (i.e., the active BSs and SCs). The ESO scheme achieves a considerable reduction up to 76% for the two scenarios, comparing to the NSO. Apart from the total network cost reduction, let us add that the BSs switching off scheme that we proposed achieves total annual energy gains up to ~ 13140 kWh, and in terms of annual cost gains up to ~ 350 euros for one individual BS.

DISCUSSION

Base on the analysis in Section VI.B, we have shown that the proposed ISO scheme outperforms the state-of-the-art approach in terms of total network and individual energy efficiency. More specifically, it achieves higher benefits for a larger number of operators, since the resource allocation results to a fairer and better allocation of the SCs capacity to the MNOs and thus, a larger number of BSs are deactivated. Furthermore, through a performance assessment, we have identified the significance of incorporating the energy efficiency maximization factor in the objectives of the resource allocation problem that is solved. Through the proposal of the chapter, better performance results are attained in terms of energy efficiency and number of switched off infrastructure. In addition, the proposed algorithm is very simple and with low complexity, thus, it can be applied very easily in current and future heterogeneous networks. The marketplace of the auction gives the freedom to all the involved parties to participate, while at the same time it gives the necessary motives in order to apply the auction-based offloading switching off scheme. At the same time, the auction scheme does not require any redundant discussions and complicated agreements between the involved parties that are compulsory in conventional switching off schemes based on traffic conditions or network characteristics. Taking into consideration the rationality of the players and their conflicting interests, in this chapter, a simple auction-based framework is introduced that enables the operators and the third-party to act independently, thus bypassing potential complex service level agreements among them.

CONCLUSION

This chapter proposed a new trading marketplace where mobile network operators can lease the unused bandwidth made available by third-party SC nodes to be able to switch off their underutilized BSs. The switching off decision via offloading problem was formulated as a combinatorial auction and an innovative payment rule was designed to guarantee both individual rationality and truthfulness for those realistic scenarios in which all the data traffic of a subset of the MNOs can be offloaded. In order to solve efficiently the multiobjective problem for large scale network scenarios, the author also proposed a simple algorithm to find the optimal solutions. In addition, an explicit cost calculation model for the SCs was given. Numerical results demonstrate that the proposed schemes well capture the economical and networking essence of the problem, thus representing a promising cost effective and energy efficiency solution to implement a trading marketplace for next-generation access networks. The proposed scheme has been evaluated in terms of throughput, energy efficiency and network cost and the results have shown that our proposal can significantly improve the network energy efficiency, comparing to the state-of-the- art approaches, guaranteeing at the same time the network throughput in realistic scenarios, motivating the operators to adopt the employed auction-based strategy for their decisions.

ACKNOWLEDGMENT

The author of this chapter would like to recognize the contributions of the following to earlier published works on this topic: Elli Kartsakli (Technical University of Catalonia, Spain), Angelos Antonopoulos (Telecommunications Technological Center of Catalonia, Spain), Luis Alonso (Technical University of Catalonia, Spain) and Christos Verikoukis (Telecommunications Technological Center of Catalonia, Spain).

REFERENCES

Alsharif, M. H., Nordin, R., & Ismail, M. (2014). A review on intelligent base stations cooperation management techniques for greener lte cellular networks. *Journal of Communication, 9*(12).

Andrews, J. G. (2013). Seven ways that HetNets are a cellular paradigm shift. *IEEE Communications Magazine, 51*(3), 136–144. doi:10.1109/MCOM.2013.6476878

Antonopoulos, A., Kartsakli, E., Bousia, A., Alonso, L., & Verikoukis, C. (2015b). Energy Efficient Infrastructure Sharing in Multi-Operator Mobile Networks. *IEEE Communications Magazine, 53*(5), 242–249. doi:10.1109/MCOM.2015.7105671

Ashraf, I., Boccardi, F., & Ho, L. (2011). Sleep mode techniques for small cell deployments. *IEEE Communications Magazine, 49*(8), 72–79. doi:10.1109/MCOM.2011.5978418

Auer, G., Giannini, V., Desset, C., Gdor, I., Skillermark, P., Olsson, M., & Fehske, A. et al. (2011). How Much Energy Is Needed To Run A Wireless Network? *IEEE Wireless Communications, 18*(5), 40–49. doi:10.1109/MWC.2011.6056691

Bao, X., Lin, Y., Lee, U., Rimac, I., & Choudhury, R. R. (2013). DataSpotting: Exploiting Naturally Clustered Mobile Devices to Offload Cellular Traffic. *Proceedings from INFOCOM'13:The IEEE International Conference on Computer Communication.*

Bartelt, J., Fehske, A., Klessig, H., Fettweis, G., & Voigt, J. (2013). Joint bandwidth allocation and small cell switching in heterogeneous networks. *Proceedings from VTC'13 Fall: The IEEE 78th Vehicular Technology Conference.* doi:10.1109/VTCFall.2013.6692255

Bousia, A., Antonopoulos, A., Alonso, L., & Verikoukis, C. (2012). Green distance-aware base station sleeping algorithm in LTE-Advanced. *Proceedings from ICC'12:The IEEE International Conference on Communications.*

Bousia, A., Kartsakli, E., Alonso, L., & Verikoukis, C. (2012a). Dynamic energy efficient distance-aware base station switch on/off scheme for LTE-Advanced. *Proceedings from GLOBECOM'12:The IEEE Global Communications Conference.*

Bousia, A., Kartsakli, E., Alonso, L., & Verikoukis, C. (2012b). Energy efficient base station maximization switch off scheme for LTE-Advanced. *Proceedings from CAMAD'12: The IEEE 17th International Workshop on Computer Aided Modeling and Design of Communication Links and Networks.*

Bousia, A., Kartsakli, E., Antonopoulos, A., Alonso, L., & Verikoukis, C. (2013). Energy Efficient Schemes for Base Station Management in 4G Broadband Systems. In Broadband Wireless Access Networks for 4G: Theory, Application and Experimentation. IGI Global.

Bousia, A., Kartsakli, E., Antonopoulos, A., Alonso, L., & Verikoukis, C. (2013). Game Theoretic Approach for Switching Off Base Stations in Multi-Operator Environments. *Proceedings from ICC'13:The IEEE International Communications Conference.* doi:10.1109/ICC.2013.6655262

Bousia, A., Kartsakli, E., Antonopoulos, A., Alonso, L., & Verikoukis, C. (2014). Sharing the small cells for energy efficient networking: How much does it cost? *Proceedings from GLOBECOM'14:The IEEE Global Communications Conference.*

Bousia, A., Kartsakli, E., Antonopoulos, A., Alonso, L., & Verikoukis, C. (2015). Game Theoretic Infrastructure Sharing in Wireless Networks with Two Operators. In *Game Theory Framework Applied to Wireless Communication Networks*. IGI Global. DOI: 10.4018/978-1-4666-8642-7

Bousia, A., Kartsakli, E., Antonopoulos, A., Alonso, L., & Verikoukis, C. (2015). Multiobjective Auction-based Switching Off Scheme in Heterogeneous Networks: To Bid or Not To Bid? *IEEE Transactions on Vehicular Technology.* doi:10.1109/TVT.2016.2517698

Bousia, A., Kartsakli, E., Antonopoulos, A., Alonso, L., & Verikoukis, C. (2015). Game Theoretic Infrastructure Sharing in Multi-Operator Cellular Networks. *IEEE Transactions on Vehicular Technology.* doi:10.1109/TVT.2015.2445837

Bousia, A., Kartsakli, E., Antonopoulos, A., Alonso, L., & Verikoukis, C. (2016). Auction-based offloading for base station switching off in Heterogeneous Networks. *Proceedings from EUCNC'16: The European Conference on Networks and Communications.*

Cai, S., Xiao, L., Yang, H., Wang, J., & Zhou, S. (2013). A cross-layer optimization of the joint macro- and picocell deployment with sleep mode for green communications. *Proceedings from WOCC'13: The 22nd Wireless and Optical Communication Conference.*

Chen, Y., Zhang, S., & Xu, S. (2010). Characterizing Energy Efficiency and Deployment Efficiency Relations for Green Architecture Design. *Proceedings from ICC'10 WORKSHOPS:The IEEE International Conference on Communications Workshops.* doi:10.1109/ICCW.2010.5503900

Cisco. (2015, February 03). *Cisco Visual Networking Index: Global Mobile Data Traffic Forecast Update, 2014-2019.* Retrieved from: http://www.cisco.com/c/en/us/solutions/collateral/service-provider/global-cloud-index-gci/Cloud_Index_White_Paper.pdf

Coon, J., Dettmann, C. P., & Georgiou, O. (2012). Full connectivity: Corners, edges and faces. *Journal of Statistical Physics, 147*(4), 758–778. doi:10.1007/s10955-012-0493-y

Correia, L. M., Zeller, D., Blume, O., Ferling, D., Jading, Y., Godor, I., & Van der Perre, L. et al. (2012). Challenges and enabling technologies for energy aware mobile radio networks. *IEEE Communications Magazine, 48*(11), 66–72. doi:10.1109/MCOM.2010.5621969

Dong, W., Rallapalli, S., Jana, R., Qiu, L., Ramakrishnan, K. K., Razoumov, L., & Won Cho, T. et al. (2013). iDEAL: Incentivized dynamic cellular offloading via auctions. *Proceedings from INFOCOM'13:The IEEE International Conference on Computer Communication.*

Fehske, A. J., Richter, F., & Fettweis, G. P. (2000). Energy efficiency improvements through micro sites in cellular mobile radio networks. *Proceeding from GLOBECOM'09 WORKSHOPS:The IEEE Global Telecommunications Conference Workshops.*

Gao, L., Iosifidis, G., Jianwei, H., & Tassiulas, L. (2013). Economics of mobile data offloading. *Proceedings from INFOCOM'13:The IEEE International Conference on Computer Communication.*

Global Action Plan. (2012). *Global Action Plan. Report.* Author.

Han, F., Safar, Z., & Ray Liu, K. J. (2013). Energy-Efficient Base-Station Cooperative Operation with Guaranteed QoS. *IEEE Transactions on Communications, 61*(8), 3505–3517. doi:10.1109/TCOMM.2013.061913.120743

Krishna, V. (2010). *Auction Theory.* Academic Press.

Loozen, T., Murdoch, R., & Orr, S. (2013). *Mobile web watch 2013 accenture.* Technical Report. Retrieved from: www.accenture.com

Marsan, M. A., Chiaraviglio, L., Ciullo, D., & Meo, M. (2009). Optimal energy savings in cellular access networks. *Proceedings from ICC'09 WORKSHOPS:The IEEE International Conference on Communications Workshops.*

Marsan, M. A., & Meo, M. (2013). Network sharing and its energy benefits: a study of European mobile network operators. *Proceedings from GLOBECOM'13:The IEEE Global Communications Conference.* doi:10.1109/GLOCOM.2013.6831460

Nokia. (2015, February). *Nokia networks: Solutions.* Report. Retrieved from: http://networks.nokia.com/portfolio/solutions/heterogeneous-networks

Oh, E., Son, K., & Krishnamachari, B. (2013). Dynamic Base Station Switching-On/Off Strategies for Green Cellular Networks. *IEEE Transactions on Wireless Communications, 19*(5), 2126–2136. doi:10.1109/TWC.2013.032013.120494

Paris, S., Martignon, F., Filippini, I., & Chen, L. (2013). A bandwidth trading marketplace for mobile data offloading. *Proceedings from INFOCOM'13:The IEEE Conference on Computer Communications.* doi:10.1109/INFCOM.2013.6566809

Pinola, J., Perala, J., Jurmu, P., Katz, M., Salonen, S., Piisilä, J., & Tuuttila, P. et al. (2013). A systematic and flexible approach for testing future mobile networks by exploiting a wrap-around testing methodology. *IEEE Communications Magazine, 51*(3), 160–167. doi:10.1109/MCOM.2013.6476882

Richter, F., Fehske, A. J., & Fettweis, G. P. (2009). Energy efficiency aspects of base station deployment strategies for cellular networks. *Proceedings from VTC'09 Fall: The IEEE 70th Vehicular Technology Conference Fall.* doi:10.1109/VETECF.2009.5379031

Sawaragi, Y., Hirotaka, I., & Tanino, T. (1985). Theory of Multiobjective Optimization. Academic Press, Inc. Retrieved from www.smallcellforum.org

Soh, Y. S., Quek, T. Q. S., Kountouris, M., & Shin, H. (2013). Energy efficient heterogeneous cellular networks. *IEEE Journal on Selected Areas in Communications*, *31*(5), 840–850. doi:10.1109/JSAC.2013.130503

Vodafone Group. (2012). *Sustainability report: Environmental footprint - performance data*. Technical Report. Retrieved from: http://www.vodafone.com/content/index/about/sustainability/sustainabilityreport/issuebyissue/environmentalfootprint/ performancedata.html

KEY TERMS AND DEFINITIONS

Auction: An auction is a process of buying and selling goods or services by offering them up for bid, taking bids, and then selling the item to the highest bidder.

Green Communications: Field of cellular networks that deals with the proposal of energy efficient solutions.

Energy Efficiency: Metric that is defined as the ratio of the transmitted bits over the average energy consumption, measured in [bits/joule].

Multiobjective Optimization: Multiobjective optimization is an area of multiple criteria decision making, that is concerned with mathematical optimization problems involving more than one objective function to be optimized simultaneously.

Switching Off Schemes: Algorithms for energy saving in cellular networks where operators switch off the BSs which become redundant due to low traffic variations.

APPENDIX A

A network with N_{BS} macro cells owned by one operator and M_{SC} SCs, located uniformly on a coverage area is considered. In the general case, where multiple operators serve the same area, it is assumed that the BSs of the different MNOs are collocated in each the macro cell. Assuming that the cell radius of the BSs is r_{BS}, the cell radius of the SCs is $r_{SC} = \alpha \cdot r_{BS}$, with $\alpha \in (0, 1)$. Respectively, the number of BSs and SCs are associated with the following equation:

$$M_{SC} = \beta \cdot N_{BS}, with\ \beta > 1. \tag{17}$$

According to connectivity theory (Coon, Dettmann, & Georgiou, 2012) (Equation 28 from (Coon, Dettmann, & Georgiou, 2012)), the probability that all nodes,
  N_{BS}, are connected is given by:

$$P_{f_c,BS} = 1 - N_{BS} \cdot e^{-4 \cdot \pi \cdot r_{BS}^2 \cdot \rho_{BS}} \cdot \left(1 + O\left(\rho_{BS}^{-1}\right)\right), \tag{18}$$

where ρ_{BS} is the BSs density and $O\left(\cdot\right)$ represent the complexity of the $P_{fc,BS}$ calculation. Equivalently, the probability that the SC network, consisting of M_{SC} SCs (with ρ_{SC} being the SCs density), is connected, is:

$$P_{f_c,SC} = 1 - M_{SC} \cdot e^{-4 \cdot \pi \cdot r_{SC}^2 \cdot \rho_{SC}} \cdot \left(1 + O\left(\rho_{SC}^{-1}\right)\right). \tag{19}$$

The objective is that the two networks should be equivalent and cover the same area, thus:

$$P_{f_c,BS} = P_{f_c,SC} \Rightarrow$$

$$1 - N_{BS} \cdot e^{-4 \cdot \pi \cdot r_{BS}^2 \cdot \rho_{BS}} = 1 - M_{SC} \cdot e^{-4 \cdot \pi \cdot r_{SC}^2 \cdot \rho_{SC}} \Rightarrow \alpha = \sqrt{\frac{1}{\beta} \cdot \left(1 + \frac{\ln \beta}{4 \cdot \pi \cdot r_{BS}^2 \cdot \rho_{BS}}\right)} \Rightarrow \tag{20}$$

$$\beta = -\frac{W\left(-4 \cdot a^2 \cdot e^{-4 \cdot \pi \cdot r_{BS}^2 \cdot \rho_{BS}} \cdot \pi \cdot r_{BS}^2 \cdot \rho_{BS}\right)}{4 \cdot \pi \cdot \alpha^2 \cdot r_{BS}^2 \cdot \rho_{BS}},$$

where $W\left(\cdot\right)$ is the Lambert-W function, defined as:

$$W\left(x\right) = \sum_{n=1}^{\infty} \frac{\left(-1\right)^{n-1} \cdot n^{n-2}}{\left(n-1\right)!} \cdot x^n. \tag{21}$$

APPENDIX B: PROOF OF THEOREM 1

Considering the Knapsack Problem is NP-Complete, so if the given optimization problem is NP-hard, it could be reduced to Knapsack Problem (Pinola, Perala, Jurmu, et al., 2013). The objective is to allocate the resources to the users, so as to achieve the best allocation that will benefit both the third-party and the operators. The resource allocation that takes into consideration the limited capacity of the SCs and the need of minimizing the power consumption is equivalent to the Knapsack Problem. Thus, the switching off control of the BSs is NP-hard.

APPENDIX C: PROOF OF THEOREM 2

To prove the truthfulness, two cases are compared: *Case 1*, where the MNO i bids $b_{i,m} = u_i$ and the solution of the problem (8) is $x_{i,m}$, and *Case 2*, where the MNO i bids $b'_{i,m} = u'_{i,m}$ and the corresponding solution is $x'_{i,m}$. In addition, let $x_{n,m}^{-i}$ denote the solution to the same problem without considering the MNO i, thus forcing $x_{i,m} = 0$, $\forall m \in M$ in the problem. Note that $x_{n,m}^{-i} = x_{n,m}^{'-i}$

Given the Equation 11 and Equation 12, the utility of i, when it bids $u_{i,m}$, is equal to:

$$U_{i,m} = \sum_{n \in N \setminus \{i\}} \sum_{m \in M} x_{n,m} \cdot u_{n,m} - \sum_{n \in N} \sum_{m \in M} x_{n,m}^{-i} \cdot u_{n,m}, \tag{22}$$

whereas, when the MNO declares $u'_{i,m}$ the utility is equal to:

$$U'_{i,m} = \sum_{n \in N \setminus \{i\}} \sum_{m \in M} x'_{n,m} \cdot u'_{n,m} - \sum_{n \in N} \sum_{m \in M} x_{n,m}^{-i} \cdot u_{n,m}. \tag{23}$$

Since, $x_{n,m}$ is the solution that maximizes the objective function (8), we have:

$$\sum_{k \in N \setminus \{i\}} \sum_{m \in M} x_{k,m} \cdot u_{k,m} \geq \sum_{k \in N \setminus \{i\}} \sum_{m \in M} x'_{k,m} \cdot u'_{k,m}, \tag{24}$$

thus, $U_{i,m} \geq U'_{i,m}$, and the MNO i cannot increase its utility by bidding unilaterally untruthfully. Therefore, bidding $u_{i,m}$ is always a weakly dominant strategy.

APPENDIX D: PROOF OF THEOREM 3

As it has been proved that the scheme is truthful, $b_{n,m} = u_{n,m}$, $\forall n \in N$, and the utility of a winning MNO is $U_{n,m} = 0$, which is non-negative, proving the individual rationality.

Chapter 9
D2D- and DTN-Based Efficient Data Offloading Techniques for 5G Networks

Bighnaraj Panigrahi
Tata Consultancy Services, India

Bhushan Jagyasi
Pristine Retail Solutions, India

Hemant Kumar Rath
Tata Consultancy Services, India

Anantha Simha
Tata Consultancy Services, India

ABSTRACT

With the advancement of smart phone technologies cellular communication has come to a stage where user bandwidth has surpassed the available bandwidth. In addition, the well-organized but stubborn architecture of cellular networks sometimes creates hindrance to the optimal usage of the network resources. Due to this, a User Equipment (UE) experiencing a poor channel to the Base Station (BTS) or evolved NodeB (eNB) or any other Access Point (AP) retransmits the data. In such scenarios, Device-to-Device (D2D) communication and offload/relay underlying the cellular networks or the access networks provides a unique solution where the affected UE can find a close proximity offloader UE to relay its data to eNB. Delay Tolerant Networks (DTN) is another framework which has potential usage in low-connectivity zones like cell edge and/or remote locations in cellular networks. This chapter investigates various possibilities where D2D and DTN can be jointly used to improve teledensity as well delayed but guaranteed services to poor or no connectivity areas.

INTRODUCTION

Today's generation is witnessing a continuous and exponential growth in cellular devices, applications, and data usage. In the future, mobile devices including surveillance cameras, smart-city/home/grid devices etc., are expected to increase by 10- to 100- to 1000- fold. This huge transition presents a formidable challenge in the field of wireless communications. Moreover, each one of us desires to stay connected all the time in a seamless manner through social networking, on-line gaming, and ubiquitous business framework, etc. With the demand in data usage increasing day-by-day and 5G knocking the

DOI: 10.4018/978-1-5225-2023-8.ch009

doors, mobile operators are facing a major challenge in providing adequate services. In addition to this, with limited spectrum available and almost saturated channel capacity, supporting extra services becomes a nightmare for the operators. At present, the mobile operators are struggling to make significant profit on voice, message, and other services due to the advancement of Over-The-Top (OTT) services like instant messaging, multimedia services such as photo sharing, video calling and other popular mobile application based free services.

To match the above demand and to generate more revenue from their operations, operators need to increase the capacity of the cellular networks which means both the access capacity from the mobile to the Base Stations (BTSs) or Access Points (APs) and the backhaul capacity from the BTSs/APs to the core network has to be increased. This can be achieved in three different ways:

1. Add new BTSs/Aps,
2. Release new spectrum,
3. Increase the spectral efficiency of the technology used.

However, these are neither feasible nor scalable due to various reasons, and hence not viable for the operators to continue in making business. Moreover, as predicted by industry and academia, all the above techniques can only add 15-20 times capacity (even with LTE and LTE-Adv technologies that is expected to roll out by the year 2017-18). Therefore it is hard to find "*a solution*" or a "*class of solutions*" which can support more than 1,000 times traffic growth. Mobile operators need to evaluate alternate solutions or ways to handle this growth in a cost effective manner. The operators not only need to find-out cost effective solutions, but also look for solutions which are complementary in nature as "*one technology fits all*" will not be able to cater the traffic growth. The seamless integration of such complementary technologies with evolved 3G and 4G can bring a new consumer experience, enable a host of new services and can be called as the evolution towards 5G.

Technologies such as Wireless Fidelity (WiFi), Small Cells, Delay Tolerant Network (DTN) based Relays, and Device-to-Device (D2D) communications have emerged as some of the complimentary solutions to the cellular technology through simultaneous transmission or offloading. Many a times, although the mobile users are communicating (sharing files) in close proximity (in a stadium, club, office, homes, etc.), they require to follow the existing cellular transmission procedures, i.e., up link from the sender mobile to the base station (BTS or eNB) first, and then down link from eNB to the receiver mobile. This is not only complex, but also resource consuming. In such scenarios, Device-to-Device (D2D) communication can be used as an alternative; can be realized as a network assisted service in which eNB facilitates the peer to peer (P2P) or Device-to-Device connectivity. In addition, other technologies such as WiFi Direct and Bluetooth can also be used in such scenarios. Since there is a proximity involved, the transmission power required in such cases is significantly low. Therefore, D2D communication not only can be used to bring connectivity to proximity users, but also it can be used to bring connectivity to users who are in an isolated area or experiencing poor channel to the eNB or BTS.

D2D can be further used for mobile data offloading in which users with poor radio channels are able to upload their data to eNB by offloading through a proximal device (mobile) that has a good radio channel. For example, as shown in Figure 1, UE_2 and UE_3, UE_6 and UE_7 can have proximity based peer-to-peer connections, whereas UE_2 to eNB connection can be facilitated by UE_3 using the concept

Figure 1. Proximity services: need of the hour

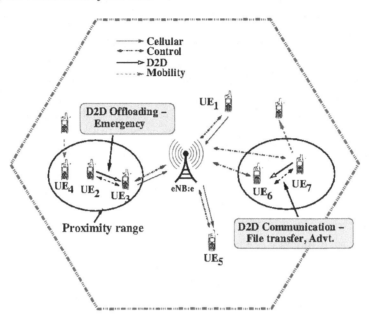

of D2D offloading. Proximity based services are not only useful for commercial services, but also are useful for emergency services as explained in the figure.

Another interesting but challenging problem operators face is to provide guaranteed connectivity to their users in remote villages, agricultural lands, mines, jungles, hilly areas, etc. It has been observed that rural and tribal folks travel for several kilometers to make a voice call. Data connectivity of 2G/3G is even worse in these areas. It has been felt that there exists a communication barrier due to the poor cellular network connectivity in several deployment locations in India and other developing countries. For instance, in remotely located tea farms and tea estates of Assam, India, telecommunication network is intermittent and very poor. Further, in the Araku constituency of Andhra Pradesh, India, which is known for its organic cultivation of coffee, rubber and spices, network is only available in selected pockets. Due to this, farmers of these regions face difficulty to get the relevant advice on their cultivation related queries. As farmer queries are mostly not delay sensitive concepts of Delay Tolerant Networks (DTN) can be extended to provide cost-effective, easy to deploy guaranteed communication in such areas.

DTN, which is getting more focus these days (Doppler et al., 2009) is initially designed for harsh and challenging conditions where continuous Internet connectivity cannot be guaranteed. To compensate data loss due to frequent disconnections, a relay node or a DTN node used to store data packets with itself until connection to a forwarding node is established again. The use of this paradigm becomes critical in challenging scenarios like satellite, military, and rural applications. In countries like India, where the lack of infrastructure makes seamless end-to-end connectivity difficult, DTN can be used as an alternative and effective solution. DTN combined with D2D communications and offloading, where D2D outlines the proximity based local communication and DTN outlines the end-to-end communication framework, can be very much applicable in many low-connectivity network zones to provide guaranteed communication and to improve the quality of the network performance.

Figure 2. Extending the reach by D2D and DTN

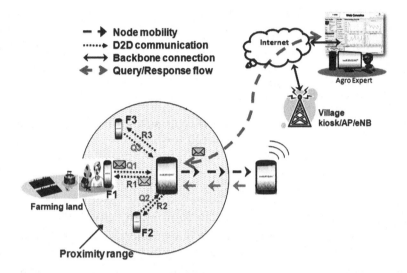

Figure 2 outlines a scenario, where the concept of DTN can be utilized to provide value added services to farmers (F1, F2, and F3) in a poor or no connectivity area. Farmers connect to the relay node R2 using proximity based services and then R2 uses the concept of store-and-forward mechanism to transfer farmers' queries to an Agro Expert.

This chapter primarily starts with D2D communications and offloading in Long Term Evolution (LTE) networks. D2D performance in terms of spectral efficiency improvement is presented and evaluated through extensive simulations. Post that, Delay Tolerant Networks concepts are presented and a use case where DTN along with D2D are jointly used to provide guaranteed end-to-end communications for the farmers is discussed. A complete framework of the above use case along with Android developments is also evaluated next. This chapter concludes with necessary future works' discussion which can be taken up by the academia and research community to provide seamless connectivity solutions required for 5G and Internet of Things (IoT).

BACKGROUND

Data offloading has been considered as one of the key solutions to handle the traffic on the networks by 3GPP (3GPP, 2000). In Sankaran et al., 2012, the basic concepts of offloading methods in Internet Protocol (IP) networks are discussed. Offloading the cellular traffic to WiFi networks are studied in Hinger et al. 2014. In a similar way, studies have also been carried out in offloading the traffic to small cells or *femto* cells (3GPP23.829, 2011). The authors in Pyattaev et al., 2013 have explored offloading the cellular traffic onto the WiFi Direct links and have analyzed their performance with respect to the LTE networks. In Rebecchi et al., authors have elaborated different types of offloading techniques. The authors have conducted a comprehensive survey of various state-of-the-art data offloading techniques. Assisted offloading has been presented in Andreev et. al., 2015 where, the authors have modeled dynamic network by Poisson point process and demonstrated offloading process by assuming cellular users in the licensed spectrum and D2D users in the unlicensed spectrum. These data offloading schemes are different from the basic D2D offloading schemes as:

- They follow a different network architecture and services and hence, availability, reliability, etc., cannot be guaranteed.
- Minimal control of cellular networks.

Since data offloading is the major theme of this chapter, state-of-the-art on various offloading techniques is presented as follows.

State-of-the-Art Wi-Fi Offloading

WiFi Offloading is a complementary network technology which delivers data originally targeted for cellular networks in a spectral efficient and cost-effective manner. It reduces the amount of data being carried on the cellular bands; hence freeing bandwidth for other applications and users. Schwartz et. al. (2012) justifies the need of WiFi offloading and discusses issues related to deploying WiFi offloading solutions at present and in the future. It considers the Capital and Operational Expenditure (CAPEX/OPEX) issues related to deployment. Further, it analyzes two deployment use-cases – WiFi offloading in New York and Sandiago, where non-standard device-initiated deployments are in place. Zwickl et. al. (2013) highlights the need of inter-operator collaboration models for selecting the spectrum (frequency bands) required in WiFi operation, when operators use carrier WiFi for offloading. It also talks about different revenue models which can be explored by the operator. Lee et. al., 2012 discusses on possible deployment scenarios and revenue model for WiFi offloading for a European and American requirement. It also mentions that delayed offloading based on traffic characterization can benefit the operator as well as the customer. Wang et. al. (2013) discusses on interference management in Heterogeneous Networks (HetNet) – between Macro and Femto cells and proposes a novel scheme via Traffic Offloading. This paper also solves a joint offloading/scheduling Small Cell and WiFi scheme to handle the interference issues and data requirements.

Lee et. al. (2010) presents a quantitative study on the performance of 3G mobile data offloading through WiFi (device-initiated) networks through test-bed level experiments and simulations. Balasubramanian et. al. (2010) investigates the possibility of WiFi access to augment 3G mobile capacity through drive-tests and analysis. Authors of Amelichev et. al. (2010) have proposed methods for handover between WiFi and 3G networks. They have also estimated the handover delays and shown that their estimates are reasonable for most network applications, except for the applications which are sensitive to delays (such as VoIP or streaming video). They have also proposed a network fitness function, which can be used by the operators while deciding between networks to choose for offload.

State-of-the-Art Small Cell Offloading

Small Cell Offloading is another alternate offloading solution, which proposes to use femto cells or small/micro cells in addition to the existing macro cell operation of the cellular networks. In general, small cells also use the same license band as that of the macro cell. Therefore, unlike the best-effort service offered by WiFi networks, small cells are provided by mobile operators as a managed service. However, small cells are comparatively new technology than WiFi, which are already deployed in many places. In Prasad et. al. (2013), the authors attempt to give proper justifications on how and why small cells can be used for mobile data offloading. They have extended their work in Prasad et. al. (2013a) and proposed a mathematical model to evaluate the pricing structure for Internet Service Providers (ISPs) who wish to expand their small cell network to offload more 4G data traffic. However, it cannot change its pricing structure due to exogenous factors, e.g., presence of a major competitor. In a recent article, (Andrews et. al., 2012), the authors proposed a distributed framework which can support multi-mode Small Cell Base Stations (SCBSs) that can transmit simultaneously on both licensed and unlicensed bands. In their proposed game theoretic procedure, called dubbed cross-system learning, they integrate cellular and WiFi networks where every SCBS,. It use an intelligent and online learning mechanism to optimize its licensed spectrum transmission, while at the same time WiFi is leveraged by offloading delay tolerant traffic.

State-of-the-Art D2D Offloading

In the last few years, significant research advancement is being witnessed in the area of Device-to-Device (D2D) communication for cellular networks. Some early works on ad-hoc networks (Lin et al., 2000; Wu et al., 2001) proposed the idea of modeling D2D communication as a means of relaying in cellular networks. Assisted offloading has been presented in Sergey et al., 2015 where the authors have modeled the dynamic network by Poisson point process and demonstrated the offloading process by assuming cellular users in licensed spectrum and the D2D users in the unlicensed spectrum. The concept of allowing local D2D communication to use cellular spectrum resources simultaneously with uplink/downlink in cellular traffic is mentioned initially by Doppler et al. (2009) and Yu et al. (2011) and has gained much interest since then. Three kinds of resource sharing modes are mentioned in literature:

1. **D2D Mode Reusing Cellular Resources:** Simultaneous D2D and cellular transmission on same Resource Block (RB), i.e., frequency band.
2. **D2D Mode Using Orthogonal Resources:** Both D2D and cellular transmissions do not overlap.
3. **Cellular Mode in which the D2D Pair Communicates through the Cellular eNB:** No separate D2D pairs defined (Panigrahi et al., 2015, 2015a).

Though the academia and research communities are investigating various issues related to offloading seriously in the near past, it is observed that the current state of the art and standards have not addressed the offloading solution significantly. While offloading improves the spectral efficiency, it also imposes challenges in terms of proper network management, provisioning, scalability, Quality of Services (QoS) guarantee, energy efficiency, spectral efficiency, device management, etc. Standardization of D2D under 3GPP started in 2011 3GPP meeting (3GPP, 2000) and a study item description on the radio aspects D2D discovery and communication has been submitted. However 3GPP's main focus is to design LTE enabled proximity services for emergency situations in which two devices can directly communicate even when the network is down (without operators' intervention). Much development to provide D2D as a commercial service has so far not gathered attention. Since the operators require control over the D2D services for billing, regulatory, and security prospective, it is necessary to bring commercial D2D into the 3GPP standard. Moreover, better user experience has to be guaranteed to D2D users, without which the users may turn to traditional D2D technologies (WiFi Direct, Bluetooth, Infrared, etc.), which are free but at a lower speed and compromised security.

To provide Internet connectivity in rural India, a Sustainable Access in Rural India (SARI) program (Conroy, 2006), a DTN like framework has been initiated in which Internet kiosks have been distributed in different villages. However, providing and maintaining kiosks in every village are not feasible. Another project called Computers on Wheels (COW), Conroy (2006) was started in 2006, in which motorcycles with Internet equipment act as mobile kiosks and travel to remote villages to collect the data from users emulating the age old Postal System where Postmen are used to visit villages to collect and deliver letters. In DTN paradigm connections can be intermittent and hence nodes store the data till connection to a forwarding node is available again. The disconnection from the Internet can be for majority of the time and data exchange can take very long time. Research on DTN started initially as the space application for Inter Planetary Networks (IPNs) (Akyildiz et al., 2003; Fall, 2003) with a low network dynamic of satellites and rovers. In mobile wireless networks, the applications of DTNs have been envisioned for Vehicular Ad-hoc NETworks (VANETs), Under Water Networks (UWNs), Packet Switched Networks (PSNs), and suburb networks for developing regions. In Gupta et al., 2015, authors have explored the feasibility of DTNs in enabling value added services to the rural farmers in a time bound manner and have used smart phones with mKRISHI® (Jagyasi et al., 2013) application to provide end-to-end guaranteed connectivity to the farmers in tea gardens of Assam. It has been observed that DTN can be an alternative solution in providing data services in poor connectivity areas and the combination of D2D with DTN can be used as an efficient offloading technique for the next generation networks.

This chapter highlights the need of DTN and D2D combination as an alternative efficient offloading scheme for the next generation networks.

MAIN FOCUS OF THE CHAPTER

Efficient Proximity-Based Communication

As discussed earlier, in a conventional mode of communication, irrespective of the distance and proximity, mobile users communicate via the regular Base Station (BTS) or eNB or AP. Due to this, even if the mobile users are at proximity and the channel between them is good, they have to communicate through the BTS. It results in more energy consumption by the mobile devices as well as the BTS. Moreover, this also impacts the spectral efficiency of the system. In such scenarios, Device-to-Device (D2D) communication plays an important role. In D2D communication, two mobiles can directly communicate between themselves using the same cellular resources (sub-carrier/channel) as peer-to-peer communication, with some assistance of the eNB or using traditional peer-to-peer communication techniques such as WiFi Direct or Bluetooth. This helps in direct transfer of data between two close-by mobiles at a higher data rate with less transmission power. Although, WiFi Direct, Bluetooth, InfraRed, etc., can be used for creating D2D services, cellular-D2D, which is being coined by the 3GPP forum is more efficient as it works under same network (as the cellular) and on same cellular spectrum.

Device-to-Device (D2D) Communication and Offloading in Cellular Networks

As per the 3GPP standard, each User Equipment (UE) reports uplink channel condition along with its location information using Sounding Reference Signal (SRS) to the eNB. Based on the SRS information the eNB discovers the proximity of the UEs and decides the mode of communication between the UEs, i.e., whether regular or D2D mode of communication. Further, based on the received Signal to Interference and Noise Ratio (SINR) at the eNB, the eNB assigns modulation schemes, transmission power, and coding rates to each UE. Note that, maximum capacity for a particular radio channel is constant corresponding to the best modulation and coding scheme selected; different users may have different effective capacities depending on their dynamic channel conditions. Post that, eNB schedules the UEs as per their QoS requirements and their profiles, and the communication continues. In this process two important resources such as energy and spectrum are utilized efficiently; optimal transmission power due to the mode of communication (D2D consumes low power due to the proximity between two communicating UEs) and spectrum re-use due to low interference caused because of the low transmission power.

Figure 3 explains different modes of communication that is possible under LTE Networks. Note that, D2D communication can be extended to single-hop as well as multi-hop offloading based communications by appropriate scheduling at the eNBs.

D2D communication can be further extended to support multi-hop or relay-based communications. In such scenarios, the cell edge UEs or UEs that are experiencing a poor channel condition can relay their data to the eNB via a close proximity relay UE who has a better channel condition with the eNB. In other words, data offloading takes place between the poor channel UE and the relaying UE for seamless connection. Figure 3 explains relay based communication in LTE Networks. Though D2D relay communication uses at-least two hops as compared to the single hop cellular communications, it can bring improvement in network performance in terms of throughput, delay and energy consumption. Novel dynamic D2D relay scheme along with adaptive modulation based uplink scheduling framework for commercial usage of D2D communication has been proposed in Panigrahi et al., 2015. Note that, optimal offloader or relay selection and scheduling schemes should be flexible enough to handle the change in data rates due to channel variations and mobility of the UEs.

To evaluate the performance of the D2D offloading scheme Panigrahi et al. (2015) have conducted extensive simulations using MATLAB with 100 different seed values. For the sake of completeness and to emphasize the performance improvement of D2D offloading schemes, a relevant simulation result is

Figure 3. Modes of communications under LTE

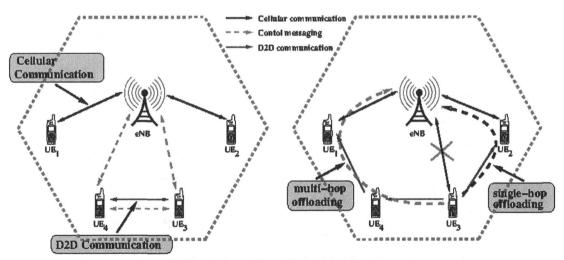

Different modes of communication

being presented in this chapter. For the simulations, a single eNB with 100 randomly positioned UEs within a radius of 250 m is considered. On an average 50% UEs are selected as active transmitters. The remaining UEs are kept as either idle or receiver UEs. The idle UEs are considered to be potential D2D relays. A radius of 30 m is assumed as the D2D transmission range. The UEs are provided with low mobility with a walk interval between [1, 3] seconds, with a speed of [0, 0.5] m/s and only in the forward direction with angle of deviation as ±45 degrees. D2D offloading vs. existing cellular network in terms of spectral efficiency improvement has been presented in Figure 4; for UEs with low SINR profiles, D2D offloading can provide better spectral efficiency. Moreover, it also shows that closer the D2D relay node, better is the spectral efficiency.

In heterogeneous network conditions, many wireless technologies such as WiFi direct, Bluetooth and cellular technologies are used simultaneously. In such a case a communication framework can be designed, in which all these alternative technologies should be used jointly to provide guaranteed connectivity in a cost-effective and spectral/power efficient manner. In such a scenario, D2D communication can be realized through the traditional WiFi Direct or Bluetooth and communication/offloading through cellular technologies. Appropriate standardization efforts are necessary to bring this engineering approach into a reality.

Delay Tolerant Networks/Communication

In recent times, Delay Tolerant Networks/Communication has started gaining lot of interest because of its ability to deal even with limited or no dedicated infrastructure. It uses *a store- forward* method of message delivery in the absence of contemporaneous end-to-end paths. The *store -forward* method of message delivery is mostly realized by the use of a single or multiple number of relay nodes, which can

Figure 4. Spectral efficiency improvement with D2D

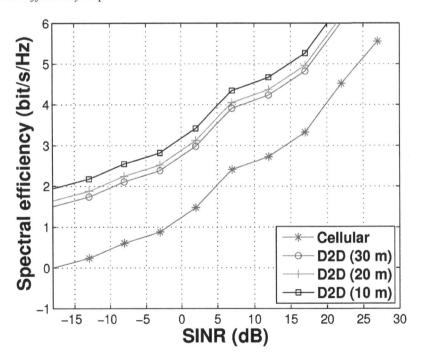

be permanent or ad-hoc in nature. These relay nodes can be satellites, mobile base stations, agent carrying a smart phone or a relay antenna, relay node/BTS/APs installed on local transport system, drones or Un-manned Arial Vehicles (UAVs), etc. Due to the nature of this kind of communication and networking, Delay Tolerant Communication is also known as Disruption Tolerant Communication or Networking. Therefore, this nature of DTN makes itself as a prime contender for emergency communication, which can be extensively used during floods, earthquakes, tsunamis, and many other natural calamities.

DTN can also be used to improve *teledensity* in areas where cellular data coverage is poor or absent by extending the age old Postal System of communication as the e-carrier in the last-mile. For example, the Sustainable Access in Rural India (SARI) program (Conroy, 2006), consists of disseminating more than 80 rural Internet kiosks distributed in the Madurai area of Tamil Nadu in India are used to bridge the gap in the last-mile of communication. Another similar project called Computers on Wheels (COW) (Conroy et. Al., 2006) was started in 2006, in which motorcycles with Internet equipment act as mobile kiosks. These mobile kiosks visit remote villages regularly to collect the data from users. These kiosks are also used to deliver the replies and acknowledgements (if any) back for the previous day messages, next day while collecting new data. Similar projects are also being undertaken by various other agencies of India in Assam, Andhra Pradesh, Maharashtra, Karnataka, etc. At present these DTN based techniques are being used to provide broadband connectivity in rural areas; an attempt to improve *teledensity* in such areas.

DTN is flexible and a lenient communication layer structure, has ability to handle worse kind of intermittent and disrupted connectivity, and most importantly is cost effective. DTN deployments can be broadly categorized as:

1. Opportunistic,
2. Scheduled.

Under Opportunist mode, relay of contact reoccurrence may never happen as in disaster recovery scenarios. Under Scheduled DTN mode, relays are scheduled and the period of connectivity can be predicted, resulting in possible data offloading scenarios which can be used to improve coverage. Both the above deployment scenarios use two broad types of communication protocols/schemes to forward the concerned data:

1. Replication based forwarding,
2. Single copy forwarding.

Under replication based forwarding, multiple relay agents can be used to forward or offload the same data; replicate the same data in various methods. Since the relay paths are different, random and are mostly noisy, the replicated messages are received at different time instants. To reconstruct the transmitted message the multiple received copies can be combined using various techniques at the receiver end which can improve the message reception capability significantly. Replication based forwarding are mostly used in satellite and inter-terrestrial communications or in emergency communications or in situations where each relay path cannot give a guarantee in relaying the data successfully to the receiver. On the other hand, single copy forwarding scheme is used where the relays are more reliable and delayed but guaranteed data delivery is possible. This chapter uses a combination of opportunistic and scheduled mode of deployment with both single copy and replication based forwarding for data offloading.

D2D-DTN: A NOVEL SOLUTION FOR FUTURE GURANTEED GREEN COMMUNICATION

This section outlines an innovative scheme which can be used to facilitate data connectivity in poor or no coverage areas using a joint D2D and DTN based approaches. As a deployment use case, time-bound agro-advisory services to farmers located in remote areas with either no or limited network coverage is being considered in this chapter. Using this innovative scheme, communication barrier is removed in an efficient manner. Though the proposed scheme is deployed for a simple but an important practical use case without considering the data rate needs and delay guarantees of 5G Networks, it can be extended to data offloading in 5G Networks as well.

This chapter considers a Rural Participatory Sensing framework, in which farmers living in a no or poor coverage area gathers various farming related information such as crop diseases, pests used, nutrient disorders and other activities using a Personalized Services Delivery Platform call mKRISHI®. This platform enables two-way information exchange between the farmers and the expert systems. The expert system includes virtual knowledge banks, Agriculture Experts, Procurement Officers (PO), etc., situated mostly in cities. Each query generated at the farmers' end may consist of geo-tagged photographs, voice clip, meta-data, etc., and has a unique pair of Event ID (EID) bounded with the User ID (UID) or Farmer ID which is assigned from the expert system or the server. In case network coverage is available, mKRISHI can allow the farmers to communicate with the expert system directly. Otherwise, mKRISHI uses a store and forward application in which queries can be stored in the local memory which needs to be communicated at a later point of time. To realize the store and forward communication in no or poor network coverage areas, a D2D-DTN based approach is being proposed. While D2D is used for collection of data locally, DTN is used to provide store and forward mechanism.

In the proposed solution, a relay node is being defined which can operate in both opportunistic as well as scheduled mode of DTN. A relay node can be any other smart phone which can be used by other fellow farmers, farm agents, or field executives, that comes in close proximity to the farmers at the remote locations. The functionalities of the relay node are as follows:

1. Collect farmers' sensed data or queries using D2D and store them till network is available.
2. Transmit the collected queries from one or more farmers to the expert system using available network technologies (viz., WiFi, cellular or any other) in a time-bound manner.
3. Collect and communicate the acknowledgements (ACKs) and advisories from the expert system to the farmers.

The proposed solution is adaptive to relay node selection, technologies, data rates, and environmental conditions. Both single and multi-hop relay node based communication is used to extend the services in remote areas. Moreover, a particular relay node may or may not visit the farming area again. Therefore both opportunistic as well as scheduled mode of DTN deployment is required. Appropriate application level security and privacy schemes are to be used to ensure data security and privacy in such scenarios.

Proposed Solution: Building Blocks

The solution is realized with three broad modules:

1.   Farmer Node,
2.   Relay Node,
3.   Expert System.

Out of these three modules, Farmer Node and Relay Node are in general use smart phones with Android Operating Systems (OS) running mKRISHI application. Farmer Node has the capability to sense and digitize the queries which need to be transmitted to the Expert System. Each event or query generated at the Farmer Node is time tagged and the mKRISHI platform stores the events in its internal memory such that, based on the network availability, it can transmit to the expert system, either directly or through a Relay Node. Figure 5 explains the block diagram of the proposed solution; the logical communication framework versus the physical communication framework visits the no or poor coverage areas, and can create multiple Device-to-Device (D2D) connections with multiple Farmer Nodes using LTE-based D2D or WiFi Direct or any other proximity based communication technique. Though several proximity connection technologies are possible, this chapter deals with WiFi Direct to connect the Farmer Nodes to the Relay Nodes. These D2D connections can be auto sensed or discovered or can be manually triggered. It uses the license free spectrum (ISM band) and self initiated discovery and signaling techniques for the D2D communication initialization. At present, it uses a very low power (fixed) transmission for the D2D communication; transmission power can be further reduced using sophisticated signaling and adaptive modulation and coding schemes. Appropriate security and privacy mechanisms are in place to authenticate the Relay as well as the Farmer Node. Once the communication link is set-up, the queries from the Farmer Nodes are transferred to the Relay Node which stores all the queries received from various Farmers and assigns priorities to the queries based on their associated time stamps. The relay node would then transmit all the queries to the server using its own network or by physically moving to an available network zone. Though multi-hop relaying is possible, at present it is out of the scope of this chapter. Similar to the forward direction flow of queries, the Relay Node also collects the ACKs/responses for the queries from the server and delivers to the Farmer Nodes within a permissible time bound.

It is to be noted that, Relay Node clears its own memory once the queries are successfully transferred to the server. Appropriate ACK based protocols such as Transmission Control Protocol (TCP) based connections are in place to ensure the guaranteed communication. Unlike the Relay Node, Farmer Nodes keep their queries in their own memory for a significant time period as they receive the ACKs and responses to their queries in a delayed time frame due to the DTN framework. Once the ACKs are received, queries are flushed at the Farmer Nodes. In addition to this, to ensure freshness in the queries, each query is also time lived, i.e., each query has a maximum life period of 24 hours. Post that, irrespective of whether the queries are transferred or not, they are flushed out from the Farmer's Node.

To make the deployment more flexible, the forward and reverse flow of message between the Farmer Node and the Server can also be made possible using two different Relay Nodes. To enable this multiple relay node options, server maintains a map of Relay Nodes and their registered Farmer Nodes. Note that, responses are required to be received by the farmer within a specified time period (T_r - 24 hours in this solution) starting from the query generation time. Else, the Farmer Node discards the query; new queries are generated again. Similar to the Responses, ACKs are also to be received by the Farmer Node within a fixed time period T_d ($T_d << T_r$). It is generally assumed that Relay Node can go online fairly quickly ($< T_d$) since it is mobile. To take care of the situation that the Relay Node due to some emergency is un-

Figure 5. Block diagram of the proposed solution relay nodes

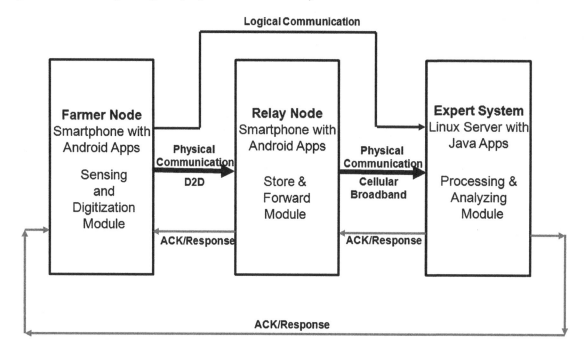

able to connect to the server within this time period, a timeout value is being used and a re-transmission to a possibly different Relay Node option is explored to ensure reliable message delivery to the server.

Figure 6 explains the control flow and depicts the timing details being used in D2D-DTN based mKRISHI solution. As shown in this figure, farmers can either connect directly to the server, if data connectivity is available (Mode1) or connect through an agent (Mode 2). This chapter focuses on Mode 2 communication. Events or queries (Ei) are being generated at the Farmer Node, communicated to the Server through the relay and corresponding ACKs (A_j) are sent by the Server to the Farmer Node (directly or through agents). As mentioned earlier, if the ACKs are not received in predefined time, the events are to be deleted from the Farmers' Node.

Proposed Solution: Practical Deployment

To realize the solution, Android based applications are developed along with the existing mKRISHI platform. These applications are deployed at the Farmers' smart phones as well as at the Relay Nodes. Relay selection, authentication, signaling for D2D communication, transmission power selection to improve battery lifetime of smart phones, prioritization of query transmission at the Relay Node based on the time stamps of the queries, and end-to-end time-bound communication for both the queries and the ACKs/Responses are the key functional modules developed. At the Expert System end, appropriate Java based applications are developed such that relay selection, ACK/Response maintenance and data analytics are performed seamlessly. These are simple and easy to deploy applications, which can be used by the farmers without much difficulty. Local language support is also being provided in the Apps, such that they can be adapted easily. Appropriate care has been taken by keeping security and privacy settings of smart phones intact while installing these Apps.

Figure 6. Control flow: D2D-DTN based solution for mKRISHI

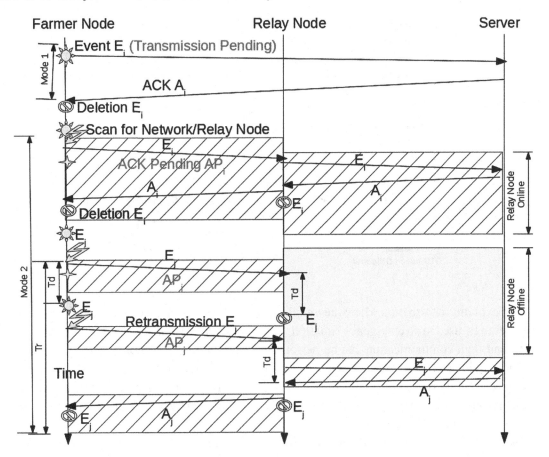

The proposed solution is deployed in the tea gardens of Assam and other areas in the North-East, Andhra Pradesh and Maharashtra are also being planned for future deployments. Cellular operators are also being approached to provide free services to the mKRISHI platform through the Relay Node such that more and more agro-advisory services can be penetrated. The proposed D2D-DTN based technique can also be enhanced for emergency situations, disaster management and for extending broadband connectivity in rural areas. Authenticated agents with D2D-DTN application enabled smart phones can also be used for relaying data from network disconnected users to a central agency.

D2D-DTN FOR 5G DATA OFFLOADING

As discussed earlier in this chapter, D2D Communication and Offloading are being proposed as part of the next generation networks to support emergency communication under 3GPP. Using D2D in combination with DTN, public safety mobile devices can rely on pre-configured network resources for connection initiation and maintaining data paths. In addition to this, the mobile devices can also be configured to manage radio resources using necessary control messages through self-discovery and signaling techniques.

Figure 7. D2D for emergency services

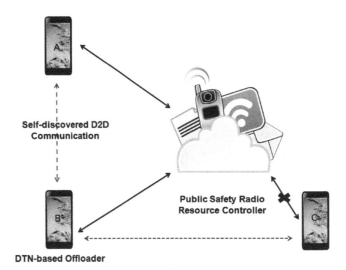

Figure 7 explains the situation where the mobile devices are aware of the channel, power and modulation schemes to be used in an emergency situation. Since network assistance is not possible, self-initiated discovery and then communication can be performed. This kind of D2D communication can also be extended to provide offloading services, where two mobile devices can interact with each other through a common relay node through a joint discovery and communication framework. The relay node can use simple pre-defined Time Division Multiplexing or Frequency Division Multiplexing techniques to realize the end-to-end communication.

Further, D2D in combination with DTN can be used to guarantee data connectivity in isolated areas such as inside lifts, basements, isolated office locations, multi-storey buildings, etc. Data connectivity can be maintained even with mobility. DTN helps in defining store-and-forwarding protocol, whereas D2D helps in creating links between the Access Points and/or other mobile devices while on move.

D2D-DTN: Improving the Teledensity

Figure 8 brings out a situation where wireless connectivity is available in a few pockets (a scenario in highways, or village roads, or jungles) and the mobile devices while on move generate data which needs to be communicated to the outside world. The data generated in the no-connectivity region are stored using the DTN framework and are offloaded to the external world once the mobile enters to a connectivity zone. All such possible combinations - D2D based on WiFi, LTE, Bluetooth or regular cellular communication can be explored in such areas. By re-creating several pockets on the highways or on the remote areas, end-to-end connectivity can be realized in a cost-effective manner; resulting in improving the teledensity.

Figure 8. DTN an enabler for data offloading and mobility

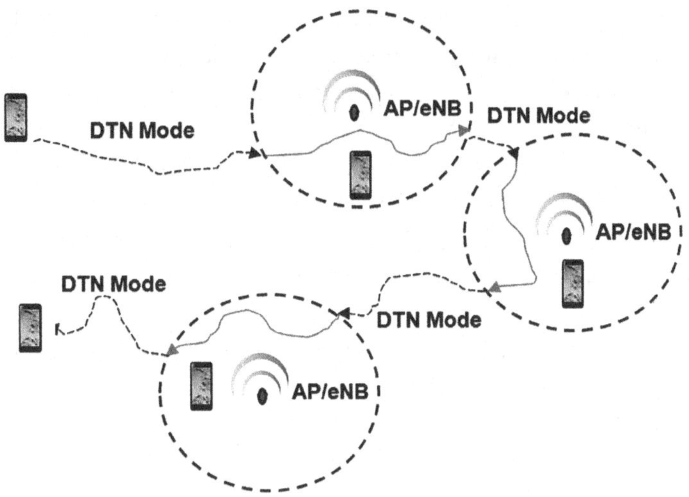

FUTURE RESEARCH DIRECTIONS

Though there are significant efforts being observed in all over the world, the current telecom world is still far away from the 5G goals. It has been observed that to achieve the goals of 5G in terms of data rates, delay, mobility, security and privacy, heterogeneous communication methodologies are the complementary solutions that operators should look for. This chapter has investigated in a similar direction and has proposed a joint D2D-DTN solution to improve teledensity and to ensure end-to-end connectivity required for agro-diversity services in India and other developing countries. However, various power and spectral efficient techniques are needed which can be used to provide commercial services as well as value added services to the citizens and telecom operators. In the digital world, bringing Government as well as social services to people poses major challenges. Apart from these, bringing affordability to the services and making them user friendly is another challenge. Scalability and our preparedness to counter the emergency situation in terms of quick connectivity, data rates, delay sensitiveness, power efficiency, and spectral efficiency during floods, cyclones, typhoons, tsunamis, earthquakes, and public gatherings also require special attention. Another important aspect which requires adequate attentions from researchers, industries, academia as well as Government is standardization of such techniques and protocols. Since many possible solutions are on the way, standardization plays a major role - to provide a level playing field to all - developers, operators, manufacturers in general and users in particular.

SOME OPEN RESEARCH PROBLEMS

Although data offloading is gathering lot of interest and is need of the hour, several challenges and open problems are still being investigated:

1. In order to have a tightly coupled co-existence and data offloading between cellular (3GPP) and non-cellular (WiFi) technologies, there should be a system level change.

2. Future 5G architectures should intelligently support the distribution of heterogeneous classes of services, including regular, highly delay sensitive or real-time and delay-tolerant flows. This needs to cope with traffic increase of several orders of magnitude.

3. Operator level and device level changes required along with energy aware dynamic discovery, appropriate scheduling, billing mechanism, privacy mechanism, incentive mechanism, and power control algorithms required to be developed to realize efficient D2D data offloading technique.

4. In case of DTN based offloading several challenges such as providing bounded delayed yet guaranteed delivery of data, assisting users in the opportunistic data retrieval, appropriate intermediate data storage mechanisms, robust data security and privacy models.

A fine comprehension of data traffic and mobility patterns of nodes is required to be developed.

CONCLUSION

This chapter outlines an innovative, easy to deploy framework which can be used for data offloading and to improve teledensity in poor or no coverage areas. The communication framework proposed here uses the combination of D2D and DTN techniques, and it can be extended to provide value added services such as e-Governance, e-Healthcare, e-Administration, e-Education, etc., at a low cost and easy to deploy manner. An Android - Java based deployment framework based on mKRISHI is also designed and deployed in the tea gardens of Assam, India. This framework is being used to provide agro-advisory services to farmers in their native languages. This framework can also be extended to provide smart-village and smart-city applications in a time and cost efficient manner. Though the proposed framework is being used to improve teledensity and agro-advisory services, seamless and end-to-end connectivity and mobility support as required for 5G and IoT services can also be planned using the D2D-DTN framework in future.

REFERENCES

Akyildiz, I. F., Akan, O. B., Chen, C., Fang, J., & Su, W. (2003). Interplanetary internet: State-of-the-art and research challenges. *Computer Networks*, *43*(2), 75–112. doi:10.1016/S1389-1286(03)00345-1

Amelichev, N., & Krinkin, K. (2010). Simulation of 3G/WLAN Offload: first steps. *8th Conference of Open Innovations Framework Program FRUCT*, Lappeenranta, Finland.

Andreev, Galinina, Pyattaev, Johnsson, & Koucheryavy. (2015). Analyzing Assisted Offloading of Cellular User Sessions onto D2D Links in Unlicensed Bands. *Journal on Selected Areas in Communications, 33*(1), 67–80.

Andreev, Galinina, Pyattaev, Johnsson, & Koucheryavy. (2015). Analyzing Assisted Offloading of Cellular User Sessions onto D2D Links in Unlicensed Bands. *IEEE Journal on Selected Areas in Communications, 33*(1), 67-80.

Andrews, G. (2012). Femto-cells: Past, Present, and Future. *IEEE Journal on Selected Areas in Communications*.

Balasubramanian, A., Mahajan, R., & Venkataramani, A. (2010). Augmenting mobile 3G using WiFi. *Proceedings of ACM MobiSys*.

Castro, M., Galluccio, L., Kassler, A., & Rametta, C. (2010, October). Opportunistic P2P Communications in Delay-Tolerant Rural Scenarios. *EURASIP Journal on Wireless Communications and Networking*, *2011*(9).

Conroy, C. (2006). *Telecentre initiatives in rural india: Failed fad or the way forward?* Natural Resources Institute, University of Greenwich.

Conroy, C. (2006). *Telecentre Initiatives in Rural India*. Natural Resources Institute, University of Greenwich.

Doppler, K., Rinne, M., Wijting, C., Ribeiro, C. B., & Hugl, K. (2009). Device-to-device communication as an underlay to LTE-advanced networks. *IEEE Communications Magazine*, *47*(10), 42–49. doi:10.1109/MCOM.2009.5350367

Fall, K. (2003, August). A delay-tolerant network architecture for challenged internets.*Proceedings of ACM SIGCOMM*. doi:10.1145/863955.863960

3. GPP. (2012, August). *3rd generation partnership project; technical specification group sa; feasibility study for proximity services (prose)(release12)*. TR22.803 V1.0.0. 3GPP.

3GPP. (2011, August). *Technical Specification Group Services and SA; Local IP Access and Selected IP Traffic Offload (LIPA-SIPTO)(Release 10)*. TR23.829 V10.0.1. 3GPP.

Gupta, P., Jagyasi, B., Panigrahi, B., Rath, H. K., Papulla, S., & Simha, A. (2015). A Revolutionary Rural Agricultural Participatory Sensing Approach Using Delay Tolerant Networks.*Proceedings of 18th IEEE International Symposium on Wireless Personal Multimedia (WPMC)*.

Hinger, D., & Kalbande, D. (2014, April). Review of Mobile Data Offloading through Wi-Fi.*Proceedings of IEEE International Conference on Circuits, Systems, Communication and Information Technology Applications (CSCITA)*, 425–429. doi:10.1109/CSCITA.2014.6839298

Jagyasi B., Mohite J., & Pappula S. (2013, October). Applications of mobile sensing technologies in precision agriculture. *CSI Communications, 22–24.*

Lee, Yi, Chong, & Jin. (2012). *Economics of WiFi Offloading: Trading Delay for Cellular Capacity*. arXiv

Lee, K., Lee, J., Yi, Y., Rhee, I., & Chong, S. (2013). Mobile Data Offloading: How Much Can WiFi Deliver. *IEEE/ACM Transactions on Networking*, *21*(2), 536–550. doi:10.1109/TNET.2012.2218122

Lee, K., Rhee, I., Lee, J., Chong, S., Yi, Y., & Offloading, M. D. (2010). How Much Can WiFi Deliver? ACM CoNEXT 2010, Philadelphia, PA.

Lin, Y.-D., & Hsu, Y.-C. (2000, March). Multihop cellular: a new architecture for wireless communications. *Proceedings of 19th IEEE INFOCOM*, *3*, 1273–1282.

Panigrahi, B., Ramamohan, R., Rath, H. K., & Simha, A. (2015, December). Efficient Device-to-Device (D2D) Offloading Mechanism in LTE Networks.*Proceedings of 18th IEEE International Symposium on Wireless Personal Multimedia (WPMC)*.

Panigrahi, B., Rath, H. K., & Simha, A. (2015, February). Interference-aware Discovery and Optimal Uplink Scheduling for D2D Communication in LTE Networks.*Proceedings of 21st IEEE National Conference on Communication (NCC)*. doi:10.1109/NCC.2015.7084877

Prasad. (2013). *Energy-Efficient Flexible Inter-Frequency Scanning Mechanism for Enhanced Small Cell Discovery*. IEEE VTC, Dresden, Germany.

Prasad, A., Tirkkonen, O., Lundén, P., Yilmaz, O., Dalsgaard, L., & Wijting, C. (2013, May). Energy Efficient Inter-Frequency Small Cell Discovery Techniques for LTE-Advanced Heterogeneous Network Deployments. *IEEE Communications Magazine, 51*(5), 72–81. doi:10.1109/MCOM.2013.6515049

Rebecchi, F., Dias de Amorim, M., Conan, V., Passarella, A., Bruno, R., & Conti, M. (2015). Data Offloading Techniques in Cellular Networks: A Survey. IEEE Communications Surveys & Tutorials, 17(2), 580-603.

Sankaran. (2012). Data Offloading Techniques in 3GPP Rel-10 Networks: A Tutorial. *IEEE Communications Magazine, 50*(6), 46-53.

Schwartz & Johansson. (2012). *Wireless 2020, Carrier WiFi Offload, Building a Business Case for Carrier WiFi offload*. Academic Press.

Traffic Offloading onto WiFi Direct. (2013). *Wireless Communications and Networking Conference Workshops (WCNCW)*, 135-140.

Wang, Sheng, Zhang, & Jiang. (2013). *IM-Torch: Interference Mitigation via Traffic Offloading in Macro/Femto-cell+WiFi HetNets*. 24th IEEE PIMRC, London, UK.

Wu, H., Qiao, C., De, S., & Tonguz, O. (2001, October). Integrated cellular and ad hoc relaying systems: ICAR. *IEEE Journal on Selected Areas in Communications, 19*(10), 2105–2115.

Yu, C.-H., Doppler, K., Ribeiro, C., & Tirkkonen, O. (2011, August). Resource sharing optimization for device-to-device communication underlaying cellular networks. *IEEE Transactions on Wireless Communications, 10*(8), 2752–2763. doi:10.1109/TWC.2011.060811.102120

Zwickl, Fuxjaeger, Gojmerac, & Reichl. (2013). *Wi-FiOffload: Tragedy of the Commons or Land of Milk and Honey?*. 24th IEEE PIMRC, London, UK.

KEY TERMS AND DEFINITIONS

Android: A mobile Operating System (OS) developed by Google, based on the Linux kernel. It is designed primarily for touch screen mobile devices such as smart phones and tablets.

Device-to-Device (D2D): A mode of communication used for proximity users which enables direct communication between nearby mobiles.

Delay Tolerant Networks (DTN): A computer network architecture approach that addresses the technical issues in heterogeneous networks in terms of lack continuous network connectivity. This is also called as Disruption Tolerant Networks.

mKRISHI: The TCS's Mobile Agro Advisory System (mKrishi) connects farmers with an ecosystem that empowers them to make sound decisions about agriculture, drive profits and conserve the environment.

Chapter 10
Resource Allocation in Multi–Tier Femtocell and Visible–Light Heterogeneous Wireless Networks

Eirini Eleni Tsiropoulou
University of Texas at Dallas, USA

Panagiotis Vamvakas
National Technical University of Athens, Greece

Symeon Papavassiliou
National Technical University of Athens, Greece

ABSTRACT

The increasing demand in mobile data traffic, data hungry services and high QoS prerequisites have led to the design of advanced multi-tier heterogeneous cellular networks. In this chapter, a multi-tier heterogeneous wireless network is examined consisting of the macrocell, multiple femtocells and multiple Visible Light Communication (VLC) cells. Distributed resource allocation approaches in two-tier femto-cells are presented focusing on (a) power allocation and interference management, (b) joint power and rate allocation, and (c) resource allocation and pricing policies. Similarly, the most prominent resource allocation approaches in two-tier VLC cells are examined, including (a) user association and adaptive bandwidth allocation, (b) joint bandwidth and power allocation, and (c) interference bounded resource blocks allocation and power control. The resource allocation problem in the two-tier heterogeneous environment where both femtocells and VLC-LANs are simultaneously present is also discussed. Finally, detailed future directions and comprehensive conclusions are provided.

DOI: 10.4018/978-1-5225-2023-8.ch010

INTRODUCTION

The demand for higher data rates, energy-efficiency and interference improved solutions in wireless networks is unrelenting. The even-increasing support of wireless services, e.g. data transfer, voice, video streaming, e-Health, glasses / touch Internet, e-gaming, etc. via wireless networks has dictated the necessity for deploying more data supportive cellular architectures. The Ericsson Mobility Report (Cerwall et. al, 2015) presented in June 2015 predicts *9.2* billion total mobile subscriptions (i.e. mobile broadband, smartphones, mobile PCs, tablets and routers) by 2020, which is an increase of *30%* compared to 2014. Furthermore, it is estimated that *90%* of the world's population over 6 years old will have a mobile phone by 2020 (ITU, 2009; CISCO, 2012).

The next generation cellular wireless networks should be appropriately designed and amended to accommodate the ongoing growth of mobile data traffic, while in parallel improve their spectral and energy-efficiency. To cope with this trend, the current technologies and standards adopted in cellular wireless networks, i.e. Long Term Evolution (LTE), LTE-Advanced (LTE-A), High Speed Packet Access (HSPA), Worldwide Interoperability for Microwave Access (WiMAX), etc. should evolve towards supporting a multi-tier cellular architecture, where system's bandwidth reusability will be supported.

Aiming at achieving system's bandwidth reusability in the same physical area, the idea of cell splitting has been proposed and it is based on the hierarchical cell deployment model, where small cells with possibly different transmission technologies lie in the coverage area of a macrocell. This hierarchical infrastructure of a wireless network constitutes a heterogeneous network, i.e. HetNet (Damnjanovic et. al, 2011). However, though system capacity may increase via such an approach, several drawbacks exist in their deployment. These may include:

- The installation and maintenance of the cell towers is prohibitively expensive,
- They do not completely solve the indoor coverage problem,
- The radio frequency interference in the same bandwidth diminishes system's capacity,
- The backhaul deployment costs cannot be avoided.

Based on the above observations, more cost-effective solutions have emerged, such as femtocells and visible light communication cells.

A femtocell consists of a short-range (*10-30m*) low-cost and low-power (*10-100mW*) Femtocell Access Point (FAP) being installed by the consumers towards achieving better indoor coverage and capacity. FAPs transmit over a licensed Radio Frequency (RF) spectrum and are connected to the macrocell network via a broadband connection, e.g. Digital Subscriber Line (DSL), cable modem or via a dedicated RF backhaul channel. The main advantages of femtocells are:

1. Lower transmission power,
2. Prolongation of mobile users' battery life,
3. Higher signal-to-interference-plus-noise ratio (SINR),
4. Increased system capacity,
5. Reduced interference,
6. Low cost installation,
7. Increased number of served users in the same physical area (Chandrasekhar et. al, 2008).

Visible Light Communication (VLC) cells, developed by the IEEE 802.15.7 standard, operate in a different frequency band (i.e. *400 - 800 THz*) compared to RF communication, thus overcoming the burden of interference with RF-based small cells. A VLC cell consists of an Optical Access Point (OAP) with small coverage area (i.e. *1 – 4 m*). In VLC systems, the communication signal is encoded on top of the illumination light, thus resulting in energy-saving "green" communication and high-speed wireless connectivity reaching speeds of *224 Gbps* (Cuthbertson, 2015). The key advantages of VLC cells are:

1. Nearly infinite bandwidth,
2. Usage of free and unregulated channels,
3. They pose no health hazards, due to the non-existence of electromagnetic radiation,
4. They pose no electromagnetic interference (EMI) and / or no radio frequency interference (RFI),
5. Extremely low transmission power,
6. Almost no cost, due to the fact that light sources already exist everywhere (Ndjiongue et. al, 2015).

This chapter aims to present the architecture of a multi-tier heterogeneous wireless network and the different system models that are proposed in the literature for each type of small-cell technology, e.g. femtocell and VLC. The main goal of this work is to formulate and present the solutions of resource allocation problems in the multi-tier heterogeneous wireless environment, where different transmission technologies are adopted, e.g. CDMA, OFDMA and SC-FDMA. The included resource allocation problems can be either single or multi-variable ones, with continuous (e.g. transmission power, transmission rate etc.) or discrete resources (e.g. resource blocks) to be allocated to the users, depending on the adopted technology, i.e. CDMA, OFDMA or SC-FDMA. Therefore, different optimization techniques are considered towards confronting these problems, e.g. game-theoretic approaches, linear programming or even simplified heuristic algorithms.

The outline of the chapter is as follows. Initially, the overall multi-tier wireless network architecture is presented and subsequently the system model of two-tier femtocell networks and of visible light communication local area networks (VLC-LANs) is introduced. Then, various distributed resource allocation scenarios in the two-tier femtocell networks are discussed classified in three main categories based on their fundamental characteristics (i.e. power allocation and interference management, joint power and rate allocation and resource allocation and pricing policies). More specifically, the problem's formulation and solution, as well as an indicative algorithm to solve each resource allocation problem are analyzed per each category. Afterwards, dynamic resource allocation approaches adopted in VLC-LANs environment are described in four representative categories (i.e. user association, adaptive bandwidth allocation, joint bandwidth and power allocation, and interference bounded resource blocks allocation and power control). A similar methodology as before is followed, that is the corresponding problem formulation being initially presented, followed by the corresponding solution alongside an indicative algorithm to obtain it. Furthermore, the resource allocation problem in heterogeneous combined femtocells and VLC-LANs is discussed in detail as well. Finally, some future directions in the area of resource allocation in multi-tier heterogeneous wireless networks are discussed and some relative conclusions are drawn.

FUTURE GENERATION WIRELESS NETWORKS

Multi-Tier Wireless Network Architecture

Mobile broadband communication has gone beyond traditional voice services and targets to more data-hungry multimedia services, due to the emergence of plethora of new services and the advanced mobile terminals' capabilities. Based on a recent statistical research, a mobile subscriber consumes about *1GB* per month in 2014, while 3 years ago the average figures were about *0.5GB* per month. Additionally, it is estimated that a mobile user stays in an indoor environment *80%* of his connection time, while stays outdoors about *20%* of the time. Based on (Cullen, 2008), *30%* of business and *45%* of household users currently encounter poor indoor coverage. Thus, in order to address the traffic and data rate demands in a wireless environment, various parameters should be considered, e.g. user behavior, mobility, diverse Quality of Service (QoS) requirements, etc. Towards confronting the aforementioned data demands, three main strategies have been proposed:

1. Improve the macrocell infrastructure,
2. Densify the deployed macrocells, and
3. Complement the macrocell infrastructure with subscribers' developed small cells, e.g. femtocells, VLC cells, etc. and create heterogeneous network, i.e. HetNet.

The first two approaches are sometimes prohibitively expensive, difficult to be realized due to physical constraints and mainly target at supporting the outdoor coverage. On the other hand, HetNets focus on alleviating the traffic demand primarily in indoor environments. Among the various types of small cells, e.g. microcells, picocells, metrocells, etc., femtocells and VLC cells have recently arisen as the most cost-efficient, low-transmission power solutions.

The multi-tier wireless network architecture, i.e. macrocell, femtocell and VLC cells (MFV architecture), is illustrated in Figure 1. Femtocells have larger coverage area than VLC cells, thus multiple VLC cells can reside even within a femtocell. Both femtocells and VLC cells improve macrocell's performance and reliability, via decongesting the macrocell, allowing the latter to redirect its resources

Figure 1. Three-tier wireless network architecture

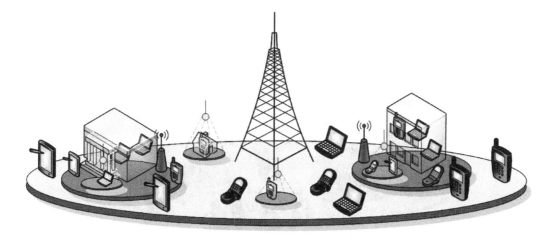

towards providing better reception for mobile users. Furthermore, they have increased cost benefits by reducing operating and capital expenditure costs of operators, as well as they set barriers to the indoor user to switch operators or maintain a dedicated wired line due to poor indoor coverage that they currently experience.

Several technical challenges may arise in the described three-tier MFV architecture (due to the dense deployment of femtocells and VLC cells), including the following:

- Resource allocation and interference management:
  ○ Co-tier and cross-tier interference mitigation.
- Cell association and admission control,
- Limited cross-tier signaling and absence of centralized control,
- Handoff and mobility management,
- Enabling self-* properties of mobile users, e.g. self-optimization, self-configuration, self-healing, etc.,
- Network performance analysis.

In this chapter, emphasis is placed on the resource allocation and interference management problem within this emerging heterogeneous wireless networking environment, as it evolves towards 5G technologies.

System Model of Two-Tier Femtocell Networks

The system model of a two-tier femtocell networks is examined, consisting of a central macrocell base station (MBS) $B_i = 0$ serving a region $\Re$ and providing cellular coverage of radius R_0. Figure 2 shows the topology of the two-tier femtocell network. Towards constructing the two-tier femtocell network, F co-channel femtocells $B_i = 1, 2, ..., F$ are deployed within the region $\Re$. Each femtocell covers a disk of radius $R_c << R_0$ meters and its corresponding coverage area is $C \subset \Re$. Let N_M and N_F denote the number of macrocell and femtocells users' equipment, i.e. MUE and FUE, respectively, and $N = N_M + N_F$

Figure 2. Two-tier femtocell network topology

the overall number of users residing within the two-tier femtocell network. The corresponding sets of MUEs and FUEs are denoted as S_M and S_F, respectively, while the overall set of users is $S = S_M \cup S_F$. In the presented system model the single macrocell topology is depicted, which can be extended to a multi-macrocell topology including the corresponding femtocells.

Three different access modes are adopted in femtocells:

1. Open access mode,
2. Closed access mode,
3. Hybrid access mode.

The open access mode is adopted in public places, e.g. museums, shopping malls, conference places, where increased data demand appears. In the open access mode, any mobile user residing in the coverage area of the femtocell access point (FAP) can be served by it and utilize FAP's bandwidth. The motivation for adopting open access mode is the improvement of indoor coverage in congested places, where macrocell's capacity is unable to support users' data demand. The closed access mode is mainly adopted in residential deployment scenarios to support the increasing demand of household users. In the closed access mode, mobile users' registration to the FAP is mandatory, thus there is a better control of the number of served users. Finally, the hybrid access mode is mainly adopted in small business deployment scenarios. In hybrid access mode, registered users have priority to access the FAP and utilize its resources; however any mobile user can also access the FAP.

Each user $i \in S$ is associated with the MBS $B_i = 0$ or one of the FAPs $B_i = 1, 2, ..., F$ and the MBS / FAP of a user i under consideration is denoted as $B_i = l$. The channel gain of the link between user i and some MBS/FAP j, where $j = 0, 1, 2, ..., F$, in the two-tier femtocell network is denoted by h_{ij}. Channel gains h_{ij} in the two-tier femtocell environment are modelled following the simplified path loss model in the IMT-2000 specification (ITU, 1997) as follows:

$$h_{ij} = \begin{cases} A \cdot \min\left(d_{i,0}^{-a}, 1\right), & i \ is \ MUE, j = 0 \\ B \cdot R_c^{-b}, & i \ is \ FUE, j \succ 0, j = l \\ C \cdot D \cdot \min\left(d_{i,j}^{-a}, 1\right), & i \ is \ MUE, j \succ 0 \\ A \cdot D \cdot \min\left(d_{i,0}^{-a}, 1\right), & i \ is \ FUE, j = 0 \\ C \cdot D^2 \cdot \min\left(d_{i,j}^{-a}, 1\right), & i \ is \ FUE, j \succ 0, j \neq l \end{cases} \tag{1}$$

The exact values of the above constants are summarized in Table 1 and have been adopted by (Chandrasekhar et. al, 2009b).

User's $i \in S$ transmission power and rate are presented by p_i and r_i, respectively and are upper and lower bounded variables, i.e. $0 \prec p_i \leq p_i^{Max}$ and $0 \prec r_i \leq r_i^{Max}$. The transmission power and data rate vector of all users residing in the two-tier femtocell network are denoted by $\mathrm{p} = [p_1, p_2, ..., p_N]$ and $\mathrm{r} = [r_1, r_2, ..., r_N]$, respectively. Let σ^2 be the variance of the Additive White Gaussian Noise (AWGN) at B_i. The interference observed by user i is given as follows:

$$I_i\left(p_{-i}\right) = \sigma^2 + \sum_{k \neq i} h_{kl} p_k \tag{2}$$

where $B_i = l\left(l = 0, 1, 2, \dots F\right)$ denotes user's i serving MBS/FAP. Therefore, the received signal-to-interference-plus-noise ratio (SINR) γ_i of user i at its serving BS/FAP $B_i = l$ is:

$$\gamma_i = \frac{W}{r_i} \cdot \frac{h_{il} p_i}{\sigma^2 + \sum_{k \neq i} h_{kl} p_k} \tag{3}$$

Table 1. Parameters/notations

Parameter	Symbol/Value
Macrocell BS	B_0
Macrocell's region	$\Re$
Macrocell's radius	R_0
Number of FAPs	F
FAP's region	C
FAP's radius	R_c
Set of MUEs and FUEs	S_M, S_F
Number of MUEs and FUEs	N_M, N_F
Channel gain between user i and BS/FAP j	h_{ij}
Macrocell and indoor femtocell path loss exponent	$a = 4$
Indoor to outdoor femtocell path loss exponent	$b = 3$
Distance of user i (if he is an MUE $i = 0$, otherwise $i \geq 1$) from BS/FAP j (if it is the BS: $j = 0$, otherwise if it is a FAP: $j \geq 1$)	$d_{i,j}$
Fixed decibel propagation loss during macrocell transmissions to the BS	$A = 28dB$
Fixed loss between FUE i to his corresponding FAP $j = i$	$B = 37dB$
Fixed path loss between FUE i to a different FAP $j \neq i$.	$C = 37dB$
Partition loss during indoor to outdoor propagation	$D = 10dB$

where $W[Hz]$ is the system's available spread spectrum bandwidth.

System Model of Visible-Light Communication Local Area Networks

In this section, the system model of Visible-Light Communication Local Area Networks (VLC-LANs), where $|U|$ users are served by $|T|$ optical access points (OAPs), is presented. It should be noted that VLC-LANs are expected to lie within the coverage area of a macrocell. The two-tier VLC topology is considered as shown in Figure 3. Let $U = \{u = 1, 2, ..., U\}$ and $T = \{t = 1, 2, ..., T\}$ denote the set of users and the set of OAPs within the two-tier VLC network, respectively. Each OAP t serves a total number of mobile users $N_t \leq U$. A spectrum of total bandwidth W is devoted per each OAP (and its corresponding cell) and is available for transmissions from the OAP to the mobile users and vice versa. Orthogonal Frequency Division Multiple Access (OFDMA) is the main transmission technique adopted in VLC-LANs (Bykhovsky et. al, 2014). OAPs' total bandwidth is divided into subcarriers, which are organized in resource blocks (RBs). The RBs are allocated to the users, while each RB can be exclusively occupied by one user per OAP. Let $R = \{r = 1, 2, ..., R\}$ denote the set of RBs (Wang et. al, 2015).

Each mobile user $u \in U$ communicates directly with an OAP $t \in T$ via a communication link $l = \{u, t\}$. Each user's transmission power $p_{u.t}^{(r)}$ over RB $r \in R$ is upper and lower bounded, i.e. $0 \prec p_{u.t}^{(r)} \leq p_{u.t}^{Max}$, due to user's physical and technical limitations. Assuming the flat-fading channel model, i.e. mobile user's channel gain is not differentiated per RB, let $H_{u,t}$ denote the gain of optical communication link l between user $u \in U$ and OAP $t \in T$. In the case of selective-fading, the gain of optical communication l would also be differentiated per RB $r \in R$, i.e. $H_{u,t}^{(r)}$. The line-of-sight (LOS) DC gain between mobile user $u \in U$ and OAP $t \in T$ is given by (Ndjiongue et. al, 2015).

$$H_{u,t} = \begin{cases} \dfrac{(m+1)A}{2\pi d^2} \cos^m(\varphi) T_s(\psi) g(\psi) \cos(\psi), & 0 \leq \psi \leq \psi_c \\ 0, & otherwise \end{cases} \quad (4)$$

Figure 3. Two-tier VLC network topology

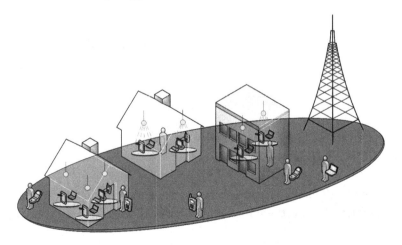

where A denotes the photodetector area, φ the angle of irradiance, $T_s(\psi)$ the signal transmission coefficient of an optical filter, ψ the angle of incidence and m is the order of the Lambertian emission, which is given by

$$m = -\frac{\ln 2}{\ln\left(\cos\phi_{1/2}\right)} \tag{5}$$

where $\phi_{1/2}$ is the transmitter semi-angle at half power. Moreover, $g(\psi)$ denotes the channel gain of an optical concentrator and is given by

$$g(\psi) = \begin{cases} \dfrac{\alpha^2}{\sin^2(\psi_c)}, & 0 \le \psi \le \psi_c \\ 0, & otherwise \end{cases} \tag{6}$$

where α denotes the refractive index of the optical concentrator, ψ_c user's field of view (FOV) and d the distance between the OAP and the user.

Moreover, the signal-to-interference-plus-noise ratio (SINR), $\gamma_{u,t}^{(r)}$ of user $u \in U$ served by the OAP $t \in T$ at RB $r \in R$ can be expressed as follows.

$$\gamma_{u,t}^{(r)} = \frac{R_{PD}H_{u,t}p_{u,t}^{(r)}}{\displaystyle\sum_{u'=1, u' \neq u, t \in T}^{U} H_{u',t}p_{u',t}^{(r)} + \xi} \tag{7}$$

where R_{PD} denotes the responsitivity of the photodiode and ξ is the cumulative noise power.

$$\xi = 2qR_{PD}I_{amb}B_{noise} + \frac{4K_B TB}{R_F} \tag{8}$$

where $q = 1.6 \cdot 10^{-19}C$, I_{amb} denotes the ambient light intensity, B_{noise} the equivalent noise bandwidth, K_B Boltzmann's constant, T the absolute temperature and R_F the transimpedance amplifier gain (Zhang et. al, 2015).

DISTRIBUTED RESOURCE ALLOCATION IN TWO-TIER FEMTOCELL NETWORKS

After introducing the multi-tier heterogeneous wireless network architecture, a representative class of resource allocation problems in two-tier femtocell networks is discussed. Illustrative utility-based distributed resource allocation problems in two-tier femtocells networks are presented, which may consider either single variable (i.e. power allocation) or two variable (i.e. joint power and rate allocation) resource management examples. Users are organized in two main categories, i.e. femtocell users (FUEs) and macro-cell users (MUEs) and they are associated with different types of utility functions based on the tier they belong to. Different access tariffs are applied for these two types of users, due to the fact that MUEs have strictly higher priority over the FUEs in accessing the underlying radio spectrum. Given the adopted utility functions by the users, distributed maximization problems of each user's utility function are formulated and solved, targeting either at inter-cell and cross-tier interference mitigation and/or guaranteeing a targeted signal-to-interference-plus-noise ratio (SINR) and/or users' Quality of Service (QoS) prerequisites' satisfaction under multiple users' requested services. Furthermore, the combined formulation and solution of resource allocation, while considering different imposed pricing policies by the service provider to the FUEs is also analyzed. FUEs are penalized with linear or convex pricing policies with respect to their transmission power, providing higher access priority to the MUEs. Additionally, different techniques (especially based on game-theoretic approaches) towards confronting the single and the two-variable resource allocation problem are examined and the benefits, in terms of power saving, increased throughput and energy-efficiency, stemming from the control of two independent variables/resources are discussed in alignment with the concept of mobile users' self-optimization.

Power Allocation and Interference Management

Considering the power control and interference mitigation problem in two-tier femtocells, the proposed approaches in the literature can be organized in four main categories, as follows.

1. QoS guarantee for MUEs,
2. Soft QoS provisioning for FUEs,
3. Distributed utility-based SINR adaptation,
4. Power control in multi-service two-tier femtocell networks.

In the following, the most characteristic approaches in the literature per category are discussed, regarding the adopted users' utility function, the optimization problem and its solution, as well as the proposed algorithm at each time. MUEs have priority over FUEs in the resource allocation problem, due to their a priori worse channel conditions, i.e. typically more distant users from the MBS compared to the FUEs from their belonging FAP. Users' access priority and services' requirements can be expressed through different SINR thresholds, as follows (Ngo et. Al, 2012):

$$
\begin{aligned}
MUE &: \gamma_i \geq \gamma_{target}^M \\
FUE &: \gamma \geq \gamma_{target}^F
\end{aligned}
\tag{9}
$$

SINR γ_i is an one-to-one function with the transmission power p_i, thus γ_{target}^M and γ_{target}^F correspond to p_{target}^M and p_{target}^F, respectively. Each user adopts a net utility function $U_i^{NET}(p)$ consisting of the pure utility function $U_i(p)$, which represents user's $i \in S$ degree of satisfaction with respect to the resource allocation and the pricing function $C_i(p)$ which corresponds to the incurred cost.

$$U_i^{NET}\left(p_i, p_{-i}\right) = U_i\left(p_i, p_{-i}\right) - C_i\left(p_i, p_{-i}\right) \tag{10}$$

Following the overall framework of mobile users' self-optimization and targeting at pure user-centric approaches, in the power control problem each user maximizes his own net utility in a distributed manner. Therefore, the power control problem can be formulated as an optimization problem, as follows.

$$\max_{0 \prec p_i \le p_i^{Max}} U_i^{NET}\left(p_i, p_{-i}\right) \tag{11}$$

QoS Guarantee for MUEs

Zheng et. al (2012) and Lu et. al (2012) have adopted a game theoretic approach to solve the optimization problem, as presented in Equation 11, due to its distributed nature. In their approach, both FUEs and MUEs adopt the same type of net utility function, while no pricing function was considered, i.e. $C_i\left(p_i, p_{-i}\right) = 0$. Furthermore, only MUEs have a specific target SINR γ_{target}^M, while FUEs do not have specific QoS prerequisites. MUEs and FUEs utility function is formulated as follows:

$$U_i^{NET}\left(p_i, p_{-i}\right) = \frac{W \log_2(1 + \gamma_i)}{p_i + p_c} \tag{12}$$

where W is system's bandwidth and p_c denotes the circuit power.

Towards solving the optimization problem Equation 11 for the net utility function Equation 12, the authors considered the first order derivative of U_i^{NET} with respect to p_i and given the quasi-concavity property of U_i^{NET} again with respect to p_i, they determined the unique maximizer $\hat{p}_i$. Thus, considering cellular link protection and in order to guarantee γ_{target}^M they concluded to the following optimal power allocation.

$$p_i^* = \begin{cases} \min\left(\max\left(\hat{p}_i, p_{target}^M\right), p_i^{Max}\right), & i \ is \ MUE \\ \min\left(\hat{p}_i, p_i^{Max}\right), & i \ is \ FUE \end{cases} \tag{13}$$

Aiming at achieving MUEs' targeted SINR γ_{target}^M, each MUE can tolerate a maximum level of interference I_{lim}, i.e. $\frac{p_{MUE}^{Max} h_{0,0}}{I_{lim} + \sigma^2} = \gamma_{target}^M$. If an MUE cannot achieve γ_{target}^M even via transmitting with his maximum power p_{MUE}^{Max}, it means that MUE's sensed interference exceeds I_{lim}, thus FUEs who exceed a threshold L, i.e. $p_i h_{0,i} \succ L$, should reduce their caused interference to the MUEs, by updating their maximum transmission power, i.e. $p_{FUE}^{Max} = p_{FUE}^* - \Delta p, \Delta p > 0$.

Power Optimization with Cellular Link Protection

1. Initialize L, $\Delta L, \Delta p$
2. Initialize $\forall i \in S$, $0 \prec p_i^{(k=0)} \leq p_i^{Max}$ and $k = 1$

While $k \leq k_{MAX}$ do
   MUEs update their transmission power according to

$$p_i^* = \min\left(\max\left(\hat{p}_i, p_{t\arg et}^M\right), p_i^{Max}\right)$$

FUEs update their transmission power according to

$$p_i^* = \min\left(\hat{p}_i, p_i^{Max}\right)$$

Update $k = k + 1$
End while

3. If $\gamma_{MUE}^* \geq \gamma_{t\arg et}^M$, MUE broadcasts status indicator $flag = 1$ and stops, else broadcasts status indicator $flag = 0$.
4. If $flag = 0$, FUEs form their status indicator $flag_i$ according to their caused interference $p_i^* h_{0,i}$, i.e. if $p_i^* h_{0,i} > L$, $flag_i = 0$ else $flag_i = 1$.

If $flag_i = 0$, FUEs with $flag_i = 0$ update their maximum transmission power $p_i^{Max} = p_i^* - \Delta p$ and $L = L - \Delta L$ and return to step 2.

Similar approach to the above considering cellular link protection has been followed by Su et. al (2012), while differentiated net utility functions have been adopted for MUEs and FUEs, respectively, as below.

$$U_i^{NET}\left(p_i, p_{-i}\right) = \begin{cases} \dfrac{W \log_2(1 + \gamma_i)}{p_i + p_c}, & i \ is \ MUE \\ \dfrac{W \log_2(1 + \gamma_i)}{p_i + p_c} - c \cdot p_i \cdot h_{0,i}, & i \ is \ FUE \end{cases} \tag{14}$$

where c is a positive scalar. The fundamental difference of this formulation, considering the power control problem Equation 11 is that FUEs' net utility function is not quasi-concave with respect to p_i. Thus, supermodular games have been adopted towards determining the optimal power p_i^*, while the algorithm "Power Optimization with Cellular Link Protection" presented before can also be adopted here, guaranteeing a γ_{target}^M to the MUEs.

Another approach that can be included in the power control problems so as to ensure MUEs' QoS prerequisites (i.e. γ_{target}^{M}, while no γ_{target}^{F} exists) is proposed by Ngo et. al (2012), where the adopted net utility functions by MUEs and FUEs are also differentiated as follows.

$$U_i^{NET}\left(p_i, p_{-i}\right) = \begin{cases} \dfrac{1}{1+\exp\left[-b_i\left(\gamma_i - c_i\right)\right]} - \alpha_i^M \cdot p_i, & i \ is \ MUE \\ W \cdot \ln(1+\gamma_i) - \alpha_i^F \cdot p_i, & i \ is \ FUE \end{cases} \tag{15}$$

where b_i, c_i, α_i^M and α_i^F are positive scalar values. As a solution to Equation 11, Ngo et. al (2012) take the first order derivative of U_i^{NET} with respect to p_i and by equating it to zero they conclude to the following users' power control updating rule.

$$p_i^{*(k+1)} = \begin{cases} \dfrac{\left(\sigma^2 + \sum\limits_{j\neq i} h_{ij} p_j^{*(k)}\right)}{h_{i,i}} \cdot \gamma_i^{(k)}, & if \ \gamma_i^{(k)} \geq \gamma_{target}^M, i \ is \ MUE \\ \dfrac{\left(\sigma^2 + \sum\limits_{j\neq i} h_{ij} p_j^{*(k)}\right)}{h_{i,i}} \cdot \gamma_{target}^M, & if \ \gamma_i^{(k)} \prec \gamma_{target}^M, i \ is \ MUE \\ \dfrac{W}{\alpha_i^F} - \dfrac{\left(\sigma^2 + \sum\limits_{j\neq i} h_{ij} p_j^{*(k)}\right)}{h_{i,i}}, & i \ is \ FUE \end{cases} \tag{16}$$

The algorithm "Power Optimization with Cellular Link Protection" presented above can be adopted in this case as well to determine users' optimal power allocation.

Soft QoS Provisioning for FUEs

Compared to the aforementioned approaches which target at QoS Guarantee for the MUEs, another perspective has been proposed in the literature regarding the power control problem in two-tier femtocells, which ensures a minimum SINR $\gamma_{target}^{F} \prec \gamma_{target}^{M}$ for FUEs. The adopted utility functions for MUEs and FUEs are as follows (Ngo et. al, 2012).

$$U_i^{NET}\left(p_i, p_{-i}\right) = \begin{cases} \dfrac{1}{1+\exp\left[-b_i\left(\gamma_i - c_i\right)\right]} - \alpha_i^M \cdot p_i, & i \ is \ MUE \\ -\left(\gamma_i - \gamma_{target}^F\right)^2 - \alpha_i^F \cdot p_i, & i \ is \ FUE \end{cases} \tag{17}$$

In order to solve the power control problem Equation 11 under the utilities introduced in Equation 17 the first order derivative of U_i^{NET} with respect to p_i is taken equal to zero and the following algorithm which determines the users' optimal power allocation is illustrated.

1. Set $p_i = 0$, $\forall i \in S$, initialize the set of active FUEs S_F and set $k = 1$.

2. Each MUE $i \in S_M$ measures $h_{i,i}^{(k)}$ and $I_i(k)$ and calculates $\hat{\gamma}_i$ as the unique solution of $\dfrac{\partial U_i}{\partial \gamma_i} = 0$.

3. If $\hat{\gamma}_i \geq \gamma_{target}^M$ then

4. MUE $i, i \in S_M$ updates his power $p_i(k+1) = \dfrac{I_i(k) \cdot \hat{\gamma}_i(k)}{h_{i,i}^{(k)}}$

5. Else if $\hat{\gamma}_i \prec \gamma_{target}^M$ and $|S_F| \succ 0$ then

6. MUE $i, i \in S_M$ updates his power $p_i(k+1) = \dfrac{I_i(k) \cdot \gamma_{target}^M}{h_{i,i}^{(k)}}$

7. Each FUE $i, i \in S_F$ updates his pricing coefficient $\alpha_i^F = k_i^F \cdot \alpha_i^F$, where $k_i^F \succ 1$ are predetermined scaling factors.

8. End if.

9. Each FUE $i, i \in S_F$ measures $h_{i,i}^{(k)}$ and $I_i(k)$ and calculates $\hat{p}_i$ as

$$\hat{p}_i = \frac{I_i(k) \cdot \gamma_{target}^F}{h_{i,i}^{(k)}} - \frac{\alpha_i^F \cdot I_i^2(k)}{2 \cdot \left(h_{i,i}^{(k)}\right)^2}$$

10. FUE $i, i \in S_F$ updates his power $p_i(k+1) = \hat{p}_i$.

11. If $\dfrac{\hat{p}_i h_{i,i}^{(k)}}{I_i(k)} \prec \gamma_{target}^F$ then FUE $i, i \in S_F$ sets $p_i(k+1) = 0$ and removes himself from the set of active FUEs, i.e. $A_F = A_F - \{i\}$.

12. End if.

Set $k := k+1$, go to step 2 and repeat until convergence.

Distributed Utility-Based SINR Adaptation

In this section, a distributed utility-based SINR adaptation of femtocells is proposed towards mitigating cross-tier interference at the macrocell from co-channel femtocells. Each MUE has a targeted SINR, γ_{target}^M while the FUEs target at maximizing their individual net utility consisting of an SINR-based reward minus the incurred cost, i.e. interference to the MUEs. As it is shown later in this section, each FUE will conclude to a channel-dependent SINR equilibrium, which strongly discourages him to use high transmission power. Therefore, the proposed approach is characterized as an SINR adaptation approach. The adopted net utility functions for both MUEs and FUEs are included below. (Chandrasekhar et. al, 2009a; Chandrasekhar et. al, 2009b; Ma et. al, 2013; Douros et. al, 2012).

$$
U_i^{NET}\left(p_i, p_{-i}\right) = \begin{cases} -\left(\gamma_i - \gamma_{target}^M\right)^2, & i \ is \ MUE \\ 1 - \exp\left[-\alpha_i\left(\gamma_i - \gamma_{target}^F\right)\right] + b_i \dfrac{-p_i \cdot h_{0,i}}{\left(\sigma^2 + \sum_{j \neq i} h_{ij} p_j\right)}, & i \ is \ FUE \end{cases} \tag{18}
$$

where α_i, b_i are positive scalars and their values express the tradeoff between FUEs' desire to maximize their achievable data rate while considering the importance of satisfying MUEs QoS prerequisites.

Towards concluding to the optimal power allocation of power control problem as described in Equation 11, the quasi-concavity of U_i^{NET} with respect to p_i is proven in (Chandrasekhar et. al, 2009a; Chandrasekhar et. al, 2009b; Ma et. al, 2013; Douros et. al, 2012). Based on the quasi-concavity property of U_i^{NET}, the unique Nash equilibrium point of Equation 11 is reached. Thus, the power update rule both for MUEs and FUEs is as follows.

$$
p_i^{(k+1)} = \begin{cases} \min\left(\dfrac{p_i^{(k)}}{\gamma_i^{(k)}} \gamma_{target}^M, p_i^{Max}\right), & i \ is \ MUE \\ \min\left(\dfrac{p_i^{(k)}}{\gamma_i^{(k)}}\left[\gamma_{target}^F + \dfrac{1}{\alpha_i}\ln\left(\dfrac{\alpha_i h_{i,i}}{b_i h_{0,i}}\right)\right]^+, p_i^{Max}\right), & i \ is \ FUE \end{cases} \tag{19}
$$

Based on the aforementioned power update rule, the same concept of algorithm "Power Optimization with Cellular Link Protection" can be adopted, while in step 2 MUEs' and FUEs' power update rule should be substituted by the corresponding formulas of Equation 19.

Power Control in Multi-Service Two-Tier Femtocell Networks

All the previously discussed approaches considered either a common utility function for both classes of users or the utility function was differentiated based on the tier that the user belongs to, i.e. MUE or FUE. At this point, a more holistic approach is presented supporting multiple services (i.e. both real-time and non-real time) with various and often diverse QoS prerequisites. Users' net utility functions are diversified not only according to the tier the users belong to, but also in relevance to the type of service they request (Tsiropoulou et. al, 2013; Tsiropoulou et. al, 2014).

$$U_i^{NET}(p_i, p_{-i}) = \begin{cases} \dfrac{W \cdot f(\gamma_i)}{p_i}, & i \ is \ MUE, real\text{-}time \ service \\[2ex] \dfrac{\log(1 + D \cdot f(\gamma_i))}{p_i}, & i \ is \ MUE, non\text{-}real\text{-}time \ service \\[2ex] \dfrac{W \cdot f(\gamma_i)}{p_i} - c(e^{p_i} - 1), & i \ is \ FUE, real\text{-}time \ service \\[2ex] \dfrac{\log(1 + D \cdot f(\gamma_i))}{p_i} - c(e^{p_i} - 1), & i \ is \ FUE, non\text{-}real\text{-}time \ service \end{cases} \tag{20}$$

where D is positive constant, c is the pricing factor for FUEs and $f(\gamma_i) = \left(1 - e^{-A\gamma_i}\right)^M$ denotes user's efficiency function (*A, M*: positive constants), which represents the successful packet transmission at fixed data rates depending on the modulation and coding schemes that are being used (Sarayadar et. al, 2002).

In order to provide a solution to the above power control problem, the optimization problem Equation 11 is confronted as a non-cooperative game, which is proven to be a supermodular game adopting the objective function Equation 20 (Tsiropoulou et. al, 2013), thus the existence of an optimal power allocation (Pareto dominant Nash equilibrium) is concluded. Finally, a distributed, iterative and complexity algorithm designed to determine the optimal management of the user's transmission powers is proposed.

FAP/MBS Part (c_{best} Identification)

1. Each FAP announces the initial pricing factor *c=0* to all FUEs residing in each cell.
2. Each FUE and MUE determines the optimal power allocation (according to the second part of the algorithm) and computes his pure utility, i.e. the net utility without the penalty (cost function) for FUEs.
3. Increase the pricing factor $c := c + \Delta c$ and each FAP announces it to its FUEs.
4. If the pure utilities of all MUEs and FUEs do not improve, then stop and set $c_{best} = c$ as the best choice of the pricing factor. Otherwise, go to step 2.

User's Part Algorithm (Power Allocation)

1. Each MUE and FUE initially transmits with a randomly selected feasible transmission power $0 \le p_i^{(0)} \le p_i^{Max}$). Set *k=0*.
2. The FAPs report to the MBS the overall interference per each femtocell and the MBS broadcasts the overall interference in the two-tier femtocell network to all users (both MUEs and FUEs), i.e. $\sum_{j \ne i} h_{ji} p_i$ and determines his best response strategy:

$$BR_i(\mathrm{p}_{-i}) = \arg\max_{p_i} U_i^{NET}(p_i, \mathrm{p}_{-i})$$

and transmits with $p_i^{(k)} = \min\left(BR_i\right)$.

Joint Power and Rate Allocation

Among the key elements that need to be considered and controlled in multi-tier heterogeneous wireless networks are users' transmission power and rate under a more holistic perspective. Towards addressing this problem several works have attempted to consider both transmission power and rate allocation mainly referring to single tier architectures, i.e. macrocell, wireless networks. Due to the complexity of the consideration of the joint power and rate allocation, the basic approaches that have been proposed in the recent literature treating the problem are summarized below:

1. The joint rate and power control is divided in two sequential problems, where the output of the first, e.g. transmission rate allocation, acts as input to the second resource allocation problem, i.e. transmission power allocation. All users determine first their transmission rate and then given their uplink transmission rate, they apply power control to allocate their uplink transmission powers (Hayajneh et. al, 2004).

2. The joint rate and power control problem is amended in a single-variable problem of the ratio of transmission rate to the transmission power (Musku et. al, 2010).

Based on this observation, it is concluded that joint power and rate control in multi-tier heterogeneous wireless networks is a challenging research topic, due to the multi-variable nature of the resource allocation problem. Therefore, the proposed approaches presented in the previous section cannot be either straightforwardly nor easily extended and adapted in the field of joint power and rate allocation.

One fundamental approach in the literature considering the joint power and rate allocation problem is its formulation of this problem as a joint power and resource blocks allocation (Salati et. al, 2012; Le et. al, 2013). Let $RB = \left\{1, 2, ..., |RB|\right\}$ denote the set of resource blocks (RBs) available to the MBS and each FAP and $RB_i = \left\{1, 2, ..., |RB_i|\right\}$ denote the set of RBs occupied by each user, either MUE or FUE. It should be noted that each RB can be allocated to at most one user per cell, either in the macrocell or in each femtocell, however different cells may reuse the same RB. This observation consists also a constraint to the following joint power and RBs allocation optimization problem Equations 23a to 23c. Each user transmits with transmission power $p_i^{(s)}$ at each occupied RB $s, s \in RB_i$ and considering each user's total transmission power, the following constraint holds true.

$$\sum_{s=1}^{|S_i|} p_i^{(s)} \le p_i^{Max}, i \in S \tag{21}$$

Furthermore, let $h_{i,j}^{(s)}$ denote the channel gain of the link between user i and some MBS/FAP j $\left(j = 0, 1, 2, ..., F\right)$ over the RB $s, s \in RB_i$, then the SINR of user i at its serving MBS / FAP $B_i = l$ over the RB $s, s \in RB_i$ is expressed below.

$$\gamma_i^{(s)} = \frac{h_{i,l}^{(s)} p_i^{(s)}}{\sigma^2 + \sum\limits_{\substack{k \neq i \\ s \in RB_i}} h_{k,l}^{(s)} p_k^{(s)}} \tag{22}$$

Based on the above, the joint power and RBs allocation problem targeting at maximizing system's sum-rate (assuming that each RB can be exclusively occupied by one user at each cell) expressed via Shannon formula can be written as follows.

$$\max_{p_i^{(s)}, RB_i} \sum_{s=1}^{|RB|} \left[\frac{W}{S} \cdot \log\left(1 + \gamma_i^{(s)}\right) \right] \tag{23a}$$

$$s.t. \sum_{s=1}^{|RB|} p_i^{(s)} \leq p_i^{Max}, \forall i \in S \tag{23b}$$

$$\gamma_i^{(s)} \geq \gamma_{th}^{(s)}, \ \forall i \in S \tag{23c}$$

It should be noted that the constraint Equation 23c implies that a minimum predetermined SINR threshold is guaranteed for each user $i, i \in S$ over each RB $s, s \in RB_i$. The optimization problem Equations 23a to 23c can be transformed into a standard mixed integer program, thus, this resource allocation problem is NP-hard.

Towards confronting the optimization problem Equations 23a to 23c various efforts have been devoted in the literature, including relaxation methods, heuristics approaches and/or slight variations of the original optimization problem. Li et. al (2012) proposed a joint power and RBs allocation problem, while considering a handover from its serving MBS to a nearby FAP. The RBs that were originally allocated to the MUEs that perform the handover to their neighbor FAP are freed by the MBS and after the handover is occurred, the RBs and power resources both at the MBS and at each FAP are reallocated. The proposed resource allocation mechanism uses the dual decomposition method to conclude to a near optimal solution. Xu et. al (2013) proposed a dynamic RBs allocation based on Stackelberg games, where the MBS acts as a leader and the FAPs as followers. In this approach, the authors considered cross-tier interference, caused by each user $i, i \in S$ considering its occupied RBs RB_i, as the objective function. After proving the existence of a Stackelberg equilibrium for this joint resource allocation scenario, they adopted the best response dynamics methodology so as to determine the optimal solution for the optimization problem of minimizing the cross-tier interference.

Another simplification for solving the joint resource allocation problem Equations 23a to 23c is to fix the one variable, e.g. RBs allocation, and focus on the single variable optimization problem, e.g. power allocation and vice versa. Ngo et. al (2014) examined an iterative approach of the aforementioned simplified methodology, concluding to a near optimal solution of the joint resource allocation problem. More specifically, they have shown that for a fixed power allocation, the optimal policy in each cell is to allocate each RB to the user with the highest SINR on that RB. Additionally, given a fixed RB allocation, an efficient methodology to solve the highly non-convex power allocation problem is to transform it into a sequence of convex problems via adopting successive convex optimization, as it is proven in (Ngo et. al, 2014).

The same concept of reformulating the two-variable resource allocation case to a single-variable has been proposed by Tsiropoulou et. al (2015), through considering the rate as a continuous variable and not implicitly expressed as the number of RBs occupied by each user. This work focuses on the uplink of multi-service two-tier wireless networks, where user's uplink transmission rate is denoted by r_i. Each user adopted a utility function expressed as follows.

$$U_i(p_i, r_i, p_{-i}, r_{-i}) = \begin{cases} \dfrac{r_i f_i(\gamma_i)}{p_i}, & i \text{ is } MUE, real\text{-}time\ service \\[2em] \dfrac{r_i \log(1 + \gamma_i)}{p_i}, & i \text{ is } MUE, non\text{-}real\text{-}time\ service \\[2em] \dfrac{r_i f_i(\gamma_i)}{p_i} - c\left(e^{\gamma_i} - 1\right), & i \text{ is } FUE, real\text{-}time\ service \\[2em] \dfrac{r_i \log(1 + \gamma_i)}{p_i} - c\left(e^{\gamma_i} - 1\right), & i \text{ is } FUE, non\text{-}real\text{-}time\ service \end{cases} \quad (24)$$

where γ_i is given by Equation 3 and c denotes the pricing factor imposed to the FUEs as an enforcing measure to reduce their uplink transmission power and mitigate the overall cross-tier interference. The corresponding two-variable optimization problem is formulated as a maximization problem of each user's utility function, as follows.

$$\max_{(p_i, r_i)} U_i(p_i, r_i p_{-i}, r_{-i}),$$
$$s.t.\ p_{i\min} \le p_i \le p_i^{Max}, r_{i\min} \le r_i \le r_i^{Max} \quad (25)$$

The ratio $\dfrac{r_i}{p_i}$ is substituted by a new variable x_i, thus user's utility function is rewritten as follows.

$$v_i(x_i) = \begin{cases} x_i\left(1 - e^{-A\frac{d_i}{x_i}}\right)^M, & i \text{ is } MUE, real\text{-}time\ service \\[2em] x_i \dfrac{\ln\left(1 + \dfrac{d_i}{x_i}\right)}{\ln 10}, & i \text{ is } MUE, non\text{-}real\text{-}time\ service \\[2em] x_i\left(1 - e^{-A\frac{d_i}{x_i}}\right)^M - c\left(e^{\frac{d_i}{x_i}} - 1\right), & i \text{ is } FUE, real\text{-}time\ service \\[2em] x_i \dfrac{\ln\left(1 + \dfrac{d_i}{x_i}\right)}{\ln 10} - c\left(e^{\frac{d_i}{x_i}} - 1\right), & i \text{ is } FUE, non\text{-}real\text{-}time\ service \end{cases} \quad (26)$$

where *A, M* are the positive constants included in the efficiency function $f_i(\gamma_i)$ and the optimization problem Equation 25 is rewritten as.

$$
\max_{x_i = \frac{r_i}{p_i}} v_i\left(x_i = \frac{r_i}{p_i}\right), \tag{27}
$$
$$
s.t.\ p_{i\min} \leq p_i \leq p_i^{Max},\ r_{i\min} \leq r_i \leq r_i^{Max}
$$

The above optimization problem is modeled as a non-cooperative game and its unique Nash equilibrium point $\left(p_i^*, r_i^*\right)$ is determined via proving that the objective function Equation 26 is quasi-concave with respect to x_i. Finally, an iterative distributed algorithm is proposed towards determining the optimal power and rate allocation in the uplink of multi-service two-tier femtocell networks.

Access Point's Part

1. Each FAP announces the initial pricing factor $c = 0$ to its respective FUEs. The pricing factor is the same for all FUEs within their corresponding FAPs that reside within the same macrocell.
2. Each user, either MUE or FUE, determines his optimal transmission power and data rate, i.e. $\left(p_i^*, r_i^*\right)$ (according to the second part of the algorithm) and computes his pure utility value, i.e. without the penalty factor.
3. The pricing factor is increased by the same value Δc, i.e. $c := c + \Delta c$. The new pricing factor is announced to all FUEs by their corresponding FAP.
4. If the pure utility values for all users, either MUEs or FUEs, are not improved, then stop and set $c_{best} = c$. Otherwise, go to step 2.

User's Part

1. At the first iteration $k=0$ of the algorithm, each user i initializes his uplink transmission power and data rate. Thus, at the first iteration $k=0$ of the algorithm we have the following power and transmission data rate vectors: $p = \left(p_1^{(0)}, p_2^{(0)}, ..., p_N^{(0)}\right)$ and $r = \left(r_1^{(0)}, r_2^{(0)}, ..., r_N^{(0)}\right)$, where $p_i^{(0)} = p_{i\min}, p_{i\min} \succ 0$ and $r_i^{(0)} = r_i^{MAX}$.
2. At the next iteration $k \succ 0$, compute the ratio $x_j^{(k)}$, as follows:

$$
x_i^{(k)} = \underset{x_i \in \left[\frac{r_{i\min}}{p_i^{MAX}}, \frac{r_i^{MAX}}{p_{i\min}}\right]}{\arg\max}\ v_i\left(x_i = \frac{r_i}{p_i}, p_{-i}^{(k)}, r_{-i}^{(k)}\right)
$$

3. Determine each user's uplink transmission power $p_i^{(k+1)}$ and data rate $r_i^{(k+1)}$ as follows:

$$
\left(p_i^{(k+1)}, r_i^{(k+1)}\right) = \begin{cases} if\ \dfrac{A\,WG_{ii}}{I\ln M} \succ \dfrac{r_i^{MAX}}{p_i^{MAX}} : \begin{cases} \left(p_i^{MAX}, x_i^{(k)}p_i^{MAX}\right), & if\ x_i^{(k)} \le \dfrac{r_i^{MAX}}{p_i^{MAX}} \\[2em] \left[\dfrac{r_i^{MAX}}{x_i^{(k)}}, r_i^{MAX}\right], & if\ x_i^{(k)} \succ \dfrac{r_i^{MAX}}{p_i^{MAX}} \end{cases} \\[4em] else \qquad\qquad\quad \left(p_i^{MAX}, x_i^{(k)}p_i^{MAX}\right) \end{cases}
$$

If the powers and transmission data rates converge, i.e.,

$$
\left| r_i^{(k)} - r_i^{(k+1)} \right| \le \varepsilon, \left| p_i^{(k)} - p_i^{(k+1)} \right| \le \varepsilon, \varepsilon = 10^{-7},
$$

then stop. Otherwise, set $k = k+1$ and go to step 2.

Resource Allocation and Pricing Policies

Pricing of system's resources is a common methodology that has been widely adopted in resource allocation problems in two-tier femtocell networks, towards mitigating FUEs caused interference to the MUEs and supporting MUEs' priority over the system's resources. Furthermore, using pricing in such problems allows to achieve a more social welfare operational point with respect to the usage of the available resources. Among the many pricing policies, such as access-based, priority-based, flat-rate, usage-based, etc. (Saraydar et. al, 2002), usage-based pricing especially with respect to user's transmission power has been mainly adopted in the literature dealing with the problem of resource allocation with pricing policies in two-tier femtocell networks. Linear or non-linear pricing schemes as functions of user's transmission power have been proposed for penalizing FUEs' transmissions, thus enforcing them to reduce their transmission power and correspondingly deliver lower cross-tier interference levels and maintain MUEs' priority to be served (Liu et. al, 2012).

Furthermore, the aforementioned usage-based pricing policies can be categorized as uniform and non-uniform pricing policies. In non-uniform pricing policies, each FUE is penalized with a different price (i.e. different pricing factor) c_i, while in uniform ones all FUEs are penalized with a common price, i.e. $c_i = c, \forall i \in S$.

Hong et. al (2009) applied a uniform linear pricing policy to the FUEs with respect to their transmission power, while MUEs have higher priority to the resource allocation problem and they are not penalized. Therefore, the proposed pricing function for FUEs is presented below.

$$
c_i\left(p_i\right) = c \cdot p_i \tag{28}
$$

where c denotes the common pricing factor for all FUEs and it is a positive constant, with the value of pricing factor c to have an effect on the potential interference to the other users. Hence, the lower values of c will lead to greater interference to others, while a higher value of c will result in small interference to the rest of the users.

Additionally, Kang et. al (2012) proposed a non-uniform linear pricing mechanism for FUEs also with respect to their uplink transmission power.

$$c_i\left(p_i\right) = c_i \cdot h_{il} \cdot p_i \tag{29}$$

where c_i is a personalized penalty for each FUE expressing the amount of the interference quota that each FUE is willing to buy considering the interference price.

On the other hand, non-linear pricing policies with respect to FUEs' transmission power have been proposed, towards penalizing FUEs for the caused cross-tier interference. Zhao et. al (2014) considered a strictly convex non-uniform pricing policy with respect to FUe's transmission power p_i, as follows.

$$c_i\left(p_i\right) = c_i \cdot \exp\left[h_{il} \cdot p_i\right] \tag{30}$$

where c_i denotes FUE's pricing factor.

A non-linear uniform pricing policy also regarding FUE's transmission power has been utilized by Tsiropoulou et. al (2014) penalizing FUEs' transmissions, via a pricing function as below.

$$c_i\left(p_i\right) = c \cdot \left(e^{p_i} - 1\right) \tag{31}$$

where c denotes a common pricing factor for all FUEs.

An even more sophisticated non-linear non-uniform pricing policy has been proposed by Liu et. al (2013) taking into consideration an interference cap Q that can be afforded by the MUEs, as well as FUEs' channel conditions before they are penalized. Therefore, the pricing function $c_i\left(p_i\right)$ is defined as an exponential function of FUE's transmission power p_i, which can be expressed as follows.

$$c_i\left(p_i\right) = c_i \cdot \left(e^{p_i} - p_i - 1\right) \tag{32}$$

where $c_i = f\left(Q\right) \cdot \dfrac{h_{i,i}}{I_i}$ is each FUE's $i, i \in S_F$ pricing factor. The pricing factor c_i considers the function $f\left(Q\right) = \dfrac{1}{Q + q}$, where q is a positive constant. The function $f\left(Q\right)$ reflects MUE's tolerance to FUEs' caused interference. In other words, as Q increases, meaning the more interference that the MUEs can tolerate, FUEs are less penalized.

Furthermore, the pricing factor c_i depends on $\dfrac{h_{i,i}}{I_i}$, where I_i is given by Equation 2. The factor $\dfrac{h_{i,i}}{I_i}$ reflects the condition of the transmission channel (i.e. the larger of it, the better condition of the transmission), thus FUEs in better condition are penalized more in order to reflect fairness between favored and unfavored FUEs.

DYNAMIC RESOURCE ALLOCATION FOR VISIBLE-LIGHT LOCAL AREA NETWORKS

Visible Light Communication applied in Local Area Networks (VLANs) has many advantages over other forms of communications and especially Radio Frequency (RF) communication, such as high signal-to-interference-plus-noise ratio (SINR), easy installation, non-existence of interference from electromagnetic waves, usage of license free frequency band, as well as high security (Zhang et. al, 2015). VLC is a new research concept, while in 2011 the first draft of PHY and MAC standard for VLC was completed by the IEEE 802.15.7 VLC task group (IEEE, 2011). The majority of the literature with respect to VLC and Radio Resource Management (RRM) over the last years has mainly focused on the physical and data link layer investigating the transmitter's (Yu et. al, 2013) and / or receiver's design, e.g. angle diversity receiver (Chen et. al, 2014), the optimal placement of light emitting diode (LED) arrays (Stefan et. al, 2013a), as well as adopting multiple-input-multiple-output (MIMO) system's approach (Tsonev et. al, 2013; Zeng et. al, 2009). Within the scope of this section is to present resource allocation approaches lying at the network layer. A radio resource management mechanism is required for a VLAN network in order to achieve the desired network objective under the constraint of available radio resources, e.g. bandwidth, resource blocks, transmission power, etc. Next, the main proposed resource allocation and user association approaches are classified and presented.

User Association in VLANs

Optical Access Points (OAPs) serve a small coverage area by their nature. Thus, mobile users who are characterized by mobility, should decide in an efficient manner which OAP they should be associated with, in order to fulfill their specific QoS prerequisites via the OAP that they communicate with (Nguyen et. al, 2013). Considering the above observations, simplified (in terms of low complexity) and efficient methodologies towards supporting users' association in VLANs should be devised. Users' Association to OAPs is a procedure that is performed before the resource allocation.

Bykhovsky et. al (2014) introduced a user association methodology, i.e. OAP selection, based on the Maximum Gain Selection (MGS) policy. More specifically, a mobile user can reside within the coverage area of multiple OAPs in a multi-cell VLAN network. The fundamental goal of OAP selection is to associate each user with the appropriate OAP towards mitigating the overall interference in the network and fulfilling user's QoS prerequisites. Following this concept, MGS policy associates each user $u \in U$ with the OAP $t \in T$ that presents the highest channel gain $H_{u,t}$ between himself, i.e. $u \in U$ and all available and feasible OAPs $t \in T$ to connect to.

The MGS policy provides a near optimum solution achieving multi-user, as well as multiple OAPs diversity and channel gain diversity. It should not be disregarded that the MGS policy is neither necessary nor sufficient for optimality. The corresponding algorithm is described as follows.

Access Point's Part

1. Create the matrix H, which is structured based on the line-of-sight (LOS) channel gain $H_{u,t}$ between each user $u \in U$ and OAP $t \in T$

$$H(u,t) = \begin{bmatrix} H_{1,1} & H_{1,2} & \cdots & H_{1,T} \\ H_{2,1} & H_{2,2} & \cdots & \cdot \\ \cdot & \cdot & \cdots & \cdot \\ \cdot & \cdot & \cdots & \cdot \\ H_{U,1} & H_{U,2} & \cdots & H_{U,T} \end{bmatrix}$$

2. Select the pair $\{user, OAP\} = \{u^*, t^*\} = \arg\max_{t\in T} H(u,t)$.

3. Erase user u^* from the corresponding row of the matrix.

If the number of rows of H is equal to zero, i.e. all users have been associated to OAPs, then stop. Otherwise, go to Step 2.

Adaptive Bandwidth Allocation

The goal of the adaptive bandwidth allocation scheme is to allocate bandwidth to the users in a scalable way, while guaranteeing the performance of the requested services and in parallel admitting maximum possible number of users in the system (Jin et. al, 2016). Each user is able to achieve a corresponding transmission rate R_u based on the assigned bandwidth W_u, as follows.

$$R_u = W_u \log_2\left(1 + \frac{\gamma_u}{W_u}\right) \tag{33}$$

where γ_u denotes the SINR of user $u \in U$, $U = [1,2,...,U]$.

The corresponding Adaptive Bandwidth Allocation problem can be formulated as follows.

$$\max R_{total} = \sum_{u=1}^{U} \frac{W_u}{U} \log_2\left(1 + \frac{U \cdot \gamma_u}{W_u}\right) \tag{34a}$$

$$\text{s.t. } \sum_{u=1}^{U} W_u \leq W_{available} \tag{34b}$$

$$R_u \geq R_u^{target}, \forall u \in U \tag{34c}$$

The objective function in Equation 34a aims to maximize the overall sum rate of all users in the VLC system, while the constraint Equation 34b ensures that the allocated bandwidth to users U does not exceed the available bandwidth and the constraint Equation 34c ensures that each user $u \in U$ achieves the requested targeted data rate R_u^{target}.

Towards solving the optimization problem Equations 34a to 34c, it is observed that it has a non-negative constraint Equation 34c. Thus, by transforming Equation 34a into a minimization problem and also transforming Equation 34c into a negative constraint, the transformed set of equations can be made a convex optimization problem (Boyde et. al, 2004). Consequently, by using the Lagrangian approximation, the optimal bandwidth allocation to the users can be determined, i.e. $W^* = \left(W_1^*, W_2^*, ..., W_U^* \right)$ (Saha et. al, 2013a).

Finally, it should be noted that in the proposed approach each user transmits with a fixed transmission power.

Joint Bandwidth and Power Allocation

The joint allocation of bandwidth and power to the users is of great importance towards utilizing system's resources even more efficiently and enabling each OAP to serve as many users as possible via mitigating the overall interference in the VLC system (Saha et. al, 2014). In an orthogonal frequency division multiple access (OFDMA) VLAN, the bandwidth W is divided into R resource blocks (RBs), which are exclusively allocated to the users of each OAP, i.e. non-reusability of the RBs in the same OAP $t \in \mathrm{T}$ is considered. Furthermore, in the case of adopting the selective-fading channel model, user's channel gain is differentiated per RB. The latter does not hold true in the case of adopting flat-fading channel model. Therefore, the RBs allocation algorithm for OFDMA-based VLANs is as follows.

RBs Allocation Algorithm for OFDMA-Based VLANs

1. Based on the "User Association / OAP Selection" algorithm described before, each OAP $t \in \mathrm{T}$ is aware of the number of users residing in it, i.e. U.
2. If $R = U$ allocate RB $r^* \in \mathrm{R}$ to user $u^* \in \mathrm{U}$ based on the maximum channel gain criterion, i.e. $\left(r^*, u^* \right) = \underset{\substack{u \in \mathrm{U} \\ t \in \mathrm{T}}}{\arg \max} \, H_{u,t}^{(r)}$.
3. Else if $R \succ U$, allocate at least one RB $r^* \in \mathrm{R}$ to each user $u^* \in \mathrm{U}$ based also on the maximum channel gain criterion, and allocate the remaining RBs, i.e. $R - U$, to the users based also on the order of their channel gain.

Else if $R \prec U$, sort the users based on their channel gain and allocate the RBs R to the first R users (each user occupies one RB) with the best channel conditions.

Towards proceeding to the power allocation, each user is associated with a generic utility function, as follows.

$$U_{u,t}^{(r)} = \frac{W \cdot f_u\left(\gamma_{u,t}^{(r)} \right)}{N_t \cdot P_{u,t}^{(r)}} \tag{35}$$

where N_t denotes the number of users served by the OAP t, W is OAP's $t \in \mathrm{T}$ bandwidth and $f_u(\cdot)$ is the efficiency function. The efficiency function represents the probability of a successful packet transmission for user $u \in U$ and is an increasing, continuous, twice differentiable sigmoidal function of his SINR $\gamma_{u,t}^{(r)}$. A user's function for the probability of a successful packet transmission depends on the transmission schemes used, i.e. modulation and coding schemes (Lee et. al, 2006).

Hence, user's optimal transmission power per RB is the one that maximizes his perceived satisfaction, which is appropriately represented via the corresponding values of the utility function Equation 35. Thus, the power allocation problem is formulated as a distributed optimization problem (Tsiropoulou et. al, 2016).

$$\max U_{u,t}^{(r)} \left(p_{u,t}^{(r)}, p_{-u,t}^{(r)} \right) \tag{36a}$$

$$s.t. \; 0 \prec p_{u,t}^{(r)} \leq \frac{p_{u,t}^{Max}}{R_{u,t}} \tag{36b}$$

where $R_{u,t}$ denotes the number of RBs allocated to user $u \in U$. Towards solving the power control problem Equations 36a to 36b, the following distributed algorithm can be used.

Distributed Power Control in VLANs

1. Each user, $u, u \in U$ has already decided the OAP that he is connected to and initially he transmits with a randomly selected feasible uplink transmission power, i.e. $0 \prec p_{u,t}^{*(r)(0)} \prec \frac{p_{u,t}^{Max}}{R_{u,t}}$. Set $k:=0$ and hence $p_{u,t}^{*(r)(0)}$, $u \in U$ and $t \in T$.

2. Given that the single central controller of the OAPs collects the information of the overall interference within the multi-cell environment, each OAP announces this information, i.e. $\sum_{\substack{u=1 \\ t \in T}}^{U} H_{u,t} p_{u,t}^{(r)}$ to all users residing within its coverage area, via broadcasting. Each user computes his sensed interference $\sum_{\substack{u'=1 \\ u' \neq u \\ t \in T}}^{U} H_{u',t} P_{u',t}^{(r)}$.

3. Set $k:=k+1$. Each user updates his uplink transmission power, i.e.

$$p_{u,t}^{*(r)(k)} = \min \left\{ \frac{\gamma_{u,t}^{(r)*} \cdot \left(\sum_{\substack{u'=1 \\ u' \neq u \\ t \in T}}^{U} H_{u',t} p_{u',t}^{(r)} + \xi \right)}{R_{PD} H_{u,t}}, \frac{p_{u,t}^{Max}}{R_u} \right\}, \; u \in U \text{ and } t \in T.$$

If $\left| p_{u,t}^{*(r)(k+1)} - p_{u,t}^{*(r)(k)} \right| \leq \varepsilon$, e.g. $\varepsilon = 10^{-5}$ then stop. Otherwise go to step 2.

Interference Bounded RBs Allocation and Power Control

Self-organizing networks include attributes like self-configurations, self-optimization, self-planning, etc. The self-organizing concept for intelligent interference coordination can be adopted aiming at reaching an efficient RBs and power allocation. The necessary information, like overall interference in the VLC system, is provided by a Smart Coordinator (SC) of the OAPs, towards enabling the users to decide on their optimal RB and power allocation.

In the interference bounded RBs and power allocation, RBs' reusability is assumed. This means that an RB can be reused within an OAP, if its interference level (announced by the SC) does not exceed a predefined level. Let $I_{u,t}^{(r)}$ denote the overall interference on RB $r, r \in R$ for user $u, u \in U$, which is expressed as follows.

$$I_{u,t}^{(r)} = \sum_{\substack{i=1 \\ i \neq u \\ t \in T}}^{U} R_{PD} \cdot H_{i,t}^{(r)} \cdot p_{i,t}^{(r)} \tag{37}$$

The SC collects the overall interference in the VLC system and broadcasts it to the users towards each user to be able to calculate its sensed interference, as in Equation 37. Therefore, the RB $r^*, r^* \in R$ is occupied by user $u^*, u^* \in U$ based on the maximum channel to interference ratio (CIR).

$$\left\{ r^*, u^* \right\} = \arg \max_{\substack{u \in U \\ r \in R}} \frac{H_{u,t}^{(r)}}{I_{u,t}^{(r)}} \tag{38}$$

The corresponding power allocation problem is modelled below.

$$\max \sum_{u=1}^{U} \sum_{r=1}^{R} \log_2 \left(1 + \gamma_{u,t}^{(r)} \right) \tag{39a}$$

$$\text{s.t.} \sum_{u=1}^{U} \sum_{r=1}^{R} H_{u,t}^{(r)} p_{u,t}^{(r)} \leq I_{thres} \tag{39b}$$

$$p_{u,t}^{(r)} \geq 0, \quad \forall u \in U, \forall r \in R \tag{39c}$$

The objective function Equation 39a targets at maximizing the overall achievable rate within the VLAN, while constraint Equation 39b considers that the overall interference will not exceed a predefined interference threshold and constraint Equation 39c reflects the feasible selection of user's transmission power. The optimization problem Equation 39a to 39c can be solved through the Lagrange relaxation, if it is transformed to a minimization problem with all constraints being negative. The optimal user's $u \in U$ transmission power per each occupied RB is given as follows.

$$p_{u,t}^{(r)*} = \left[\frac{1}{\lambda \cdot H_{u,t}^{(r)}} - \frac{I_{u,t}^{(r)}}{R_{PD} \cdot H_{u,t}^{(r)}} \right]^{+} \tag{40}$$

where $\left[x \right]^{+} = \max \left\{ x, 0 \right\}$ and λ is the Lagrangian multiplier (Saha et. al, 2013b; Mondal et. al, 2012).

RESOURCE ALLOCATION FOR HETEROGENEOUS COMBINED VISIBLE-LIGHT AND RADIO FREQUENCY FEMTOCELLS

The two previous sections of this book-chapter mainly focused on efficient resource allocation approaches in two-tier wireless networks, emphasizing either on the use of femtocell architecture or VLANs technology. However, with the advent of heterogeneous networks and the increasing demand to higher data rates, the co-existence of Optical Wireless (OW) and Radio Frequency (RF) technologies, especially in indoor environments has arisen as a promising solution towards increasing system's bandwidth, as well as alleviating congestion (Stefan et. al. 2013). There are plenty of every-day and real life scenarios, where VLC and RF systems can coexist towards providing multiple QoS requests' fulfillment. For example, the WiFi congestion observed in the rooms of the hotels can be alleviated by providing a non-interfering VLC system in each room combined with the existing lighting system. Also, WiFi congestion can be resolved in mass transportation, e.g. bus, subway, via combining VLC systems in existing RF communication (Wang et. al, 2015; Rahaim et. al, 2011).

Based on the aforementioned examples, an alternative two-tier architecture is created consisting of femtocells and VLC cells. The problem of resource allocation in this two-tier architecture becomes even more complicated however. In the following, an indoor scenario is considered, where combined VLC cells and radio-frequency femtocells are employed for providing indoor coverage. A limited-delay resource allocation problem is formulated for the indoor multi-tier heterogeneous wireless network and the effective capacity approach is applied towards converting the statistical delay constraints into equivalent average rate constraints (Jin et. al, 2015). The resource allocation problem is formulated as non-linear programming (NLP) problem and it is shown that the objective function, as well as the corresponding constraints are concave, thus convex optimization techniques can be utilized in order to provide a stable solution to the problem. Thus, in this section a representative resource allocation problem in two-tier heterogeneous wireless network is described, formulated and solved.

Let us denote the network set as $M = \left\{ m = 1, 2 \right\} = \left\{ VLC, femtocell \right\}$, where *m=1* stands for VLC cells and *m=2* for femtocells. The set of users by $N = \left\{ 1, ..., n, .., N \right\}$ who are connected to a single network at a time. User's association to a network is reflected by the network selection index $x_{m,n} = \left\{ 1, 0 \right\}$ indicating that user n is connected to network m. Let $\Delta \left(\theta \right)$ denote the effective capacity, which can be interpreted as the maximum constant packet-arrival rate that the system can support while guaranteeing some given delay-related QoS prerequisites indicated by the QoS exponent θ. The effective capacity is defined as follows.

$$\Delta\left(\theta\right) = -\frac{1}{\theta} \cdot \ln \mathrm{E}\left[e^{-\theta \cdot r}\right] \tag{41}$$

where $E\left[\bullet\right]$ is the expectation operator and r the throughput.

Each user adopts an appropriately formulated utility function, which depends on the network that the user connects to, i.e. m, and the instantaneous transmission probability $\beta_{m,n}$ of the network m transmitting to user n.

$$U_{m,n}\left(\beta_{m,n}\right) = \phi_{\alpha}\left(\Delta_{m,n}\right) \tag{42}$$

where $\phi_{\alpha}\left(\bullet\right)$ denotes the α-proportional fairness function, which is an enough generic fairness concept, including max-min ($\alpha \to \infty$), proportional ($\alpha = 1$) and throughput maximization ($\alpha = 0$) fairness (Jin et. al, 2015). $\phi_{\alpha}\left(\bullet\right)$ is a smooth, monotonically increasing and concave function.

$$\phi_{\alpha}\left(\Delta_{m,n}\right) = \begin{cases} \log\left(\Delta_{m,n}\right), & if \ \alpha = 1 \\ \dfrac{\Delta_{m,n}}{1-\alpha}, & if \ \alpha \geq 0, \alpha \neq 1 \end{cases} \tag{43}$$

As a result, the resource allocation problem can be formulated as a maximization problem of the sum of utilities of all users, as follows.

$$\max_{\vec{x},\vec{\beta}} \sum_{n\in\mathrm{N}} \phi_{\alpha}\left(\sum_{m\in\mathrm{M}} x_{m,n}\Delta_{m,n}\right) \tag{44a}$$

$$\text{s.t.} \sum_{m\in\mathrm{M}} x_{m,n}\Delta_{m,n} \geq R_{n}, \forall n \in \mathrm{N} \tag{44b}$$

$$\sum_{n\in\mathrm{N}} x_{m,n}\beta_{m,n} \leq 1, \forall m \in \mathrm{M} \tag{44c}$$

$$\sum_{m\in\mathrm{M}} x_{m,n} = 1 \tag{44d}$$

$$x_{m,n} = \left\{1,0\right\}, 0 \leq \beta_{m,n} \leq 1 \tag{44e}$$

where $\Delta_{1,n}$ and $\Delta_{2,n}$ represent the effective capacity of VLC cell and femtocell, respectively, and detailed expressions can be found in (Jin et. al, 2015). The constraint Equation 44b ensures that the heterogeneous network can satisfy user's $n \in \mathrm{N}$ bit-rate R_{n}, while constraint Equation 44c expresses that the total transmission probability for each network should be less than *1*. Moreover, constraint Equation 44d reflects that each user is connected only to one network for each transmission, while constraint

Equation 44e states the feasible values of the independent variables of the problem. Given that $x_{m,n}$ is a binary variable and $\beta_{m,n}$ is a real-valued positive variable, the optimization problem Equations 44a to 44e becomes a mixed-integer non-linear programming (MINLP) problem, which is mathematically intractable.

Towards solving the optimization problem Equation 44a to 44e, a relaxation of the binary constraint $x_{m,n} = \{1,0\}$ is assumed, considering continuous values of $x_{m,n}$ within the interval $[0,1]$. The solutions of the relaxed problem are close to the original problem, i.e. Equations 44a to 44e, as shown in (Yu et. al, 2006). Furthermore, it should be noted that for each user $n \in N$ there is exactly one value $x_{m,n} = 1$. Such a specific network is denoted by m' and $\phi_\alpha \left(\sum_{m \in M} x_{m,n} \Delta_{m,n} \right) = \phi_\alpha \left(\Delta_{m',n} \right)$ holds true. Based on the above analysis, the optimization problem Equations 44a – 44e can be rewritten as follows.

$$\max_{\vec{x}, \vec{\beta}} \sum_{m \in M} \sum_{n \in N} x_{m,n} \phi_\alpha \left(\Delta_{m,n} \right) \tag{45a}$$

$$\text{s.t.} \sum_{m \in M} x_{m,n} \Delta_{m,n} \geq R_n, \forall n \in N \tag{45b}$$

$$\sum_{n \in N} x_{m,n} \beta_{m,n} \leq 1, \forall m \in M \tag{45c}$$

$$\sum_{m \in M} x_{m,n} = 1 \tag{45d}$$

$$x_{m,n} = \{1,0\}, 0 \leq \beta_{m,n} \leq 1 \tag{45e}$$

The reformulated optimization problem Equations 45a to 45e is a concave optimization problem with respect to the two independent variables $x_{m,n}$ and $\beta_{m,n}$ and can be easily solved following the Lagrangian formulation. Therefore, the optimal solutions x and β of Equations 45a to 45e can be determined.

FUTURE DIRECTIONS

Despite the special attention that has been placed over the last few years in the design and mass deployment of multi-tier wireless networks, there exist several technical challenges of high research and practical importance, that still need to be addressed, in order to improve the operation and efficiency of such networks. At this point we briefly present some indicative future research and development directions based on the current trend of technology, however this list is by no means exhaustive, and it is expected that even more interesting research topics will arise in the upcoming years within the continuously evolving research and innovation field of multi-tier heterogeneous networks.

- **Distributed Interference Management:** With the advent of Internet of Things (IoT), Radio Frequency Identification (RFID) technology, Machine-to-Machine (M2M) and Device-to-Device (D2D) communication, every machine / user is expected to request a data hungry application from its belonging network. Therefore, the number of mobile users / machines is expected to increase dramatically and correspondingly their caused interference within the multi-tier wireless network. Thus, distributed interference management schemes are required to deal with the co-tier and cross-tier interference. The distributed interference management schemes should satisfy the hard QoS requirements of macrocell users, as well as the soft QoS requirements of femtocells' or VLC cells' users, while simultaneously enhancing the capacity and coverage of the network.

- **Load Balancing, Cell Association and Admission Control:** Due to the dense deployment of the femtocells and VLC cells, as well as the dramatic increase of the number of the mobile users in the overall multi-tier network, more efficient schemes compared to the traditional multicell environment should be devised towards enabling:
  - The load balancing among the cells,
  - The cell association of the users,
  - The admission control.

Considering load balancing and cell association schemes, techniques like maximum gain or SINR or utility selection, i.e. the mobile user being connected to the cell where he appears to have maximum channel gain or SINR or utility value, can be adopted. Furthermore, the optimal admission control schemes should consider multi-tier network's topology, i.e. users' distribution and MBS / FAPs / OAPs location, as well as the available information to the mobile users and the corresponding traffic patterns.

- **Lack of Centralized Control, Self-Optimization:** A centralized controller in dense deployed multi-tier heterogeneous wireless networks is not feasible due to the large number of FAPs and OAPs, which are also owned by different providers. Thus, the resource allocation and interference management proposed approaches should be distributed in nature and support mobile users' self-optimization. The exchanged signaling among MBS / FAPs / OAPs and the corresponding users residing in their coverage area should be minimized, as well as the exchanged information among different tiers of the networks. The decision-making process should primarily lie at mobile user's side, who is able to sense his surrounding environment and choose his optimal strategy.

- **Mobility and Handoff Management:** Due to the small coverage areas of femtocells and VLC cells, which conclude to often users' handoffs among cells, the effective and efficient mobility management and handover schemes are of great importance. The following handover scenarios may appear:
  - Macrocell to femtocell,
  - Macrocell to VLC cell,
  - Femtocell to VLC cell.

Furthermore, the network complexity and signaling cost should be also considered in the design of the aforementioned schemes, while mobile devices' different access modes capability will affect the corresponding deployments.

CONCLUSION

This chapter aims to introduce to the reader the main resource allocation topics addressed in multi-tier femtocell and visible light communication (VLC) heterogeneous wireless networks. Initially, the multi-tier heterogeneous wireless networks architecture was presented. The system model of two-tier femtocell wireless networks, as well as the system model of two-tier VLC local area networks were discussed highlighting their fundamental characteristics. The main distributed resource allocation approaches proposed in two-tier femtocell networks were organized in the following three categories:

- Power allocation and interference management,
- Joint power and rate allocation,
- Resource allocation and pricing policies.

Following similar methodology with respect to the presentation, the main resource allocation approaches in two-tier VLC cells were organized in four categories as follows:

- User association in VLANs,
- Adaptive bandwidth allocation,
- Joint bandwidth and power allocation,
- Interference bounded resource blocks allocation and power control.

Moreover, the problem of resource allocation, where femtocells and VLC cells coexist, was also introduced. It is noted that in this chapter, for reader's convenience, we attempted to follow a common presentation methodology with respect to the discussion of all the examined resource allocation approaches, i.e. definition of the problem and corresponding objective function, formulation of the optimization problem, its solution, and presentation of an indicative algorithm to obtain the solution. Finally, future directions were provided following the concept of the existence of multi-tier heterogeneous wireless networks as they emerge in the 5G networking era.

REFERENCES

Boyd, S., & Vandenberghe, L. (2004). *Convex Optimization*. New York, NY: Cambridge University Press. doi:10.1017/CBO9780511804441

Bykhovsky, D., & Arnon, S. (2014). Multiple Access Resource Allocation in Visible Light Communication Systems. *Journal of Lightwave Technology*, 32(8), 1594–1600. doi:10.1109/JLT.2014.2308282

Cerwall, P., & Jonsson, P. (2015). *Ericsson Mobility Report on the Pulse of the Networked Society*. Retrieved June 2015, from http://www.ericsson.com/res/docs/2015/ericsson-mobility-report-june-2015.pdf

Chandrasekhar, V., Andrews, J. G., & Gatherer, A. (2008). Femtocell networks: A survey. *IEEE Communications Magazine*, 46(9), 59–67. doi:10.1109/MCOM.2008.4623708

Chandrasekhar, V., Andrews, J. G., Muharemovict, T., Shen, Z., & Gatherer, A. (2009a). Power control in two-tier femtocell networks. *IEEE Transactions on Wireless Communications*, 8(8), 4316–4328. doi:10.1109/TWC.2009.081386

Chandrasekhar, V., Andrews, J. G., Shen, Z., Muharemovict, T., & Gatherer, A. (2009b). Distributed Power Control in Femtocell-Underlay Cellular Networks. *IEEE Global Telecommunications Conference*, 1-6. doi:10.1109/GLOCOM.2009.5425923

Cisco. (2012). *Cisco Visual Networking Index: Global Mobile Data Traffic Forecast Update, 2011–2016.* Technical Report, Cisco Systems Inc.

Cullen, J. (2008). *Radioframe presentation.* London, UK: Femtocell Europe.

Cuthbertson, A. (2015). *LiFi internet: First real-world usage boasts speed 100 times faster than WiFi.* Academic Press.

Damnjanovic, A., Montojo, J., Wei, Y., Ji, T., Luo, T., Vajapeyam, M., & Malladi, D. et al. (2011). A survey on 3GPP heterogeneous networks. *IEEE Wireless Communications*, 18(3), 10–21. doi:10.1109/MWC.2011.5876496

Douros, V. G., Toumpis, S., & Polyzos, G. C. (2012). Power control under best response dynamics for interference mitigation in a two-tier femtocell network. *10th International Symposium on Modeling and Optimization in Mobile, Ad Hoc and Wireless Networks*, 398-405.

Hayajneh, M., & Abdallah, C. T. (2004). Distributed joint rate and power control game-theoretic algorithms for wireless data. *IEEE Communications Letters*, 8(8), 511–513. doi:10.1109/LCOMM.2004.833817

Hong, E. J., Yun, S. Y., & Cho, D. H. (2009). Decentralized power control scheme in femtocell networks: A game theoretic approach. *IEEE 20th International Symposium on Personal, Indoor and Mobile Radio Communications*, 415-419.

IEEE. (2011). *IEEE 802.15 WPAN Task Group 7 (TG7) Visible Light Communication.* IEEE Standards Association. Retrieved 9 Dec 2011 from http://www.ieee802.org/15/pub/TG7.html

ITU. (2009). *Telecommunications Indicators Update 2009.* Available at: http://www.itu.int/ITU-D/ict/statistics/

ITU Recommendation M.1225. (1997). *Guidelines for evaluation of radio transmission technologies for IMT-2000.* Author.

Jin, F., Li, X., Zhang, R., Dong, C., & Hanzo, L. (2016). Resource Allocation Under Delay-Guarantee Constraints for Visible-Light Communication. *IEEE Access*, 99, 1-12.

Jin, F., Zhang, R., & Hanzo, L. (2015). Resource Allocation Under Delay-Guarantee Constraints for Heterogeneous Visible-Light and RF Femtocell. *IEEE Transactions on Wireless Communications*, 14(2), 1020–1034. doi:10.1109/TWC.2014.2363451

Kang, X., Zhang, R., & Motani, M. (2012). Price-Based Resource Allocation for Spectrum-Sharing Femtocell Networks: A Stackelberg Game Approach. *IEEE Journal on Selected Areas in Communications*, 30(3), 538–549. doi:10.1109/JSAC.2012.120404

Le, L. B., Niyato, D., Hossain, E., Kim, D. I., & Hoang, D. T. (2013). QoS-Aware and Energy-Efficient Resource Management in OFDMA Femtocells. *IEEE Transactions on Wireless Communications*, *12*(1), 180–194. doi:10.1109/TWC.2012.120412.120141

Lee, J. W., Mazumdar, R. R., & Shroff, N. B. (2006). Joint Resource Allocation and Base-Station Assignment for the Downlink in CDMA Networks. *IEEE/ACM Transactions on Networking*, *14*(1), 1–14. doi:10.1109/TNET.2005.863480

Li, L., Xu, C., & Tao, M. (2012). Resource Allocation in Open Access OFDMA Femtocell Networks. *IEEE Wireless Communications Letters*, *1*(6), 625–628. doi:10.1109/WCL.2012.091312.120394

Liu, D., Zheng, W., Zhang, H., Ma, W., & Wen, X. (2012). Energy efficient power optimization in two-tier femtocell networks with interference pricing.*8th International Conference on Computing and Networking Technology*, 247-252.

Liu, J., Zheng, W., Li, W., Wang, X., Xie, Y., & Wen, X. (2013). Distributed uplink power control for two-tier femtocell networks via convex pricing.*IEEE Wireless Communications and Networking Conference*, 458-463.

Lu, Z., Sun, Y., Wen, X., Su, T., & Ling, D. (2012). An energy-efficient power control algorithm in femtocell networks.*7th International Conference on Computer Science & Education*, 395-400. doi:10.1109/ICCSE.2012.6295100

Ma, Y., Lv, T., & Lu, Y. (2013). Efficient power control in heterogeneous Femto-Macro cell networks. *IEEE Wireless Communications and Networking Conference*, 4215-4219.

Mondal, R. K., Chowdhury, M. Z., Saha, N., & Jang, Y. M. (2012). Interference-aware optical resource allocation in visible light communication.*International Conference on ICT Convergence*, 155-158. doi:10.1109/ICTC.2012.6386803

Musku, M. R., Chronopoulos, A. T., Popescu, D. C., & Stefanescu, A. (2010). A game-theoretic approach to joint rate and power control for uplink CDMA communications. *IEEE Transactions on Communications*, *58*(3), 923–932. doi:10.1109/TCOMM.2010.03.070205

Ndjiongue, A. R., Ferreira, H. C., Ngatched, T. M. N., & Webster, J. G. (2015). *Visible Light Communications (VLC) Technology*. John Wiley & Sons, Inc. doi:10.1002/047134608X.W8267

Ngo, D. T., Khakurel, S., & Le-Ngoc, T. (2014). Joint Subchannel Assignment and Power Allocation for OFDMA Femtocell Networks. *IEEE Transactions on Wireless Communications*, *13*(1), 342–355. doi:10.1109/TWC.2013.111313.130645

Ngo, D. T., Le, L. B., Le-Ngoc, T., Hossain, E., & Kim, D. I. (2012). Distributed Interference Management in Two-Tier CDMA Femtocell Networks. *IEEE Transactions on Wireless Communications*, *11*(3), 979–989. doi:10.1109/TWC.2012.012712.110073

Nguyen, T., Chowdhury, M. Z., & Jang, Y. M. (2013). A novel link switching scheme using pre-scanning and RSS prediction in visible light communication networks. *EURASIP Journal on Wireless Communications and Networking*, 1–17.

Rahaim, M. B., Vegni, A. M., & Little, T. D. C. (2011). A hybrid Radio Frequency and broadcast Visible Light Communication system. *IEEE GLOBECOM Workshops*, 792-796.

Saha, N., Mondal, R. K., Ifthekhar, M. S., & Jang, Y. M. (2014). Dynamic resource allocation for visible light based wireless sensor network.*International Conference on Information Networking*, 75-78. doi:10.1109/ICOIN.2014.6799668

Saha, N., Mondal, R. K., & Jang, Y. M. (2013). Opportunistic channel reuse for a self-organized visible light communication personal area network.*Fifth International Conference on Ubiquitous and Future Networks*, 131-134. doi:10.1109/ICUFN.2013.6614796

Saha, N., Mondal, R. K., & Jang, Y. M. (2013). Adaptive Bandwidth Allocation for QoS Guaranteed VLC Based WPAN. *The Journal of Korean Institute of Communications and Information Science*, *38C*(8), 719–724. doi:10.7840/kics.2013.38C.8.719

Salati, A. H., Nasiri-kenari, M., & Sadeghi, P. (2012). Distributed subband, rate and power allocation in OFDMA based two-tier femtocell networks using Fractional Frequency Reuse.*IEEE Wireless Communications and Networking Conference*, 2626-2630. doi:10.1109/WCNC.2012.6214243

Saraydar, C. U., Mandayam, N. B., & Goodman, D. J. (2002). Efficient power control via pricing in wireless data networks. *IEEE Transactions on Communications*, *50*(2), 291–303. doi:10.1109/26.983324

Stefan, I., Burchardt, H., & Haas, H. (2013). Area spectral efficiency performance comparison between VLC and RF femtocell networks.*IEEE International Conference on Communications*, 3825-3829. doi:10.1109/ICC.2013.6655152

Stefan, I., & Haas, H. (2013). Analysis of Optimal Placement of LED Arrays for Visible Light Communication. *IEEE 77*[th] *Vehicular Technology Conference*, 1-5.

Su, T., Zheng, W., Li, W., Ling, D., & Wen, X. (2012). Energy-efficient power optimization with Pareto improvement in two-tier femtocell networks. *IEEE 23rd International Symposium on Personal Indoor and Mobile Radio Communications,* 2512-2517.

Tsiropoulou, E. E., Katsinis, G. K., Filios, A., & Papavassiliou, S. (2014). On the Problem of Optimal Cell Selection and Uplink Power Control in Open Access Multi-service Two-Tier Femtocell Networks. *ADHOC-NOW*, 114-127.

Tsiropoulou, E. E., Katsinis, G. K., Vamvakas, P., & Papavassiliou, S. (2013). Efficient uplink power control in multi-service two-tier femtocell networks via a game theoretic approach. *IEEE 18th International Workshop on Computer Aided Modeling and Design of Communication Links and Networks*, 104-108.

Tsiropoulou, E. E., Vamvakas, P., Katsinis, G. K., & Papavassiliou, S. (2015). Combined power and rate allocation in self-optimized multi-service two-tier femtocell networks. *Computer Communications*, *72*, 38–48. doi:10.1016/j.comcom.2015.05.012

Tsiropoulou, E. E., Gialagkolidis, I., Vamvakas, P., & Papavassiliou, S. (2016). Resource Allocation in Visible Light Communication Networks: NOMA vs OFDMA Transmission Techniques. *Ad-hoc, Mobile, and Wireless Networks*, *9724*, 32-46.

Tsonev, D., Sinanovic, S., & Haas, H. (2013). Practical MIMO Capacity for Indoor Optical Wireless Communication with White LEDs. *IEEE 77th Vehicular Technology Conference*, 1-5.

Wang, Y., Videv, S., & Haas, H. (2015). Dynamic load balancing with handover in hybrid Li-Fi and Wi-Fi networks. *IEEE 25th Annual International Symposium on Personal, Indoor, and Mobile Radio Communication*, 575-579.

Xu, P., Fang, X., Chen, M., & Xu, Y. (2013). A Stackelberg game-based spectrum allocation scheme in macro/femtocell hierarchical networks. *Computer Communications*, *36*(14), 1552–1558. doi:10.1016/j.comcom.2012.10.002

Yu, W., & Lui, R. (2006). Dual methods for nonconvex spectrum optimization of multicarrier systems. *IEEE Transactions on Communications*, *54*(7), 1310–1322. doi:10.1109/TCOMM.2006.877962

Yu, Z., Baxley, R. J., & Zhou, G. T. (2013). Multi-user MISO broadcasting for indoor visible light communication.*IEEE International Conference on Acoustics, Speech and Signal Processing*, 4849-4853. doi:10.1109/ICASSP.2013.6638582

Zeng, L., Obrien, D., Minh, H. L., Faulkner, G. E., Lee, K., Jung, D., & Won, E. T. et al. (2009). High data rate multiple input multiple output (MIMO) optical wireless communications using white led lighting. *IEEE Journal on Selected Areas in Communications*, *27*(9), 1654–1662. doi:10.1109/JSAC.2009.091215

Zhang, R., Wang, J., Wang, Z., Xu, Z., Zhao, C., & Hanzo, L. (2015). Visible light communications in heterogeneous networks: Paving the way for user-centric design. *IEEE Wireless Communications*, *22*(2), 8–16. doi:10.1109/MWC.2015.7096279

Zhao, J., Zheng, W., Wen, X., Chu, X., Zhang, H., & Lu, Z. (2014). Game Theory Based Energy-Aware Uplink Resource Allocation in OFDMA Femtocell Networks. *International Journal of Distributed Sensor Networks*, 1–8.

Zheng, W., Su, T., Li, W., Lu, Z., & Wen, X. (2012). Distributed energy-efficient power optimization in two-tier femtocell networks.*IEEE International Conference on Communications*, 5767-5771. doi:10.1109/ICC.2012.6364882

KEY TERMS AND DEFINITIONS

Cell Selection: A methodology towards indicating to the mobile users the optimal cell to connect to.

Cellular Link Protection: A resource allocation framework applied to a cell towards guaranteeing the Quality of Service needs of mobile users.

Energy Efficiency: The way of managing and restraining the growth in energy consumption.

Hierarchical Cell Architecture: The architecture of a multi-layered cellular network where users may be served by various layers such as macro, micro, or pico layer, depending on the network capacity and their Quality of Service prerequisites.

Interference Management: A set of techniques towards mitigating interference.

Internet of Things: A development of the Internet in which all objects have network connectivity, allowing them to send and receive data.

Local Area Networks: A wireless network that links devices and mobile users within a building or group of adjacent buildings.

Multi-Tier Networks: Wireless networks organized in a multi-layered structure.

Resource Allocation: A plan for using available system's resources, for example bandwidth, power, to achieve goals like mobile users' Quality of Service prerequisites' satisfaction.

Chapter 11
Fault Tracking Framework for Software–Defined Networking (SDN)

Amitava Mukherjee
IBM India Private Limited, India

Sudip Dutta
IBM India Private Limited, India

Rashid A. Saeed
Ministry of Higher Education and Scientific Research, Sudan

Mrinal K. Naskar
Jadavpur University, India

ABSTRACT

The emergence of software-defined networking (SDN) raises a set of fundamental questions, including architectural issues like whether control should be centralized or distributed, and whether control and data planes should be separated. Several open problems exist in SDN space, ranging from architectural questions that are fundamental to how networks scale and evolve to implementation issues such as how we build distributed "logically centralized" control planes. Moreover, since SDN is still in its early stage, there is an opportunity to make fault tracking framework a more integral part of the overall design process. Although SDN's goal is to simplify the management of networks, the challenge is that the SDN software stack itself is a complex distributed system, operating in asynchronous, heterogeneous, and failure-prone environments. In this chapter we will focus on three key areas: 1) SDN architecture, 2) scalable SDN systems to understand which pieces of control plane can be run logically centralized fashions, and 3) fault tracking framework to track down the failures in SDN.

INTRODUCTION

The emergence of software-defined networking (SDN) brings out opportunities to both industry and academia to improve the functionalities in networking and cut down the cost of networking operation too. With this, SDN raises a set of fundamental questions, including architectural issues like whether control should be centralized or distributed, and whether control and data planes should be separated. "SDN starts from two simple ideas: generalize network hardware so it provides a standard collection of packet processing functions instead of a fixed set of narrow features, and decouple the software that

DOI: 10.4018/978-1-5225-2023-8.ch011

controls the network from the devices that implement it. This design makes it possible to evolve the network without having to change the underlying hardware and enables expressing network algorithms in terms of appropriate abstractions for particular applications" (Casado, M.,2014). The SDN concepts are new and still under research, and standard development stage in academic while industries are working to develop product under trial, but not in position to commercialize them. From one perspective, it is visible from different initiatives how SDN is able to foster innovation in networks at a level that has not been seen in the last decade. On the other hand, industries are usually too concerned with time to market rather than providing conceptually elegant solutions (Wickboldt, J. A., 2015). Particularly, the majority of efforts are focused on providing solutions and services over SDN networks, whereas network management specifically fault management is not given much attention. However, as widely recognized, management must not be an afterthought (Schonwalder, J., et al., 2009).

The OpenFlow (ONF) was first introduced in March 2008, from the network research group of Stanford University and collaborators. The first time the concept of "network operating system (NOX)" appeared in this context was through the proposal of the NOX controller (Cisco, 2013). NOX provided a concept how to enable the development of software to control OpenFlow-based networks. The ONF is also responsible for the maintenance of OpenFlow standards, technical specifications of the Open-Flow Switch, and the conformance testing of SDN enabled devices. The architecture of SDN consists of three layers: the application layer, the control layer, and the infrastructure layer. The function of the two lower layers are called OpenFlow controller and OpenFlow Switch, corresponding to the control and data planes of traditional IP/MPLS network switches and routers. With the OpenFlow standard, the OpenFlow controller instructs the OpenFlow Switch to define the standard functional messages such as packet-received, send-packet-out, modify-forwarding-table, get-stats, etc. (Sun, S., 2015).

In addition to the ONF, the Internet Engineering Task Force (IETF), the International Telecommunications Union Telecommunication Standardization Sector (ITU-T), the European Telecommunications Standards Institute (ETSI), and the China Communications Standards Association (CCSA) have also started standardization work on SDN. IETF issued an RFC concerning the requirements and application issues relating to SDN from an operator's perspective (IETF, 2014), while ITU-T has not published a formal recommendation since the project began in 2012. Table 1 summarizes the formally published SDN standards (Sun, S., 2015).

Table 1. Current main standards for SDN

Standardization Organization	Main Related Standards and Activities	Functionality
ONF	Software-Defined Networking: The New Norm for Networks (white paper) Interoperability Event Technical Paper v0.4/ v1.0	Definition and interoperability
ITU	ITU-T Resolution 77	Standardization for SDN
IETF	IETF RFC 7149	Perspective
ETSI	NFV ISG	Ues cases and framework and requirements
CCSA	TC6 WG1	Application scenarios and framework protocol

Sun, S., 2015.

Currently, SDN has found its best practices in campus networks and data centers, and has drawn increasing attention recently. SDN is regarded as a promising technology to solve current and emerging problems. However, necessary extensions are still required for future heterogeneous networks (HetNets) (Sun, S., 2015).

NEC was the first to develop a commercial switch with native Open-Flow support, in April 2009. In 2011 some Internet giants, such as Google, announced the adoption of SDN inside their data centers and backbones. In the same year a few standardization efforts started in. ONF is basically dedicated to promote and evolve the concept of SDN by standardizing the OpenFlow technology (Wickboldt, J. A., 2015). Near 2012 other major players such as Cisco, Juniper, Hewlett-Packard, and VMW appeared to put themselves in a leading position in that promising but not yet matured networking paradigm (Wickboldt, J. A., 2015). In the beginning of 2013 the IRTF started the Software-Defined Networking Research Group (SDNRG), while the Linux Foundation launched the Open Daylight project. All these standardization efforts are supposed to be vendor independent, although most of the aforementioned companies actually embody the majority of the working groups and committees.

Several open problems exist in the SDN space, ranging from architectural questions that are fundamental to how networks scale and evolve to implementation issues such as how we might build distributed "logically centralized" control planes. For example, how much programmability should an SDN system provide, and where? Other questions include how distributed state management systems (such as controllers) should implement state consistency and which APIs and corresponding abstractions should be standardized, if any (Meyer, D., 2013). In this respect, moving control logic out of hardware and into software enables concise policy specifications and significantly more sophisticated testing and fault tracking tools. Moreover, since SDN is still in its early stage (compared to traditional networking approaches), there is an opportunity to make fault tracking framework a more integral part of the overall design process. Although SDN's goal is to simplify the management of networks, the challenge is that the SDN software stack itself is a complex distributed system, operating in asynchronous, heterogeneous, and failure-prone environments (Wickboldt, J. A., 2015; Scott, R. C., 2012). In order to address these issues we will focus on three key areas: i) SDN architecture; ii) scalable SDN systems to understand which pieces of control plane can be run 'logically centralized' fashions and iii) fault tracking framework to track down the failures in SDN (Scott, R. C., 2012; Kazemian, P., 2012).

To select SDN architecture out of among three architectural issues like OpenFlow/SDN (OF/SDN), Control Plane/SDN (CP/SDN) and Overlay/SDN (OL/SDN). OF/SDN is characterized by the complete separation of the control and data planes, open interfaces to the forwarding plane (that is, Open-Flow), and centralized control. In CP/SDN, designers seek to make the existing, distributed control plane programmable. CP/SDN will provide mechanisms for using that arbitration engine to inject routing state into the system as well as read possibly abstracted state from it. OL/SDN represents a design point that encompasses those models in which a virtual network is overlaid on the network (which might be physical, virtual, or both). In this case, the designers overlay a new control plane on top of existing control and data planes, and (in theory) have minimal interaction with the "underlay" network (Meyer, D., 2013).

To define scalable SDN systems to understand which pieces of control plane can be used to run in logically centralized fashion Path Computation Element (PCE) (Dasgupta, S., 2007) can be used a traffic engineering technology under consideration as a candidate for measured separation of control and data planes, with the goal of making the network (more) programmable and architecturally centralized. PCE retains the resilience and scale of the underlying distributed control plane while still providing programmability and a global network view for use in traffic engineering. To design fault tracking framework to track down the failures in SDN.

Control applications on SDN should handle four types of network failures (Kazemian, P., 2012; Koponen, T., 2010):

1. Forwarding element failures,
2. Link failures,
3. Physical layer instance failures of SDN, and
4. Failures in connectivity between network elements in physical layer infrastructure and physical layer instance instances (and between the physical layer instance instances themselves).

This step introduces a general framework, called fault tracking framework, which provides a set of tools and insights to model and check networks for a variety of failure conditions in a protocol-independent way in SDN.

Figure 1. Three-layer SDN reference model
Xia, W., et al., 2015.

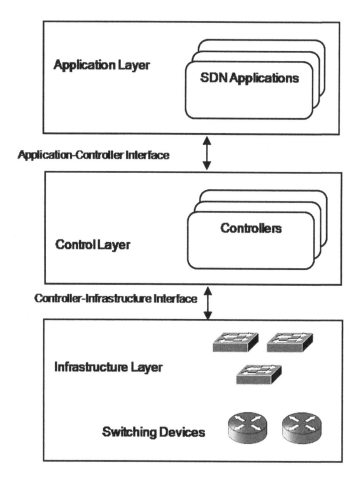

SDN ARCHITECTURE

The reference model for SDN, as suggested by ONF is shown in Figure 1. This model consists of three layers, namely an infrastructure layer, a control layer, and an application layer; they stack over each other.

The infrastructure layer in this SDN reference model consists of data planes of switching devices i.e., switches, routers, etc. The functions of these switching devices are mostly two-fold (refer to Figure 2). First, these devices collect network status, store them temporally and subsequently send them to controllers. The network status includes information in regards to network topologies, traffic statistics, and network usages. Second, these devices process packets based on the rules provided by a controller. The control layer bridges the application layer and the infrastructure layer, via two interfaces. Towards downward interacting with the infrastructure layer termed as the south-bound interface, it specifies functions for controllers to access functions provided by switching devices. The functions include reporting network status and importing packet forwarding rules. In upward interacting with the application layer called the north-bound interface, it provides service access points in various forms, for example, an Application Programming Interface (API). SDN applications can access network status information reported from switching devices through this API, make system tuning decisions based on this information, and carry out these decisions by setting packet forwarding rules to switching devices using this API. Since multiple controllers will exist for a large administrative network domain, an "east-west" communication interface among the controllers will also be needed for the controllers to share network information and coordinate their decision-making processes (Yin, H., et al., 2012; Xie, H., et al., 2012).

The application layer contains SDN applications designed to fulfill user requirements. Through the programmable platform provided by the control layer, SDN applications are able to access and control switching devices at the infrastructure layer. Example of SDN applications could include dynamic access control, seamless mobility and migration, server load balancing, and network virtualization.

At the lowest layer in the SDN reference model, the infrastructure layer consists of switching devices (e.g., switches, routers, etc.), which are interconnected to build a single network. The connections among switching devices are through different transmission medias, including copper wire, wireless radio, and also optical fiber. The Figure 3 illustrates an SDN enabled reference network.

Figure 2. Two-fold function of switching device
Xia, W., et al., 2015.

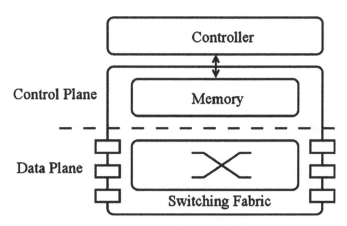

Figure 3. Typical SDN architecture
Xia, W., et al., 2015.

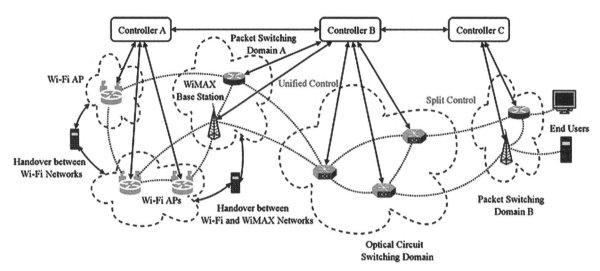

The Figure 3 illustrates the architectural design (Xia, W., et al., 2015) of an SDN switching device, consisting of two logical components for the data plane and the control plane. In the data plane, the switching device, in particular, through its processor, performs packet forwarding, based on the forwarding rules defined by the control layer. The underlying ideas of SDN —separating the control and data planes — have turned up in telecommunications in prior technologies, but it will be challenging in design issues as it would represent (Scott, R. C., 2012). Three architecture models in SDN are predominated in the design space:

1.   OpenFlow/SDN (OF/SDN),
2.   Control Plane/SDN (CP/ SDN),
3.   Overlay/SDN (OL/SDN).

OpenFlow/SDN

This is characterized by complete separation of control and data planes and open access to the forwarding plane, to overlay models that are less concerned with existing control and data planes. Equally diverse design would emerge new design ideas about what kinds of APIs would exist and which abstractions they do or would implement. OpenFlow is arising as the protocol (or API) of choice between controller and forwarding elements. New services, feature velocity and cost reduction are expected benefits of SDN (Meyer, D., 2013).

This OF/SDN covers the components and the basic functions of the switch, and the OpenFlow protocol to manage an OpenFlow switch from a remote controller. An OpenFlow Switch consists of one or more flow tables and a group table, which perform packet lookups and forwarding, and an OpenFlow channel to an external controller (Figure 4). The switch communicates with the controller and the controller manages the switch via the OpenFlow protocol.

Figure 4. Key components of OpenFlow switch

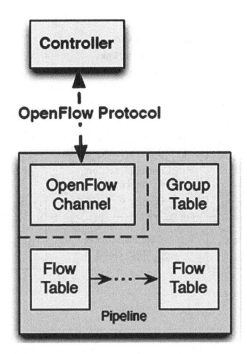

Using the OpenFlow protocol, the controller can add, update, and delete flow entries in flow tables, both reactively (in response to packets) and proactively. Each flow table in the switch contains a set of flow entries; each flow entry consists of match fields, counters, and a set of instructions to apply to matching packets.

We take the concept of BGP-based Routing Control Platforms (RCP) (Caesar, M., 2005) with the visibility and direct control capabilities (i.e., actual forward table (FT) installation, rich matching and instructions) of an OF/SDN (Caesar, M., 2005). OF/SDN is a new technology, that allows getting back to basics, with potential to multidisciplinize or even extrapolate on IP control. SDN-driven APIs provide a unique opportunity to reheat cold topics around IP routing (e.g. BGP) by deploying and evaluating in real conditions (past and new) research results (Rothenberg, C. E., et al., 2012). OpenFlow opens a real possibility to the direct modification of current routing services by users and operators without the costly dependence on vendors. While inter-domain protocols are quite robust in the loop/error handling of misbehaving implementations, for IGPs that may not really be the same.

The left half of Figure 5 shows a typical Tier-1 ISP network divided into data-plane core, control-plane core, and the edge, consisting of devices known as Provider Edge (PE) routers, that peer with external ASes and are configured to provide services to Customer Edge (CE) devices. There are three cases of Border Gateway Protocol (BGP) deployment within ASes today: full mesh, confederation, and route reflection, which are the most popular way to distribute BGP routes between routers of the same AS. Avoiding routing pitfalls (e.g., oscillations, loops, and path inefficiencies) requires topology design, route reflector (RR) placement, and link-metric assignment. RRs have been deployed in the data path and placed on the edge to core boundaries. That model has started to evolve taking RRs out of the data paths to deliver application requiring PE-PE encapsulation (e.g., L3 VPN). With edge to edge MPLS or

Figure 5. Routing architectures: current (left) vs. OpenFlow/SDN-based "BGP-free edge" (right)
Feamster, N., 2004.

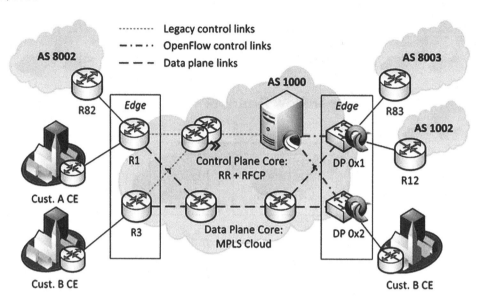

IP encapsulation also used to carry Internet traffic, this model has been gradually extended other BGP address families, including IPv4/v6 Internet routing. Control plane RRs are placed in arbitrary core locations of large networks. The major issue of such deployment models relies in the fact that best path selection (e.g. hot potato) is performed by the RRs from the reference point of inter gateway protocol (IGP) and gets propagated to each RR client in different locations. Clearly, that such best path is not optimal for a lot of RR clients. In essence, RCPs are based on three architectural principles (Feamster, N., 2004): i) path computation based on a consistent view of network state, ii) controlled interactions between routing protocol layers, and iii) expressive specification of routing policy. The SoftRouter (Lakshman, T. V., et al. 2004) is another noteworthy architectural work that promotes the separation and logical centralization of control plane using the IETF ForCES protocol. An OF/SDN approach to IP routing control can easily be implemented eBGPspeaking applications, providing full route control and direct manipulation of the actual FIBs (now OpenFlow tables), augmented with flexible flow match and rich instruction capabilities beyond basic next-hop forwarding. Replacing iBGP with OpenFlow can be seen as an (orthogonal) advancement of phases 2 and 3 in the RCP taxonomy (Feamster, N., 2004), heading towards an effective "BGP-free edge" architectural proposal for intra-domain BGP deployments. The BGP control plane is removed from both core and edge devices and shifted into a higher control layer running on one or more generic computing machines. Only their final product gets distributed via OpenFlow to datapath switches. As shown in the right half of Figure 5, the new control plane is added in the form of a BGP controller (further referred to RFCP) that acts as a gateway between existing RRs and OpenFlow controllers programming datapaths. The scale of such deployment can vary and completely be controlled by network operator.

Control Plane/SDN (CP/SDN)

The second architecture model in this SDN space is Control Plane/SDN (CP/SDN) where designers make the existing, distributed control plane programmable. Interface to the Routing System (I2RS) (I2RS, 2016) is a protocol designed to make the *routing information base* (RIB) programmable and enable new kinds of network provisioning and operation (Meyer, D., 2013). The basic idea (Schonwalder, J., et al., 2009) is that because the RIB is already an arbitration engine for various routing state sources, CP/SDN will provide mechanisms for using that arbitration engine to inject routing state into the system as well as read possibly abstracted state from it. Thus, the routing system includes control plane protocols and processes that compute routes and paths for data packets, wherever the processes implementing those protocols and processes may be running. Examples of protocols in this class include the Border Gateway Protocol-Link State (BGP-LS) and Application-Layer Traffic Optimization (ALTO).

IETF working group has stated that "I2RS facilitates real-time or event driven interaction with the routing system through a collection of protocol-based control or management interfaces. These allow information, policies, and operational parameters to be injected into and retrieved (as read or by notification) from the routing system while retaining data consistency and coherency across the routers and routing infrastructure, and among multiple interactions with the routing system. The I2RS interfaces will co-exist with existing configuration and management systems and interfaces. The users of the I2RS interfaces will be management applications, network controllers, and user applications that make specific demands on the network (Caesar, M., 2005)." The I2RS working group works to develop basic building-blocks necessary to enable the specific use cases, and that will lead to an understanding of the abstract informational models and requirements for encodings and protocols for the I2RS interfaces. That can be used by designers in CP/SDN model in SDN architecture (Meyer, D., 2013). The IETF working group is to develop this standard. To get detail information we refer readers to check the standard given in (Caesar, M., 2005).

To explain CP/SDN model, we use the concept on which a group of researchers had worked (Koponen, T., 2010) on. They used the idea of Distributed Control Platform (DCP) to understand how DCP realizes a production-quality control platform requires two aspects of its design: the context in which it fits into the network, and the API it provides to application designers. There are four components in a network controlled by DCP, and they have distinct roles. These are the four basic components of an SDN based network.

1. **Physical Infrastructure:** This includes network switches and routers, as well as any other network elements (such as load balancers) that support an interface allowing DCP to read and write the state controlling the element's behavior (such as forwarding table (FE) entries).
2. **Connectivity Infrastructure:** The communication between the physical networking elements and DCP (the "control traffic") transits the connectivity infrastructure. Standard routing protocols (such as IS-IS or OSPF) are suitable for building and maintaining forwarding state in the connectivity infrastructure.
3. **DCP:** DCP is a distributed system which runs on a cluster of one or more physical servers, each of which may run multiple control instances. This is responsible for giving the control logic programmatic access to the network (both reading and writing network state).

4.   **Control Logic:** The network control logic is implemented on top of DCP's API. This control logic determines the desired network behavior; DCP merely provides the primitives needed to access the appropriate network state.

In CP/SDN model, we have to have the contribution of control plane like DCP that define a useful and general API for network control that allows for the development of scalable applications. DCP's API around a view of the physical network, allowing control applications to read and write state to any element in the network (Koponen, T., 2010). This API is therefore data-centric, providing methods for keeping state consistent between the in-network elements and the control application (running on multiple DCP instances) (Koponen, T., 2010). More specifically, this API consists of a data model that represents the network infrastructure, with each network element corresponding to one or more data objects. The control logic can: read the current state associated with that object; alter the network state by operating on these objects; and register for notifications of state changes to these objects.

In addition, since DCP supports control scenarios, the platform allows the control logic to customize the data model and have control over the placement and consistency of each component of the network state. The copy of the network state tracked by DCP is stored in RIB used by IP routers. However, rather than just storing prefixes to destinations, the RIB crates a graph of all network entities within a network topology. The RIB is used for this control model and the basis for DCP's distribution model. The control applications are implemented by reading and writing to the RIB (for example modifying forwarding state or accessing port counters), and DCP provides scalability and resilience by replicating and distributing the RIB between multiple running instances (as configured by the application). DCP handles the replication and distribution of RIB data, it relies on the application-specific logic to both detect and provide conflict resolution of network state as it is exchanged between two instances, as well as between a DCP instance and a network element. It is assumed that the RIB only contains physical entities in the network.

Overlay/SDN

Third architecture model in SDN Overlay/SDN (OL/SDN). D. Mayer described in his work (Meyer, D., 2013) that "OL/SDN represents a design point that encompasses those models in which a virtual network is overlaid on the network (which might be physical, virtual, or both). In this case, the designers overlay a new control plane on top of existing control and data planes, and (in theory) have minimal interaction with the "underlay" network. (Note that the degree to which an OL/SDN control or data plane requires knowledge or control of network state in the underlay network is a topic of vigorous debate.) The IETF's Network Virtualization Overlays (NVO3) working group is involved in standardizing OL/SDN models. Of course, these are discrete points in the design space; we can mix and match the features they represent to yield interesting architectures. For example, in some use cases, it might make sense to direct traffic down traffic-engineered tunnels using OpenFlow at the network edges and the Path Computation Element (PCE; http://datatracker.ietf.org/wg/pce/charter/) to build the tunnels themselves. On the other hand, OL/SDN architectures are typically less concerned with the programmability of the "underlay" control or data planes; rather, scaling here is achieved by overlaying a new programmable control plane and, in some cases, a virtual data plane such as the Open Virtual Switch (OVS)."

SCALABLE SDN SYSTEMS

In an efficient distributed flow table management, an interaction with the central controller is required, some packets will be dropped due to the cached policy decisions at the switches. A load balancing network controller (LNC) may perform a routing decision for each new TCP flow, incurring one packet drop per TCP flow.

Casado et al. (Casado, M., 2014) estimated that these control messages would generate as many multi-million flows per second in large data centers with virtual machines. On the other hand, some controllers, i.e., NOX (Meyer, D., 2013) and Nettle (Wickboldt, J. A., 2015), were able to process on the order of very few flows per second(Casado, M., 2014). The SDN controller may face a problem due to these dropped packets which may cause a bottleneck and reduce scaling to large networks.

Andreas (Rothenberg, C. E., et al., 2012) came out with McNettle which designed scalable performance based on multicore CPUs that implemented an extensible OpenFlow messaging service. McNettle contribution was to handle very large number of switches in network with millions of events per second. The user-defined OpenFlow event handlers in McNettle used Haskell, which is a high-level functional programming tool. In order to reduce memory traffic, core synchronizations, and synchronizations in the Glasgow Haskell Compiler (GHC) runtime system, McNettle dynamically and systematically executes (Scott, R. C., 2012):

- Event handlers on multiple cores,
- Scheduling event handlers on cores,
- Managing message buffers, and
- Parsing and serializing control messages.

Controller scalability can be achieved by many ways however the key instrumental will be a parallel processing at switch-level:

- Design a parallel controller's thread model,
- Parallel memory management, and
- Event processing loops to localize controller the processing paths for multiple client switches which efficiently reduce the number and frequency of accesses to a state shared across by many "client" switches.

Switch-level parallelism of SDN controller's principles can be examined by many parameters such as:

- Buffering and batching input and output message streams,
- Scheduling, and
- Load balancing across cores.

Logical Centralization Concept

The centralized processing concept states that events must be processed by the centralized control plane. This may cause bottleneck when many events under scaling settings are needed to be processed central-

Figure 6. Comparisons in controller with core based scalability
Senan, S. H., 2012.

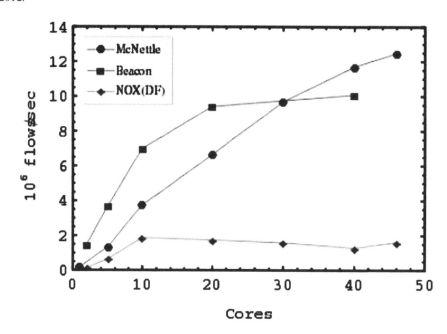

ized, and accessing the same centralized control plane. To improve the scaling system, one should reduce the number of events that are accessing the control plane.

Figure 6 shows the throughput for McNettle, NOX destiny- fast branch, and Beacon learning controller as a function of the number of cores.

As shown in Figure 6, NOX-MT (Rothenberg, C. E., et al., 2012), Beacon (Dasgupta, S., 2007), and Maestro (Dzulkhifli, N. F., 2014) scale network controllers used multi-core servers. In particular, NOX-MT was modified multithreaded successor of NOX to better utilize multi-core central processing units by batching system calls and by using Boost (Koponen, T., 2010). Beacon (Al-fares, M., 2010) statically assigned each switch to the controller and used one OS thread per core.

To offer load balance, systems distributed load across multiple control servers, it might implement OpenFlow network controllers across multi-servers (Conway, 2010; Wilson, C., et al., 2011). For example, Onix (Koponen, T., 2010) would implement SDN across multiple distributed controllers that were to provide scalability and fault-tolerance processing, however they had lost the simplicity of the centralized SDN controllers. ElastiCon (Ahmed, E. S. A., 2014) implemented switch-specific controllers in different servers as distributed controller solution according to load being distributed or balanced.

In SDN, algorithmic policies are quite difficult to be distributed among switch flow tables and hence will require more packets to be processed centrally, which causes scalability challenges and generates many bottlenecks. For example, Ethane (Chowdhury, N., 2009) to make sure of concrete security policy it has enforced a centralized security processing for each new application (i.e., UDP) flow, requiring at least one centralized execution of the algorithmic policy per UDP flow. Hence, to consider different types of packet processing functions or large scale networks, the central server must scale the execution smoothly if the SDN as a whole is to scale up.

Path Computation Element (PCE)

Constraint-based path computation is a fundamental building block for traffic engineering systems such as Multiprotocol Label Switching (MPLS) and Generalized MPLS (GMPLS) networks. Path computation in large, multi-domain, multi-region, or multi-layer networks is a complex task and may require special computational components and cooperation among the different network domains, so they need an architecture for a Path Computation Element (PCE)-based model to cope up with these design issues. This architecture model should describe a set of building blocks for the PCE architecture solution (Tootoonchian, 2012).

Figure 7. PCE node model: composite PCE node

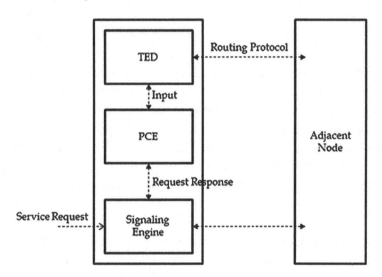

Figure 8. PCE node model: external PCE node

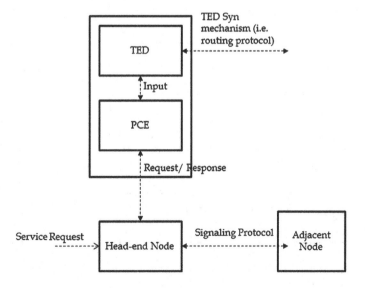

The PCE is an entity (component, application, or network node) that is capable of computing a network path or route based on a network graph, and of applying computational constraints during the computation. The PCE entity is an application (Yu, M., 2010) that can be located within a network node or component in an out-of-network server, etc. For example, a PCE would be able to compute the path of a Traffic Engineering MPLS Label Switched Path (TE LSP) by operating on the Traffic Engineering Database (TED) and considering bandwidth and other constraints applicable to the TE LSP service request. TED contains the topology and resource information of the domain. The TED may be fed by Interior Gateway Protocol (IGP) extensions or potentially by other means. Figures 7and Figure 8 show the PCE composite node.

A network domain is a collection of network entities within one zone of address management or path computation responsibility i.e., the broadcast domain. Examples of domains can be IGP areas, Autonomous Systems (ASs), and multiple ASs within same service provider network (Curtis, A. R., 2011). Domains of path computation responsibility may also exist as sub-domains of areas or AS. In order to fully characterize PCE, the following important considerations must be examined:

- Path computation can be implemented in intra-domain, inter-domain, and inter-layer contexts.
- Inter-domain path computation may involve the association of topology, routing, and policy information from multiple domains from which relationships may be figured out in order to help in implementing and modeling the path computation.
- Inter-layer path computation, where multiple layers are considered, is taking into account of topology and resource information at each layer. Overlapping or cross domains are one of the promising areas in the future. In the inter-domain scenario, the domains may belong to a single or to multiple service providers.

In single PCE path computation, a single PCE is used to compute one path at a time in a domain. There may be multiple PCEs in a domain, however only one PCE per domain is executed in any single path computation. In multiple PCE path computation, multiple PCEs threads are executed to compute one path in a domain. Centralized computation model: it is a model whereby all paths in a domain are

Figure 9. Multiple PCE path computation

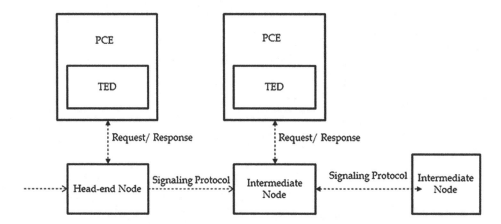

Figure 10. Multiple PCE path computation with inter-PCE communication

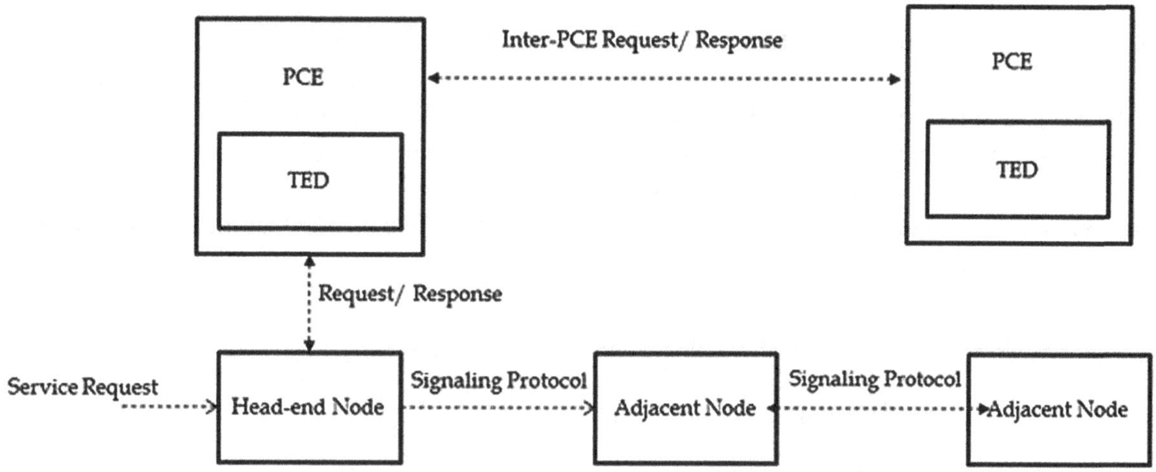

processed and executed in centralized PCE (Tavakkoli, A., 2009). Conversely, distributed computation model: it is a model that computes paths in a shared domain with multiple PCEs. Paths that span across multiple domains may be computed using the distributed model with one or more PCEs responsible for each domain, or the centralized model by defining a domain that encompasses all the other domains. Figures 9 and 10 show multiple PCE path computation.

From these definitions, a centralized computation model inherently uses single PCE path computation. However, a distributed computation model could use either single PCE path computation or multiple PCE path computations. There would be no such option available in centralized model that uses multiple PCEs together.

The PCE can be located at the head-end of the path; however, it can be located somewhere else within the domain. For example, a conventional intra-domain solution is to have path computation performed by the head-end i.e., the label switching router (LSR) of an MPLS TE LSP. In this case, the head-end LSR contains a PCE. But solutions also exist where other nodes on the path must contribute to the path computation, making them PCEs in their own right. At the same time, the path computation may be made by some other PCE physically separated from the computed path. The path computed by the PCE may be an explicit path or a loose path, where a hop may be an abstract node such as an AS (Koponen, T., 2010).

A PCE-based path computation model can be implemented alone or collaboratively with other nodes i.e., the path of inter-AS TE LSP may be computed by using of hybrid models where PCE-based path computation can be used in conjunction other different path computation models. A PCE could be implemented on a router, an LSR or on a dedicated network server, or any other entity in the SDN architecture.

FAULT TRACKING FRAMEWORK

Forwarding Element Failures

In the SDN architecture, "Forward Elements (FE)" generally refer to switching elements, those send packets from one of port to another port based on the forwarding tables set by the controllers. Failures in the switches have adverse effects in the entire network. The failure in the data plane elements means that no traffic moves from one network element to another. The faults in the forwarding elements may occur in the following three scenarios.

- The connection between controller and switch fails,
- The switch is not working,
- Switch has wrong forwarding table set by the controller.

The Connection between Controller and Switch Fails

Depending on the network configuration, if a switch is controlled by one and only one controller, then switch continues to work with the forwarding table available before the fault occurs. When a fault occurs with any one of the switches, or the connectivity between the switch and controller is lost, then controller may consider the switch as a faulty one. As an action to recover this fault, the controller may reprogram the forwarding tables of other switches connected to it to avoid packet flow through the faulty switch. Apart from that controller may inform other controllers about the error condition and other controllers may reprogram the flow tables in the switches (attached to them) to avoid the faulty switch while forwarding the packets. The change (due to the faulty switch) in the underlying network must be informed to other controllers so that paths could be recalculated, and the changes in the network are propagated to all other controllers. If controllers perform these reprogramming of flow tables to the switches connected

Figure 11. SDN with all connected elements

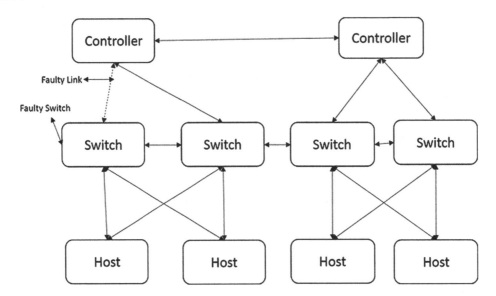

Figure 12. SDN with single link

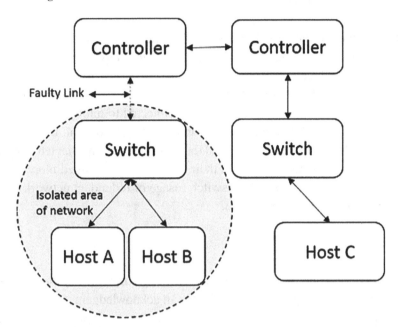

to them and propagate the same information to other connected controllers, then during a time interval, the fault information will be spread across the entire network. In effect, all the forwarding tables in the data planes are adjusted to avoid the faulty switch. We assume that all the network elements (hosts) are connected to other elements in multiple paths (refer to Figure 11).

If this assumption is not true and if the hosts connected to the switch are not connected to the network by any other link (Refer to Figure 12), then the faulty node becomes a "single point of failure", and in that situation, nodes (hosts) connected to the faulty switch can be isolated from the rest of the network.

However in reality, switches are connected to multiple controllers. Hence, if connection between controller and switch is lost, then controller may ask another controller to control this switch. In this case one of the controller acts as "master" and other controllers act as "slaves" controllers for a switch. In case, master controller loses the connectivity from the switch, then other "slave" controller may become the "master" controller for this switch from which controller has lost connectivity. OpenFlow specification 1.2 onwards has the provision of connecting to multiple controllers (Open Networking Foundation, 2015). Naga Katta et al. had shown in their work (Katta, N., et al., 2015) that the OpenFlow protocol had some inconsistency that might lead to wrong packet processing decisions.

The Switch Is Not Working

In this type of failure, the controller is expected to detect the situation and propagate the error to other controllers as described above.

Switch Has Wrong Forwarding Table Set by the Controller

This kind of error occurs due to errors in the controller software. The detail discussion about this kind of failure is given in section 4.3 below.

Fault Detection of FE Failure

Fault detection at FE is an important task for all SDN controllers and switches. Timely detection of faults and triggering recovery process is one of essential goals of any SDN recovery. In this section, various schemes are discussed for fault detection at FEs.

In general, the simplest method of detection of active connection between controller and switches, could be using echo request/reply. In case of switches connected to multiple controllers, exchanges of such keep-alive packets lead to significant overhead in the network (Kotani, D., et al., 2015). Kotani et al., in their work (Kotani, D., et al., 2015), proposed the following scheme that led to less amount of echo message usage to identify connection failure. In their scheme, they assumed more than one controllers (redundant) controllers were associated with a switch (usage of redundant network elements to avoid a "single point of failure", is a common practice).

Fast Failure Detection

When a switch detects a port (link) down, then it sends message through all other links (channels) at the same time, to all the connected controller and waits for an acknowledgement. This port down message reaches to one or more controllers connected to it. Controllers, upon receiving the message sends back an acknowledgement to the switch. In this case the switch may safely expect that, the fault event had been propagated to the controller. In case, the switch does not receive any acknowledgement message, event after a predefined timeout period, then the switch regards all the channels to the connected controller has failed and enters into a predefined "standalone fail safe mode". When a controller receives a message that is sent to multiple channels such as a port status message, the controller notifies the arrival of the message to other controllers. When a controller receives a notification of arrival of a message from other controllers and the controller has not received the notified message from the switch (that is directly connected to it), the controller waits for a certain period (timeout). If the message has not been arrived at the controller until the timeout expires, the channel to the switch from the controller has been lost, and controller avoids using this channel.

Using Link-Layer Discovery (LLD)

Using Link-Layer Discovery Protocol (LLDP) messages to discover failures of link and node and triggering path restoration actions could be another approach that could be employed by the SDN controllers. However, using this mechanism has scalability issue (Kempf, J., 2011), all the LLDP messages collected by the switches should be passed through the controller to take necessary decision for path restoration. This may lead to lots of message processing by the controller affecting the performance of the controller, if the network is large. James Kempf et al. (Kempf, J., 2011) proposed a mechanism to implement the link monitoring on the switches in place of controllers and sent necessary messages to other switches when link failed.

In the approaches as mentioned above, the error detection and recovery mechanism are implemented either in switches or in controllers. Instead of keeping the responsibility of fault detection inside the controller/switches, a special type of element (monitoring element) could be placed in the management plane of SDN. This monitoring element could take the responsibility of monitoring the network links and communication failure identification. Upon error identification, it could notify the controllers using

Figure 13. Layers of SDN architecture

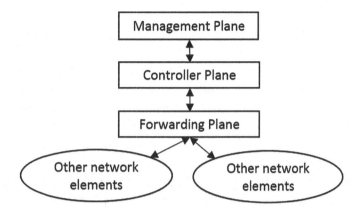

control messages. Receiving such messages from the monitoring element, controllers may initiate flow table correction in the attached switches. The monitoring element may utilize "Header Space Analysis" (Kazemian, P., 2012) to detect link failure and inform the controller about the change the in the network topology. As mentioned above, on receiving the network change notification from the monitoring element, controllers may take the necessary actions and re program the switches attached to them to reflect the network change.

Link Failure

Detection of link failure is one of the most important aspects of any fault tracking framework for SDN. All the elements of a network those are directly or indirectly connected, depends on the availability of the links to transmit all sorts of information (that would be data packet or control information). In this sub section, whenever the link is referred, it will denote any kind of physical medium of transmission available in todays' market (that will be wireless or wired medium) and by the link protocol, we would mean both physical and MAC layer protocol.

Without any loss of generality, any SDN architecture contains three different logical categories of links as depicted in Figure 13.

1. Link connected between management plane and control plane (If they reside on different physical machines).
2. Link connected between control plane and forwarding plane (If they reside on different physical elements).
3. Link connected directly from forwarding plane to other network elements (These elements (e.g. host machines) reside on the physical network layer).

The significance of link failure in the above mentioned three link categories, have different implications in the architecture of SDN, and the failure recovery strategies would be different for obvious reasons. For example, a link failure between forwarding plane and other host means that there is a loss of reachability between two elements. The reachability could be restored by using another path in the network. In order to do so, controller plane should be involved to calculate the alternate path, and the forwarding tables in the FEs should be reprogramed.

For the link failure between forwarding plane equipment (e.g., an OpenFlow Switch) and to other network elements (e.g., another OpenFlow switch), the detection of failure typically depends on the type of the medium used. For example, sending echo request at an interval and not receiving a reply within a stipulated time interval could be used as a simple mechanism to identify the unavailability of a link. Measuring physical parameters like signal to noise ratio (SNR) or measuring signal strength (in case of a wireless medium) could be used to identify the availability of link. There are many standard mechanisms available that determine the link failures, e.g., "link fault signaling (802.3ae/ ba)" for Ethernet (Cisco, 2013). Most of switches available in today's market place contain interrupt driven notification for link failure with a less than 10 millisecond detection delay (Cisco, 2013). Utilizing the capabilities of these switches, forward planes (e.g. an OpenFlow Switch) may identify link failure and inform the controller plane to take next actions (Padma, V., 2015).

Another important and widely used protocol that is to identify the link failure is Bidirectional Forwarding Detection (BFD). BFD provides a single mechanism to identify failure between any two adjacent forwarding planes connected through any medium. It is a low latency and low overhead protocol (BFD, 2015). Recent research works in the area of "Fast Failure Detection on SDN" are based on BFD (Desai, M., 2010; Scott, R. C., 2012).

There could be four approaches of link failure recovery process (Padma, V., 2015). They are:

1. Restoration approach,
2. Data plane mechanism,
3. Path protection, and
4. Link protection.

Restoration Approach

As described above it is the simpler and intuitive approach for the recovery of link failure. The forwarding plane equipment directly notifies the failure to the controller plane in command, and controller plane takes the necessary action (Sharma, S., 2011; Sharma, S., 2013). In the event of such notification, controller identifies the possible flows involving that link, calculates an alternate path and reprograms the forwarding plane flow tables. For an Ethernet based network the recovery time takes around 200ms (Sharma, S., 2011; Sharma, S., 2013). This approach has worked well for a smaller network; for a larger and complex network this approach may flood the controller with the notification of reconfiguration that may lead to poor performance in SDN.

Data Plane Mechanism

When a link fails, the switch connected to that link sends notification to those switches, which send packets through that failed link. The notified switches then modify the forwarding tables to drop the packets which are directed through the failed link. This mechanism ensures the reduced number of dropped packets, however it depends on the controller to reconstruct an alternative path to recover from the failure (BFD, 2015).

Path Protection

The alternate back up paths are pre-computed and stored in switch by the controller. In the event of the failure, switches automatically reallocate backup forwarding entries to send the packets to the destination bypassing the faulty link. This mechanism has comparatively better recovery time (50 milliseconds (Wickboldt, J. A., 2015)) as it needs not require the involvement of the controller during the recovery. However, this approach may not be practical for a larger network, as the computation of backup paths and storage of each of the alternate paths require more resources of the switch and the controller.

Link Protection

In this scheme, for each pair of nodes, controllers computes multiple paths and all are stored in the switch flow table. In case of a link failure between two nodes, one of the alternative paths is used to send packets. This takes lesser recovery time than path protection scheme, as every switch in the working path can directly route the traffic through the back up path (Sgambelluri, A., 2013). But this increases the number of flow entries in the flow table and additionally more computing power is required for the controller to calculate all possible paths.

Different Solution Schemes

To track the fault at various levels in SDN architecture, there are many mechanisms at various levels available that are discussed in this subsection.

Fault Tracking and Recovery in Controller Plane

As discussed in the earlier sub-sections, controllers in the controller plane play the important role to keep running the network. Faults in controllers jeopardize the functioning of the entire network. The stack of programs is running in controller planes in SDN architecture, there could be two different causes for the failure of a controller/controller plane. They are:

1. Failure of the network elements in the controller plane,
2. Defect/bug in the controller software.

Hence, the localization of the fault is another necessary measure of any fault tracking mechanism.

Failure in Network Elements in the Controller Plane

In a common, simple SDN architecture, a logically centralized controller manages and dictates a distributed set of switches to provide higher level services to end-host applications. The controller can program the switches (though running commands) to adapt to traffic demands and failures (those observed through events). For example, an SDN controller receives events related to underlying physical topology changes, traffic statistics, and packets requiring special attention, and it responds with the run of appropriate commands (e.g., install new forwarding table entry) on the switches. This common architecture assumes global visibility of all network events that are passed through the controllers, and the controllers have direct control over the switch logic, render entire management of the network. In spite of centralized control, a single controller easily becomes "single point of failure" and leads to service disruptions or incorrect processing of packets (Casado, M., 2007; Scott, C., 2014).

Many works have implemented existing mechanisms of distributed computing. For example, the controllers may choose to store their internal memory content (generally referred as controller state) into a persistent storage (at a regular interval). In case of a controller failure, controllers may restore their state by loading the stored content from the persistent storage. In this way controllers may resume their work without needing them to re-build their state from the scratch. Onix (Koponen, T., 2010) and ONOS (Berde, P., 2014) used this mechanism. Another approach could be i) to model each controller as a replicated state machine (RSM) and ii) consistently replicate the set of inputs (packets, events etc.) to each controller. "Provided each replicated controller executes these inputs deterministically and in an identical order, their internal state would remain consistent" (Katta, N., et al., 2015). Hence in the event of controller crash, any one of the controller in the RSM set can continue operate without disrupting the service of the controller plane. Consistent state maintenance of the controller provides the half of the solution. To implement a logically centralized controller, handling of switch state is an essential task in the event of the failure. During the period between a controller failure and its recovery, the probability of losing the events and states of the switches attached to the controllers, is very high. Simple solution for this could be to run a consensus protocol involving the switches for every event would be prohibitively expensive and not practical one (Katta, N., et al., 2015). On the other hand, using distributed storage to replicate switch states also, would be prohibitive for a large scale SDN. Hence, after a controller crash, the new master controller of a switch may not have the sufficient information to resume programming of the switch state. Reading the switch forwarding state would not provide enough information about all commands (control commands such as port status update etc.) sent by the old master controller before its failure. In addition, while the system can roll back the controller state, the switches cannot easily "roll back" to a safer checkpoint. After all, what does it mean to rollback a packet that was already sent? Since an event from one switch can trigger commands to other switches, simultaneous failure of the master controller and a switch can cause inconsistency in the rest of the network and that might lead to an unpredictable behavior (Katta, N., et al., 2015) of the entire network.

Defect/Bug in the Controller Software

Since the whole SDN architecture relies on the dynamically programing the data plane elements by the controller, any defect in the controller software, may lead to a non-functioning network. For example, due to some bug in the controller software, erroneous flow tables may be installed in the switches. Due to erroneous flow tables, switches may fail to deliver a packet or may loop infinitely to deliver a packet. Hence, when we are discussing about a fault tracking framework/program at any level of SDN, the ability to detect the software bug is also an important aspect of fault tracking in SDN. While deploying an SDN or after introducing new protocol, controller software, a set of diagnostic tool could be used to test whether there is any error in the newly introduced protocol and/or software. A set of failures may be introduced purposefully (by simulation or by any other method) in the network to check whether the newly introduced element (controller, protocol, s/w logic) can detect the error or not. Robert Colin Scott (Scott, R. C., 2012) et al. presented an automated way for detecting bugs in the controller software. In their approach, they have used a simulation based tool (a.k.a. W3), where a set of network events (e.g. link failures) are introduced. As result of the network change, the controller and switches performs some actions (e.g. flow table update commands by controller to switch etc.) as per the login implemented in the controllers. These events by the controller and switches are recorded. By observing the recorded events, W3 can detect and localize the error in the software installed in various planes (i.e. management, controller or forwarding plane) of SDN.

Fault Tracking and Recovery in Data Plane

Fault tracking in the data plane by the switches are divided into two categories:

1. The "link down" (or port down) fault,
2. "Disconnection from the controllers".

In the case of "link down", the data planes in switches have very little to do in their own for tracking the fault. It informs the link failure to the controller attached to it. (Refer to section 4.1 for various approaches). The controller takes the necessary action (by changing the flow tables installed in the switch to avoid the faulty link) to reprogram the switch and the switch starts sending the packets in the new path (avoiding the faulty link) as per the update flow table installed by the controller. In the case of "disconnection from the controllers" situation where the switch remains in working state but the links connected to the switch-commanding controller(s) are lost, then the switch may enter into a pre-configured stand-alone mode. Once the connectivity with the controller is restored, the controller will reprogram the flow table of the switch based on the latest network state. Other than the connectivity failure, a switch may fail for various reasons. For example a switch may fail due to power failure or hardware failure. In that cases when the switch becomes active again, the controller reprograms it and the switch starts working further. Unlike the controller, where the state of the controller needs to be saved for a quicker recovery, switches may not need to store their state as their state is controlled by a controller.

REFERENCES

I2RS. (2016). Retrieved from: http://datatracker.ietf.org/wg/i2rs/charter/

Ahmed, E. S. A., & Saeed, R. A. (2014). A Survey of Big Data Cloud Computing Security. *International Journal of Computer Science and Software Engineering*, *3*(1), 78–85.

Al-fares, M., Radhakrishnan, S., Raghavan, B., Huang, N., & Vahdat, A. (2010), Hedera: Dynamic flow scheduling for data center networks. *Proc. of Networked Systems Design and Implementation (NSDI) Symposium*.

Berde, P., Gerola, M., Hart, J., Higuchi, Y., Kobayashi, M., Koide, T., … Parulkar, G. (2014). ONOS: Towards an Open, Distributed SDN OS. *HotSDN*.

BFD. (2015). Retrieved from: https://tools.ietf.org/html/rfc5880

Caesar, M., Caldwell, D., Feamster, N., Rexford, J., Shaikh, A., & Merwe, J. (2005). Design and implementation of a routing control platform. *NSDI*.

Casado, M., Foster, N., & Guha, A. (2014). Abstractions for Software-Defined Networks. *Communications of the ACM, 57*(10), 86–95. doi:10.1145/2661061.2661063

Casado, M., Freedman, M. J., Pettit, J., Luo, J., McKeown, N., & Shenker, S. (2007). *Ethane: Taking Control of the Enterprise*. SIGCOMM. doi:10.1145/1282380.1282382

Chowdhury, N., Rahman, M., & Boutaba, R. (2009). Virtual Network Embedding with Coordinated Node and Link Mapping.*Proc. 28th IEEE Conf. Computer Communications (INFOCOM 09)*, 783–791. doi:10.1109/INFCOM.2009.5061987

Cisco. (2013). *Cisco Visual Networking Index: Forecast and Methodology, 2012–2017*. White Paper. Retrieved from: http://www.cisco.com/en/US/solutions/collateral/ns341/n s525/ns537/ns705/ns827/white_paper_c11-481360.pdf

Cisco. (2013). *Network Failure Detection*. Retrieved from: http://monsterdark.com/wp-content/uploads/Network-Failure-Detection.pdf

Conway, K., Kalyanasundharam, N., Donley, G., Lepak, K., & Hughes, B. (2010). Cache hierarchy and memory subsystem of the and Opteron processor. *IEEE Micro, 30*(2), 16–29. doi:10.1109/MM.2010.31

Curtis, A. R. (2011). DevoFlow: Scaling Flow Management for High-Performance Networks.*Proc. ACM SIGCOMM*, 254–65. doi:10.1145/2018436.2018466

Dasgupta, S., & Oliveira, J. (2007). Path-Computation-Element-Based Architecture for Interdomain MPLS/GMPLS Traffic Engineering: Overview and Performance. *IEEE Network, 21*(4), 38–45. doi:10.1109/MNET.2007.386468

Desai, M., & Nandagopal, T. (2010). Coping with link failures in centralized control plane architectures.*Second International Conference on Communication Systems and Networks (COMSNETS)*, 1–10. doi:10.1109/COMSNETS.2010.5431977

Dzulkhifli, N. F., Alsaqour, R., Alsaqour, O., Shaker, H., & Saeed, R. A. (2014). Network Services and Applications: Web Caching. *Middle-East Journal of Scientific Research, 18*(10), 1517–1523.

Feamster, N., Balakrishnan, H., Rexford, J., Shaikh, A., & van der Merwe, J. (2004). *The case for separating routing from routers*. FDNA. doi:10.1145/1016707.1016709

Hasan, M. K., Saeed, R. A., Hashim, A.-H. A., Islam, S., Alsaqour, R. A., & Alahdal, T. A. (2012). Femtocell Network Time Synchronization Protocols and Schemes. *Research Journal of Applied Sciences Engineering and Technology, 4*(23), 5136–5143.

Internet Engineering Task Force (IETF). (2014). *Software-Defined Networking: A Perspective from within a Service Provider Environment*. IETF.

Katta, N. (2015). Ravana: Controller Fault-Tolerance in Software-Defined Networking.*Proceedings of the 1st ACM SIGCOMM Symposium on Software Defined Networking Research*. doi:10.1145/2774993.2774996

Kazemian, P., Varghese, G., & McKeown, N. (2012). Header Space Analysis: Static Checking For Networks.*Proceeding of ACM NSDI*.

Kempf, J., Bellagamba, E., Kern, A., Jocha, D., Takacs, A., & Skoldstrom, P. (2011), Scalable fault management for OpenFlow.*IEEE Int. Conf. on Communications (ICC)*, 6606–6610.

Koponen, T., Casado, M., Gude, N., Stribling, J., Poutievskiy, L., Zhuy, M., & Shenker, S. et al. (2010), Onix: A Distributed Control Platform for Large-scale Production Networks.*Proceedings of ACM OSDI*.

Kotani, D. (2015). Fast Failure Detection of OpenFlow Channels.*Proceedings of the Asian Internet Engineering Conference AINTEC*. doi:10.1145/2837030.2837035

Lakshman, T. V. (2004). The SoftRouter architecture. *HotNets-III*.

Meyer, D. (2013). Standard: The Software-Defined-Networking Research Group. *IEEE Internet Computing*, *17*(6), 84–87. doi:10.1109/MIC.2013.122

ONF. (2011). *Software-Defined Networking: The New Norm for Networks.* White Paper. Retrieved from: https://www.opennetworking.org/images/stories/downloads/whitepapers/ wp-sdn-newnorm.pdf

Open Networking Foundation. (2015). *OpenFlow Switch Specification Version 1.5.1*. Author.

Padma, V., & Yogesh, P. (2015), Proactive Failure Recovery in OpenFlow Based Software Defined Networks.*3rd International Conference on Signal Processing, Communication and Networking (ICSCN)*. doi:10.1109/ICSCN.2015.7219846

Rothenberg, C. E. (2012). Revisiting Routing Control Platforms with the Eyes and Muscles of Software-Defined Networking. *ACM HotSDN*, 13-18.

Schonwalder, J., Fouquet, M., Rodosek, G., & Hochstatter, I. (2009). Future Internet = Content + Services + Management. *IEEE Communications Magazine*, *47*(7), 27–33. doi:10.1109/MCOM.2009.5183469

Scott, C., Wundsam, A., Raghavan, B., Panda, A., Or, A., Lai, J., & Shenker, S. et al. (2014). *Troubleshooting Blackbox SDN Control Software with Minimal Causal Sequences*. SIGCOMM. doi:10.1145/2619239.2626304

Scott, R. C., Wundsam, A., Zarifis, K., & Shenker, S. (2012). *What, Where, and When: Software Fault Localization for SDN*. Technical Report No. UCB/EECS-2012-178.

Senan, S. H., Abdella, A. H., Zeki, A. M., Saeed, R. A., Hameed, S. A., & Daoud, J. I. (2012). A framework of a route optimization scheme for nested mobile network. Lecture Notes in Computer Science, 7667, 689-696.

Sgambelluri, A., Giorgetti, A., Cugini, F., Paolucci, F., & Castoldi, P. (2013). OpenFlow-Based Segment Protection in Ethernet Networks. *Journal of Optical Communications and Networking*, *5*(9), 1066–1075. doi:10.1364/JOCN.5.001066

Sharma, S., Staessens, D., Colle, D., Pickavet, M., & Demeester, P. (2011). Software Defined Networking: Meeting Carrier Grade Requirements.*Proceedings of 18th IEEE Workshop on Local Metropolitan Area Networks*, 1–6.

Sharma, S., Staessens, D., Colle, D., Pickavet, M., & Demeester, P. (2013). OpenFlow: Meeting Carrier-Grade Recovery Requirements. *Journal of Computer Communications*, *36*(6), 656–665. doi:10.1016/j.comcom.2012.09.011

Sun, S., Gong, L., Rong, B., & Lu, K. (2015). An Intelligent SDN Framework for 5G Heterogeneous Networks. *IEEE Communications Magazine, 53*(11), 142–147. doi:10.1109/MCOM.2015.7321983

Tavakkoli, A. (2009), Applying NOX to the Datacenter.*Proc. ACM HotNets-VIII Workshop.*

Tootoonchian. (2012). On Controller Performance in Software-Defined Networks. *Proc. USENIX Hot-ICE.*

Van Adrichem, N. L. M. (2014). *Fast Recovery in Software-Defined Networks.* EWSDN. doi:10.1109/EWSDN.2014.13

Wickboldt, J. A., de Jesus, W. P., Isolani, P. H., Bonato Both, C., Rochol, J., & Granville, L. Z. (2015). Software-Defined Networking: Management Requirements and Challenges. *IEEE Communications Magazine, 53*(1), 278–285. doi:10.1109/MCOM.2015.7010546

Wickboldt, J. A., de Jesus, W. P., Isolani, P. H., Both, C. B., Rochol, J., & Granville, L. Z. (2015). Software-Defined Networking: Management Requirements and Challenges. *IEEE Communications Magazine, 53*(1), 278–285. doi:10.1109/MCOM.2015.7010546

Wilson, C. (2011), Better Never than Late: Meeting Deadlines in Datacenter Networks.*Proc. ACM SIGCOMM,* 50–61. doi:10.1145/2018436.2018443

Xia, W. (2015). A Survey on Software-Defined Networking. *IEEE Communication Surveys & Tutorials,* 27-50.

Xie, H. (2012). Software-defined networking efforts debuted at IETF 84. *IETF J.* Retrieved from: http://www.internetsociety.org/fr/node/45708

Yin, H. (2012). *SDNi: A Message Exchange Protocol for Software Defined Networks (SDNS) across Multiple Domains.* Retrieved from: http://www.cisco.com/en/US/solutions/collateral/ ns341/ns525/ns537/ns705/ns827/white_paper_c11-481360.pdf

Yu, M. (2010). Scalable Flow-Based Networking with DIFANE.*Proc. ACM SIGCOMM Conf.,* 351–362.

Chapter 12
Experimental Study of SDN-Based Evolved Packet Core Architecture for Efficient User Mobility Support

Sakshi Chourasia
Indian Institute of Technology Madras, India

Krishna Moorthy Sivalingam
Indian Institute of Technology Madras, India

ABSTRACT

The mobility management architecture in current generation LTE networks results in high signaling traffic. In this chapter, we present an Evolved Packet Core (EPC) architecture based on Software Defined Networking (SDN) concepts. The proposed EPC architecture centralizes the control plane functionality of the EPC thereby eliminating the use of mobility management protocols and reducing mobility related signaling overheads. The architecture utilizes the global network knowledge with SDN for mobility management. The proposed architecture has been implemented in the ns-3 simulator. A prototype testbed has also been implemented using the Floodlight SDN controller, a Software Defined Radio platform and relevant software.

INTRODUCTION

It is expected that the number of global mobile 4G connections based on LTE networks will grow from approximately 203 million in 2013 to 1.5 billion by 2018 at a CAGR of 50 percent (Cisco Systems, 2014). It is also expected that more than half of all this traffic will be offloaded from mobile-connected devices (almost 17 exabytes) to the fixed network using WiFi and femtocells (Cisco Systems, 2014). Thus, the network's data and control planes should be suitably designed. In particular, signaling cost incurred for session establishment and for handover from one network to another (e.g. LTE to WiFi) should be

DOI: 10.4018/978-1-5225-2023-8.ch012

reduced significantly. The objective of this chapter is to design a scalable architecture that incorporates efficient control signaling mechanisms to help meet the future network's requirements. The proposed architecture is based on software defined networking (SDN) concepts.

The core components of the 3GPP–EPC architecture are the Mobility Management Entity (MME), Serving Gateway (SGW) and Packet Gateway (PGW) (Savic, 2011). The SGW is used for intra-mobility purposes (within the same LTE network) and the PGW for connectivity to the Internet. In 3GPP–EPC, each connection is an EPS bearer that consists of a data radio bearer (DRB), GPRS Tunneling Protocol (GTP) and a Proxy Mobile IPv6 (PMIPv6) tunnel (Oliva, Bernardos, Calderon, Melia, & Zuniga, 2011). The PMIPv6 protocol is standardized by IETF to provide network-based IP mobility support (Oliva, et al., 2011). PMIPv6 is used in 3GPP–EPC to integrate 3GPP with non–3GPP access networks. The GTP protocol is used in 3GPP–EPC to provide intra-network IP mobility. For each EPS Bearer, the maintenance of these tunnels leads to high control plane signaling overheads. Maintenance of these GPRS Tunneling Protocol (GTP) and Proxy Mobile IPv6 (PMIPv6 or PMIP) tunnels are required whenever events such as connection establishment, connection release and handover occur in the network.

An analysis of messaging events in an LTE Evolved Packet Core (EPC, also called 3GPP–EPC in this chapter) showed that main contributors to the signaling overhead are connection establishment/release, handover and tracking area update events (Nowoswiat & MIlliken, 2013). Thus, for next generation networks, an architecture that supports low signaling cost while handling such events (like connection establishment/release, handovers, etc.) is required.

This chapter proposes an EPC architecture that is based on Software Defined Networking (SDN) principles (Open Networking Foundation, 2012), (Kobayashi, 2014). SDN systems operate by separating the data and control planes. It also provides several advantages in terms of network programmability, network virtualization and others. The OpenFlow protocol (Open Networking Foundation, 2014) has emerged as an industry standard for interactions between the SDN controller and the routing/switching hardware elements in the network.

In the proposed architecture, the control plane functionalities of MME, SGW and PGW are moved to a centralized logical controller referred to as the EPC Controller; the SGW and PGW are replaced with an OpenFlow switch (Open Networking Foundation, 2014). To overcome the problem of signaling due to GTP or PMIPv6 maintenance, the use of GTP or PMIPv6 mobility management protocol is eliminated in the proposed EPC architecture. Instead mechanisms based on SDN concepts are designed to provide IP mobility, QoS and security. The EPC Controller handles flow-based routing. When the UE moves within or outside the network (from LTE to WiFi and similar), the IP address remains unchanged. The packets are forwarded along the updated routes as specified by the EPC Controller. The SDN approach can also provide fine-granularity QoS support (delay, jitter, throughput, etc.) using various mechanisms as described in (Egilmez, Dane, Gorkemli, & Tekalp, 2012), (Bari, Chowdhury, Ahmed, & Boutaba, 2013), (Ishimori, Faria, Furtado, Cerqueira, & Abelem, 2012).

A comparison of signaling overheads in the existing and proposed LTE architectures is presented. The architecture has also been implemented in the ns-3 simulator and related performance results in terms of user throughput and delay are presented.

Section 2 presents the background and related work on 3GPP-EPC architecture and Software Defined Networks (SDN). Section 3 presents a detailed analysis of the signaling overhead in the existing LTEarchitecture. Section 4 presents the proposed SDN based EPC architecture. Section 5 describes the model to determine signaling cost in the existing and proposed EPC architectures. Section 6 presents the ns3 network simulation based performance analysis. Sections 7 and 8 present the details and results of theexperimental EPC testbed implemented using off-the-shelf components and public domain EPC software. Section 9 concludes the chapter.

BACKGROUND AND RELATED WORK

This section presents some background material on LTE networks and its backhaul architecture, SDN networks, and related work.

Overview of 3GPP-EPC Architecture

The 3GPP Evolved Packet Core (EPC) architecture mainly consists of Mobility Management Entity (MME), Serving Gateway (SGW), Packet Gateway (PGW) and the Home Subscriber Server (HSS) as shown in Figure 1. The MME is connected to different eNodeBs (i.e. base stations) and the SGW using the S1-MME and S11 interface respectively. The eNodeB is connected to SGW using the S1-U interface, and the SGW to the PGW via S5/S8 interface. As explained earlier, the data packets travel from the user equipment (UE) to the PGW via the eNodeB and the SGW. The MME exchanges the relevant control signals with the UE and also selects the SGW and PGW that will serve a given UE. The MME is also involved in the handover process as the UE moves within the LTE network. In order to improve performance in the LTE networks and for load balancing purposes, mobile data offloading from LTE to a

non-3GPP network such as WiFi is often done. This requires a seamless handover where existing flows on the LTE network are moved to the WiFi network and vice-versa. As mentioned earlier, the PMIPv6 protocol standardized by IETF and the GTP protocol are used for providing seamless network mobility. In the PMIPv6 approach, IP mobility is supported entirely by the network without participation from the user. The PMIPv6 architecture consists of entities including the Local Mobility Anchor (LMA) and Mobility Access Gateway (MAG). The LMA acts as an anchor for a UE; that is, all traffic to/from the UE go through the LMA. The LMA sends packets to the UE via the MAG. For a given UE's connection, there is one LMA and multiple MAGs since the UE can move between different MAGs. The MAG nodes support the mobility agent functions by taking care of mobility related signaling. When the UE moves between MAGs, the network establishes a new tunnel between the new MAG and its LMA. The Figure 1 also shows an LTE user who has moved to a WiFi network and communicates with the Internet through its Wireless Access Gateway (WAG). The PGW is connected to the WAG using an S8 interface to support inter-mobility with WiFi network. In PMIPv6 protocol, during the inter-mobility between LTE and WiFi networks the PGW acts as a Local Mobility Anchor (LMA) and the SGW acts as a Mobility Access Gateway (MAG). The S1-U interface runs over GTP while S5/S8 runs over either GTP or PMIPv6 (3GPP, 2013).

The specific drawbacks in terms of higher signaling overhead are described later.

SOFTWARE DEFINED NETWORKS

It has been long felt that innovation has been stifled in computer networking due to reluctance on the part of network equipment vendors to try new ideas on a large scale. One of the main objectives of software

Figure 1. 3GPP-EPC architecture

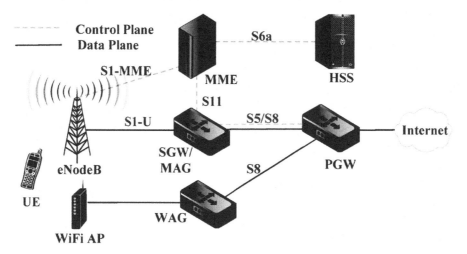

defined networking (SDN) is to increase the levels of innovation in network protocols and architectures. The main concept of SDN is the separation of control and data planes (Open Networking Foundation, 2012). The idea is to make switches and routers commodity items that implement basic forwarding and packet classification functions, while the network control resides in programmable software based controllers, residing outside these routers. The communication between the controller and the switches is achieved using the OpenFlow protocol. OpenFlow is part of the specifications released by the Open Networking Foundation (ONF) (Open Networking Foundation, 2014). Some of the advantages are: decoupling of tight integration of hardware and software seen in current routers; providing more programmatic interfaces to the underlying network hardware; enabling development of different type of user written network applications providing more control over network operations; and network virtualization enabling multiple protocol stacks to share the same physical networking infrastructure. A detailed discussion of SDNs is beyond the scope of this chapter and the reader is referred to (Nunes, Mendonca, Nguyen, Obraczka, & Turletti, 2014), (Jammal, Singh, Shami, Asal, & Li, 2014). The proposed LTE EPC architecture attempts to apply the key principles of SDN to wireless cellular networks. The specific objective is to build a scalable EPC architecture that supports efficient user mobility support between different networks.

Related Work

There have been several ideas recently proposed for the use of SDN in wireless networks, as briefly summarized here. In (Sama, Said, Guillouard, & Suciu, 2014), the current control protocols in eNB-MME and MME-SGW interfaces are replaced by OpenFlow in order to introduce flexibility and programmability aspects. The UE's S1 and S5 data bearers (GTP tunnels) are kept in the network equipment during the application's idle period to reduce the signaling overhead. The work in (Kempf, Johansson, Pettersson, Luning, & Nilsson, 2012) describes an integration of LTE control plane with OpenFlow and setting up GTP using OpenFlow. However, these two approaches do not completely utilize the advantages of SDN since they use GTP to provide IP mobility instead of using the global network view available with SDN.

Also, they need to extend the OpenFlow switch to include the virtual ports to allow encapsulation and decapsulation of GTP header and to allow flow-based routing using GTP Tunnel End Point Identifier.

The SoftCell architecture (Jin, Li, Vanbever, & Rexford, 2013) provides a scalable framework for supporting fine-grained policies in LTE core network by using core switches which forwards traffic based on hierarchical addresses and policy tags. The work in (Basta, Kellerer, Hoffmann, Hoffmann, & Schmidt, 2013) analyses the functionalities of PGW and SGW, and proposes four different frameworks to realize GTP function via SDN. The work described in (Varis, Manner, & Heinonen, 2011) eliminates the GTP tunnel and discusses a Layer-2 approach for mobility within the network, and transport in the mobile backhaul. For network-based flow mobility, (Zuniga, Bernardos, Costa, & Reznik, 2013) a partially distributed model that splits the control plane and data plane of the mobility anchors is presented in (Zuniga, Bernardos, Costa, & Reznik, 2013). This allows mobility anchors to optimally route the data traffic while relying on the single central entity. The SoftMoW (Moradi, Li, & Mao, 2014) architecture proposes a hierarchy of controllers to support IP based mobility between the different LTE networks. In (Nguyen, & Kim, 2015), a new Openflow-enabled mobile packet core network (OEPC) is proposed. The authors have analyzed the signaling load based on the number of messages for five common procedures in detail, including the initial attachment, UE-triggered service request, network-triggered service request, handover, and the tracking area update. A survey of SDN and virtualization based LTE mobile network architectures is presented in (Nguyen, Do, & Kim, 2016). It also discusses open issues such as compatibility, deployment model, and unified control plane that need to be addressed in order to implement the SDN and virtualization based mobile network in reality. Mobility management mechanisms that play a central role in the 5G networks are discussed in (Contreras, Cominardi, Qian, & Bernardos, 2016). The authors have also implemented a Software-Defined Mobility Management architecture on a test-bed.

In our proposed architecture, we are centralizing the EPC control plane with the inter-mobility anchor control plane, and thus optimally routing the data traffic while relying on the single central entity. We also use the controller to manage the IP based flow mobility between the LTE and other mobile access networks. The test-bed implementation for the proposed architecture is described in detail.

SIGNALING OVERHEAD IN EXISTING LTE FRAMEWORK

This section describes the various mobility related activities and the corresponding signaling processes and overhead involved. In this study, we are interested in initial attach procedure, access bearer set up, intra-LTE handover procedure and inter-RAT handover procedure since these are the main events that occur in the EPC network.

Initial Attach and New Access Bearer

The Initial Attach Procedure is shown in Figure 2. The UE initiates the attach procedure to register with the network to receive services. This procedure consists of UE authentication, UE registration and EPS Bearer establishment processes. After authentication, the UE registers itself with the network and the network allocates IP address to the UE and establishes the first Packet Data Network (PDN) connection. The first Packet Data Network (PDN) connection is also known as Default Bearer.

Figure 2. Initial attach and access bearer set up procedure in existing LTE architecture

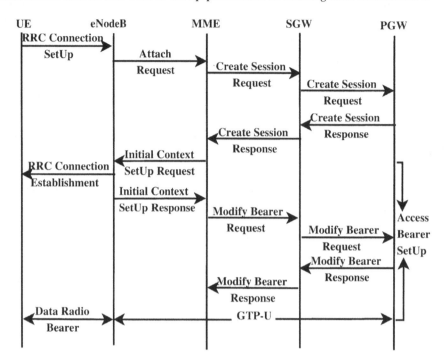

Whenever UE wants to set up a new bearer (i.e., Dedicated Bearer), it sends a NAS Service Request message to the MME. Then MME sets up a new connection as described in Figure 2. In 3GPP–EPC, a new access bearer set up means establishment of new EPS Bearer.

Intra-LTE Handover Procedure

There are many types of intra-LTE handover procedures in 3GPP–EPC architecture. Here we are considering the average case of intra-LTE handover scenario of 3GPP–EPC architecture i.e., X2 based handover with SGW relocation. We call this scenario as average case because chances of its occurrence is lesser than X2 based handover without SGW relocation but higher than inter-MME/SGW based handover. The intra-LTE handover procedure is described in Figure 3. In this scenario the UE moves between the eNodeB's which are connected to different SGW's. The source eNodeB (S-eNodeB) sends Handover Request message to the target eNodeB (T-eNodeB). The target eNodeB replies by sending Handover Request Ack message. The target eNB after receiving the eNB status from the source eNB, sends the Path Switch Request Message to the MME for creating the UE session via target SGW (T-SGW).

Inter-RAT Handover Procedure

In 3GPP–EPC architecture, PMIPv6 is used for network-based inter-mobility management. S5/S8 interface will consist of PMIPv6 instead of GTP. The inter-RAT handover procedure is described in Figure 4. This procedure consists of deletion of PMIPv6 tunnel which is present between previous MAG (SGW) and LMA (PGW); and establishment of PMIPv6 tunnel between new MAG and LMA (PGW).

Figure 3. Intra-LTE handover procedure in existing 3GPP

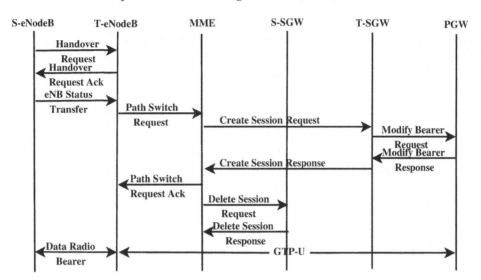

Figure 4. Inter-RAT handover procedure in existing 3GPP

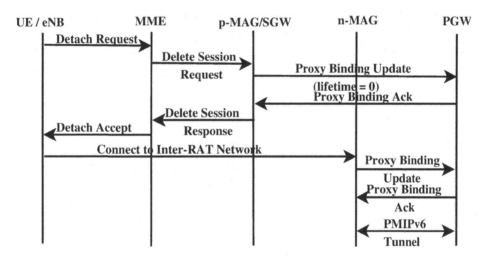

Drawbacks

The major drawbacks of the 3GPP–EPC architecture are the high volume of control signaling and event occurrence delay. This happens due to the maintenance of GTP or PMIPv6 tunnel. In all the above events, most of the messages are tunnel management messages. GTP or PMIPv6 tunnel is used to provide IP mobility but at the cost of control signaling and tunneling load.

PROPOSED EPC ARCHITECTURE

This section presents the proposed EPC architecture based on software defined networking (SDN) concepts.

Architectural Model

The proposed EPC architecture consists of a logically centralized EPC Controller and OpenFlow Switches (OF-Switches) as shown in Figure 5. The EPC Controller is connected to eNBs and OF-Switches via TCP links. The proposed EPC architecture eliminates the use of GTP or PMIPv6 tunnels for IP mobility. In the proposed architecture, OF-Switches provide the feature of IP mobility by forwarding the packets based on tuples as specified by EPC Controller. The components of the proposed EPC architecture are described in detail below.

EPC Controller

The EPC Controller is the main component of the proposed EPC architecture. The EPC Controller performs the tasks of UE Authentication, Mobility Management, IP Address Allocation and Charging Support. The EPC Controller receives the UE authentication and mobility information via TCP connected to the eNB. The EPC Controller routes the flows of an UE, based on its location, which provides the facility of IP mobility. The EPC Controller has the global view of the complete network consisting of OF-Switches, eNBs and UEs.

Figure 5. Proposed EPC architecture

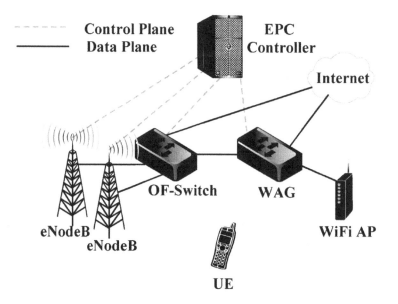

OpenFlow Switch

The OpenFlow switch, on receiving a new flow request, forwards it to the EPC Controller. The EPC Controller, based on information from the flow, identifies the corresponding UE and then routes the flow according to the UE's location; and also updates the corresponding flow table entries of the OpenFlow switches.

eNodeB

The eNodeB performs the same radio functionality as in the 3GPP–EPC architecture. Each eNodeB is connected to one OF-Switch. The eNodeB, after receiving the uplink flow, directly forwards it to the OF-Switch through which it is connected. The OF-Switch, after receiving a new flow, forwards it to the EPC Controller; the latter handles it according to its flow information. The eNodeB maintains a table consisting of two fields Flow Match Header (ofp_match) and E-UTRAN Radio Access Bearer Identifier (E-RAB ID). The table is updated by the EPC Controller whenever a new flow arrives. Whenever a downlink flow arrives, it is mapped to the corresponding radio bearer using E-RAB ID and then delivered to the corresponding UE.

EVENTS CALL FLOW

The call flow for the initial attach procedure, new flow entry procedure, intra-LTE handover procedure and inter-RAT handover procedure are described below.

Initial Attach Procedure

The Initial Attach Procedure is shown in Figure 6. The EPC Controller, after receiving the Attach Request message, authenticates the UE and allocates the IP address by sending Assign IP message. The Assign IP messages consist of IMSI, IP Address, UE Security Capabilities and Security Key information elements.

Figure 6. Initial attach procedure

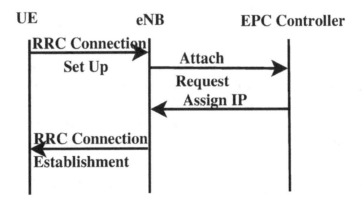

Figure 7. New flow entry procedure

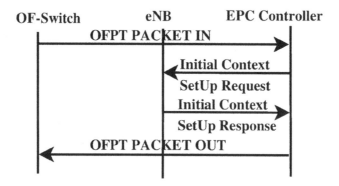

New Flow Entry Procedure

The New Flow Entry Procedure is shown in Figure 7. Whenever a new flow arrives the OF-Switch sends the OFPT_PACKET_IN message to the EPC Controller. The EPC Controller sends the Initial Context Set Up Request message to the eNB, which updates the table with the ofp_match and E-RAB ID entry corresponding to the new flow. The EPC Controller sends OFPT_PACKET_OUT message to the OF-Switches after receiving the Initial Context Set Up Response.

Intra-LTE Handover Procedure

The Intra-LTE Handover Procedure is shown in Figure 8. The source eNB (S-eNB) sends the Handover Required message to the EPC Controller. The EPC Controller sends the Handover Request message to the target eNB (T-eNB) for enquiring about the availability of resources. The target eNB sends the Handover Request Acknowledge message to the EPC Controller. If the resources are available at the target eNB, the EPC Controller sends the OFPT_PACKET_OUT message to the OF-Switches for re-routing the data flow towards the target eNB. The EPC Controller informs the status of handover process to the source eNB by sending Handover Command message. The source eNB sends the status of the UE to the EPC Controller; this status is forwarded to target eNB. The target eNB will send the Handover Notify message to the EPC Controller when the UE has been identified by the target eNB and the handover has been successfully completed.

Inter-RAT Handover Procedure

The Inter-RAT Handover Procedure is shown in Figure 9. When a UE moves from one access network (e.g. LTE) to a new access network (e.g. WiFi), it will send the Detach Request message to the EPC Controller. The EPC Controller based on the location information of the UE makes the binding entry for the UE at the new access networks by sending the message Binding Entry. The binding entry provides the same IP address to the UE at the new access network. After receiving the Binding Entry Response, the EPC Controller sends the OFPT_PACKET_OUT message to the OF-Switches to re-route the flow towards the new access network.

Figure 8. Intra-LTE handover procedure in the proposed architecture

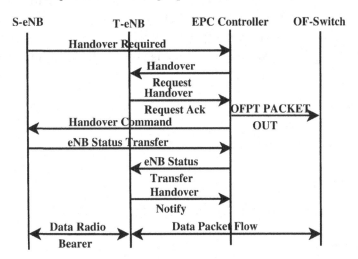

Figure 9. Inter-RAT handover procedure in the proposed architecture

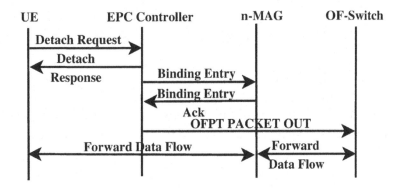

SIGNALING OVERHEAD ANALYSIS

In this section, we analyze the proposed architecture in terms of signaling overhead. We compare the performance of proposed EPC architecture with the 3GPP–EPC architecture.

Signaling Cost

The signaling cost is defined as the total size of all the control messages required for the completion of an event. When evaluating this cost, we do not consider the NAS, RRC Connection Set up, Attach/Detach Request/Response and authentication messages since the size of these messages is the same in both the architectures.

Let λ_n be the session arrival rate for each UE. The UE arrival process follows a Poisson distribution with rate λ_u. For the 3GPP EPC architecture, the message size specified in 3GPP specifications (3GPP, 2012a), (3GPP, 2012b), (3GPP, 2015) and (Sama, Said, Guillouard, & Suciu, 2014) are shown in Table 1. For the proposed EPC architecture, the messages OFPT_PACKET_IN and OFPT_PACKET_OUT are determined from (Open Networking Foundation, 2014); the rest of the message sizes are obtained from (3GPP, 2012a), (3GPP, 2012b), (3GPP, 2015) by removing the information element MME UE S1AP ID and replacing E-RAB ID List with ofp_match List in messages. The size of the proposed EPC messages is shown in Table 2. We evaluate the signaling cost for the following four scenarios:

1.   Initial Attach Procedure,
2.   New Access Bearer Set Up/New Flow Entry Procedure,
3.   Intra-LTE Handover Procedure,
4.   Inter-RAT Handover Procedure.

3GPP–EPC Architecture

The signaling cost of the various scenarios based on the discussion done in Section 3 is as follows:

Initial Attach Procedure

A new UE needs to attach itselfto obtain service from the access network as shown in Figure 2. The signaling cost involved in the attach procedure is:

$$C_1 = M_{csr} + M_{csp} + M_{csr'} + M_{csp'} + M_{icsr} + M_{icsp} + M_{mbr} + M_{mbp} + M_{mbr'} + M_{mbp'}$$

New Access Bearer Set Up Procedure

To set up a new connection UE sends request to the eNB which is forwarded to PGW via MME and SGW as shown in Figure 2. The signaling cost involved in this procedure is:

$$C_2 = M_{icsr} + M_{icsp} + M_{mbr} + M_{mbp} + M_{mbr'} + M_{mbp'}$$

Intra-LTE Handover Procedure

The process involved in intra-LTE handover is shown in Figure 3. The signaling cost involved when a UE move within the network is:

$$C_3 = M_{hr} + M_{hack} + M_{est} + M_{psr} + M_{csr} + M_{csp} + M_{mbr'} + M_{mbp'} + M_{dsr} + M_{dsp} + M_{pack}$$

Inter-RAT Handover Procedure

The process involved in inter-RAT handover is shown in Figure 4. The signaling cost involved when UE moves to different access network is as follows:

$$C_4 = M_{dsr} + M_{pbu} + M_{pba} + M_{dsp} + M_{pbu} + M_{pba}$$

Proposed Architecture

The signaling cost of the various scenarios based on the discussion done in Section 5.2 is as follows:

Initial Attach Procedure

A new UE needs to attach itself to obtain service from the access network as shown in Figure 6. The signaling cost involved in the attach procedure is as follows:

$$C_1 = OF_{aip}$$

New Flow Entry Procedure

Whenever a new flow arrives, the OF-Switch sends a request to the EPC Controller and the controller adds an entry in OF-Switch. The detailed procedure is shown in Figure 7. The signaling cost involved in this procedure is as follows:

$$C_2 = OF_{in} + OF_{icsr} + OF_{icsp} + OF_{out}$$

Intra-LTE Handover Procedure

The process involved in intra-LTE handover is shown in Figure 8. The signaling cost involved when a UE move within the network is as follows:

$$C_3 = OF_{hrq} + OF_{hr} + OF_{hack} + OF_{hc} + OF_{out}$$

Inter-RAT Handover Procedure

The process followed during inter-RAT handover is shown in Figure 9. The signaling cost involved when UE moves to different access network is as follows:

$$C_4 = OF_{pbu} + OF_{pba} + OF_{out}$$

The total signaling cost for each UE of the architecture is given by:

$$TSC_{ue} = P_1.C_1 + P_2.C_2 + P_3.C_3 + P_4.C_4 \qquad (1)$$

The total signaling cost for N UEs in the network is given by:

$$T_{SC} = N.TSC_{ue} \qquad (2)$$

Here, P_1 is the probability of occurrence of scenario 1 and $P_1 = 1$ because we can consider a UE in the network only if it is attached to the network. P_2 is the probability of occurrence of scenario 2. We assume the session arrival rate for each UE follows Poisson distribution with rate λ_n. Thus $P_2 = \lambda_n.e^{-\lambda_n}$. P_3 and P_4 are the probability of occurrence of scenario 3 and 4 respectively. The P 3 and P 4 are given by, as described in 3GPP (2012b):

$$P_3 = \frac{\mu_c}{\mu_d}, P_4 = \frac{\mu_c + \lambda_u}{\mu_d + \lambda_u}$$

The variables μ_c and μ_d represent the border crossing rate of a UE out of a subnet and an access network respectively. These are given by:

$$\mu_c = 2\frac{\nu}{\sqrt{\pi.\alpha_R}}, \mu_d = \frac{\mu_c}{\sqrt{\beta}}$$

Here, ν is the average velocity of the UE. The access network consist of β number of eNB having the coverage area of $\alpha R = \pi R^2$ with radius of R.

Table 1. Message sizes (Bytes) in the 3GPP EPC architecture

Messages	Notation	Src-Dst	Size
Tunnel Management Messages			
Create Session Request	M_{csr}	MME-SGW	335
Create Session Response	M_{csp}	SGW-MME	241
Create Session Request	$M_{csr'}$	SGW-PGW	335
Create Session Response	$M_{csp'}$	PGW-SGW	224
Modify Bearer Request	M_{mbr}	MME-SGW	101
Modify Bearer Response	M_{mbp}	SGW-MME	81
Modify Bearer Request	$M_{mbr'}$	SGW-PGW	67
Modify Bearer Response	$M_{mbp'}$	PGW-SGW	81

continued on following page

Table 1. Continued

Messages	Notation	Src-Dst	Size
Delete Session Request	M_{dsr}	MME-SGW	90
Delete Session Response	M_{dsp}	SGW-MME	18
Delete Session Request	$M_{dsr'}$	SGW-PGW	90
Delete Session Response	$M_{dsp'}$	PGW-SGW	18
Context Management Messages			
Initial Context Set Up Request	M_{icsr}	MME-eNB	145
Initial Context Set Up Response	M_{icsp}	eNB-MME	86
Handover Messages			
Path Switch Request	M_{psr}	eNB-MME	~48
Path Switch Request Ack	M_{pack}	MME-eNB	~54
Handover Request	M_{hr}	MME-eNB	~84
Handover Request Ack	M_{hack}	eNB-MME	~34
eNB Status Transfer	M_{est}	eNB-MME	22
Proxy Binding Update	M_{pbu}	PGW-MAG	38
Proxy Binding Ack	M_{pba}	MAG-PGW	38

PERFORMANCE EVALUATION

This section presents the performance comparison of the proposed architecture.

Signaling Overheads

This section presents the numerical results of the analysis done in Section 5. The total signaling cost is calculated using Equation 2 for both the architectures. The analysis is done for 50% pedestrian and 50% vehicular users in the network. The default values and parameters used for performance evaluation are shown in Table 3. Messages size is shown in Tables 1 and 2. Figure 10 shows that the total signaling for 3GPP–EPC architecture increases at a higher rate as compared to proposed EPC architecture, with increasing number of users. For 10,000 users the signaling cost of 3GPP EPC architecture is 18 MBytes;

the corresponding cost in the proposed architecture is around 1 MByte. The signaling overhead increases proportionally with the number of UEs. If the number of UEs are very high (of the order of millions), this can become a critical bottleneck for the existing 3GPP EPC architecture.

Simulation Based Results

The proposed architecture has been implemented in an ns-3 simulator (NS-3 Network Simulator (n.d.)) for more detailed evaluation. In ns-3 simulator, EPC Controller is implemented on top of the ns-3 OpenFlow controller and then connected with 100 eNBs, 11 OF-Switches. The topology also consists of 100 WiFi APs to test the inter-RAT handover delay of the proposed EPC architecture. Each UE generates traffic at the rate of 500 Kbps. To test the scalability of the EPC Controller, 50% of the users sends handover

Table 2. Message size (Bytes) in proposed EPC architecture

Messages	Notation	Src-Dst	Size
OF Assign IP	OF_{aip}	eNB-Ctr	44
OF Initial Context Set Up Request	OF_{icsr}	Ctr-eNB	82
OF Initial Context Set Up Response	OF_{icsp}	eNB-Ctr	42
Handover Required	OF_{hrq}	eNB-Ctr	~20
Handover Request	OF_{hr}	Ctr-eNB	~62
Handover Request Ack	OF_{hack}	eNB-Ctr	~42
Handover Command	OF_{hc}	Ctr-eNB	~46
Handover Notify	OF_{hn}	eNB-Ctr	30
eNB Status Transfer	OF_{est}	eNB-Ctr	22
Proxy Binding Update	OF_{pbu}	Ctr-MAG	38
Proxy Binding Ack	OF_{pba}	MAG-Ctr	38
OFP_PACKET_IN	OF	OF_Switch-Ctr	32
OFP_PACKET_OUT	OF_{out}	Ctr-OF_Switch	24

Figure 10. Total signaling cost varying the number of users

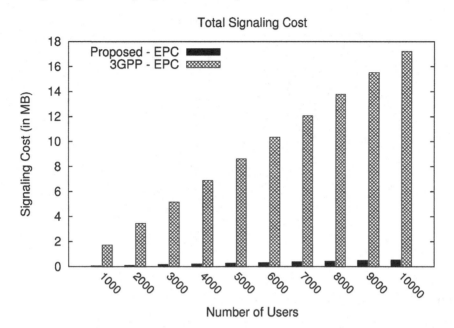

Table 3. System parameters

Parameters	Values
R	$500m$
$\nu\left(Vehicular\right)$	$30km\,/\,h$
$\nu\left(Pedestrian\right)$	$1km\,/\,h$
$\lambda_n, \lambda_u, \beta$	$0.03, 1.66, 5$

requests each second to the EPC Controller. It can be seen from Figure 11 that the average per-user throughput for the different users is equivalent or higher in case of the handover scenario than from the without handover scenario. Thus we can say that the EPC Controller per second is able to handle the handover requests from these users, thereby increasing the throughput of the network.

The delay for the four different events is presented in Table 4. The delay for 3GPP EPC architecture is determined from ns-3 simulations by constructing a topology consisting of PGW/SGW, MME and 100 eNBs. It can be seen that the proposed architecture reduces the delay for the various procedures; from 6.044 to 2 ms for initial attach and new access bearer set up. Similar reduction is seen in the case of the handover procedures.

For experimental studies, we plan to build the EPC Controller on top of the IRIS controller (Lee, Park, Shin, & Yang, 2014) that can support up to 5 million flows per second; this will further help in reducing the delay for processing the different events.

Figure 11. Average per-user throughput, varying the number of users

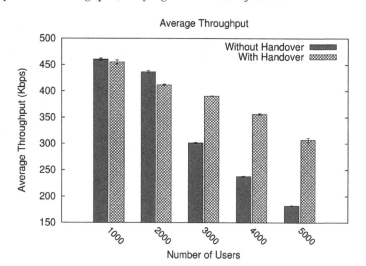

Table 4. Delay in the occurrence of various events

Event	3GPP–EPC	Proposed–EPC
Initial Attach Procedure	6.044 ms	2 ms
New Access Bearer Set Up/New Flow Entry Procedure	6.044 ms	2 ms
Intra-LTE Handover Procedure	177.21 ms	26 ms
Inter-RAT Handover Procedure	565 ms	26 ms

EXPERIMENTAL EPC TESTBED

This section presents the detail of the implementation of the SDN–based EPC. The initial prototype of the proposed architecture is implemented. The testbed setup is shown in Figure 12. The prototype implements the SDN–based EPC on top of the Java–based Floodlight (Floodlight - Open Source Software for Building Software-Defined Networks, (n.d.)) SDN controller and the LTE base station is created with the help of open-source package called OpenLTE (OpenLTE, (n.d.)) and USRP, a Software Defined Radio platform. The OpenLTE is used to run the LTE protocol stack layer of the eNodeB; the USRP is used for transmission and reception of the messages with the mobile devices. Lets discuss how each of the component is implemented for the testbed setup in detail.

LTE Base Station

LTE Base Station is created using OpenLTE. OpenLTE is an open-source implementation of the 3GPP LTE specifications in C++. OpenLTE emulates the eNodeB stack on a
Linux Machine. The requirements of OpenLTE are as follows:

- Linux PC with multicore processor,
- USRP B210 (Software Defined Radio platform),
- 2 vert900 antennas,
- UHD driver,
- GNU Radio 3.7.2 or higher,
- USB port 3.0.

The USRP B210 is an RF hardware which provides a platform for Software Defined Radio. The USRP B210 works with Linux PC with the help of USRP Hardware Driver (UHD). The GNU Radio (GNU Radio (n.d.)) is an open-source software development toolkit that provides Linux PC the functionality of signal processing blocks to implement software radios. The OpenLTE code is modified to send and receive the authentication and attach procedure messages from the SDN-based EPC.

SDN-Based EPC

SDN-based EPC is setup with minimal functionality on top of the floodlight SDN controller. Floodlight is an enterprise-class, Apache-licensed, Java-based OpenFlow Controller. The Floodlight is used as a base to implement the EPC Controller. The Floodlight SDN controller requires a Linux PC with Ubuntu 10.04 (Natty) or higher. The OpenLTE implements the MME as a layer of the eNodeB (like RRC). But for the implementation of the proposed architecture testbed setup, we need the EPC functionality such as the functions of MME, SGW and PGW to be running on top of the Floodlight controller. Thus, we removed the MME from the OpenLTE and implemented it as core functionality of the Floodlight SDN controller. The MME module sends and receives messages from the OpenLTE. The MME module performs the task of the UE Authentication, interpretation of the UE NAS messages and UE Attach Procedure. The functionality of the PGW to act as a firewall is implemented as a module in the Floodlight SDN controller. The HSS database is also implemented as core functionality of the Floodlight SDN controller to maintain the valid user list. The features supported by Floodlight SDN controller are as follows:

- Support for OpenStack,
- Can handle mixed OpenFlow and non-OpenFlow networks,
- Offers a module loading system.

OpenFlow Switch

OpenFlow Switch is emulated on a Linux PC with the help of an open-source package Open vSwitch. Open vSwitch (Open vSwitch, (n.d.)) is a production quality, multilayer open source virtual switch. To implement the Open vSwitch, we require Linux PC. The features of Open vSwitch are as follows:

- Full support for OpenFlow 1.3,
- Partial support for OpenFlow 1.4 and 1.5.,
- IPv6 support,
- Fine-grained QoS control.

LTE User Equipment

The LG G2 mobile is used as LTE user equipment for the testbed setup. The LG G2 mobile has android 4.2.2 running. A blank sim is configured with the test IMSI and attached to the LG G2 to be able to connect the OpenLTE. The ping and ftp server android applications are installed to test the data connection.

SCENARIOS TESTED

This section discusses the scenarios for which the prototype of the proposed architecture is tested. The scenarios tested are as follows:

1.   The connection of mobile user with the LTE network which has the SDN–based EPC.
2.   Mobile user data connection with the other user.

Scenario 1

In this scenario, we test whether the SDN-based EPC of the LTE network is able to authenticate and provide the LTE network connection to the mobile user. The testbed demo of the scenario discussed above is explained with the help of figures. In Figure 14, the Floodlight SDN controller and OpenLTE starts. The OpenLTE is configured with the parameters like reception gain, transmission gain, etc. Figure 15 shows that the Floodlight controller is listening for the OpenLTE connections. Once the OpenLTE

Figure 12. Testbed setup

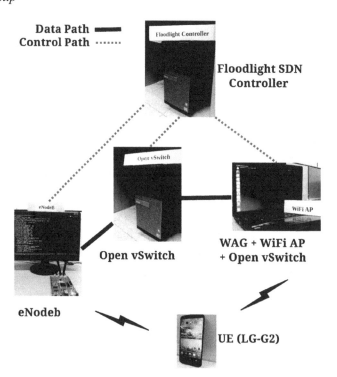

starts it connects with the Floodlight controller which performs the basic functionality of the EPC. The whole setup of proposed SDN–based LTE EPC network is now ready for the initial attach process.

Once the mobile users comes into the LTE network it sends the Attach Request message to the Floodlight controller via OpenLTE and the controller responds by sending the OF Assign IP message which assigns the IP address to the user and connects it with the network. The connected user is shown in Figure 13. The average connection time is observed to be 691.99 ms.

Scenario 2

In this scenario, we test whether the mobile user has the data connection and is able to send and receive the data packets from the other user. Here, we assume that the other user is the external Linux PC connected via Open vSwitch. The mobile user has the IP Address 192.168.1.10 while the external Linux PC is connected on the different network with the IP Address 10.6.21.54. To test the data connection the ping application is used. The mobile user ping the external Linux PC with the different packet sizes and the result is shown in Table 5. The Figure 16 shows the tcpdump for the ping from UE (IP:192.168.1.10) to the external Linux PC machine (IP: 10.6.21.54). The Figure 17 shows the flow entry made at the Open vSwitch by the floodlight controller when the ping application runs. The Figure 18 shows that the external Linux PC (IP: 10.6.21.54) is able to ping the mobile user (IP: 192.168.1.10). The FTP and TCP

Figure 13. Screenshot of UE getting attached

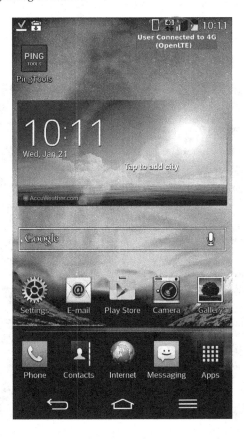

Table 5. Round Trip Time (RTT) for Ping from mobile user to external Linux PC

Ping Packet Size	RTT (ms)
28 Bytes	162 ms
48 Bytes	764 ms
68 Bytes	1380 ms
78 Bytes	2334 ms

chat application also works for the small size file and messages between the mobile user and the external Linux PC. The test for a larger file and message transfer was also conducted but it did not succeed. This is because the OpenLTE data channel only provides support for smaller size packet. In future, we will try enhancing the data channel capacity of the OpenLTE and send the larger data between the mobile user and external Linux PC.

CONCLUSION

The current LTE network architecture has serious limitations due to high control signaling, delay and protocol stack overhead. This is because each control transaction (from UE Attach Procedure to UE Detach Procedure) in the 3GPP–EPC architecture starts from UE and goes till the edge of the network. In this chapter, we have presented architecture to overcome the limitations of 3GPP–EPC architecture

Figure 14. Screenshot showing start of OpenLTE and Floodlight

Figure 15. Screenshot showing working of OpenLTE and Floodlight

Figure 16. Screenshot showing tcpdump for ping from mobile user to the external Linux PC

```
     192.168.1.10 > 10.6.21.54: ICMP echo request, id 56847, seq 1, length 64
18:13:58.786951 IP (tos 0x0, ttl 63, id 61371, offset 0, flags [none], proto ICMP (1), length 84)
     10.6.21.54 > 192.168.1.10: ICMP echo reply, id 56847, seq 1, length 64
18:13:59.021681 IP (tos 0xc0, ttl 64, id 1967, offset 0, flags [none], proto ICMP (1), length 90)
```

Figure 17. Screenshot showing flow entry at Open vSwitch

```
Feb 04 18:39:49|00015|vconn|DBG|unix:/var/run/openvswitch/b.mgmt: sent (Success): NXST_FLOW request (xid=0x4):
Feb 04 18:39:49|00016|vconn|DBG|unix:/var/run/openvswitch/b.mgmt: received: NXST_FLOW reply (xid=0x4):
 cookie=0x20000000000000, duration=8.081s, table=0, n_packets=1, n_bytes=98, idle_timeout=5,priority=1,ip,in_port=2,dl_src=08:00:27:ad:3c:44,dl
_dst=90:b1:1c:95:e2:db,nw_src=10.6.21.54,nw_dst=192.168.1.10 actions=output:1
 cookie=0x20000000000000, duration=3.965s, table=0, n_packets=1, n_bytes=98, idle_timeout=5,priority=1,ip,in_port=1,dl_src=90:b1:1c:95:e2:db,dl
_dst=08:00:27:ad:3c:44,nw_src=192.168.1.10,nw_dst=10.6.21.54 actions=output:2
NXST_FLOW reply (xid=0x4):
 cookie=0x20000000000000, duration=8.081s, table=0, n_packets=1, n_bytes=98, idle_timeout=5,priority=1,ip,in_port=2,dl_src=08:00:27:ad:3c:44,dl
_dst=90:b1:1c:95:e2:db,nw_src=10.6.21.54,nw_dst=192.168.1.10 actions=output:1
 cookie=0x20000000000000, duration=3.965s, table=0, n_packets=1, n_bytes=98, idle_timeout=5,priority=1,ip,in_port=1,dl_src=90:b1:1c:95:e2:db,dl
_dst=08:00:27:ad:3c:44,nw_src=192.168.1.10,nw_dst=10.6.21.54 actions=output:2
```

Figure 18. Screenshot showing external Linux PC pings mobile user

```
ubuntu@ubuntu:~$ ping -c 3 192.168.1.10
PING 192.168.1.10 (192.168.1.10) 56(84) bytes of data.
64 bytes from 192.168.1.10: icmp_req=1 ttl=63 time=172 ms

--- 192.168.1.10 ping statistics ---
3 packets transmitted, 1 received, 66% packet loss, time 2007ms
rtt min/avg/max/mdev = 172.756/172.756/172.756/0.000 ms
```

by using the concepts of SDN. The proposed architecture centralizes the functionality of EPC control plane and inter-mobility anchor at the logical controller and replaces the SGW and PGW with the OF Switch. Centralization of functionality reduces the high control signaling and delay. Global network view property of EPC Controller helps eliminate the tunneling requirements thus overcoming the limitations of protocol stack overhead. The evaluation results show that the proposed architecture reduces the signaling cost, delay during the occurrence of the various events.

ACKNOWLEDGMENT

This work was supported in part by DST-EPSRC funded India-UK Advanced Technology Centre of Excellence in Next Generation Networks, Systems and Services (IU-ATC). The help extended by Mr. C.S.Ganesh and Mr. Anix Anbiah, Ph.D. students in CSE Dept, IIT Madras, towards revising this manuscript is gratefully acknowledged.

REFERENCES

3GPP. (2012a). *3GPP TS 36.414, Evolved Universal Terrestrial Radio Access Network (E-UTRAN);S1 Data Transport (Release 10)*. Retrieved from http://www.etsi.org/deliver/etsi_ts/136400_136499/1364 14/10.01.00_60/ts_136414v100100p.pdf

3GPP. (2012b). *3GPP TS 36.413, Evolved Universal Terrestrial Radio Access Network (E-UTRAN);S1 Application Protocol (S1AP)(Release 10)*. Retrieved from http://www.etsi.org/deliver/etsi_ts/136400_1 36499/136413/10.00.01_60/ts_136413v100001p.pdf

3GPP. (2013). *3GPP TS 23.401, GPRS Enhancements for E-UTRAN Access (Release 11)*. Retrieved from http://www.etsi.org/deliver/etsi_ts/123400_123499/123401/11.11.00_60/ts_123401v111100p.pdf

3GPP. (2015). *3GPP TS 29.275, Proxy Mobile IPv6 (PMIPv6) based Mobility and Tunnelling protocols; Stage 3 (Release 11)*. Retrieved from https://portal.3gpp.org/desktopmodules/Specifications/SpecificationDetails.aspx?specificationId=1693

Bari, M. F., Chowdhury, S. R., Ahmed, R., & Boutaba, R. (2013). PolicyCop: An Autonomic QoS Policy Enforcement Framework for Software Defined Networks.*Proc. IEEE International Conference on SDN for Future Networks and Services (SDN4FNS)*, 1-7. doi:10.1109/SDN4FNS.2013.6702548

Basta, A., Kellerer, W., Hoffmann, M., Hoffmann, K., & Schmidt, E. D. (2013). A Virtual SDN-Enabled LTE EPC Architecture: A Case Study for S-/P-Gateways Functions.*Proc. IEEE Conference on SDN for Future Networks and Services (SDN4FNS)*, 1-7. doi:10.1109/SDN4FNS.2013.6702532

Cisco Systems. (2014). *Cisco Networking Index: Global Mobile Data Traffic Forecast Update, 2015–2020 white paper*. Retrieved from http://www.cisco.com/c/en/us/solutions/collateral/service-provider/visual-networking-index-vni/white_paper_c11-520862.html

Contreras, L. M., Cominardi, L., Qian, H., & Bernardos, C. J. (2016). Software-Defined Mobility Management: Architecture Proposal and Future Directions. *Mobile Networks and Applications*, *21*(2), 226–236. doi:10.1007/s11036-015-0663-7

Egilmez, H. E., Dane, S. T., Gorkemli, B., & Tekalp, A. M. (2012). OpenQoS: OpenFlow Controller Design and Test Network for Multimedia Delivery with end-to-end Quality of Service over Software Defined Networks.*Proc. APSIPA Annual Summit and Conference*, 1-8.

Floodlight - Open Source Software for Building Software-Defined Networks. (n.d.). Retrieved from http://www.tomsitpro.com/articles/open-source-cloud-computing-software,2-754-7.html

GNU Radio. (n.d.). Retrieved from http://www.gnuradio.org/

Ishimori, A., Faria, F., Furtado, I., Cerqueira, E., & Abelem, A. (2012). Automatic QoS Management on OpenFlow Software-Defined Networks.*Proc. API Software Defined Networking Event Demo*.

Jammal, M., Singh, T., Shami, A., Asal, R., & Li, Y. (2014). Software defined networking: State of the art and research challenges. *Elsevier Computer Networks*, *72*, 74–98. doi:10.1016/j.comnet.2014.07.004

Jin, X., Li, L. E., Vanbever, L., & Rexford, J. (2013). Softcell: Scalable and Flexible Cellular Core Network Architecture.*Proc. ACM conference on Emerging Networking Experiments and Technologies (CoNXT)*, 1-13. doi:10.1145/2535372.2535377

Kempf, J., Johansson, B., Pettersson, S., Luning, H., & Nilsson, T. (2012). Moving the Mobile Evolved Packet Core to the Cloud.*Proc. IEEE International Conference on Wireless and Mobile Computing, Networking and Communications (WiMob)*, 784-791. doi:10.1109/WiMOB.2012.6379165

Kobayashi, M., Seetharaman, S., Parulkar, G., Appenzeller, G., Little, J., Van Reijendam, J., & McKeown, N. et al. (2014). Maturing of OpenFlow and Software-defined Networking through deployments. *Elsevier Computer Networks*, *61*, 151–175. doi:10.1016/j.bjp.2013.10.011

La Oliva, A. D., Bernardos, C. J., Calderon, M., Melia, T., & Zuniga, J. C. (2011). IP Flow Mobility: Smart Traffic Offload For Future Wireless Networks. *IEEE Communications Magazine*, *49*(10), 124–132. doi:10.1109/MCOM.2011.6035826

Lee, B., Park, S. H., Shin, J., & Yang, S. (2014). IRIS: The OpenFlow-based Recursive SDN controller. *Proc. IEEE 16th International Conference on Advanced Communication Technology (ICACT)*, 1227-1231. doi:10.1109/ICACT.2014.6779154

Makaya, C., & Pierre, S. (2008). An Analytical Framework for Performance Evaluation of IPv6-based Mobility Management Protocols. *IEEE Transactions on Wireless Communications*, *7*(3), 972–983. doi:10.1109/TWC.2008.060725

Moradi, M., Li, L. E., & Mao, Z. M. (2014). SoftMoW: A Dynamic and Scalable Software Defined Architecture for Cellular WANs.*Proc. ACM SIGCOMM Workshop on Hot Topics in Software Defined Networking (HotSDN)*, 1-2. doi:10.1145/2620728.2620763

Nguyen, V., Do, T. X., & Kim, Y. (2016). SDN and virtualization-based LTE mobile network architectures: A comprehensive survey. *Wireless Personal Communications*, *86*(38), 1401–1438. doi:10.1007/s11277-015-2997-7

Nguyen, V., & Kim, Y. (2015). Proposal and evaluation of SDN based mobile packet core networks. *EURASIP Journal on Wireless Communications and Networking, 172,* 1–18.

Nowoswiat, D., & Milliken, G. (2013). *Alcatel-Lucent: Managing the Signaling Traffic in Packet Core.* Retrieved from http://www2.alcatel-lucent.com/techzine/managing-lte-core-network-signaling-traffic/

NS-3 Network Simulator. (n.d.). Retrieved from http://www.nsnam.org

Nunes, B., Mendonca, M., Nguyen, X. N., Obraczka, K., & Turletti, T. (2014). A survey of software-defined networking: Past, present, and future of programmable networks. *IEEE Commun. Surveys Tuts., 16*(3), 1617–1634. doi:10.1109/SURV.2014.012214.00180

Open Networking Foundation. (2012). *Software-Defined Networking: The New Norm for Networks.* Retrieved from https://www.opennetworking.org/images/stories/downloads/sdn-resources/white-papers/wp-sdn-newnorm.pdf

Open Networking Foundation. (2014). *OpenFlow specifications.* Retrieved from https://www.opennetworking.org/images/stories/downloads/sdn-resources/onf-specifications/openflow/openflow-switch-v1.3.4.pdf

Open Networking Foundation. (n.d.). Retrieved from https://www.opennetworking.org/

Open vSwitch. (n.d.). Retrieved from http://openvswitch.org

OpenLTE. (n.d.). *An open source 3GPP LTE implementation.* Retrieved from http://openlte.sourceforge.net

Sama, M. R., Said, S., Hadj, B., Guillouard, K., & Suciu, L. (2014). Enabling Network Programmability in LTE/EPC Architecture Using OpenFlow. *Proc. 12th International Symposium on Modeling and Optimization in Mobile, Ad Hoc, and Wireless Networks (WiOpt),* 389-396. doi:10.1109/WIOPT.2014.6850324

Savic, Z. (2011). *LTE Design and Deployment Strategies* [Power Point slides]. Retrieved from http://www.cisco.com/web/ME/expo2011/saudiarabia/pdfs/LTE_Design_and_Deployment_Strategies-Zeljko_Savic.pdf

Varis, N., Manner, J., & Heinonen, J. (2011). A Layer-2 Approach for Mobility and Transport in the Mobile Backhaul. *Proc. International Conference on ITS Telecommunications (ITST),* 268-273. doi:10.1109/ITST.2011.6060066

Zuniga, J. C., Bernardos, C. J., Costa, R., & Reznik, A. (2013). Distributed Mobility Management: A Standards Landscape. *IEEE Communications Magazine, 51*(3), 80–87. doi:10.1109/MCOM.2013.6476870

Compilation of References

10.3.0., G. T. (2011). *Lte evolved universal terrestrial radio access (eutra) physical layer procedures (release 10)*. Author.

3GPP TS 23.401 V8.1.0. (2008). *General Packet Radio Service (GPRS) enhancements for Evolved Universal Terrestrial Radio Access Network (E-UTRAN) access*. 3GPP.

3GPP TS 36.213. (2011). *Version 10.1.0 R10: Evolved Universal Terrestrial Radio Access (E-UTRA); Physical layer procedures*.

3GPP TSG RAN WG1 Meeting #47, R1-063275. (2006). *Discussion on control signaling for persistent scheduling of VoIP*. Riga, Latvia: 3GPP.

3GPP TSG RAN WG1 Meeting #47bis, R1-070098. (2007). *Discussion on control signaling for persistent scheduling of VoIP*. Sorrento, Italy: 3GPP.

3GPP. (2011, August). *Technical Specification Group Services and SA; Local IP Access and Selected IP Traffic Offload (LIPA-SIPTO)(Release 10)*. TR23.829 V10.0.1. 3GPP.

3GPP. (2012, August). *3rd generation partnership project; technical specification group sa; feasibility study for proximity services (prose)(release12)*. TR22.803 V1.0.0. 3GPP.

3GPP. (2012a). *3GPP TS 36.414, Evolved Universal Terrestrial Radio Access Network (E-UTRAN);S1 Data Transport (Release 10)*. Retrieved from http://www.etsi.org/deliver/etsi_ts/136400_136499/136414/10.01.00_60/ts_136414v100100p.pdf

3GPP. (2012b). *3GPP TS 36.413, Evolved Universal Terrestrial Radio Access Network (E-UTRAN);S1 Application Protocol (S1AP)(Release 10)*. Retrieved from http://www.etsi.org/deliver/etsi_ts/136400_136499/136413/10.00.01_60/ts_136413v100001p.pdf

3GPP. (2013). *3GPP TS 23.401, GPRS Enhancements for E-UTRAN Access (Release 11)*. Retrieved from http://www.etsi.org/deliver/etsi_ts/123400_123499/123401/11.11.00_60/ts_123401v111100p.pdf

3GPP. (2015). *3GPP TS 29.275, Proxy Mobile IPv6 (PMIPv6) based Mobility and Tunnelling protocols; Stage 3 (Release 11)*. Retrieved from https://portal.3gpp.org/desktopmodules/Specifications/SpecificationDetails.aspx?specificationId=1693

Access, E. U. (2010). *Further advancements for E-UTRA physical layer aspects*. 3GPP Technical Specification TR, 36, V2.

Adhikary, A. D., Dhillon, H. S., & Caire, G. (2015). Massive-MIMO meets HetNet: Interference coordination through spatial blanking. *IEEE Journal on Selected Areas in Communications*, *33*(6), 1171–1186. doi:10.1109/JSAC.2015.2416986

Afolabi, R. O., Dadlani, A., & Kiseon, K. (2013). Multicast scheduling and resource allocation algorithms for OFDMA-based systems: A survey. *IEEE Communications Surveys and Tutorials*, *15*(1), 240–254. doi:10.1109/SURV.2012.013012.00074

Ahmed, E. S. A., & Saeed, R. A. (2014). A Survey of Big Data Cloud Computing Security. *International Journal of Computer Science and Software Engineering*, *3*(1), 78–85.

Akhshabi, S., Begen, A. C., & Dovrolis, C. (2011). An experimental evaluation of rate-adaptation algorithms in adaptive streaming over HTTP. ACM MMSys2011.

Akyildiz, I. F., Akan, O. B., Chen, C., Fang, J., & Su, W. (2003). Interplanetary internet: State-of-the-art and research challenges. *Computer Networks*, *43*(2), 75–112. doi:10.1016/S1389-1286(03)00345-1

Akyildiz, I. F., Lee, W.-Y., Vuran, M. C., & Mohanty, S. (2006). Next generation/dynamic spectrum access/cognitive radio wireless networks: A survey. *Computer Networks*, *50*(13). 2127–2159. doi:10.1016/j.comnet.2006.05.001

Al-Abri, F., Edirisingh, E., De Cock, J., Notebaert, S., & Van de Walle, R. (2011). Optimal H.264/AVC video transcoding system. *IEEE International Conference on Consumer Electronics (ICCE)*. doi:10.1109/ICCE.2011.5722613

Alaya-Feki, A. B. H., Jemaa, S. B., Sayrac, B., Houze, P., & Moulines, E. (2008). Informed spectrum usage in cognitive radio networks: Interference cartography. *IEEE 19th International Symposium on Personal, Indoor and Mobile Radio Communications*, 1–5.

Al-fares, M., Radhakrishnan, S., Raghavan, B., Huang, N., & Vahdat, A. (2010), Hedera: Dynamic flow scheduling for data center networks. *Proc. of Networked Systems Design and Implementation (NSDI) Symposium.*

Alsharif, M. H., Nordin, R., & Ismail, M. (2014). A review on intelligent base stations cooperation management techniques for greener lte cellular networks. *Journal of Communication*, *9*(12).

Amelichev, N., & Krinkin, K. (2010). Simulation of 3G/WLAN Offload: first steps. *8th Conference of Open Innovations Framework Program FRUCT*, Lappeenranta, Finland.

Andreev, Galinina, Pyattaev, Johnsson, & Koucheryavy. (2015). Analyzing Assisted Offloading of Cellular User Sessions onto D2D Links in Unlicensed Bands. *IEEE Journal on Selected Areas in Communications, 33*(1), 67-80.

Andreev, Galinina, Pyattaev, Johnsson, & Koucheryavy. (2015). Analyzing Assisted Offloading of Cellular User Sessions onto D2D Links in Unlicensed Bands. *Journal on Selected Areas in Communications, 33*(1), 67–80.

Andrews, G. (2012). Femto-cells: Past, Present, and Future. *IEEE Journal on Selected Areas in Communications.*

Andrews, J. G. (2013). Seven ways that HetNets are a cellular paradigm shift. *IEEE Communications Magazine*, *51*(3), 136–144. doi:10.1109/MCOM.2013.6476878

Antonopoulos, A., Kartsakli, E., Bousia, A., Alonso, L., & Verikoukis, C. (2015b). Energy Efficient Infrastructure Sharing in Multi-Operator Mobile Networks. *IEEE Communications Magazine*, *53*(5), 242–249. doi:10.1109/MCOM.2015.7105671

Asadi, A., & Mancuso, V. (2013, November). WiFi Direct and LTE D2D in action. In Wireless Days (WD). 2013 IEEE IFIP, 1-8.

Ashraf, I., Boccardi, F., & Ho, L. (2011). Sleep mode techniques for small cell deployments. *IEEE Communications Magazine*, *49*(8), 72–79. doi:10.1109/MCOM.2011.5978418

Auer, G., Giannini, V., Desset, C., Gdor, I., Skillermark, P., Olsson, M., & Fehske, A. et al. (2011). How Much Energy Is Needed To Run A Wireless Network? *IEEE Wireless Communications*, *18*(5), 40–49. doi:10.1109/MWC.2011.6056691

Automatic Terminal Information Service (ATIS). (2012). *Report on Wireless Network Energy Efficiency*. Available online: http://www.atis.org/topsc/Docs/Deliverables/ATIS-I-0000033.pdf

Babun, L. (2015). Extended Coverage for Public Safety and Critical Communications Using Multi-hop and D2D Communications. *FIU Electronics thesis and dissertation, 2015.*

Balasubramanian, A., Mahajan, R., & Venkataramani, A. (2010). Augmenting mobile 3G using WiFi.*Proceedings of ACM MobiSys.*

Banerjee, N., De, S., De, P., & Dhamale, K. (2012). Dynamic Source and Channel Rate Adaptation for Video Streaming over Wireless Fading Channels. *IEEE 14th International Conference on High Performance Computing and Communications,* 734 - 739.

Bao, X., Lin, Y., Lee, U., Rimac, I., & Choudhury, R. R. (2013). DataSpotting: Exploiting Naturally Clustered Mobile Devices to Offload Cellular Traffic. *Proceedings from INFOCOM'13:The IEEE International Conference on Computer Communication.*

Barbieri, A. G. (2012). Coordinated downlink multi-point communications in heterogeneous cellular networks.*Information Theory and Applications Workshop (ITA),* 7-16. doi:10.1109/ITA.2012.6181826

Bari, M. F., Chowdhury, S. R., Ahmed, R., & Boutaba, R. (2013). PolicyCop: An Autonomic QoS Policy Enforcement Framework for Software Defined Networks.*Proc. IEEE International Conference on SDN for Future Networks and Services (SDN4FNS),* 1-7. doi:10.1109/SDN4FNS.2013.6702548

Baron, L., Boubekeur, F., Klacza, R., Rahman, M. Y., Scognamiglio, C., Kurose, N., & Fdida, S. (2015, September). Demo: OneLab: Major Computer Networking Testbeds for IoT and Wireless Experimentation.*Proceedings of the 21st Annual International Conference on Mobile Computing and Networking,* 199-200. doi:10.1145/2789168.2789180

Bartelt, J., Fehske, A., Klessig, H., Fettweis, G., & Voigt, J. (2013). Joint bandwidth allocation and small cell switching in heterogeneous networks. *Proceedings from VTC'13 Fall: The IEEE 78th Vehicular Technology Conference.* doi:10.1109/VTCFall.2013.6692255

Basta, A., Kellerer, W., Hoffmann, M., Hoffmann, K., & Schmidt, E. D. (2013). A Virtual SDN-Enabled LTE EPC Architecture: A Case Study for S-/P-Gateways Functions.*Proc. IEEE Conference on SDN for Future Networks and Services (SDN4FNS),* 1-7. doi:10.1109/SDN4FNS.2013.6702532

Begen, A. C., Akgul, T., & Baugher, M. (2011). Watching video over the Web, Part I: Streaming protocols. *IEEE Internet Computing,* *15*(2), 54–63. doi:10.1109/MIC.2010.155

Ben-Shimol, Y., Kitroser, I., & Dinitz, Y. (n.d.). Two-dimensional mapping for wireless OFDMA system. *IEEE Transactions on Broadcasting,* *32*(3), 388–396.

Berde, P., Gerola, M., Hart, J., Higuchi, Y., Kobayashi, M., Koide, T., … Parulkar, G. (2014). ONOS: Towards an Open, Distributed SDN OS. *HotSDN.*

BFD. (2015). Retrieved from: https://tools.ietf.org/html/rfc5880

Bhattacharjee, S., Debroy, S., & Chatterjee, M. (2011) Trust computation through anomaly monitoring in distributed cognitive radio networks. *IEEE 22nd International Symposium on Personal, Indoor and Mobile Radio Communications,* 593–597.

Bhattacharjee, S., & Kwiat, K. (2013). Utilizing misleading information for cooperative spectrum sensing in cognitive radio networks.*IEEE International Conference on Communications (ICC).*2612–2616. doi:10.1109/ICC.2013.6654929

Bhattacharjee, S., Sengupta, S., & Chatterjee, M. (2013). Vulnerabilities in cognitive radio networks: A survey. *Computer Communications,* *36*(13). 1387–1398. doi:10.1016/j.comcom.2013.06.003

Biagioni, A., Fantacci, R., Marabissi, D., & Tarchi, D. (2009). Adaptive subcarrier allocation schemes for wireless OFD-MA systems in WiMAX networks. *IEEE Journal on Selected Areas in Communications*, 27(2), 217–225. doi:10.1109/JSAC.2009.090212

Bi, S., Ho, C., & Zhang, R. (2015). Wireless powered communication: Opportunities and challenges. *IEEE Communications Magazine*, 53(4), 117–125. doi:10.1109/MCOM.2015.7081084

Bjornson, E., Matthaiou, M., & Debbah, M. (2013). A new look at dual-hop relaying: Performance limits with hardware impairments. *IEEE Transactions on Communications*, 61(11), 4512–4525. doi:10.1109/TCOMM.2013.100913.130282

Björnson, E., Zetterberg, P., & Bengtsson, M. (2012, December). Optimal coordinated beamforming in the multicell downlink with transceiver impairments. In *Global Communications Conference (GLOBECOM)*, (pp. 4775-4780). IEEE. doi:10.1109/GLOCOM.2012.6503874

Blume, O., Eckhardt, H., Klein, S., Kuehn, E., & Wajda, W. M. (2010). Energy savings in mobile networks based on adaptation to traffic statistics. *Bell Labs Tech. J.*, 15(2), 7794. doi:10.1002/bltj.20442

Bouras, C., Konidaris, A., & Kostoulas, D. (2004). Predictive prefetching on the web and its potential impact in the wide area. *World Wide Web (Bussum)*, 7(2), 143–179. doi:10.1023/B:WWWJ.0000017208.87570.7a

Bousia, A., Kartsakli, E., Alonso, L., & Verikoukis, C. (2012b). Energy efficient base station maximization switch off scheme for LTE-Advanced. *Proceedings from CAMAD'12: The IEEE 17th International Workshop on Computer Aided Modeling and Design of Communication Links and Networks*.

Bousia, A., Kartsakli, E., Antonopoulos, A., Alonso, L., & Verikoukis, C. (2013). Energy Efficient Schemes for Base Station Management in 4G Broadband Systems. In Broadband Wireless Access Networks for 4G: Theory, Application and Experimentation. IGI Global.

Bousia, A., Kartsakli, E., Antonopoulos, A., Alonso, L., & Verikoukis, C. (2013). Game Theoretic Approach for Switching Off Base Stations in Multi-Operator Environments. *Proceedings from ICC'13:The IEEE International Communications Conference*. doi:10.1109/ICC.2013.6655262

Bousia, A., Kartsakli, E., Antonopoulos, A., Alonso, L., & Verikoukis, C. (2015). Game Theoretic Infrastructure Sharing in Wireless Networks with Two Operators. In *Game Theory Framework Applied to Wireless Communication Networks*. IGI Global. DOI: 10.4018/978-1-4666-8642-7

Bousia, A., Antonopoulos, A., Alonso, L., & Verikoukis, C. (2012). Green distance-aware base station sleeping algorithm in LTE-Advanced. *Proceedings from ICC'12:The IEEE International Conference on Communications*.

Bousia, A., Kartsakli, E., Alonso, L., & Verikoukis, C. (2012a). Dynamic energy efficient distance-aware base station switch on/off scheme for LTE-Advanced. *Proceedings from GLOBECOM'12:The IEEE Global Communications Conference*.

Bousia, A., Kartsakli, E., Antonopoulos, A., Alonso, L., & Verikoukis, C. (2014). Sharing the small cells for energy efficient networking: How much does it cost? *Proceedings from GLOBECOM'14:The IEEE Global Communications Conference*.

Bousia, A., Kartsakli, E., Antonopoulos, A., Alonso, L., & Verikoukis, C. (2015). Multiobjective Auction-based Switching Off Scheme in Heterogeneous Networks: To Bid or Not To Bid? *IEEE Transactions on Vehicular Technology*. doi:10.1109/TVT.2016.2517698

Bousia, A., Kartsakli, E., Antonopoulos, A., Alonso, L., & Verikoukis, C. (2015a). Game Theoretic Infrastructure Sharing in Multi-Operator Cellular Networks. *IEEE Transactions on Vehicular Technology*. doi:10.1109/TVT.2015.2445837

Boyd, S., & Vandenberghe, L. (2004). *Convex Optimization.* New York, NY: Cambridge University Press. doi:10.1017/CBO9780511804441

Buddhikot, M., Kolodzy, P., Miller, S.,Ryan, K., and Evans, J., (2005). Dimsumnet: new directions in wireless networking using coordinated dynamic spectrum. Proceedings from *World of Wireless Mobile and Multimedia Networks, WoWMoM*, 78–85.

Bykhovsky, D., & Arnon, S. (2014). Multiple Access Resource Allocation in Visible Light Communication Systems. *Journal of Lightwave Technology, 32*(8), 1594–1600. doi:10.1109/JLT.2014.2308282

Caesar, M., Caldwell, D., Feamster, N., Rexford, J., Shaikh, A., & Merwe, J. (2005). Design and implementation of a routing control platform. *NSDI.*

Cai, S., Xiao, L., Yang, H., Wang, J., & Zhou, S. (2013). A cross-layer optimization of the joint macro- and picocell deployment with sleep mode for green communications. *Proceedings from WOCC'13: The 22nd Wireless and Optical Communication Conference.*

Calvanese Strinati, E., & Greco, P. (2010). Green resource allocation for ofdma wireless cellular networks. In *Personal Indoor and Mobile Radio Communications (PIMRC).* IEEE 21st International Symposium on. doi:10.1109/PIMRC.2010.5671817

Casado, M., Foster, N., & Guha, A. (2014). Abstractions for Software-Defined Networks. *Communications of the ACM, 57*(10), 86–95. doi:10.1145/2661061.2661063

Casado, M., Freedman, M. J., Pettit, J., Luo, J., McKeown, N., & Shenker, S. (2007). *Ethane: Taking Control of the Enterprise.* SIGCOMM. doi:10.1145/1282380.1282382

Castro, M., Galluccio, L., Kassler, A., & Rametta, C. (2010, October). Opportunistic P2P Communications in Delay-Tolerant Rural Scenarios. *EURASIP Journal on Wireless Communications and Networking, 2011*(9).

Cerwall, P., & Jonsson, P. (2015). *Ericsson Mobility Report on the Pulse of the Networked Society.* Retrieved June 2015, from http://www.ericsson.com/res/docs/2015/ericsson-mobility-report-june-2015.pdf

Chandrasekhar, V., Andrews, J. G., & Gatherer, A. (2008). Femtocell networks: A survey. *IEEE Communications Magazine, 46*(9), 59–67. doi:10.1109/MCOM.2008.4623708

Chandrasekhar, V., Andrews, J. G., Muharemovict, T., Shen, Z., & Gatherer, A. (2009a). Power control in two-tier femtocell networks. *IEEE Transactions on Wireless Communications, 8*(8), 4316–4328. doi:10.1109/TWC.2009.081386

Chandrasekhar, V., Andrews, J. G., Shen, Z., Muharemovict, T., & Gatherer, A. (2009b). Distributed Power Control in Femtocell-Underlay Cellular Networks.*IEEE Global Telecommunications Conference*, 1-6. doi:10.1109/GLOCOM.2009.5425923

Chen, R., Park, J. M., & Bian, K. (2008). Robust distributed spectrum sensing in cognitive radio networks. *The 27th Conference on Computer Communications. IEEE, INFOCOM.*

Chen, Y., Farley, T., & Ye, N. (2004). Qos requirements of network applications on the internet. *Inf. Knowl. Syst. Manag., 4,* 5576. Available: http://portal.acm.org/citation. cfm?id=1234242.1234243

Chen, Y., Zhang, S., & Xu, S. (2010). Characterizing Energy Efficiency and Deployment Efficiency Relations for Green Architecture Design. *Proceedings from ICC'10 WORKSHOPS:The IEEE International Conference on Communications Workshops.* doi:10.1109/ICCW.2010.5503900

Cheng, G., Liu, W., Li, Y., & Cheng, W. (2007). Spectrum aware on-demand routing in cognitive radio networks. *2nd IEEE International Symposium on New Frontiers in Dynamic Spectrum Access Networks, DySPAN*, 571–574. doi:10.1109/DYSPAN.2007.80

Chen, T., Haesik, H., & Yang, Y. (2010). Energy efficiency metrics for green wireless communications. *Proceedings International Conference on Wireless Communications and Signal Processing (WCSP)*. doi:10.1109/WCSP.2010.5633634

Chowdhury, K. R., & Akyildiz, I. F. (2011). Crp: A routing protocol for cognitive radio ad hoc networks. *IEEE Journal on Selected Areas in Communications*, 29(4). 794–804. doi:10.1109/JSAC.2011.110411

Chowdhury, N., Rahman, M., & Boutaba, R. (2009). Virtual Network Embedding with Coordinated Node and Link Mapping. *Proc. 28th IEEE Conf. Computer Communications (INFOCOM 09)*, 783–791. doi:10.1109/INFCOM.2009.5061987

Cisco Systems. (2014). *Cisco Networking Index: Global Mobile Data Traffic Forecast Update, 2015–2020 white paper*. Retrieved from http://www.cisco.com/c/en/us/solutions/collateral/service-provider/visual-networking-index-vni/white_paper_c11-520862.html

Cisco. (2012). *Cisco Visual Networking Index: Global Mobile Data Traffic Forecast Update, 2011–2016*. Technical Report, Cisco Systems Inc.

Cisco. (2013). *Cisco Visual Networking Index: Forecast and Methodology, 2012–2017*. White Paper. Retrieved from: http://www.cisco.com/en/US/solutions/collateral/ns341/n s525/ns537/ns705/ns827/white_paper_c11-481360.pdf

Cisco. (2013). *Network Failure Detection*. Retrieved from: http://monsterdark.com/wp-content/uploads/Network-Failure-Detection.pdf

Cisco. (2015, February 03). *Cisco Visual Networking Index: Global Mobile Data Traffic Forecast Update, 2014-2019*. Retrieved from: http://www.cisco.com/c/en/us/solutions/collateral/service-provider/global-cloud-index-gci/Cloud_Index_White_Paper.pdf

Conroy, C. (2006). *Telecentre Initiatives in Rural India*. Natural Resources Institute, University of Greenwich.

Conroy, C. (2006). *Telecentre initiatives in rural india: Failed fad or the way forward?* Natural Resources Institute, University of Greenwich.

Conte, A. (2011). Cell wilting and blossoming for energy efficiency. *IEEE Wireless Communications*, 18(5), 50-57.

Contreras, L. M., Cominardi, L., Qian, H., & Bernardos, C. J. (2016). Software-Defined Mobility Management: Architecture Proposal and Future Directions. *Mobile Networks and Applications*, 21(2), 226–236. doi:10.1007/s11036-015-0663-7

Conway, K., Kalyanasundharam, N., Donley, G., Lepak, K., & Hughes, B. (2010). Cache hierarchy and memory subsystem of the and Opteron processor. *IEEE Micro*, 30(2), 16–29. doi:10.1109/MM.2010.31

Coon, J., Dettmann, C. P., & Georgiou, O. (2012). Full connectivity: Corners, edges and faces. *Journal of Statistical Physics*, 147(4), 758–778. doi:10.1007/s10955-012-0493-y

Correia, L. M., Zeller, D., Blume, O., Ferling, D., Jading, Y., Godor, I., & van der Perre, L. et al. (2010). Challanges and enabling technologies for energy aware mobile radio networks. *IEEE Communications Magazine*, 48(11), 6672. doi:10.1109/MCOM.2010.5621969

Cover, T., & Gamal, A. E. (1979). Capacity theorems for the relay channel. *IEEE Transactions on Information Theory*, 25(5), 572–584. doi:10.1109/TIT.1979.1056084

Cullen, J. (2008). *Radioframe presentation*. London, UK: Femtocell Europe.

Curtis, A. R. (2011). DevoFlow: Scaling Flow Management for High-Performance Networks.*Proc. ACM SIGCOMM*, 254–65. doi:10.1145/2018436.2018466

Cuthbertson, A. (2015). *LiFi internet: First real-world usage boasts speed 100 times faster than WiFi*. Academic Press.

Dahlman, E. (2008). *3G evolution: HSPA and LTE for mobile broadband*. Academic Press.

Dai, J., Liu, F., Li, B., Li, B., & Liu, J. (2012). Collaborative caching in wireless video streaming through resource auctions. *IEEE Journal on Selected Areas in Communications*, *30*(2), 458–466. doi:10.1109/JSAC.2012.120226

Damnjanovic, A., Montojo, J., Wei, Y., Ji, T., Luo, T., Vajapeyam, M., & Malladi, D. et al. (2011). A survey on 3GPP heterogeneous networks. *IEEE Wireless Communications*, *18*(3), 10–21. doi:10.1109/MWC.2011.5876496

Dasgupta, S., & Oliveira, J. (2007). Path-Computation-Element-Based Architecture for Interdomain MPLS/GMPLS Traffic Engineering: Overview and Performance. *IEEE Network*, *21*(4), 38–45. doi:10.1109/MNET.2007.386468

Dean, J., & Ghemawat, S. (2008). MapReduce: Simplified Data Processing on Large Clusters. *Communications of the ACM*, *52*(1), 107–113. doi:10.1145/1327452.1327492

Debroy, S., & Chatterjee, M. (2014). Spectrum map aided multi-channel multi-hop routing in distributed cognitive radio networks. *IEEE 25th Annual International Symposium on Personal, Indoor, and Mobile Radio Communication (PIMRC)*. 947–952.

Debroy, S., Bhattacharjee, S., & Chatterjee, M. (2016). *Spectrum map and its application in resource management in cognitive radio networks. IEEE Transactions on Cognitive Communications and Networking*.

Deb, S. M., Monogioudis, P., Miernik, J., & Seymour, J. P. (2014). Algorithms for enhanced inter-cell interference coordination (eICIC) in LTE HetNets. *IEEE/ACM Transactions on Networking*, *22*(1), 137–150. doi:10.1109/TNET.2013.2246820

Denkovski, D., Atanasovski, V., Gavrilovska, L., Riihijrvi, J., & Mhnen, P. (2012). Reliability of a radio environment map: Case of spatial interpolation techniques.*7th International ICST Conference on Cognitive Radio Oriented Wireless Networks and Communications (CROWNCOM)*.248–253. doi:10.4108/icst.crowncom.2012.248452

Denolle, M. A., Fan, W., & Shearer, P. M. (2015). Dynamics of the 2015 M7. 8 Nepal earthquake. *Geophysical Research Letters*, *42*(18), 7467–7475. doi:10.1002/2015GL065336

De, S., Saini, R., & Sharma, A. (2014, October). Source-aware adaptive power allocation in OFDM systems for rate constrained applications. *IEEE Communications Letters*, *18*(10), 1855–1858. doi:10.1109/LCOMM.2014.2358648

Desai, M., & Nandagopal, T. (2010). Coping with link failures in centralized control plane architectures.*Second International Conference on Communication Systems and Networks (COMSNETS)*, 1 –10. doi:10.1109/COMSNETS.2010.5431977

Dong, W., Rallapalli, S., Jana, R., Qiu, L., Ramakrishnan, K. K., Razoumov, L., & Won Cho, T. et al. (2013). iDEAL: Incentivized dynamic cellular offloading via auctions. *Proceedings from INFOCOM'13:The IEEE International Conference on Computer Communication*.

Doppler, K., Rinne, M., Wijting, C., Ribeiro, C. B., & Hugl, K. (2009). Device-to-device communication as an underlay to LTE-advanced networks. *IEEE Communications Magazine*, *47*(10), 42–49. doi:10.1109/MCOM.2009.5350367

Douros, V. G., Toumpis, S., & Polyzos, G. C. (2012). Power control under best response dynamics for interference mitigation in a two-tier femtocell network.*10th International Symposium on Modeling and Optimization in Mobile, Ad Hoc and Wireless Networks*, 398-405.

Dzulkhifli, N. F., Alsaqour, R., Alsaqour, O., Shaker, H., & Saeed, R. A. (2014). Network Services and Applications: Web Caching. *Middle-East Journal of Scientific Research*, *18*(10), 1517–1523.

Egilmez, H. E., Dane, S. T., Gorkemli, B., & Tekalp, A. M. (2012). OpenQoS: OpenFlow Controller Design and Test Network for Multimedia Delivery with end-to-end Quality of Service over Software Defined Networks.*Proc. APSIPA Annual Summit and Conference*, 1-8.

Etoh, M., Ohya, T., & Nakayama, T. (2008). Energy consumption issues on mobile network systems. *Proceedings of International Symposium on Applications and the Internet (SAINT)*, 365-368. doi:10.1109/SAINT.2008.84

Faint, S., Reten, O., & Willink, T. (2010). Impact of the number of sensors on the network cost and accuracy of the radio environment map.*23rd Canadian Conference on Electrical and Computer Engineering (CCECE)*.1–5. doi:10.1109/ CCECE.2010.5575188

Fall, K. (2003, August). A delay-tolerant network architecture for challenged internets.*Proceedings of ACM SIGCOMM*. doi:10.1145/863955.863960

Fan, X. C. (2007). An inter-cell interference coordination technique based on users' ratio and multi-level frequency allocations.*2007 International Conference on Wireless Communications, Networking and Mobile Computing*, 799-802. doi:10.1109/WICOM.2007.206

FCC. (2007). *FCC adopts rule for unlicensed use of television white spaces.* Retrieved from: http://www.fcc.gov/

Feamster, N., Balakrishnan, H., Rexford, J., Shaikh, A., & van der Merwe, J. (2004). *The case for separating routing from routers.* FDNA. doi:10.1145/1016707.1016709

Federal Communications Commission (FCC). (2004). *Notice of proposed rule making.* eT Docket no. 04113. FCC.

Fehske, A. J., Richter, F., & Fettweis, G. P. (2000). Energy efficiency improvements through micro sites in cellular mobile radio networks. *Proceeding from GLOBECOM'09 WORKSHOPS:The IEEE Global Telecommunications Conference Workshops.*

Floodlight - Open Source Software for Building Software-Defined Networks. (n.d.). Retrieved from http://www.tomsitpro. com/articles/open-source-cloud-computing-software,2-754-7.html

Forster, C., Dickie, I., Maile, G., Smith, H., & Crisp, M. (n.d.). *Understanding the Enviromental Impact of Communication Systems.* Ofcom Study Report. Available online: http://stakeholders.ofcom.org.uk/binaries/research/technology-research/environ.pdf

Frenger, P. (2011). Reducing Energy Consumption in LTE with Cell DTX. *IEEE 73rd Vehicular Technology Conference (VTC Spring)*, 1-5. doi:10.1109/VETECS.2011.5956235

Ganesan, G., & Li, Y. (2007). Cooperative spectrum sensing in cognitive radio, part I: Two user networks. *IEEE Transactions on Wireless Communications*, *6*(6). 2204–2213. doi:10.1109/TWC.2007.05775

Gao, L., Iosifidis, G., Jianwei, H., & Tassiulas, L. (2013). Economics of mobile data offloading. *Proceedings from INFOCOM'13:The IEEE International Conference on Computer Communication.*

Gao, N., & Wang, X. (2011). Optimal subcarrier-chunk scheduling for wireless OFDMA systems. *IEEE Transactions on Wireless Communications*, *10*(7), 2116–2123. doi:10.1109/TWC.2011.050511.100458

Ghasemi, A., & Sousa, E. (2005). Collaborative spectrum sensing for opportunistic access in fading environments.*IEEE International Symposium on New Frontiers in Dynamic Spectrum Access Networks, DySPAN*, 131–136. doi:10.1109/ DYSPAN.2005.1542627

Ghosh, A. R., Ratasuk, R., Mondal, B., Mangalvedhe, N., & Thomas, T. (2010). LTE-advanced: Next-generation wireless broadband technology. *IEEE Wireless Communications*, *17*(3), 10–22. doi:10.1109/MWC.2010.5490974

Global Action Plan. (2012). *Global Action Plan. Report*. Author.

GNU Radio. (n.d.). Retrieved from http://www.gnuradio.org/

Gollakota, S., Reynolds, M. S., Smith, J. R., & Wetherall, D. J. (2014). The emergence of RF-powered computing. *Computer*, *47*(1), 32–39. doi:10.1109/MC.2013.404

Google. (2015). *Google spectrum database*. Retrieved from: https://www.google.com/get/spectrumdatabase/

Gouache, S., Bichot, G., Bsila, A., & Howson, C. (2011). Distributed & adaptive HTTP streaming.*IEEE International Conference on Multimedia and Expo (ICME)*.

Guan, L., Zhang, J., Li, J., Liu, G., & Zhang, P. (2007, September). Spectral efficient frequency allocation scheme in multihop cellular network. In *2007 IEEE 66th Vehicular Technology Conference* (pp. 1446-1450). IEEE. doi:10.1109/VETECF.2007.308

Gündüz, D., Yener, A., Goldsmith, A., & Poor, H. V. (2013). The multiway relay channel. *IEEE Transactions on Information Theory*, *59*(1), 51–63. doi:10.1109/TIT.2012.2219156

Guo, Y., Kang, G., Zhang, N., Zhou, W., & Zhang, P. (2010). Outage performance of relay-assisted cognitive-radio system under spectrum-sharing constraints. *Electronics Letters*, *46*(2), 182–184. doi:10.1049/el.2010.2159

Gupta & Calvanese Strinati. (2012). Base-Station Duty-Cycling and Traffic Buffering as a Means to Achieve Green Communications. *2012 IEEE Vehicular Technology Conference (VTC Fall)*.

Gupta, H., Rao, N. P., Shashidhar, D., & Mallika, K. (2008). The Disastrous M 7.9 Sichuan Earthquake of 12 May 2008. *Journal of the Geological Society of India*, *72*, 325–330.

Gupta, P., Jagyasi, B., Panigrahi, B., Rath, H. K., Papulla, S., & Simha, A. (2015). A Revolutionary Rural Agricultural Participatory Sensing Approach Using Delay Tolerant Networks.*Proceedings of 18th IEEE International Symposium on Wireless Personal Multimedia (WPMC)*.

Guvenc, I. (2011). Capacity and fairness analysis of heterogeneous networks with range expansion and interference coordination. *IEEE Communications Letters*, *15*(10), 1084–1087. doi:10.1109/LCOMM.2011.082611.111387

Han, C., Harrold, T., Armour, S., Krikidis, I., Videv, S., Grant, P. M., & Hanzo, L. et al. (2011). Green radio: Radio techniques to enable energy-efficient wireless networks. *IEEE Communications Magazine*, *49*(6), 4654. doi:10.1109/MCOM.2011.5783984

Han, F., Safar, Z., & Ray Liu, K. J. (2013). Energy-Efficient Base-Station Cooperative Operation with Guaranteed QoS. *IEEE Transactions on Communications*, *61*(8), 3505–3517. doi:10.1109/TCOMM.2013.061913.120743

Harrold, T., Cepeda, R., & Beach, M. (2011). Long-term measurements of spectrum occupancy characteristics.*IEEE Symposium on New Frontiers in Dynamic Spectrum Access Networks, DySPAN*, 83–89.

Hasan, M. K., Saeed, R. A., Hashim, A.-H. A., Islam, S., Alsaqour, R. A., & Alahdal, T. A. (2012). Femtocell Network Time Synchronization Protocols and Schemes. *Research Journal of Applied Sciences Engineering and Technology*, *4*(23), 5136–5143.

Hasan, M., Hossain, E., & Kim, D. I. (2014). Resource Allocation Under Channel Uncertainties for Relay-Aided Device-to-Device Communication Underlaying LTE-A Cellular Networks. *IEEE Transactions on Wireless Communications*, *13*(4), 2322–2338. doi:10.1109/TWC.2014.031314.131651

Hasan, Z., Boostanimehr, H., & Bhargava, V. K. (2011, November). Green Cellular Networks, A Survey, Some Research Issuesand Challenges.*IEEE Communications Surveys and Tutorials*,*13*(4),524–540. doi:10.1109/SURV.2011.092311.00031

Hayajneh, M., & Abdallah, C. T. (2004). Distributed joint rate and power control game-theoretic algorithms for wireless data. *IEEE Communications Letters*, *8*(8), 511–513. doi:10.1109/LCOMM.2004.833817

Hinger, D., & Kalbande, D. (2014, April). Review of Mobile Data Offloading through Wi-Fi.*Proceedings of IEEE International Conference on Circuits, Systems, Communication and Information Technology Applications (CSCITA)*, 425–429. doi:10.1109/CSCITA.2014.6839298

Hirata, H., Totani, K., Maehata, T., Shimura, T., Take, M., Jurokawa, Y., & Hirata, Y. et al. (2010). *Development of high efficiency amplifier for cellular base stations*. SEI Tech. Rev.

Hoang, A. T., Liang, Y. C., Wong, D. T. C., Zeng, Y., & Zhang, R. (2009). Opportunistic spectrum access for energy-constrained cognitive radios. *IEEE Transactions on Wireless Communications*, *8*(3), 1206–1211. doi:10.1109/TWC.2009.080763

Hoang, D. T., Niyato, D., Wang, P., & Kim, D. I. (2014). Opportunistic channel access and RF energy harvesting in cognitive radio networks. *IEEE Journal on Selected Areas in Communications*, *32*(11), 2039–2052. doi:10.1109/JSAC.2014.141108

Holland, M. M., Aures, R. G., & Heinzelman, W. B. (2006, September). Experimental investigation of radio performance in wireless sensor networks. In Wireless Mesh Networks. *WiMesh 2006. 2nd IEEE Workshop on,* 140-150.

Hong, E. J., Yun, S. Y., & Cho, D. H. (2009). Decentralized power control scheme in femtocell networks: A game theoretic approach. *IEEE 20th International Symposium on Personal, Indoor and Mobile Radio Communications*, 415-419.

Hoydis, J. K. (2011, June). Outage performance of cooperative small-cell systems under Rician fading channels. *2011 IEEE 12th international workshop on signal processing advances in wireless communications*, 551-555.

Huang, K. (2013, June). Mobile ad hoc networks powered by energy harvesting: Battery-level dynamics and spatial throughput. In *2013 IEEE International Conference on Communications (ICC)* (pp. 3121-3125). IEEE.

Huang, K., & Lau, V. K. (2014). Enabling wireless power transfer in cellular networks: Architecture, modeling and deployment. *IEEE Transactions on Wireless Communications*, *13*(2), 902–912. doi:10.1109/TWC.2013.122313.130727

Huang, K., & Zhou, X. (2015). Cutting the last wires for mobile communications by microwave power transfer. *IEEE Communications Magazine*, *53*(6), 86–93. doi:10.1109/MCOM.2015.7120022

Hunter, T. E., Sanayei, S., & Nosratinia, A. (2006). Outage analysis of coded cooperation. *IEEE Transactions on Information Theory*, *52*(2), 375–391. doi:10.1109/TIT.2005.862084

I2RS. (2016). Retrieved from: http://datatracker.ietf.org/wg/i2rs/charter/

IEEE 802.22. (2011). *IEEE 802.22, working group on wireless regional area networks (WRAN)*. Retrieved from: http://grouper.ieee.org/groups/802/22

IEEE P802.22a/D2. (2013). *IEEE draft standard for wireless regional area networks part 22: Cognitive wireless ran medium access control (MAC) and physical layer (PHY) specifications: Policies and procedures for operation in the TV bands - Amendment: Management and control plane interfaces and procedures and enhancement to the management information base (MIB)*. IEEE.

IEEE. (2011). *IEEE 802.15 WPAN Task Group 7 (TG7) Visible Light Communication*. IEEE Standards Association. Retrieved 9 Dec 2011 from http://www.ieee802.org/15/pub/TG7.html

Internet Engineering Task Force (IETF). (2014). *Software-Defined Networking: A Perspective from within a Service Provider Environment*. IETF.

Ishimori, A., Faria, F., Furtado, I., Cerqueira, E., & Abelem, A. (2012). Automatic QoS Management on OpenFlow Software-Defined Networks.*Proc. API Software Defined Networking Event Demo.*

ITU Recommendation M.1225. (1997). *Guidelines for evaluation of radio transmission technologies for IMT-2000.* Author.

ITU. (2009). *Telecommunications Indicators Update 2009.* Available at: http://www.itu.int/ITU-D/ict/statistics/

Jagyasi B., Mohite J., & Pappula S. (2013, October). Applications of mobile sensing technologies in precision agriculture. *CSI Communications,* 22–24.

Jain, R., Chiu, D. M., & Hawe, W. R. (1984). *A quantitative measure of fairness and discrimination for resource allocation in shared computer system. Eastern Res. Lab.* Digital Equipment Corp.

Jammal, M., Singh, T., Shami, A., Asal, R., & Li, Y. (2014). Software defined networking: State of the art and research challenges. *Elsevier Computer Networks, 72,* 74–98. doi:10.1016/j.comnet.2014.07.004

Jang, J., & Lee, K. B. (2003). Transmit power adaptation for multiuser OFDM systems. *IEEE Journal on Selected Areas in Communications, 21*(2), 171–178. doi:10.1109/JSAC.2002.807348

Jeffrey, A., & Zwillinger, D. (Eds.). (2007). *Table of integrals, series, and products.* Academic Press.

Jeon, S.-W., Devroye, N., Vu, M., Chung, S.-Y., & Tarokh, V. (2011). Cognitive networks achieve throughput scaling of a homogeneous network. *IEEE Transactions on Information Theory, 57*(8). 5103–5115. doi:10.1109/TIT.2011.2158874

Jiang, D., Wang, H., Malkamaki, E., & Tuomaala, E. (2007). Principle and Performance of Semi-Persistent Scheduling for VoIP in LTE System. *International Conference on Wireless Communications, Networking and Mobile Computing, WiCom 2007,* 2861 - 2864. doi:10.1109/WICOM.2007.710

Jin, F., Li, X., Zhang, R., Dong, C., & Hanzo, L. (2016). Resource Allocation Under Delay-Guarantee Constraints for Visible-Light Communication. *IEEE Access, 99,* 1-12.

Jin, F., Zhang, R., & Hanzo, L. (2015). Resource Allocation Under Delay-Guarantee Constraints for Heterogeneous Visible-Light and RF Femtocell. *IEEE Transactions on Wireless Communications, 14*(2), 1020–1034. doi:10.1109/TWC.2014.2363451

Jin, X., Li, L. E., Vanbever, L., & Rexford, J. (2013). Softcell: Scalable and Flexible Cellular Core Network Architecture.*Proc. ACM conference on Emerging Networking Experiments and Technologies (CoNXT),* 1-13. doi:10.1145/2535372.2535377

Jones, C. G., Liu, R., Meyerovich, L., Asanovic, K., & Bod'ık, R. (2009). Parallelizing the web browser.*First USENIX Workshop on Hot Topics in Parallelism (HotPar '09).*

Kang, X., Zhang, R., & Motani, M. (2012). Price-Based Resource Allocation for Spectrum-Sharing Femtocell Networks: A Stackelberg Game Approach. *IEEE Journal on Selected Areas in Communications, 30*(3), 538–549. doi:10.1109/JSAC.2012.120404

Karvounas, D., Georgakopoulos, A., Tsagkaris, K., Stavroulaki, V., & Demestichas, P. (2014). Smart management of D2D constructs: An experiment-based approach. *IEEE Communications Magazine, 52*(4), 82–89. doi:10.1109/MCOM.2014.6807950

Katta, N. (2015). Ravana: Controller Fault-Tolerance in Software-Defined Networking.*Proceedings of the 1st ACM SIGCOMM Symposium on Software Defined Networking Research.* doi:10.1145/2774993.2774996

Kazemian, P., Varghese, G., & McKeown, N. (2012). Header Space Analysis: Static Checking For Networks.*Proceeding of ACM NSDI.*

Kempf, J., Bellagamba, E., Kern, A., Jocha, D., Takacs, A., & Skoldstrom, P. (2011), Scalable fault management for OpenFlow.*IEEE Int. Conf. on Communications (ICC)*, 6606–6610.

Kempf, J., Johansson, B., Pettersson, S., Luning, H., & Nilsson, T. (2012). Moving the Mobile Evolved Packet Core to the Cloud.*Proc. IEEE International Conference on Wireless and Mobile Computing, Networking and Communications (WiMob)*, 784-791. doi:10.1109/WiMOB.2012.6379165

Khan, F. (2009). *LTE for 4G Mobile Broadband Air Interface Technologies and Performance.* Cambridge University Press. doi:10.1017/CBO9780511810336

Kim, K. J., Duong, T. Q., Elkashlan, M., Yeoh, P. L., & Nallanathan, A. (2013, December). Two-way cognitive relay networks with multiple licensed users. In *2013 IEEE Global Communications Conference (GLOBECOM)* (pp. 992-997). IEEE.

Kivanc, D., Li, G., & Liu, H. (2003). Computationally efficient bandwidth allocation and power control for OFDMA. *IEEE Transactions on Wireless Communications, 2*(6), 1150–1158. doi:10.1109/TWC.2003.819016

Kobayashi, M., Seetharaman, S., Parulkar, G., Appenzeller, G., Little, J., Van Reijendam, J., & McKeown, N. et al. (2014). Maturing of OpenFlow and Software-defined Networking through deployments. *Elsevier Computer Networks, 61*, 151–175. doi:10.1016/j.bjp.2013.10.011

Koponen, T., Casado, M., Gude, N., Stribling, J., Poutievskiy, L., Zhuy, M., & Shenker, S. et al. (2010), Onix: A Distributed Control Platform for Large-scale Production Networks.*Proceedings of ACM OSDI.*

Kosta, C. H., Hunt, B., Quddus, A. U. I., & Tafazolli, R. (2013). On interference avoidance through inter-cell interference coordination (ICIC) based on OFDMA mobile systems. *IEEE Communications Surveys and Tutorials, 15*(3), 973–995. doi:10.1109/SURV.2012.121112.00037

Kotani, D. (2015). Fast Failure Detection of OpenFlow Channels.*Proceedings of the Asian Internet Engineering Conference AINTEC.* doi:10.1145/2837030.2837035

Krishna, V. (2010). *Auction Theory.* Academic Press.

Kumar, N., Zeadally, S., & Rodrigues, J. J. P. C. (2015). QoS-aware hierarchical web caching scheme for online video streaming applications in internet based vehicular ad hoc networks. *IEEE Transactions on Industrial Electronics, 62*(12), 7892–7900. doi:10.1109/TIE.2015.2425364

La Oliva, A. D., Bernardos, C. J., Calderon, M., Melia, T., & Zuniga, J. C. (2011). IP Flow Mobility: Smart Traffic Offload For Future Wireless Networks. *IEEE Communications Magazine, 49*(10), 124–132. doi:10.1109/MCOM.2011.6035826

Lakshman, T. V. (2004). The SoftRouter architecture. *HotNets-III.*

Lee, K., Rhee, I., Lee, J., Chong, S., Yi, Y., & Offloading, M. D. (2010). How Much Can WiFi Deliver? ACM CoNEXT 2010, Philadelphia, PA.

Lee, Yi, Chong, & Jin. (2012). *Economics of WiFi Offloading: Trading Delay for Cellular Capacity.* arXiv

Lee, B., Park, S. H., Shin, J., & Yang, S. (2014). IRIS: The OpenFlow-based Recursive SDN controller. *Proc. IEEE 16th International Conference on Advanced Communication Technology (ICACT)*, 1227-1231. doi:10.1109/ICACT.2014.6779154

Lee, J. W., Mazumdar, R. R., & Shroff, N. B. (2006). Joint Resource Allocation and Base-Station Assignment for the Downlink in CDMA Networks. *IEEE/ACM Transactions on Networking, 14*(1), 1–14. doi:10.1109/TNET.2005.863480

Lee, K., Lee, J., Yi, Y., Rhee, I., & Chong, S. (2013). Mobile Data Offloading: How Much Can WiFi Deliver. *IEEE/ACM Transactions on Networking, 21*(2), 536–550. doi:10.1109/TNET.2012.2218122

Lee, S., & Zhang, R. (2015). Cognitive wireless powered network: Spectrum sharing models and throughput maximization. *IEEE Transactions on Cognitive Communications and Networking*, *1*(3), 335–346. doi:10.1109/TCCN.2015.2508028

Le, L. B., Niyato, D., Hossain, E., Kim, D. I., & Hoang, D. T. (2013). QoS-Aware and Energy-Efficient Resource Management in OFDMA Femtocells. *IEEE Transactions on Wireless Communications*, *12*(1), 180–194. doi:10.1109/TWC.2012.120412.120141

Le, T., Mayaram, K., & Fiez, T. (2008). Efficient far-field radio frequency energy harvesting for passively powered sensor networks. *IEEE Journal of Solid-State Circuits*, *43*(5), 1287–1302. doi:10.1109/JSSC.2008.920318

Letaief, K. B., & Zhang, W. (2009). Cooperative communications for cognitive radio networks. *Proceedings of the IEEE*, *97*(5), 878–893. doi:10.1109/JPROC.2009.2015716

Li, P., Guo, S., Cheng, Z., & Vasilakos, A. V. (2013). Joint relay assignment and channel allocation for energy-efficient cooperative communications. Proceedings IEEE Wireless Communications and Networking Conference (WCNC), 626-630. doi:10.1109/WCNC.2013.6554636

Li, Y., Quang, T. T., Kawahara, Y., Asami, T., & Kusunoki, M. (2009). Building a spectrum map for future cognitive radio technology. *Proceedings of ACM workshop Cognitive radio networks,* 1–6. doi:10.1145/1614235.1614237

Li, C. Z. (2014). User-centric intercell interference coordination in small cell networks. *2014 IEEE International Conference on Communication*, 5747-5752. doi:10.1109/ICC.2014.6884238

Li, C. Z., Zhang, J., Haenggi, M., & Letaief, K. B. (2015). User-centric intercell interference nulling for downlink small cell networks. *IEEE Transactions on Communications*, *63*(4), 1419–1431. doi:10.1109/TCOMM.2015.2402121

Li, J., Matthaiou, M., & Svensson, T. (2014). I/Q imbalance in two-way AF relaying. *IEEE Transactions on Communications*, *62*(7), 2271–2285. doi:10.1109/TCOMM.2014.2325036

Li, L., Xu, C., & Tao, M. (2012). Resource Allocation in Open Access OFDMA Femtocell Networks. *IEEE Wireless Communications Letters*, *1*(6), 625–628. doi:10.1109/WCL.2012.091312.120394

Lim, J., & Kim, M. (2008). An Optimal Adaptation Framework for Streaming Multiple Video Objects. *IEEE Transactions on Circuits and Systems for Video Technology*, *18*(5), 699–703. doi:10.1109/TCSVT.2008.918847

Lin, Y.-D., & Hsu, Y.-C. (2000, March). Multihop cellular: a new architecture for wireless communications. *Proceedings of 19th IEEE INFOCOM*, *3*, 1273–1282.

Lin, S. C., & Chen, K. C. (2014). Spectrum-map-empowered opportunistic routing for cognitive radio ad hoc networks. *IEEE Transactions on Vehicular Technology*, *63*(6). 2848–2861. doi:10.1109/TVT.2013.2296597

Liu, K., & Lee, J. (2015). On Improving TCP Performance Over Mobile Data Networks. *IEEE Transactions on Mobile Computing*, (9), 1-14.

Liu, K., & Lee, J. Y. B. (2011). Mobile accelerator: A new approach to improve TCP performance in mobile data networks. *IEEE 7th International Wireless Communications and Mobile Computing Conference.*

Liu, Z & Ji, Y(2014). Intercell Interference Coordination under Data Rate Requirement Constraint in LTE-Advanced Heterogeneous Networks. *2014 IEEE 79th Vehicular Technology Conference (VTC Spring).* IEEE.

Liu, Z., Cheung, G., & Ji, Y. (2013). Optimizing distributed source coding for interactive multiview video streaming over lossy networks. IEEE Transactions on Circuits and Systems for Video Technology, 23(10), 1781-1794. doi:10.1109/TCSVT.2013.2269019

Liu, Z., Cheung, G., Chakareski, J. and Ji, Y., 2012, December. Multiple description coding of free viewpoint video for multi-path network streaming. In Global Communications Conference (GLOBECOM), 2012 IEEE (pp. 2150-2155). IEEE. doi:10.1109/GLOCOM.2012.6503434

Liu, Z., Cheung, G., Chakareski, J., & Ji, Y. (2015). Multiple description coding and recovery of free viewpoint video for wireless multi-path streaming. IEEE Journal of Selected Topics in Signal Processing, 9(1), 151-164. doi:10.1109/JSTSP.2014.2330332

Liu, A. L., Lau, V. K. N., Ruan, L., Chen, J., & Xiao, D. (2014). Hierarchical radio resource optimization for heterogeneous networks with enhanced inter-cell interference coordination (eICIC). *IEEE Transactions on Signal Processing*, *62*(7), 1684–1693. doi:10.1109/TSP.2014.2302748

Liu, D., Zheng, W., Zhang, H., Ma, W., & Wen, X. (2012). Energy efficient power optimization in two-tier femtocell networks with interference pricing.*8th International Conference on Computing and Networking Technology*, 247-252.

Liu, J., Zheng, W., Li, W., Wang, X., Xie, Y., & Wen, X. (2013). Distributed uplink power control for two-tier femtocell networks via convex pricing.*IEEE Wireless Communications and Networking Conference*, 458-463.

Liu, Y., & Dai, Y. (2014). On the complexity of joint subcarrier and power allocation for multi-user OFDMA systems. *IEEE Transactions on Signal Processing*, *62*(3), 583–596. doi:10.1109/TSP.2013.2293130

Liu, Z. F., Feng, J., Ji, Y., & Zhang, Y. (2014). EAF: Energy-aware adaptive free viewpoint video wireless transmission. *Journal of Network and Computer Applications*, *46*, 384–394. doi:10.1016/j.jnca.2014.07.010

Li, Y. N. (2012). *CoMP and interference coordination in heterogeneous network for LTE-advanced. 2012 IEEE Globecom Workshops*, 1107–1111. doi:10.1109/GLOCOMW.2012.6477733

Lohmar, T., Einarsson, T., Frojdh, P., Gabin, F., & Kampmann, M. (2011). Dynamic adaptive HTTP streaming of live content.*IEEE International Symposium on WoWMoM*. doi:10.1109/WoWMoM.2011.5986186

Loozen, T., Murdoch, R., & Orr, S. (2013). *Mobile web watch 2013 accenture*. Technical Report. Retrieved from: www.accenture.com

López-Pérez, D. (2011). Inter-cell interference coordination for expanded region picocells in heterogeneous networks. *2011 20th International Conference on Computer Communications and Networks (ICCCN)*. IEEE.

Lopez-Perez, D. G., Guvenc, I., & Chu, X. (2012). Mobility management challenges in 3GPP heterogeneous networks. *IEEE Communications Magazine*, *50*(12), 70–78. doi:10.1109/MCOM.2012.6384454

Lopez-Perez, D. G., Guvenc, I., de la Roche, G., Kountouris, M., Quek, T., & Zhang, J. (2011). Enhanced intercell interference coordination challenges in heterogeneous networks. *IEEE Wireless Communications*, *18*(3), 22–30. doi:10.1109/MWC.2011.5876497

Lorincz, Garma, & Petrovic. (2012). Measurements and Modelling of Base Station Power Consumption under Real Traffic Loads. *Sensors, 12*, 4281-4310. doi:10.3390/s120404281

Luo, W. J. (2013). An adaptive ABS-CoMP scheme in LTE-Advanced heterogeneous networks. *IEEE 24th Annual International Symposium on Personal, Indoor, and Mobile Radio Communications (PIMRC)*, 2769-2773.

Luo, S., Zhang, R., & Lim, T. J. (2013). Optimal save-then-transmit protocol for energy harvesting wireless transmitters. *IEEE Transactions on Wireless Communications*, *12*(3), 1196–1207. doi:10.1109/TWC.2013.012413.120488

Lu, Z., Sun, Y., Wen, X., Su, T., & Ling, D. (2012). An energy-efficient power control algorithm in femtocell networks.*7th International Conference on Computer Science & Education*, 395-400. doi:10.1109/ICCSE.2012.6295100

Makaya, C., & Pierre, S. (2008). An Analytical Framework for Performance Evaluation of IPv6-based Mobility Management Protocols. *IEEE Transactions on Wireless Communications*, 7(3), 972–983. doi:10.1109/TWC.2008.060725

Marsan, M. A., & Meo, M. (2013). Network sharing and its energy benefits: a study of European mobile network operators. *Proceedings from GLOBECOM'13: The IEEE Global Communications Conference*. doi:10.1109/GLOCOM.2013.6831460

Marsan, M. A., Chiaraviglio, L., Ciullo, D., & Meo, M. (2009). Optimal energy savings in cellular access networks. *Proceedings from ICC'09 WORKSHOPS: The IEEE International Conference on Communications Workshops*.

Mateos, G., Bazerque, J. A., & Giannakis, G. B. (2009). Spline-based spectrum cartography for cognitive radios. *Conference Record of the Forty-Third Asilomar Conference on Signals, Systems and Computers*, 1025–1029.

Matthaiou, M., Papadogiannis, A., Bjornson, E., & Debbah, M. (2013). Two-way relaying under the presence of relay transceiver hardware impairments. *IEEE Communications Letters*, 17(6), 1136–1139. doi:10.1109/LCOMM.2013.042313.130191

Ma, Y. (2008). Rate maximization for downlink OFDMA systems. *IEEE Transactions on Vehicular Technology*, 57(5), 3267–3274. doi:10.1109/TVT.2007.914054

Ma, Y., Lv, T., & Lu, Y. (2013). Efficient power control in heterogeneous Femto-Macro cell networks. *IEEE Wireless Communications and Networking Conference*, 4215-4219.

Medepally, B., & Mehta, N. B. (2010). Voluntary energy harvesting relays and selection in cooperative wireless networks. *IEEE Transactions on Wireless Communications*, 9(11), 3543–3553. doi:10.1109/TWC.2010.091510.100447

Meshkova, E., Ansari, J., Denkovski, D., Riihijarvi, J., Nasreddine, J., Pavloski, M., & Mhnen, P. et al. (2011). Experimental spectrum sensor testbed for constructing indoor radio environmental maps. *IEEE Symposium on New Frontiers in Dynamic Spectrum Access Networks (DySPAN)*. 603–607. doi:10.1109/DYSPAN.2011.5936253

Meyer, D. (2013). Standard: The Software-Defined-Networking Research Group. *IEEE Internet Computing*, 17(6), 84–87. doi:10.1109/MIC.2013.122

Mohanram, C., & Bhashyam, S. (2005). A sub-optimal joint subcarrier and power allocation algorithm for multiuser OFDM. *IEEE Communications Letters*, 9(8), 685–687. doi:10.1109/LCOMM.2005.1496582

Mondal, R. K., Chowdhury, M. Z., Saha, N., & Jang, Y. M. (2012). Interference-aware optical resource allocation in visible light communication. *International Conference on ICT Convergence*, 155-158. doi:10.1109/ICTC.2012.6386803

Moon, A. M. (2014). Cell Range Expansion and Time Partitioning for Enhanced Inter-cell Interference Coordination in Heterogeneous Network. *2014 47th Hawaii International Conference on System Sciences*, 5109-5113.

Moradi, M., Li, L. E., & Mao, Z. M. (2014). SoftMoW: A Dynamic and Scalable Software Defined Architecture for Cellular WANs. *Proc. ACM SIGCOMM Workshop on Hot Topics in Software Defined Networking (HotSDN)*, 1-2. doi:10.1145/2620728.2620763

Musku, M. R., Chronopoulos, A. T., Popescu, D. C., & Stefanescu, A. (2010). A game-theoretic approach to joint rate and power control for uplink CDMA communications. *IEEE Transactions on Communications*, 58(3), 923–932. doi:10.1109/TCOMM.2010.03.070205

Nasir, A. A., Zhou, X., Durrani, S., & Kennedy, R. A. (2013). Relaying protocols for wireless energy harvesting and information processing. *IEEE Transactions on Wireless Communications*, 12(7), 3622–3636. doi:10.1109/TWC.2013.062413.122042

Ndjiongue, A. R., Ferreira, H. C., Ngatched, T. M. N., & Webster, J. G. (2015). *Visible Light Communications (VLC) Technology*. John Wiley & Sons, Inc. doi:10.1002/047134608X.W8267

Ng, D. W. K., Lo, E. S., & Schober, R. (2013). Wireless information and power transfer: Energy efficiency optimization in OFDMA systems. *IEEE Transactions on Wireless Communications, 12*(12), 6352–6370. doi:10.1109/TWC.2013.103113.130470

Ngo, D. T., Khakurel, S., & Le-Ngoc, T. (2014). Joint Subchannel Assignment and Power Allocation for OFDMA Femtocell Networks. *IEEE Transactions on Wireless Communications, 13*(1), 342–355. doi:10.1109/TWC.2013.111313.130645

Ngo, D. T., Le, L. B., Le-Ngoc, T., Hossain, E., & Kim, D. I. (2012). Distributed Interference Management in Two-Tier CDMA Femtocell Networks. *IEEE Transactions on Wireless Communications, 11*(3), 979–989. doi:10.1109/TWC.2012.012712.110073

Nguyen, D. K., Matthaiou, M., Duong, T. Q., & Ochi, H. (2015, June). RF energy harvesting two-way cognitive DF relaying with transceiver impairments. In *2015 IEEE International Conference on Communication Workshop (ICCW)* (pp. 1970-1975). IEEE. doi:10.1109/ICCW.2015.7247469

Nguyen, T., Chowdhury, M. Z., & Jang, Y. M. (2013). A novel link switching scheme using pre-scanning and RSS prediction in visible light communication networks. *EURASIP Journal on Wireless Communications and Networking*, 1–17.

Nguyen, V., Do, T. X., & Kim, Y. (2016). SDN and virtualization-based LTE mobile network architectures: A comprehensive survey. *Wireless Personal Communications, 86*(38), 1401–1438. doi:10.1007/s11277-015-2997-7

Nguyen, V., & Kim, Y. (2015). Proposal and evaluation of SDN based mobile packet core networks. *EURASIP Journal on Wireless Communications and Networking, 172*, 1–18.

Nisan, N., & Ronen, A. (2007). Computationally Feasible VCG Mechanisms. *Journal of Artificial Intelligence Research, 29*(1), 19–47.

Nokia. (2015, February). *Nokia networks: Solutions*. Report. Retrieved from: http://networks.nokia.com/portfolio/solutions/heterogeneous-networks

Notebaert, S., De Cock, J., Beheydt, S., De Lameillieure, J., & Van de Walle, R. (2009). *Mixed architectures for H.264/AVC digital video translating*. Multimedia Tools and Application.

Nowoswiat, D., & Milliken, G. (2013). *Alcatel-Lucent: Managing the Signaling Traffic in Packet Core*. Retrieved from http://www2.alcatel-lucent.com/techzine/managing-lte-core-network-signaling-traffic/

NS-3 Network Simulator. (n.d.). Retrieved from http://www.nsnam.org

Nunes, B., Mendonca, M., Nguyen, X. N., Obraczka, K., & Turletti, T. (2014). A survey of software-defined networking: Past, present, and future of programmable networks. *IEEE Commun. Surveys Tuts., 16*(3), 1617–1634. doi:10.1109/SURV.2014.012214.00180

Oh, E., Krishnamachari, B., Liu, X., & Niu, Z. (2011). Toward dynamic energy-efficient operation of cellular network infrastructure. *IEEE Communications Magazine, 49*(6), 5661. doi:10.1109/MCOM.2011.5783985

Oh, E., Son, K., & Krishnamachari, B. (2013). Dynamic Base Station Switching-On/Off Strategies for Green Cellular Networks. *IEEE Transactions on Wireless Communications, 19*(5), 2126–2136. doi:10.1109/TWC.2013.032013.120494

Okino, K. N. (2011). Pico cell range expansion with interference mitigation toward LTE-Advanced heterogeneous networks. *2011 IEEE International Conference on Communications Workshops (ICC)*, 1-5. doi:10.1109/iccw.2011.5963603

ONF. (2011). *Software-Defined Networking: The New Norm for Networks*. White Paper. Retrieved from: https://www.opennetworking.org/images/stories/downloads/whitepapers/ wp-sdn-newnorm.pdf

Open Networking Foundation. (2012). *Software-Defined Networking: The New Norm for Networks.* Retrieved from https://www.opennetworking.org/images/stories/downloads/sdn-resources/white-papers/wp-sdn-newnorm.pdf

Open Networking Foundation. (2014). *OpenFlow specifications.* Retrieved from https://www.opennetworking.org/images/stories/downloads/sdn-resources/onf-specifications/openflow/openflow-switch-v1.3.4.pdf

Open Networking Foundation. (2015). *OpenFlow Switch Specification Version 1.5.1.* Author.

Open Networking Foundation. (n.d.). Retrieved from https://www.opennetworking.org/

Open vSwitch. (n.d.). Retrieved from http://openvswitch.org

OpenLTE. (n.d.). *An open source 3GPP LTE implementation.* Retrieved from http://openlte.sourceforge.net

Padma, V., & Yogesh, P. (2015), Proactive Failure Recovery in OpenFlow Based Software Defined Networks. *3rd International Conference on Signal Processing, Communication and Networking (ICSCN).* doi:10.1109/ICSCN.2015.7219846

Panigrahi, B., Sharma, A., & De, S. (2012). Interference aware power controlled forwarding for lifetime maximisation of wireless ad hoc networks. *IET Wireless Sensor Systems, 2*(1), 22-30.

Panigrahi, B., Ramamohan, R., Rath, H. K., & Simha, A. (2015, December). Efficient Device-to-Device (D2D) Offloading Mechanism in LTE Networks. *Proceedings of 18th IEEE International Symposium on Wireless Personal Multimedia (WPMC).*

Panigrahi, B., Rath, H. K., & Simha, A. (2015, February). Interference-aware Discovery and Optimal Uplink Scheduling for D2D Communication in LTE Networks. *Proceedings of 21st IEEE National Conference on Communication (NCC).* doi:10.1109/NCC.2015.7084877

Paradiso, J. A., & Starner, T. (2005). Energy scavenging for mobile and wireless electronics. *IEEE Pervasive Computing / IEEE Computer Society [and] IEEE Communications Society, 4*(1), 18–27. doi:10.1109/MPRV.2005.9

Paris, S., Martignon, F., Filippini, I., & Chen, L. (2013). A bandwidth trading marketplace for mobile data offloading. *Proceedings from INFOCOM'13: The IEEE Conference on Computer Communications.* doi:10.1109/INFCOM.2013.6566809

Phillips, C., Ton, M., Sicker, D., & Grunwald, D. (2012). Practical radio environment mapping with geostatistics. *IEEE International Symposium on Dynamic Spectrum Access Networks (DYSPAN).* 422–433. doi:10.1109/DYSPAN.2012.6478166

Pinola, J., Perala, J., Jurmu, P., Katz, M., Salonen, S., Piisilä, J., & Tuuttila, P. et al. (2013). A systematic and flexible approach for testing future mobile networks by exploiting a wrap-around testing methodology. *IEEE Communications Magazine, 51*(3), 160–167. doi:10.1109/MCOM.2013.6476882

Pokhariyal, A., Kolding, T., & Mogensen, P. (2006). Performance of downlink frequency domain packet scheduling for the UTRAN long term evolution. *Personal, Indoor and Mobile Radio Communications, 2006 IEEE 17th International Symposium on,* 1-5. doi:10.1109/PIMRC.2006.254113

Prasad. (2013). *Energy-Efficient Flexible Inter-Frequency Scanning Mechanism for Enhanced Small Cell Discovery.* IEEE VTC, Dresden, Germany.

Prasad, A., Tirkkonen, O., Lundén, P., Yilmaz, O., Dalsgaard, L., & Wijting, C. (2013, May). Energy Efficient Inter-Frequency Small Cell Discovery Techniques for LTE-Advanced Heterogeneous Network Deployments. *IEEE Communications Magazine, 51*(5), 72–81. doi:10.1109/MCOM.2013.6515049

Qi, J., & Aissa, S. (2012). On the power amplifier nonlinearity in MIMO transmit beamforming systems. *IEEE Transactions on Communications, 60*(3), 876–887. doi:10.1109/TCOMM.2012.021712.110006

Qi, J., Aissa, S., & Alouini, M. S. (2012, April). Analysis and compensation of I/Q imbalance in amplify-and-forward cooperative systems. In *2012 IEEE Wireless Communications and Networking Conference (WCNC)* (pp. 215-220). IEEE. doi:10.1109/WCNC.2012.6214150

Raghunathan, V., Ganeriwal, S., & Srivastava, M. (2006). Emerging techniques for long lived wireless sensor networks. *IEEE Communications Magazine, 44*(4), 108–114. doi:10.1109/MCOM.2006.1632657

Rahaim, M. B., Vegni, A. M., & Little, T. D. C. (2011). A hybrid Radio Frequency and broadcast Visible Light Communication system. *IEEE GLOBECOM Workshops*, 792-796.

Rawat, A. S., Anand, P., Chen, H., & Varshney, P. K. (2011). Collaborative spectrum sensing in the presence of byzantine attacks in cognitive radio networks. *IEEE Transactions on Signal Processing, 59*(2). 774–786. doi:10.1109/TSP.2010.2091277

Rebecchi, F., Dias de Amorim, M., Conan, V., Passarella, A., Bruno, R., & Conti, M. (2015). Data Offloading Techniques in Cellular Networks: A Survey. IEEE Communications Surveys & Tutorials, 17(2), 580-603.

Rhee, W., & Cioffi, J. M. (2000). Increase in capacity of multiuser OFDM system using dynamic subchannel allocation. *Proc. IEEE VTC 2000-Spring, 2*, 1085–1089. doi:10.1109/VETECS.2000.851292

Richter, F., Fehske, A. J., & Fettweis, G. P. (2009). Energy efficiency aspects of base station deployment strategies for cellular networks. *Proceedings from VTC'09 Fall: The IEEE 70th Vehicular Technology Conference Fall*. doi:10.1109/VETECF.2009.5379031

Riihijarvi, J., & Mahonen, P. (2008). Exploiting spatial statistics of primary and secondary users towards improved cognitive radio networks. *Cognitive Radio Oriented Wireless Networks and Communications, CrownCom*, 1 –7.

Riihijarvi, J., Mahonen, P., Wellens, M., & Gordziel, M. (2008). Characterization and modelling of spectrum for dynamic spectrum access with spatial statistics and random fields.*IEEE19th International Symposium on Personal, Indoor and Mobile Radio Communications, PIMRC*, 1 –6. doi:10.1109/PIMRC.2008.4699912

Romero, L. R. (2011). *A dynamic adaptive HTTP streaming video service for Google Android* (M.S. Thesis). Royal Institute of Technology (KTH), Stockholm, Sweden.

Rothenberg, C. E. (2012). Revisiting Routing Control Platforms with the Eyes and Muscles of Software-Defined Networking. *ACM HotSDN*, 13-18.

Roy, S. N. (2008). Energy logic: A road map to reducing energy consumption in telecommunications networks. In *Proceedings of Emerson Network Power*. IEEE 30th Telecommunications Energy Conference (INTELEC), San Diego, CA. doi:10.1109/INTLEC.2008.4664025

Sadr, S., Anpalagan, A., & Raahemifar, K. (2009). Suboptimal rate adaptive resource allocation for downlink OFDMA systems. *International Journal of Vehicular Technology, 2009*, 1–10. doi:10.1155/2009/891367

Saha, N., Mondal, R. K., Ifthekhar, M. S., & Jang, Y. M. (2014). Dynamic resource allocation for visible light based wireless sensor network.*International Conference on Information Networking*, 75-78. doi:10.1109/ICOIN.2014.6799668

Saha, N., Mondal, R. K., & Jang, Y. M. (2013). Adaptive Bandwidth Allocation for QoS Guaranteed VLC Based WPAN. *The Journal of Korean Institute of Communications and Information Science, 38C*(8), 719–724. doi:10.7840/kics.2013.38C.8.719

Saha, N., Mondal, R. K., & Jang, Y. M. (2013). Opportunistic channel reuse for a self-organized visible light communication personal area network.*Fifth International Conference on Ubiquitous and Future Networks*, 131-134. doi:10.1109/ICUFN.2013.6614796

Saini, R., & De, S. (2014). Subcarrier based resource allocation. *Proc. Nat. Conf. Commun.*, 1-6.

Salati, A. H., Nasiri-kenari, M., & Sadeghi, P. (2012). Distributed subband, rate and power allocation in OFDMA based two-tier femtocell networks using Fractional Frequency Reuse.*IEEE Wireless Communications and Networking Conference*, 2626-2630. doi:10.1109/WCNC.2012.6214243

Sama, M. R., Said, S., Hadj, B., Guillouard, K., & Suciu, L. (2014). Enabling Network Programmability in LTE/EPC Architecture Using OpenFlow. *Proc. 12th International Symposium on Modeling and Optimization in Mobile, Ad Hoc, and Wireless Networks (WiOpt)*, 389-396. doi:10.1109/WIOPT.2014.6850324

Sankaran. (2012). Data Offloading Techniques in 3GPP Rel-10 Networks: A Tutorial. *IEEE Communications Magazine, 50*(6), 46-53.

Saraydar, C. U., Mandayam, N. B., & Goodman, D. J. (2002). Efficient power control via pricing in wireless data networks. *IEEE Transactions on Communications, 50*(2), 291–303. doi:10.1109/26.983324

Savic, Z. (2011). *LTE Design and Deployment Strategies* [Power Point slides]. Retrieved from http://www.cisco.com/web/ME/expo2011/saudiarabia/pdfs/LTE_Design_and_Deployment_Strategies-Zeljko_Savic.pdf

Sawaragi, Y., Hirotaka, I., & Tanino, T. (1985). Theory of Multiobjective Optimization. Academic Press, Inc. Retrieved from www.smallcellforum.org

Schenk, T. (2008). *RF imperfections in high-rate wireless systems: impact and digital compensation.* Springer Science & Business Media. doi:10.1007/978-1-4020-6903-1

Schonwalder, J., Fouquet, M., Rodosek, G., & Hochstatter, I. (2009). Future Internet = Content + Services + Management. *IEEE Communications Magazine, 47*(7), 27–33. doi:10.1109/MCOM.2009.5183469

Schwartz & Johansson. (2012). *Wireless 2020, Carrier WiFi Offload, Building a Business Case for Carrier WiFi offload.* Academic Press.

Schwarz, H., Marpe, D., & Wiegand, T. (2007). Overview of the Scalable Video Coding Extension of the H. 264/AVC Standard. *IEEE Transactions on Circuits and Systems for Video Technology, 17*(9), 1103–1120. doi:10.1109/TCSVT.2007.905532

Scott, R. C., Wundsam, A., Zarifis, K., & Shenker, S. (2012). *What, Where, and When: Software Fault Localization for SDN.* Technical Report No. UCB/EECS-2012-178.

Scott, C., Wundsam, A., Raghavan, B., Panda, A., Or, A., Lai, J., & Shenker, S. et al. (2014). *Troubleshooting Blackbox SDN Control Software with Minimal Causal Sequences.* SIGCOMM. doi:10.1145/2619239.2626304

Seah, W. K., Eu, Z. A., & Tan, H. P. (2009, May). Wireless sensor networks powered by ambient energy harvesting (WSN-HEAP)-Survey and challenges. In *Wireless Communication, Vehicular Technology, Information Theory and Aerospace & Electronics Systems Technology, 2009. Wireless VITAE 2009. 1st International Conference on* (pp. 1-5). IEEE.

Senan, S. H., Abdella, A. H., Zeki, A. M., Saeed, R. A., Hameed, S. A., & Daoud, J. I. (2012). A framework of a route optimization scheme for nested mobile network. Lecture Notes in Computer Science, 7667, 689-696.

Sgambelluri, A., Giorgetti, A., Cugini, F., Paolucci, F., & Castoldi, P. (2013). OpenFlow-Based Segment Protection in Ethernet Networks. *Journal of Optical Communications and Networking, 5*(9), 1066–1075. doi:10.1364/JOCN.5.001066

Shannon, C. E. (2001). A mathematical theory of communication. *SIGMOBILE Mob. Comput. Commun., 5*(1). 3–55. doi:10.1145/584091.584093

Shared Spectrum Company. (2007). *Spectrum Occupancy Measurements Loring Commerce Centre Limestone, Maine.* Retrieved from: http://www.sharedspectrum.com/papers/spectrum-reports/

Sharma, A., De, S., Gupta, H. M., & Gangopadhyay, R. (2014). Multiple description transform coded transmission over OFDM broadcast channels. *Elsevier Physical Commun., 12*, 79–92. doi:10.1016/j.phycom.2014.05.001

Sharma, S., Staessens, D., Colle, D., Pickavet, M., & Demeester, P. (2011). Software Defined Networking: Meeting Carrier Grade Requirements.*Proceedings of 18th IEEE Workshop on Local Metropolitan Area Networks*, 1–6.

Sharma, S., Staessens, D., Colle, D., Pickavet, M., & Demeester, P. (2013). OpenFlow: Meeting Carrier-Grade Recovery Requirements. *Journal of Computer Communications, 36*(6), 656–665. doi:10.1016/j.comcom.2012.09.011

Shen, Z. J., Andrews, G., & Evans, B. L. (2003). Optimal power allocation in multiuser OFDM systems. *Proc. IEEE Globecom*, 337–341.

Shen, Z., Andrews, J. G., & Evans, B. L. (2005). Adaptive resource allocation in multiuser OFDM systems with proportional rate constraints.*IEEE Transactions on Wireless Communications, 4*(6), 2726–2736. doi:10.1109/TWC.2005.858010

Shi, Q., Liu, L., Xu, W., & Zhang, R. (2014). Joint transmit beamforming and receive power splitting for MISO SWIPT systems. *IEEE Transactions on Wireless Communications, 13*(6), 3269–3280. doi:10.1109/TWC.2014.041714.131688

Singh, V. K., Chawla, H., & Bohara, V. A. (2016). *A Proof-of-Concept Device-to-Device Communication Testbed.* arXiv preprint arXiv:1601.01398

Singhal, C., De, S., Trestian, R., & Muntean, G.-M. (2014). Joint Optimization of User-Experience and Energy-Efficiency in Wireless Multimedia Broadcast.*IEEE Transactions on Mobile Computing, 13*(7), 1522–1535. doi:10.1109/TMC.2013.138

Singhal, C., Kumar, S., De, S., Panwar, N., Tonde, R., & De, P. (2014). Class-based shared resource allocation for cell-edge users in OFDMA networks. *IEEE Transactions on Mobile Computing, 13*(1), 48–60. doi:10.1109/TMC.2012.210

Smith, J. R. (Ed.). (2013). *Wirelessly Powered Sensor Networks and Computational RFID.* Springer Science & Business Media. doi:10.1007/978-1-4419-6166-2

Soh, Y. S., Quek, T. Q. S., Kountouris, M., & Shin, H. (2013). Energy efficient heterogeneous cellular networks. *IEEE Journal on Selected Areas in Communications, 31*(5), 840–850. doi:10.1109/JSAC.2013.130503

Song, G., & Li, Y. G. (2003). Adaptive subcarrier and power allocation in OFDM based on maximizing utility. *Proc. IEEE VTC 2003-Spring, 2*, 905–909.

Song, G., & Li, Y. G. (2005). Cross-layer optimization for OFDM wireless networks, Part I: Theoretical framework. *IEEE Transactions on Wireless Communications, 4*(2), 614–624. doi:10.1109/TWC.2004.843065

Song, G., & Li, Y. G. (2005). Cross-layer optimization for OFDM wireless networks, Part II: Algorithm development. *IEEE Transactions on Wireless Communications, 4*(2), 625–634. doi:10.1109/TWC.2004.843067

Stefan, I., & Haas, H. (2013). Analysis of Optimal Placement of LED Arrays for Visible Light Communication. *IEEE 77th Vehicular Technology Conference*, 1-5.

Stefan, I., Burchardt, H., & Haas, H. (2013). Area spectral efficiency performance comparison between VLC and RF femtocell networks.*IEEE International Conference on Communications*, 3825-3829. doi:10.1109/ICC.2013.6655152

Stockhammer, T. (2011). Dynamic adaptive streaming over HTTP – standards and design principles. ACM MMSys.

Su, T., Zheng, W., Li, W., Ling, D., & Wen, X. (2012). Energy-efficient power optimization with Pareto improvement in two-tier femtocell networks. *IEEE 23rd International Symposium on Personal Indoor and Mobile Radio Communications, 2512-2517.*

Sudevalayam, S., & Kulkarni, P. (2011). Energy harvesting sensor nodes: Survey and implications. *IEEE Communications Surveys and Tutorials, 13*(3), 443–461. doi:10.1109/SURV.2011.060710.00094

Sugano, M., Kawazoe, T., Ohta, Y., & Murata, M. (2006). Indoor localization system using RSSI measurement of wireless sensor network based on ZigBee standard. *Target, 538, 050.*

Suh, Y. H., & Chang, K. (2002). A high-efficiency dual-frequency rectenna for 2.45-and 5.8-GHz wireless power transmission. *IEEE Transactions on Microwave Theory and Techniques, 50*(7), 1784–1789. doi:10.1109/TMTT.2002.800430

Sultan, A. (2012). Sensing and transmit energy optimization for an energy harvesting cognitive radio. *IEEE Wireless Communications Letters, 1*(5), 500-503.

Sun, G., & Van de Beek, J. (2010). Simple distributed interference source localization for radio environment mapping. *Wireless Days (WD).* 1–5.

Sun, S., Gong, L., Rong, B., & Lu, K. (2015). An Intelligent SDN Framework for 5G Heterogeneous Networks. *IEEE Communications Magazine, 53*(11), 142–147. doi:10.1109/MCOM.2015.7321983

Tavakkoli, A. (2009), Applying NOX to the Datacenter.*Proc. ACM HotNets-VIII Workshop.*

Thang, T. C., Ho, Q.-D., Kang, J. W., & Pham, A. T. (2012). Adaptive streaming of audiovisual content using MPEG DASH. *IEEE Transactions on Consumer Electronics, 58*(1), 78–85. doi:10.1109/TCE.2012.6170058

Thang, T. C., Le, H. T., Nguyen, H. X., Pham, A. T., Kang, J. W., & Ro, Y. M. (2013). Adaptive video streaming over HTTP with dynamic resource estimation. *Journal of Communication and Networks, 15*(6), 635–644. doi:10.1109/JCN.2013.000112

Tootoonchian. (2012). On Controller Performance in Software-Defined Networks. *Proc. USENIX Hot-ICE.*

Traffic Offloading onto WiFi Direct. (2013). *Wireless Communications and Networking Conference Workshops (WCNCW),* 135-140.

Tsiropoulou, E. E., Gialagkolidis, I., Vamvakas, P., & Papavassiliou, S. (2016). Resource Allocation in Visible Light Communication Networks: NOMA vs OFDMA Transmission Techniques. *Ad-hoc, Mobile, and Wireless Networks, 9724,* 32-46.

Tsiropoulou, E. E., Katsinis, G. K., Filios, A., & Papavassiliou, S. (2014). On the Problem of Optimal Cell Selection and Uplink Power Control in Open Access Multi-service Two-Tier Femtocell Networks. *ADHOC-NOW,* 114-127.

Tsiropoulou, E. E., Katsinis, G. K., Vamvakas, P., & Papavassiliou, S. (2013). Efficient uplink power control in multiservice two-tier femtocell networks via a game theoretic approach. *IEEE 18th International Workshop on Computer Aided Modeling and Design of Communication Links and Networks,* 104-108.

Tsiropoulou, E. E., Vamvakas, P., Katsinis, G. K., & Papavassiliou, S. (2015). Combined power and rate allocation in self-optimized multi-service two-tier femtocell networks. *Computer Communications, 72,* 38–48. doi:10.1016/j.comcom.2015.05.012

Tsonev, D., Sinanovic, S., & Haas, H. (2013). Practical MIMO Capacity for Indoor Optical Wireless Communication with White LEDs. *IEEE 77th Vehicular Technology Conference,* 1-5.

Usman, M., & Koo, I. (2014). Access strategy for hybrid underlay-overlay cognitive radios with energy harvesting. *IEEE Sensors Journal*, *14*(9), 3164–3173. doi:10.1109/JSEN.2014.2324565

Van Adrichem, N. L. M. (2014). *Fast Recovery in Software-Defined Networks*. EWSDN. doi:10.1109/EWSDN.2014.13

Varis, N., Manner, J., & Heinonen, J. (2011). A Layer-2 Approach for Mobility and Transport in the Mobile Backhaul. *Proc. International Conference on ITS Telecommunications (ITST)*, 268-273. doi:10.1109/ITST.2011.6060066

Visotsky, E., Kuffner, S., & Peterson, R. (2005). On collaborative detection of tv transmissions in support of dynamic spectrum sharing.*IEEE International Symposium on New Frontiers in Dynamic Spectrum Access Networks, DySPAN*, 338–345. doi:10.1109/DYSPAN.2005.1542650

Vodafone Group. (2012). *Sustainability report: Environmental footprint - performance data*. Technical Report. Retrieved from: http://www.vodafone.com/content/index/about/sustainability/sustainabilityreport/issuebyissue/environmentalfootprint/ performancedata.html

Wali, P., & Das, D. (2015). PS-SPS: Power saving-semi persistent schedulr for VoLTE in LTE-Advanced. *2015 IEEE International Conference on Electronics, Computing and Communication Technologies (CONECCT)*. doi:10.1109/CONECCT.2015.7383916

Wang, H., Kong, J., Guo, Y., & Chen, X. (2013). Mobile Web Browser Optimizations in the Cloud Era: A Survey. *IEEE 7th International Symposium on Service Oriented System Engineering (SOSE)*.

Wang, J. S. (2012). Enhanced dynamic inter-cell interference coordination schemes for LTE-advanced. *2012 IEEE 75th Vehicular Technology Conference (VTC Spring)*, 1-6.

Wang, M., & Yan, Z. (2015). Security in D2D Communications: A Review. Trustcom/BigDataSE/ISPA, 2015 IEEE, 1199-1204.

Wang, Sheng, Zhang, & Jiang. (2013). *IM-Torch: Interference Mitigation via Traffic Offloading in Macro/Femto-cell+WiFi HetNets*. 24th IEEE PIMRC, London, UK.

Wang, Y. (2012, May). Performance analysis of enhanced inter-cell interference coordination in LTE-Advanced heterogeneous networks. *2012 IEEE 75th Vehicular Technology Conference (VTC Spring)*, 1-5.

Wang, Y., Videv, S., & Haas, H. (2015). Dynamic load balancing with handover in hybrid Li-Fi and Wi-Fi networks. *IEEE 25th Annual International Symposium on Personal, Indoor, and Mobile Radio Communication*, 575-579.

Wang, C. X., Haider, F., Gao, X., You, X.-H., Yang, Y., Yuan, D., & Hepsaydir, E. et al. (2014). Cellular architecture and key technologies for 5G wireless communication networks. *IEEE Communications Magazine*, *52*(2), 122–130. doi:10.1109/MCOM.2014.6736752

Wang, Y., Kim, J.-G., Chang, S.-F., & Kim, H.-M. (2007). Utility-Based Vid Adaptation for Universal Multimedia Access (UMA) and Content-Based Utility Function Prediction for Real-Time Video Transcoding. *IEEE Transactions on Multimedia*, *9*(2), 213–220. doi:10.1109/TMM.2006.886253

Wang, Z., Lin, F. X., Zhong, L., & Chishtie, M. (2011). Why are web browsers slow on smartphones?*Proceedings of the 12th Workshop on Mobile Computing Systems and Applications (HotMobile '11)*, 91–96. doi:10.1145/2184489.2184508

Wang, Z., Lin, F. X., Zhong, L., & Chishtie, M. (2012). How far can client-only solutions go for mobile browser speed?*Proceedings of the 21st international conference on World Wide Web (WWW '12)*, 31–40. doi:10.1145/2187836.2187842

Wei, Z., Zhang, Q., Feng, Z., Li, W., & Gulliver, T. A. (2013). On the construction of radio environment maps for cognitive radio networks.*IEEE Wireless Communications and Networking Conference (WCNC).*4504–4509. doi:10.1109/WCNC.2013.6555304

Wickboldt, J. A., de Jesus, W. P., Isolani, P. H., Bonato Both, C., Rochol, J., & Granville, L. Z. (2015). Software-Defined Networking: Management Requirements and Challenges. *IEEE Communications Magazine, 53*(1), 278–285. doi:10.1109/MCOM.2015.7010546

Wilson, C. (2011), Better Never than Late: Meeting Deadlines in Datacenter Networks.*Proc. ACM SIGCOMM*, 50–61. doi:10.1145/2018436.2018443

Wong, C. Y., Cheng, R. S., Letaief, K. B., & Murch, R. D. (1999). Multiuser OFDM with adaptive subcarrier, bit, and power allocation. *IEEE Journal on Selected Areas in Communications, 17*(10), 1747–1758. doi:10.1109/49.793310

Wong, I. C., Shen, Z., Evans, B. L., & Andrews, J. G. (2004). A low complexity algorithm for proportional resource allocation in OFDMA systems. *Proc. IEEE Wksp. Sig. Proc. Sys. Design and Implementation.* doi:10.1109/SIPS.2004.1363015

Wu, H., Qiao, C., De, S., & Tonguz, O. (2001, October). Integrated cellular and ad hoc relaying systems: ICAR. *IEEE Journal on Selected Areas in Communications, 19*(10), 2105–2115.

Wu, D., Hou, Y. T., Zhu, W., Zhang, Y.-Q., & Peha, J. M. (2001). Streaming video over the Internet: Approaches and directions. *IEEE Transactions on Circuits and Systems for Video Technology, 11*(3), 282–300. doi:10.1109/76.911156

Wu, X., Tavildar, S., Shakkottai, S., Richardson, T., Li, J., Laroia, R., & Jovicic, A. (2013). FlashLinQ: A synchronous distributed scheduler for peer-to-peer ad hoc networks. *IEEE/ACM Transactions on Networking, 21*(4), 1215–1228. doi:10.1109/TNET.2013.2264633

Wu, Y. C. (2015). User-centric interference nulling in downlink multi-antenna heterogeneous networks.*2015 IEEE International Symposium on Information Theory (ISIT)*, 2817-2821. doi:10.1109/ISIT.2015.7282970

Xia, W. (2015). A Survey on Software-Defined Networking. *IEEE Communication Surveys & Tutorials*, 27-50.

Xie, H. (2012). Software-defined networking efforts debuted at IETF 84. *IETF J.* Retrieved from: http://www.internet-society.org/fr/node/45708

Xu, C. Z., Zhao, F., Guan, J., Zhang, H., & Muntean, G.-M. (2013). QoE-driven user-centric VoD services in urban multihomed P2P-based vehicular networks. *IEEE Transactions on Vehicular Technology, 62*(5), 2273–2289. doi:10.1109/TVT.2012.2228682

Xu, P., Fang, X., Chen, M., & Xu, Y. (2013). A Stackelberg game-based spectrum allocation scheme in macro/femtocell hierarchical networks. *Computer Communications, 36*(14), 1552–1558. doi:10.1016/j.comcom.2012.10.002

Yang, L., Alouini, M. S., & Qaraqe, K. (2012). On the performance of spectrum sharing systems with two-way relaying and multiuser diversity. *IEEE Communications Letters, 16*(8), 1240–1243. doi:10.1109/LCOMM.2012.052112.120746

Yilmaz, H. B., & Tugcu, T. (2015). Location estimation-based radio environment map construction in fading channels. *Wirel. Commun. Mob. Comput., 15*(3). 561–570. doi:10.1002/wcm.2367

Yin, H. (2012). *SDNi: A Message Exchange Protocol for Software Defined Networks (SDNS) across Multiple Domains.* Retrieved from: http://www.cisco.com/en/US/solutions/collateral/ ns341/ns525/ns537/ns705/ns827/white_paper_c11-481360.pdf

Yu, C.-H., Doppler, K., Ribeiro, C., & Tirkkonen, O. (2011, August). Resource sharing optimization for device-to-device communication underlaying cellular networks. *IEEE Transactions on Wireless Communications, 10*(8), 2752–2763. doi:10.1109/TWC.2011.060811.102120

Yu, M. (2010). Scalable Flow-Based Networking with DIFANE.*Proc. ACM SIGCOMM Conf.*, 351–362.

Yu, W., & Lui, R. (2006). Dual methods for nonconvex spectrum optimization of multicarrier systems. *IEEE Transactions on Communications, 54*(7), 1310–1322. doi:10.1109/TCOMM.2006.877962

Yu, Z., Baxley, R. J., & Zhou, G. T. (2013). Multi-user MISO broadcasting for indoor visible light communication.*IEEE International Conference on Acoustics, Speech and Signal Processing*, 4849-4853. doi:10.1109/ICASSP.2013.6638582

Zakerinasab, M. R., & Wang, M. (2015). Dependency-Aware Distributed Video Transcoding in the Cloud. *IEEE Annual Conference on Local Computer Network.*

Zeadally, S., Hunt, R., Chen, Y., Irwin, A., & Hassan, A. (2012). Vehicular ad hoc networks (VANETs): Status, results, and challenges. *Telecommunication Systems, 50*(4), 217–241. doi:10.1007/s11235-010-9400-5

Zeng, L., Obrien, D., Minh, H. L., Faulkner, G. E., Lee, K., Jung, D., & Won, E. T. et al. (2009). High data rate multiple input multiple output (MIMO) optical wireless communications using white led lighting. *IEEE Journal on Selected Areas in Communications, 27*(9), 1654–1662. doi:10.1109/JSAC.2009.091215

Zhang, Q., Xiang, Z., Zhu, W., & Gao, L. (2004). Cost-Based Cache replacement and Server Selection for Multimedia Proxy across Wireless Internet. *IEEE Transactions on Multimedia, 6*(4), 587–598. doi:10.1109/TMM.2004.830816

Zhang, R., Wang, J., Wang, Z., Xu, Z., Zhao, C., & Hanzo, L. (2015). Visible light communications in heterogeneous networks: Paving the way for user-centric design. *IEEE Wireless Communications, 22*(2), 8–16. doi:10.1109/MWC.2015.7096279

Zhang, Y. J., & Letaief, K. B. (2004). Multiuser adaptive subcarrier-and-bit allocation with adaptive cell selection for OFDM systems. *IEEE Transactions on Wireless Communications, 3*(5), 1566–1175. doi:10.1109/TWC.2004.833501

Zhao, J., Zheng, W., Wen, X., Chu, X., Zhang, H., & Lu, Z. (2014). Game Theory Based Energy-Aware Uplink Resource Allocation in OFDMA Femtocell Networks. *International Journal of Distributed Sensor Networks*, 1–8.

Zheng, W., Su, T., Li, W., Lu, Z., & Wen, X. (2012). Distributed energy-efficient power optimization in two-tier femtocell networks.*IEEE International Conference on Communications*, 5767-5771. doi:10.1109/ICC.2012.6364882

Zhong, C., Ratnarajah, T., & Wong, K. K. (2011). Outage analysis of decode-and-forward cognitive dual-hop systems with the interference constraint in Nakagami-fading channels. *IEEE Transactions on Vehicular Technology, 60*(6), 2875–2879. doi:10.1109/TVT.2011.2159256

Zhou, H. J., Ji, Y., Wang, X., & Zhao, B. (2015). Joint Resource Allocation and User Association for SVC Multicast Over Heterogeneous Cellular Networks. *IEEE Transactions on Wireless Communications, 14*(7), 3673–3684. doi:10.1109/TWC.2015.2409834

Zhou, X., Zhang, R., & Ho, C. K. (2013). Wireless information and power transfer: Architecture design and rate-energy tradeoff. *IEEE Transactions on Communications, 61*(11), 4754–4767. doi:10.1109/TCOMM.2013.13.120855

Zhu, H., & Wang, J. (2009). Chunk-based resource allocation in OFDMA systems Part I: Chunk allocation. *IEEE Transactions on Communications, 57*(9), 2734–2744. doi:10.1109/TCOMM.2009.09.080067

Zhu, H., & Wang, J. (2012, February). (2112) Chunk-based resource allocation in OFDMA systems Part II: Joint chunk, power and bit allocation. *IEEE Transactions on Communications, 60*(2), 499–509. doi:10.1109/TCOMM.2011.112811.110036

Zoican, S. (2008). The role of programmable digital signal processors (dsp) for 3 g mobile communication systems. *ACTA Tech.Napoc.*, *49*, 4956.

Zou, Y., Valkama, M., & Renfors, M. (2008). Digital compensation of I/Q imbalance effects in space-time coded transmit diversity systems. *IEEE Transactions on Signal Processing*, *56*(6), 2496–2508. doi:10.1109/TSP.2007.916132

Zuniga, J. C., Bernardos, C. J., Costa, R., & Reznik, A. (2013). Distributed Mobility Management: A Standards Landscape. *IEEE Communications Magazine*, *51*(3), 80–87. doi:10.1109/MCOM.2013.6476870

Zwickl, Fuxjaeger, Gojmerac, & Reichl. (2013). *Wi-FiOffload: Tragedy of the Commons or Land of Milk and Honey?*. 24th IEEE PIMRC, London, UK.

About the Contributors

Chetna Singhal works as an Assistant Professor at Indian Institute of Technology (IIT) Kharagpur. She has completed her Ph.D from IIT Delhi in May, 2015 and has worked as a Postdoctoral Researcher in Department of Electrical Engineering, IIT Delhi till October 2015. She received her M.Tech. in Computer Technology from Electrical Engineering Department, IIT Delhi in 2010 and B.Eng. in Electronics and Telecommunications from University of Pune in 2008. She worked in IBM Software Lab, New Delhi, as a Software Engineer, from June 2010 to July 2011. Her research interests are in heterogeneous wireless networks, multimedia transmissions, resource allocation, and wireless handovers.

Swades De received his PhD in Electrical Eng. from the State Univ. of New York at Buffalo in 2004. He is currently an associate professor of Electrical Engineering at IIT Delhi. Dr. De's research interests are broadly in communication networks, with emphasis on performance modeling and analysis. Current directions include energy harvesting communication networks, broadband wireless access and routing, cognitive/white-space access networks, and smart grid networks. Dr. De currently serves as a senior editor of IEEE Communications Letters and an associate editor respectively of Springer Photonic Network Communications journal and IETE Technical Review journal. He is a senior member of IEEE, IEEE Communications and Computer Societies, USA, and a member of IEICE, Japan.

* * *

Pradip Kumar Barik received the B.Tech degree in Electronics and Communication engineering from Kalyani Govt. Engg. College, West Bengal in 2012 and M.Tech degree in Communication Engineering from NITK Surathkal in 2014. He is Gold Medalist from NITK Surathkal. He was with Broadcom India PVT LTD as Intern in Cellular Protocol developing and Testing division from June 2013 to May 2014. He worked as Asst Professor at CMR Institute of technology, Bangalore from July 2014 to December 2015. He is currently pursuing the PhD degree from E&EC department, IIT Kharagpur. His current research interest include adaptive multimedia services over heterogeneous broadband network, cross-layer optimization in wireless network, Software defined mobile network.

Vivek Ashok Bohara received the PhD degree from the school of EEE, Nanyang Technological University (NTU), Singapore in 2011. From 2011 to 2013, he was a Post-Doctoral researcher (Marie Curie fellowship) in ESIEE Paris, University Paris-East, France. He joined IIIT-Delhi in 2013 where he is currently working as an Assistant Professor. His research interests include next generation communication technologies, cognitive radio, cooperative communication and digital predistortion algorithms for wideband power amplifiers. He received 1st Prize in National Instruments ASEAN Virtual Instrumentation Applications Contest in 2007 and 2010. He was also the recipient of best poster award at IEEE ANTS 2014 and Comsnets 2015 conferences.

Alexandra Bousia got her PhD degree in wireless communications at the Technical University of Catalonia (UPC) in 2016. She also got her B.S. and M.S. degrees from the Department of Computer & Com. Engineering, Univ. of Thessaly, in 2008 and 2009, respectively. Since 2011 she has been involved in several national and European projects. She received the best paper award at IEEE GLOBECOM 2014 and the EuCNC/EURACON Best Student Paper Award at EuCNC 2016. Her research interests include wireless networks, MAC protocols, energy efficient protocols, and RRM algorithms.

Mainak Chatterjee received the BSc degree in physics (Hons.) from the University of Calcutta, the ME degree in electrical communication engineering from the Indian Institute of Science, Bangalore, and the PhD degree from the Department of Computer Science and Engineering from the University of Texas at Arlington. He is an associate professor in the Department of Electrical Engineering and Computer Science, University of Central Florida, Orlando. His research interests include economic issues in wireless networks, applied game theory, cognitive radio networks, dynamic spectrum access, and mobile video delivery. He has published more than 150 conferences and journal papers. He got the Best Paper Awards in IEEE Globecom 2008 and IEEE PIMRC 2011. He received the AFOSR sponsored Young Investigator Program (YIP) Award. He co-founded the ACM Workshop on Mobile Video (MoVid). He serves on the editorial board of Elseviers Computer Communications and Pervasive and Mobile Computing Journals. He has served as the TPC co-chair of several conferences including ICDCN 2014, IEEE WoWMoM 2011, WONS 2010, IEEE MoVid 2009, Cognitive Radio Networks Track of IEEE Globecom 2009, and ICCCN 2008. He also serves on the executive and technical program committee of several international conferences.

Sakshi Chourasia received her M.S. (By Research) degree in Computer Science and Engineering from Indian Institute of Technology Madras. Her research interests include LTE Networks, Software Defined Networking and Network Function Virtualization. She received her B.E. degree in 2012 from Chhattisgarh Swami Vivekanand Technical University. Currently she is Software Engineer in IBM Systems. She is a student member of the IEEE.

Saptarshi Debroy received his PhD degree in Computer Engineering from University of Central Florida in 2014, MTech degree from Jadavpur University, India in 2008, and BTech degree from West Bengal University of Technology, India in 2006. He is currently Assistant Professor at City University of New York (CUNY). Before joining CUNY, he was a Post Doctoral Fellow at University of Missouri-Columbia. He has published close to 30 international conferences and peer-reviewed journal papers including the Best Paper Award in IEEE PIMRC 2011. His current research interests include cybersecurity, cloud computing, dynamic spectrum access, and Big Data networking. He also serves on the executive and technical program committee of several international conferences.

Mianxiong Dong received B.S., M.S. and Ph.D. in Computer Science and Engineering from The University of Aizu, Japan. He is currently an Associate Professor in the Department of Information and Electronic Engineering at the Muroran Institute of Technology, Japan. Prior to joining Muroran-IT, he was a Researcher at the National Institute of Information and Communications Technology (NICT), Japan. He was a JSPS Research Fellow with School of Computer Science and Engineering, The University of Aizu, Japan and was a visiting scholar with BBCR group at University of Waterloo, Canada supported by JSPS Excellent Young Researcher Overseas Visit Program from April 2010 to August 2011. Dr. Dong was selected as a Foreigner Research Fellow (a total of 3 recipients all over Japan) by NEC C&C Foundation in 2011. His research interests include Wireless Networks, Cloud Computing, and Cyber-physical Systems. His research results have been published in 120 research papers in international journals, conferences and books. He has received best paper awards from IEEE HPCC 2008, IEEE IC-ESS 2008, ICA3PP 2014, GPC 2015, and IEEE DASC 2015. Dr. Dong serves as an Associate Editor for IEEE Communications Surveys and Tutorials, IEEE Network, IEEE Access, and Cyber-Physical Systems (Taylor & Francis), as well as a leading guest editor for ACM Transactions on Multimedia Computing, Communications and Applications (TOMM), IEEE Transactions on Emerging Topics in Computing (TETC), IEEE Transactions on Computational Social Systems (TCSS), Peer-to-Peer Networking and Applications (Springer) and Sensors, as well as a guest editor for IEICE Transactions on Information and Systems, Mobile Information Systems, and International Journal of Distributed Sensor Networks. He has been serving as the Program Chair of IEEE SmartCity 2015 and Symposium Chair of IEEE GLOBECOM 2016. Dr. Dong is currently a research scientist with A3 Foresight Program (2011-2016) funded by Japan Society for the Promotion of Sciences (JSPS), NSFC of China, and NRF of Korea.

Sudip Dutta is an application architect for an IBM Technical Support domain project. He has 12 years of experience in design and development, prototyping, providing technical strategy, solutions for creating and leveraging assets in client solutions, as well as providing technical leadership. His technological interest includes development of Java/J2EE based web frameworks, responsive UI design, Software-defined networks. cloud based solutions.

Naveen Gupta is presently pursuing PhD in Wireless Communication from IIIT Delhi since July 2013. He has completed B.Tech in Electronics and Communication from IETE, New Delhi in 2007 and M.Tech in Advanced Communication System from NIT Warangal in 2011. He is currently working on opportunistic spectrum sharing and resource allocation schemes for cognitive radio system and device to device communication.

Bhushan Jagyasi has been currently working as a Lead Data Scientist at Pristine Retail Solutions. Bhushan has earlier worked as an Associate Consultant and Scientist in the Digital Farming group of TCS Innovation Labs India for the major part of his research career. In his tenure at TCS Research, he focused on challenging societal problems towards agriculture sustainability. His one of the serendipitous solution involving a novel method for mitigation of crop disease and pest infestations has been awarded with the MIT's India TR35 Young Innovator award in 2010. Bhushan holds a Ph.D. from the Department of Electrical Engineering, Indian Institute of Technology Bombay. He was awarded with the Philips India Fellowship while pursuing his doctoral studies. His research interests include - Machine Learning, Sensor Networks, Algorithms, Signal Processing, and Statistical Analysis.

Nalin Dushantha K. Jayakody received the Ph. D. degree in Electronics, Electrical and Communications Engineering in 2014, from the University College Dublin, Ireland. He received his MSc degree in Electronics and Communications Engineering from the Department of Electrical and Electronics Engineering, Eastern Mediterranean University, Turkey in 2010 (under the University full graduate scholarship) and ranked as the first merit position holder of the department, and B. E. electronics engineering degree (with first-class honors) from Pakistan in 2009 and was ranked as the merit position holder of the University (under SAARC Scholarship. From 2014 - 2016, he was a Postdoc Research Fellow at the Coding & Information Transmission group, University of Tartu, Estonia and University of Bergen, Norway. From summer 2016, he is a Professor at the Department of Software Engineering, Institute of Cybernetics, National Research Tomsk Polytechnic University, Russia where he also serves as the Director of Tomsk Infocom Lab. Dr. Jayakody is a Member of IEEE and he has served as session chair or technical program committee member for various international conferences, such as IEEE PIMRC 2013/2014, IEEE WCNC 2014/2016, IEEE VTC 2015 etc.

Yusheng Ji received her B.E., M.E., and D.E. degrees in electrical engineering from the University of Tokyo. She joined the National Center for Science Information Systems, Japan (NACSIS), in 1990. Currently, she is a professor at the National Institute of Informatics, Japan (NII), and at the Graduate University for Advanced Studies (SOKENDAI). Her research interests include network architectures, resource management, and performance analysis for wired and wireless communication networks.

Zhi Liu received the B.E., in computer science and technology from the University of Science and Technology of China, China, in 2009 and Ph.D. degree in informatics in National Institute of Informatics and The Graduate University for Advanced Studies (Sokendai) Tokyo, Japan. He is currently an Junior Researcher (Assistant Professor) at Waseda University, Tokyo, Japan. He was a JSPS research fellow in National Institute of Informatics and The Graduate University for Advanced Studies (Sokendai) from Apr. 2012 to Nov. 2014. From Oct.2009 to Mar. 2014, he was a research assistant in National Institute of Informatics and The Graduate University for Advanced Studies (Sokendai).

Amitava Mukherjee is Senior Manager of IBM India from Oct 2002. And has over 33 years of experience in leading and managing competencies in IBM GBS India, and Application/Implementation and R&D projects for Domestic/International Clients. Amitava had been on sabbatical from IBM India (Jan 2003-Mar 2005), and visited University of New South Wales, Sydney as visiting Professor (2003-2004) and Royal Institute of Technology, Stockholm as Senior Researcher (2004-2005). He was Senior and Principal Consultant at PwC India from May 1995 to Jun 1999 and Jul 1999 to Sep 2002 respectively. From 1983 to 1995, he was with the Department of Electronics and Telecommunication Engineering, Jadavpur University, Kolkata, India in research and teaching positions. Amitava's contributions are in the design of network architecture, routing protocol and paging strategy in the field of large communication networks specifically in Wireless Sensor, Cellular communication, Mobile Ad hoc and Pervasive, and Optical Networks. Currently, his main focus of research is on 5G wireless networks, controllability of complex network, cognitive radio network, nano communication network, software defined networking (SDN), information centric networking (ICN),compressive sampling (CS). He has around 150 published papers in journals and conference proceedings of international repute, four patents, five books and two book chapters in pervasive computing, wireless communication, societal engineering, nano communication network and controllability of complex network respectively. He is a Senior Member of IEEE Communications Society and member of ACM. He has been serving as member of Technical Program Committee for a large number of conferences like ICC, GLOBECOM, WPMC, etc. He is the reviewer of major IEEE Transactions on (TON, TMC, TWC, PDS, etc.). He is currently serving 1913 WG on IEEE Standard on Software-Defined Quantum Communication (SDQC). He served as an active member of 1906.1 IEEE Standard WG on Nano networking, the emerging field of research from 2012-2015. He was founder Vice-Chairman of IEEE Communication Society, Kolkata. Amitava was one of experts of Program Analysis Task Force (PATF) of IEEE Communication Society, Head Quarter, New York. Amitava had received Ph. D degree in Computer Science from Jadavpur University, Kolkata, India.

Dang Nguyen, B.E. (2008) and M.S. (2012) in Electronics and Telecommunication from University of Technology and University of Science, Ho Chi Minh, Vietnam, respectively. Ph.D. (2016) in Information System from Kyushu Institute of Technology, Japan. He has joined Aalborg University as an Industrial Postdoc since August 2016. His research topics include 5G, cognitive networks, and relay networks.

Bighnaraj Panigrahi is currently working as a Researcher at CTO Networks Lab, TCS, Bangalore. At TCS, he is working in various projects in Wireless Networks such as Information Centric Networks (ICN), Device-to-Device (D2D) communications, and WiFi offloading, etc. Before joining TCS he was a Research Scientist-I at SDSMT, USA, and was working there on a NASA funded project on Delay Tolerant TCP protocol for Deep Space Communications. Panigrahi holds a BSc degree in Physics and two Master degrees (MSc and MTech) in Electronic Science and Computer Science, respectively. He obtained his PhD from IIT Delhi (2012) where he worked on cross-layer optimization problems in Wireless Sensor and Ad-hoc Networks. He has research experience of more than 7 years in different fields of wireless networks such as Wireless Sensor and Ad-hoc Networks, Deep Space Communications, Cognitive Radio Networks, Information Centric Networks, Cellular and LTE Networks, etc. He has keen interest in performance modeling, cross-layer optimization, theoretical modeling, simulation and test-bed implementation, etc. Bighnaraj also has academic interests and was working as an Assistant Professor in IMS Engg. Colg, UP, India, where he taught several courses in the areas of computer science and guided several Bachelors and Masters students. He has several national and international conference and journals papers to his credit and recently filed several patents in the area of Information Centric Networks (ICN) and D2D Communications. He is a reviewer for several reputed conferences and journals. He also served as a TPC member for IEEE ANTS 2014, ICIT 2014, and ICDCIT 2015. He is also actively participating in standards' bodies like TSDSI and 3GPP (through TSDSI).

Symeon Papavassiliou is a professor in the School of Electrical and Computer Engineering at the National Technical University of Athens. From 1995 to 1999, he was a senior technical staff member at AT&T Laboratories, New Jersey, while till 2004 he was an associate professor in the ECE Department at the New Jersey Institute of Technology, USA. He has an established record of publications in the area of computer and communication networks with more than 250 technical journal and conference published papers. He received the Best Paper Award in IEEE INFOCOM'94, the AT&T Division Recognition and Achievement Award in 1997, the US National Science Foundation Career Award in 2003, the Best Paper Award in IEEE WCNC 2012, the Excellence in Research Grant in Greece in 2012 and the Best Paper Award in ADHOCNETS 2015. Dr. Papavassiliou also served on the board of the Greek National Regulatory Authority on Telecommunications and Posts (2006– 2009).

Hemant Kumar Rath is a Senior Member IEEE and IARCS, holds MTech (2004) and PhD (2009) from IIT Bombay, India (Communication Engineering) and BE in EL&TCE (1997) from VSSUT Burla, Sambalpur, Odisha. He has close to 15 years of experience in academics, research and industry. At present, Hemant is a Senior Scientist at TCS Networks Lab, Bangalore, where he is working since Dec 2010. Hemant was also working as an Associate Professor at KIIT Bhubaneswar (2009-10), a premier academic institute in Eastern India, an Associate Manager (2000-02) in UACT (a joint collaboration of Usha Martin with IIT Madras) and Scientist (1998-2000) at CEERI Center, New Delhi. His current research interests include: QoS in Networks, LTE/WiMAX Scheduling, Self-Optimization, Propagation Model Design, Speech Processing, M2M Communication, Cloud Computing, Modeling of Social Network Traffic, Information Centric Networks, Software Defined Networks, etc. He has published many research papers and presented many talks in national and international conferences/seminars such as IEEE Globecom, ICC, COMSWARE, COMSNETS, NCC, PIMRC, INDICON, ACM ICDCN, ITU-T, BWCI-COAI Workshop etc., and has filled several patents through TCS in the areas of communication and networks. Hemant has extensive knowledge and experience in network modeling, algorithm design, stability analysis, kernel level programming, simulations using Matlab, NS2, NS3, Qualnet and Opnet, etc. Hemant has also served as Industry Panel Speaker at ICC 2012 (Toronto), IEEE COMSNETS 2013 (Bangalore), ACM Sumo-CPS, etc. He has also served as PhD examiner at IITs, NITs.

Rashid A. Saeed received his PhD majoring in Communications and Network Engineering at Universiti Putra Malaysia (UPM), 2007, Malaysia. He was a Senior Researcher in MIMOS Berhad where he has been involved in research and development in wireless communications systems, including WiMAX and WLAN heterogeneous networks, wireless mesh network from Jan. 2007 to Jan. 2009 where he has been awarded the "Gold Badge" from MIMOS CEO for outstanding IPs achievements. Currently, he is deputy general director of scientific research and innovation, Ministry of higher education and scientific research. He also works as Senior researcher in Telekom Malaysia™, Research and Development Innovation Centre, Cyberjaya. He is also associate professor in Sudan University of Science and Technology (SUST). Dr. Rashid is IEEE member since 2001 and Corporate Member of IEM (I.E.M).

Anantha Simha, Member IEEE, is a Post Graduate in Electrical Engineering from IIT Madras, India and BE in Digital Electronics from University of Bangalore, India. He has 30+ years of experience in industry in the areas of microprocessor based hardware design, embedded protocol software, enterprise network design, network optimization, performance analysis, data center network design, Software Defined Networks (SDN), etc. For the last 20+ years he has been working with TCS. Currently he is heading the Networks Lab, Bangalore under CTO organization of Tata Consultancy Services (TCS). His current research interests includes: QoS in Networks, Scheduling, self-Optimization, Large Scale Network Design, Cloud Computing, Software Defined Networks, ICN Architecture Design, Next Generation Networks etc. He has published many research papers in national and international conferences/ seminars such as IEEE ICC, Globecom, NCC, ANTS, COMSNETS, PIMRC, CSNT, etc., and has filed several patents through TCS in the areas of communication networks. Anantha has presented in various technical events, and is actively involved in standardization activities through Telecommunications Standards Development Society, India - TSDSI (Indian SDO) and Global ICT Standardization Forum for India (GSFI).

329

Vibhutesh Kumar Singh, born in India, is a Founder at Digital iVision Labs (divilabs.com). His technical hobbies includes Microcontroller, MATLAB & FPGA programming. He been an active member at WiRoCOMM research group at IIIT Delhi, have given his significant contribution towards various research activities. He is currently working with, a Leading Hydraulic Engineering Firm as an Embedded Software Engineer, at New Delhi.

Krishna M. Sivalingam is Professor and Head in the Department of CSE, IIT Madras, Chennai, INDIA. Previously, he was a Professor in the Dept. of CSEE at University of Maryland, Baltimore County, Maryland, USA from 2002 until 2007; with the School of EECS at Washington State University, Pullman, USA from 1997 until 2002; and with the University of North Carolina Greensboro, USA from 1994 until 1997. He has also conducted research at Lucent Technologies' Bell Labs in Murray Hill, NJ, and at AT&T Labs in Whippany, NJ. He received his Ph.D. and M.S. degrees in Computer Science from State University of New York at Buffalo in 1994 and 1990 respectively; and his B.E. degree in Computer Science and Engineering in 1988 from Anna University's College of Engineering Guindy, Chennai (Madras), India. While at SUNY Buffalo, he was a Presidential Fellow from 1988 to 1991. His research interests include wireless networks, wireless sensor networks, optical wavelength division multiplexed networks, and performance evaluation. His work has been supported by several sources including AFOSR, DST India, IBM, NSF, Cisco, Intel, Tata Power Company and Laboratory for Telecommunication Sciences. He holds three patents in wireless networks and has published several research articles including more than fifty journal publications. He has co-edited a book on Next Generation Internet Technologies in 2010; on Wireless Sensor Networks in 2004; on optical WDM networks in 2000 and 2004. He is serving or has served as a member of the Editorial Board for journals including ACM Wireless Networks Journal, IEEE Transactions on Mobile Computing, and Elsevier Optical Switching and Networking Journal. He is presently serving as Editor-in-Chief of Springer Photonic Network Communications Journal and EAI Endorsed Transactions on Ubiquitous Environments. He is a Fellow of IEEE, a Fellow of INAE and an ACM Distinguished Scientist.

Yoshiaki Tanaka received the B.E., M.E., and D.E. degrees in electrical engineering from the University of Tokyo, Tokyo, Japan, in 1974, 1976, and 1979, respectively. He became a staff at Department of Electrical Engineering, the University of Tokyo, in 1979, and has been engaged in teaching and researching in the fields of telecommunication networks, switching systems, and network security. He was a guest professor at Department of Communication Systems, Lund Institute of Technology, Sweden, from 1986 to 1987. He was also a visiting researcher at Institute for Posts and Telecommunications Policy, from 1988 to 1991, and at Institute for Monetary and Economic Studies, Bank of Japan, from 1994 to 1996. He is presently a professor at Department of Communications and Computer Engineering, Waseda University, and a visiting professor at National Institute of Informatics. He received the IEEE Outstanding Student Award in 1977, the Niwa Memorial Prize in 1980, the IEICE Achievement Award in 1980, the Okawa Publication Prize in 1994, the TAF Telecom System Technology Award in 1995 and in 2006, the IEICE Information Network Research Award in 1996, in 2001, in 2004, and in 2006, the IEICE Communications Society Activity Testimonial in 1997 and in 1998, the IEICE Switching System Research Award in 2001, the IEICE Best Paper Award in 2005, the IEICE Network System Research

Award in 2006, in 2008, and in 2011, the IEICE Communications Society Activity Award in 2008, the Commendation by Minister for Internal Affairs and Communications in 2009, the APNOMS Best Paper Award in 2009 and in 2012, the IEICE Distinguished Achievement and Contributions Award in 2013, and the CANDAR/ASON Best Paper Award in 2014. He is a Fellow of IEICE.

Eirini Eleni Tsiropoulou is a senior research associate at Wireless Networks Laboratory (WNL), UTD, an internationally recognized research group specializing in ad hoc and sensor networks, since January 2016. She obtained her Diploma, MBA in techno-economics and PhD degree in Electrical and Computer Engineering from National Technical University of Athens in 2008, 2010 and 2014 respectively. Two of her papers received the Best Paper Award at IEEE Wireless Communications and Networking Conference (WCNC 2012) in April 2012 and at the 7th International Conference on Ad Hoc Networks (ADHOCNETS 2015) in September 2015. Her main research interests include wireless and heterogeneous networking focusing on power and resource allocation schemes, smart data pricing, Internet of Things and dense wireless networks architectures.

Panagiotis Vamvakas received his diploma Degree in Electrical and Computer Engineering from the National Technical University of Athens (NTUA), Greece and an M.Sc. Degree in Management, Technology and Economics from ETH Zurich, Switzerland, in 2011 and 2015, respectively. His main scientific interests lie in the area of resource allocation in wireless networks, energy efficient and heterogeneous networks, and smart data pricing. Currently he is a research associate at the Network Management and Optimal Design Laboratory, National Technical University of Athens.

Xiaoyan Wang received the BE degree from Beihang University, China, and the ME and Ph. D. from the University of Tsukuba, Japan. He is currently working as the assistant professor with the Department of Media and Telecommunications engineering at Ibaraki University, Japan. His research interests include wireless communications and networks, with emphasis on cognitive radio networks, network security and privacy, and cooperative communications.

Hao Zhou (M'15) received the B.S. and Ph.D. degrees in computer science from the University of Science and Technology of China, Hefei, China, in 1997 and 2002, respectively. He was a Project Lecturer with the National Institute of Informatics, Japan, from 2014 to 2016. He is currently an associate professor with the University of Science and Technology of China. His research interests are in the area of software engineering, protocol testing, and wireless networking.

Index

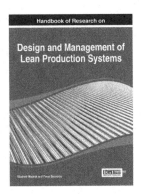
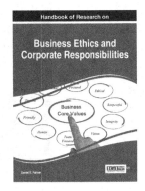

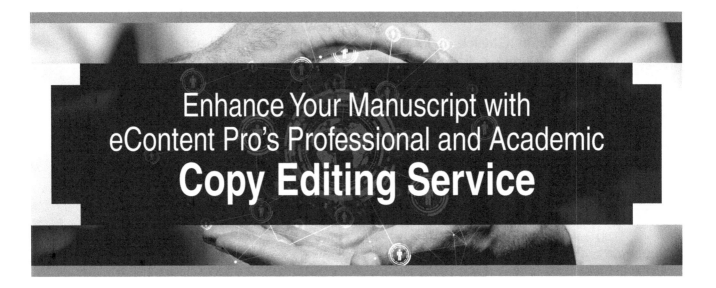

Printed in the United States
By Bookmasters